COMMUNICATING IN SMALL GROUPS

Principles and Practices

NINTH EDITION

STEVEN A. BEEBE

Texas State University–San Marcos

JOHN T. MASTERSON

Texas Lutheran University

PEARSON

Boston   New York   San Francisco
Mexico City   Montreal   Toronto   London   Madrid   Munich   Paris
Hong Kong   Singapore   Tokyo   Cape Town   Sydney

Editor-in-Chief: Karon Bowers
Acquisitions Editor: Jeanne Zalesky
Project Manager: Lisa Sussman
Marketing Manager: Suzan Czajkowski
Production Editor: Beth Houston
Editorial Production Service: Lifland et al., Bookmakers
Composition Buyer: Linda Cox
Manufacturing Buyer: JoAnne Sweeney
Electronic Composition: Publishers' Design and Production Services, Inc.
Interior Design: Publishers' Design and Production Services, Inc.
Photo Researcher: Poyee Oster
Cover Administrator: Linda Knowles

For related titles and support materials, visit our online catalog at www. ablongman. com.

Between the time website information is gathered and then published, it is not unusual for some sites to have closed. Also, the transcription of URLs can result in typographical errors. The publisher would appreciate notification where these errors occur so that they may be corrected in subsequent editions.

Library of Congress Cataloging-in-Publication Data

Beebe, Steven A., 1950–
  Communicating in small groups : principles and practices / Steven A. Beebe, John T. Masterson.
  —9th ed.
    p. cm.
  Includes bibliographical references and index.
  ISBN-13: 978-0-205-54721-0
  ISBN-10: 0-205-54721-4
  1. Small groups. 2. Communication in small groups. 3. Group relations training. I. Masterson, John T., 1946– II. Title.

  HM736.B43 2009
  302.3'4—dc22   2007034138

Printed in the United States of America

10 9 8 7 6 5 4 3 2 1   VHP   11 10 09 08 07

Dedicated to Sue and Nancy

NEW TO THIS EDITION

According to MCI Worldcom Conferencing research, most professionals spend nearly 3 hours each day in meetings. There's also evidence that the higher you advance in any organization, the *more* time you'll spend working in groups and teams. Top-level managers spend almost two-thirds of their day in meetings or working collaboratively with others. It is our goal to help prepare you, in one book and one semester, for the time you will spend communicating and working in small groups. Given that challenge, it is incumbent on us to ensure that our book includes the most recent research, relevant examples, and pedagogical tools to help you succeed.

The ninth edition of *Communicating in Small Groups: Principles and Practices* has been revised to reflect the impact of rapidly changing technology and globalization. We include new research, features, and content to address the issues of virtual communication and diversity, which are at the forefront of small group communication studies. Pages xxvi–xxvii of the Preface provide detailed chapter-by-chapter information on what is new to the ninth edition. A brief overview of some of the most important changes follows:

- New four-color design grabs and maintains students' attention and enhances the overall learning experience for visual learners.

- Revised and expanded coverage of technology highlights the use and impact of virtual groups in small group communication.

- New material about diversity and group communication helps students understand the challenges and opportunities presented by working with people from different cultures and backgrounds.

- New examples, illustrations, and cartoons communicate better with today's student learners.

- New and updated references for every chapter highlight the latest insights about communicating in small groups.

- New or updated case studies in every chapter give students the opportunity to practice applying principles through application and discussion.

- New group assessment instruments clinch students' understanding of core concepts and skills.

BRIEF CONTENTS

CONTENTS

CHAPTER TWELVE   Leadership   283

PREFACE

The title of our book, *Communicating in Small Groups: Principles and Practices*, suggests that using a carefully crafted balance of both principles and practices effectively can enhance group communication competence. From our first edition to this, our ninth edition, providing a balance between principles and practice, theory and skills, and knowledge and application has been our consistent goal. We are pleased that the first eight editions have been praised and so widely used by both teachers and students.

We have written the ninth edition of our best-selling book to serve as the primary text for a college-level course that focuses on group and team communication. We continue to seek a balanced approach to presenting the latest research about communicating in small groups, with an emphasis on the latest teamwork research, while also identifying strategies and practices that bring the principles to life.

A BALANCE OF PRINCIPLES AND PRACTICES

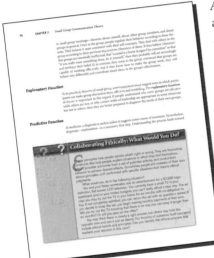

A balanced tension between theory and application, structure and interaction, and task and process are especially evident in the study of and participation in small groups. Some small group communication books emphasize theory. We believe that emphasizing theory without helping students apply principles can result in highly informed yet unskilled group members. Other texts tilt toward emphasizing skills. While it's true our students often clamor for techniques to enhance their ability to work with others, such skill-oriented approaches do not give students the underlying substantive scaffolding to inform their newfound applications. When we summarize research conclusions, we hear our students' voices echoing in our heads, asking "So what?" In response to those voices, we ask ourselves how the research conclusions we cite help enhance the quality of collaboration. We seek to present principles and practices of small group communication that make a difference in the lives of our students, who will spend much of their lives collaborating with others.

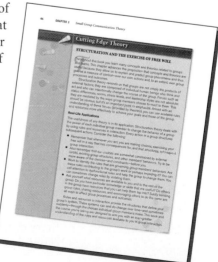

We both abhor boring meetings that are adrift from the goals they are intended to achieve. Consequently, we draw on our over 60 years of combined university administrative experience as we sift through both classic and contemporary research to keep our focus on application ("So what?"), while also anchoring our prescriptions in principled theory. Our goal is to provide a comprehensive yet laser-sharp digest of the latest thinking about group and team communication.

ℙOPULAR FEATURES WE'VE RETAINED

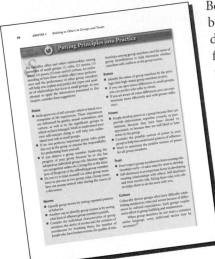

Both our students and our faculty colleagues tell us that two of the things they like best about our book are its get-to-the-point writing style and its comprehensive distillation of group and team communication research. We also receive praise for the clear applications of the research we describe. Our chapter-ending section, "Putting Principles into Practice," remains a signature feature that helps students and instructors sort through a wealth of information for immediate application.

We've done our best to keep the features instructors and students like best about our book: a lively, engaging writing style; references to the most recent research we can find; key insights about the research we identify, without unnecessary detail to overwhelm readers; and an emphasis on presenting not too much and not too little information about groups and teams. As we have in previous editions, we've revised and updated our pedagogical features, including chapter objectives, discussion questions, and end-of-chapter activities.

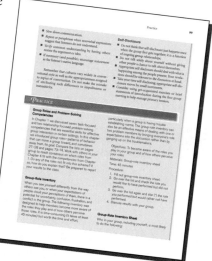

𝔾LOBAL CHANGES WE'VE MADE

In our effort to continually improve the book, we've included several new features, revisions, and additions in the ninth edition. Here's an overview of what's new in this edition.

New Colorful Design

We are so pleased with the eye-catching new design that adds interest and pizzazz to our words. Many students are visually oriented, and we believe our new design will not only help grab and maintain students' attention but also enhance their overall learning experience.

New Research Conclusions

We've done our best to find the latest research conclusions about small group communication and to add them to our already comprehensive overview of research applications. Every chapter includes new and updated references to the latest insights about communicating in small groups.

New Case Studies

Each chapter includes a new or updated case study that helps students practice applying principles through application and discussion. We've written the case studies so that they link to a key concept or skill emphasized in the chapter. Following each case study are discussion questions to guide students' application of the principles embedded in each case.

Revised and Expanded Coverage of Technology

The use of virtual groups continues to be among the fastest growing research areas of small group communication. As we have in several previous additions, we've enriched our coverage of technology by adding the latest research findings to our Virtual Communication special feature.

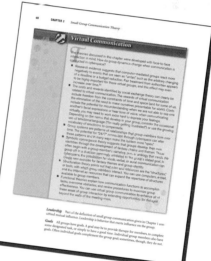

New Material about Diversity and Group Communication

Throughout the text we weave information and issues related to diversity into our conversations about a variety of theories and applications. Rather than segregating diversity information in special features, we've integrated our discussion of culture and diversity into every chapter.

New Group Assessment Instruments

We continue to include the comprehensive and widely praised "Competent Group Communicator" instrument, now in Chapter 11. However, we've added new group assessment instruments throughout the book to help clinch students' understanding of core concepts and skills.

CHAPTER-BY-CHAPTER REVISIONS

A brief summary of several specific changes we've made to each chapter of the ninth edition follows:

Chapter One: Introducing Group and Team Principles and Practices
- Revised discussion of the definition of communication
- Expanded discussion of team skills

Chapter Two: Small Group Communication Theory
- Polished discussion of small group communication theories

Chapter Three: Group Formation
- New section about group re-formation and how membership changes affect a group

Chapter Four: Relating to Others in Groups and Teams
- New material on formal and informal roles
- New information on general and operationalized norms

Chapter Five: Improving Group Climate
- New material on building trust in virtual, computer-mediated teams

Chapter Six: Enhancing Group and Team Communication Skills
- New material about conversation styles
- Expanded discussion of listening skills, including listening styles
- Expanded discussion of research about personal space in small groups
- Revised discussion of seating arrangements in small groups

Chapter Seven: Managing Conflict
- Revised discussion of the definition of conflict
- New information about what triggers conflict
- Revised and expanded discussion about conflict management styles
- Revised discussion of how to manage emotions during conflict
- New research about using the skill of extended "I" language
- New research about reaching consensus in e-groups

Chapter Eight: Preparing to Collaborate
- New research conclusions about sharing information with others in a group
- New research conclusions about the importance of identifying special skills among group members
- New research conclusions about the role of supportive communication during group deliberations
- New research conclusions about how to best discuss questions of fact, value, policy, and conjecture
- Revised discussion of using Web resources to gather research

Chapter Nine: Making Decisions and Solving Problems

- New summary of methods of group decision making
- New research about critical thinking and group decision making
- New research conclusions about online groups and decision making
- New research conclusions about how to increase group efficiency
- New application of economic theory and decision theory to groups
- Increased discussion of secondary tension in groups
- New discussion of dialectical theory applied to groups
- New research conclusions about the role of storytelling and group process

Chapter Ten: Using Problem-Solving Techniques

- Revised discussion of group interaction and group structure
- New example of flowcharting a group decision process

Chapter Eleven: Enhancing Creativity in Groups and Teams

- New discussion of the difference between creativity and innovation
- New research conclusions about cultural diversity and creativity
- New summary of how to enhance creativity skills
- New research conclusions about the importance of adding new members to a group to enhance creative thinking
- New research conclusions about tolerance of uncertainty and creativity
- New research conclusions about brainstorming

Chapter 12: Leadership

- New section on leadership and self deception

SUPPLEMENTAL RESOURCES FOR INSTRUCTORS

Instructor's Manual and Test Bank

For each chapter in the text, the *Instructor's Manual and Test Bank*, by Valerie Giroux, University of Miami, provides a chapter summary, learning objectives, and discussion activities and exercises for group and team work. The Test Bank portion offers hundreds of test questions in multiple-choice, true/false, short-answer, and essay formats.

Computerized Test Bank

The Computerized Test Bank, by Andrea M. McClanahan, East Stroudsburg University of Pennsylvania, features a user-friendly interface that enables instructors to view, edit, and add questions, transfer questions to tests, and print tests in a variety of fonts. Search and Sort features allow instructors to locate questions quickly and arrange them in a preferred order. The test questions from the printed Test Bank are also available electronically through our computerized testing system, TestGen EQ. The fully networkable test generating software is now available on a multiplatform CD-ROM.

PowerPoint Presentation Package

A PowerPoint presentation by Valerie Giroux, University of Miami, provides lecture slides based on key concepts in the text. The presentation can be downloaded free of charge from the Instructor's Resource Center at www.ablongman.com/irc.

MyCommunicationKit

MyCommunicationKit, by Douglas Threet, Evergreen Valley College, is an electronic supplement that offers book-specific learning objectives, chapter summaries, flashcards, and practice tests as well as video clips and activities to aid student learning and comprehension. Also included in MyCommunicationKit are Research Navigator and Weblinks that give you access to powerful and reliable research material. Go to http://www.mycommunicationkit .com to access this password-protected site.

Research Navigator™

Pearson's Research Navigator is the easiest way for students to start a research assignment or research paper. This password-protected Web site provides extensive help on the research process and four exclusive databases of credible and reliable source material, including the EBSCO Academic Journal and Abstract Database, *New York Times* Search by Subject Archive, "Best of the Web" Link Library, and *Financial Times* Article Archive and Company Financials. This site can be accessed at http://www.researchnavigator.com.

A&B Small Group Communication Video Library

This small group communication collection presents video case studies of groups working in diverse contexts and highlights key concepts of communication, including group problem solving, leadership roles, diversity, power, conflict, virtual group communication, and more. For adopters only; some restrictions apply. Contact your Pearson representative for details.

A&B Small Group Communication Study Site

by Rita Rahoi-Gilchrest, Winona State University

This Web site features small group communication study materials for students, including flashcards and a complete set of practice tests (including multiple choice, true/false, and essay questions) for all major topics. Students will also find Web links to valuable sites for further exploration of major topics. The site can be accessed at http://www.absmallgroups .com.

ACKNOWLEDGMENTS

Our collaboration not only as colleagues but also as friends for over three decades continues to make this book a labor of love. We met as new college professors sharing an office at the University of Miami in 1977. Today, although we live only miles apart in different communities and work at different universities, we remain united by a common bond of friendship. This book is the result of collaboration between us as authors, and among a support team of scholars, editors, colleagues, reviewers, students, and family members.

We are grateful to those who have reviewed this edition of our book to help make it a more useful instructional resource. Specifically, we thank Phillip G. Clampitt, University of Wisconsin–Green Bay; Alan C. Lerstrom, Luther College; Nancy A. Mallory, Monroe Community College; Lynnea McHenry, Hawkeye Community College; and Douglas F. Threet, Evergreen Valley College.

We continue to be thankful for the talented editorial staff at Allyn and Bacon. We are especially grateful to Lisa Sussman, who offered a wealth of creative ideas and suggestions to make this a better book. We are continually thankful for the ongoing support of Karon Bowers, Editor-in-Chief for Communication.

Steve thanks his colleagues and students at Texas State University–San Marcos for their encouragement and support. Dan Love and Sue Stewart are gifted teachers who offer advice, encouragement, and friendship. Kosta Tovstiadi provided expert assistance in helping to gather research for this new edition; we appreciate his ongoing friendship and expertise. We also want to acknowledge Dennis and Laurie Romig of Performance Resources for their rich knowledge and practical insight about groups and teams. Jim Bell, who teaches in Texas State's McCoy College of Business Administration, is a valued friend and gifted teacher who offers many ideas about teamwork. Sue Hall, Bob Hanna, and Sondra Howe are administrative assistants and invaluable colleagues at Texas State who provide ongoing structure and interaction to maintain Steve's productivity.

John thanks his friends, colleagues, and students at Texas Lutheran University, who continue to challenge and inspire him daily. Janet Hill, in particular, keeps him on track and, most of the time, out of trouble.

Finally, as in our previous editions, we offer our appreciation and thanks to our families, who continue to teach us about the value of teamwork and collaboration. Our sons have taken their place in the world, and our spouses continue to be equal partners in all we do. John's sons, John III and Noah, are now older than we both were when we began the first edition of this book. John III and Noah continue to make their dad smile with pride at their successes. Nancy Masterson continues, as always, as John's greatest love, best friend, and most respected critic. Steve's son Matt teaches others the value of finding melody and harmony in life with the music embedded in his soul. Steve's son Mark continues to teach his dad the importance of endurance and the ever-present power of renewal, even when life presents challenges. Susan Beebe has been an integral part of the author team in this and every previous edition for over thirty years. She continues to be Steve's personal Grammar Queen, life's love, and best friend.

Steve Beebe, *San Marcos, Texas*

John T. Masterson, *Seguin, Texas*

CHAPTER ONE

Introducing Group and Team Principles and Practices

"We are all dependent on one another, every soul of us on Earth."

—George Bernard Shaw

OBJECTIVES

After studying this chapter, you will be able to:

- Define small group communication.
- Discuss the characteristics of a team.
- List and describe the advantages and disadvantages of working with others in groups and teams.
- Compare and contrast primary and secondary groups.
- Describe differences between individualistic and collectivistic cultures.
- Describe five virtual communication methods.
- Identify nine group communication competencies.

HUMAN BEINGS *are creatures who collaborate. We need to establish relationships with others. We are raised in family groups, we are educated and entertained in groups, and we work and worship in groups. We collaborate in groups—we work jointly together to discuss important issues, solve particular problems, or perform certain tasks.*

Regardless of your career choice, it is likely you will spend a considerable part of your work life collaborating with others: The typical manager spends a quarter of the work week in group meetings. Top-level leaders spend up to two-thirds of their time—an average of three days a week—in meetings or preparing for meetings.[1]

Perhaps your experiences of working in groups has not been positive. Susan Sorenson coined the term **grouphate** *to mean the dread and repulsion many people feel about working in groups, teams, or meetings.*[2] *The good news is that grouphate diminishes among group members who receive training and instruction about working in groups. The purpose of this book, therefore, is to help you learn the communication principles and become skilled in the practices that make working in groups productive and enjoyable.*

Communication is the focus of this book. Communication makes it possible for groups and teams to exist and function. If you use the book as a tool to help you learn to communicate in small groups, you will distinguish yourself as a highly valued group member.

WHAT IS SMALL GROUP COMMUNICATION?

Consider these situations:

- Following multiple terrorist attacks, a Task Force Against Terrorism convened by the president begins meeting to study the problem.
- Tech.com is considering making a takeover bid for Digital.com. The chief executive officer calls company executives together to examine the virtues and pitfalls of the possible merger.
- To prepare for the final exam in your algebra class, you and several class members meet three nights each week to study.

Each of these three examples involves a group of people meeting and communicating for a specific purpose. And as group members communicate with one another, they are communicating transactively; they are simultaneously responding to one another and expressing ideas, information, and opinions. Although the purposes of the groups in these three scenarios are quite different, the groups have something in common—something that distinguishes them from a cluster of people waiting for a bus or riding in an elevator, for example. Just what is that "something"? What are the characteristics that make a group a group? We define **small group communication** as *communication among a small group of people who share a common purpose, who feel a sense of belonging to the group, and who exert influence on one another*. Let's explore this definition in more detail.

Communication

Reduced to its essence, **communication** is the process of acting on information.[3] Someone does or says something, and there is a response from someone else in the form of an action, a word, or a thought. Merely presenting information to others does not mean there is communication: Information is not communication. "But I told you what I wanted!" "I put it in the memo. Why didn't you do what I asked?" "It's in the syllabus." Such expressions of exasperation assume that if you send a message, someone will receive it. However, communication does not operate in a linear, input-output process. What you send is rarely what others understand.

Human Communication: Making Sense and Sharing That Sense with Others   **Human communication** is the process of making sense out of the world and sharing that sense with others by creating meaning through the use of verbal and nonverbal messages.[4] Let's examine the key elements of this definition.

Communication Is about Making Sense: We make sense out of what we experience when we interpret what we see, hear, touch, smell, and taste. Typically, in a small group, multiple people are sending multiple messages, often at the same time. To make sense out of the myriad of messages we experience, we look for patterns or structure; we relate what happens to us at any given moment to something we've experienced in the past.

Communication Is about Sharing Sense: We share what we experience by expressing it to others and to ourselves. We use words as well as nonverbal cues (such as gestures, facial expressions, clothing, music) to convey our thoughts and feelings to others.

Communication Is about Creating Meaning: Meaning is created in the hearts and minds of both the message source and the message receiver. We don't send meaning, we create it based on our experiences, background, and culture.

Communication Is about Verbal and Nonverbal Messages: Words and nonverbal behaviors are symbols that we use to communicate and derive meaning that makes sense to us. A **symbol** is something that represents a thought, concept, object, or experience. The words on this page are symbols that you are using to derive meaning that makes sense to you. Nonverbal symbols such as our use of gestures, posture, tone of voice, clothing, and jewelry primarily communicate emotions—our feelings of joy or sadness, our likes and dislikes, or whether we're interested or uninterested in others.

Human Communication Is Transactional   Live, in-person, human communication is **transactional**, meaning that when we communicate, we send and receive messages simultaneously. As you talk to someone, you respond to that person's verbal and nonverbal messages, even while you speak. In the context of a small group, even if you remain silent or nod off to sleep, your nonverbal behavior provides information to others about your emotions and interest, or lack of interest. The transactive nature of communication suggests that you cannot *not* communicate. Ultimately, people judge you by your behavior, not by your intent. And since you behave in some way (even when you're asleep), there is the potential for someone to make sense out of your behavior.

Human Communication Can Be Mediated Through Different Channels   Key elements of communication include the source, message, receiver, and channel. The **source** of the message is the originator of the ideas and feelings expressed. The **message** is the information being communicated. The **receiver** of the message is the person or persons who interpret the message. The **channel** is the means by which the message is expressed to the receiver.

Do groups need to communicate face to face to be considered a group? Even though most small group interaction involves in-person discussion, more and more small group meetings occur in a **mediated setting**—a setting in which the channel of communication is a phone line, fiber-optic cable, TV signal, the Internet, or other means of sending messages to others; the interaction is not face to face. In the twenty-first century, it has become increasingly easy and efficient to collaborate using the Internet, telephone conference calls, video teleconferences, and other technological means of communicating. So, yes: A group *can* be a group without meeting face to face. In the past three decades we have learned more about how mediated communication can enhance group communication. For example, there is evidence that groups linked together only by e-mail or a computer network can generate more and better ideas than groups that meet face to face.[5] Such communication may, however, be hindered by sluggish feedback or delayed replies, which are not problems when we collaborate in person. And although more ideas may be generated in a mediated meeting, complex problems and relationship issues are better handled in person than on the Internet or through another mediated network.[6] In most cases, in-person communication affords the best opportunity to clarify meaning and resolve uncertainty and misunderstanding. We will discuss the use of technology in groups and teams in a section in this chapter and throughout the book in a special feature called Virtual Communication.

Human Communication: Essential for Effective Group Outcomes   Does the quality of communication really affect what a group accomplishes? Because this is a book about group communication, you won't be surprised that our answer is yes. Researchers have debated, however, the precise role of communication in contributing to a group's success.[7] Success depends on a variety of factors besides communication, such as the personality of the group members, how motivated the members are to contribute, how much information members have, and the innate talent group members have for collaboration. Nevertheless, several researchers have found that the way group members communicate with each other is crucial in determining what happens when people collaborate.[8]

A Small Group of People

A group includes at least three people; two people are a **dyad.** The addition of a third person immediately adds complexity and an element of uncertainty to the transactive communication process. The probability increases that two will form a coalition against one. And although the dynamics of group roles, norms, power, status, and leadership are also present in two-person transactions, they become increasingly important in affecting the outcome of the transaction when three or more people communicate.

If at least three people are required for a **small group,** what is the maximum number of members a group may have and still be considered small? Scholars do not agree on a specific number. However, having more than 12 people (some say 13, others say 20) in a group significantly decreases individual members' interaction. The larger the group, the less influence each individual has on the group and the more likely it is that subgroups will develop.[9] With 20 or more people, the communication more closely resembles a public-speaking situation, when one person addresses an audience, providing less opportunity for all members to participate freely. The larger the group, the more likely it is that group members will become passive rather than actively involved in the discussion.

Meeting with a Common Purpose

The president's terrorism task force, the Tech.com company executives' group, and your algebra study group have one thing in common: Their members have a specific purpose for meeting. They share a concern for the objectives of the group. Although a group of people waiting for a bus or riding in an elevator may share the goal of transportation, they do not have a *collective* goal. Their individual destinations are different. Their primary concerns are for themselves, not for others. As soon as their individual goals are realized, they leave the bus or elevator. On the other hand, a goal keeps a committee or discussion group together until that goal is realized. Many groups fail to remain together because they never identify their common purpose. While participants in small groups may have somewhat different motives for their membership, a common purpose cements the group together.

Feeling a Sense of Belonging

Not only do group members need a mutual concern to unite them, they also need to feel they belong to the group. Commuters waiting for a bus probably do not feel part of a collective effort. Members of a small group, however, need to have a sense of *identity* with the group; they should be able to feel it is their group. Members of a small group are aware that a group exists and that they are members of the group.

Exerting Influence

Each member of a small group, in one way or another, potentially influences others. Even if a group member sits in stony silence while other group members actively verbalize opinions and ideas, the silence of that one member may be interpreted as agreement by another. As we will discuss in Chapter 6, nonverbal messages have a powerful influence on a group's climate.

At its essence, the process of influencing others defines leadership. To some degree, each member of a small group exerts some leadership in the group because of his or her potential to influence others.[10] Although some groups have an elected or appointed leader, most group members have some opportunity to share in how the work gets done and how group members relate to each other. Thus, if we define the role of leader rather broadly, each group member has an opportunity to fill the role of leader by offering contributions and suggestions. Regardless of its size, a group achieves optimal success when each person accepts some responsibility for influencing and leading others.

To repeat our definition: *Small group communication is defined as communication among a small group of people who share a common purpose, who feel a sense of belonging to the group, and who exert influence on one another.*

WHAT ABOUT TEAMS?

"Go, team!" You can hear this chant at most sports events. Whether playing a touch football game or in the Super Bowl, members of sports teams are rewarded for working together. Corporate America has also learned that working in teams can enhance productivity, efficiency, worker satisfaction, and corporate profits. Regardless of whether its members play football or construct web pages, a **team** *is a coordinated group of individuals organized to work together to achieve a specific, common goal.* Teamwork is increasingly emphasized as a way to accomplish tasks and projects because teamwork works.[11] An effectively functioning team gets results.[12] Research clearly documents the increased use of teams in corporate America during the past two decades, especially in larger, more complex organizations.[13]

Because we have clearly defined small group communication, you may be wondering, "What's the difference between a group and a team?" Often people use the terms *group* and *team* interchangeably. But are they different concepts, or is there merely a semantic difference between a group and a team? Our view is that teams are often more highly structured than typical small groups. All teams are small groups, but not all groups operate as a team.

Business and nonprofit organizations tend to use the term *team* rather than *group* to identify individuals who work together to achieve a common task. Corporate training departments often spend much time and money to train their employees to be better team members. What skills do such training programs focus on? Most programs cover the communication principles and practices that we will emphasize in this book: problem solving, decision making, listening, and conflict management. In addition to using communication skills, team members set goals, evaluate the quality of their work, and establish team operating procedures.[14]

Highly effective teams usually have at least four attributes that give the term *team* distinct meaning. Let's take a closer look at how distinctions are sometimes made between teams and groups.

1. Team goals are clear and specific (win the game, win the championship).
2. Teams have well-defined team-member responsibilities, such as positions on a sports team (first base, shortstop, and so on).
3. The rules for and expectations about how the team operates are spelled out; sports team competitions usually have a referee to enforce the rules of the game.
4. Teams usually develop a clear way of coordinating their efforts; sports teams discuss and practice how to work together.

Teams Develop Clear, Well-Defined Goals   Team goals are clear, specific, and measurable. They are also more than could be achieved by any individuals on the team. A sports team knows that the goal is to win the game. An advertising team's goal is to sell the most product. Yes, all groups, too, have a goal, but the goal may be less measurable or clear. A team develops a clear goal so that the members know when they've achieved it.

Teams Develop Clearly Defined Roles, Duties, and Responsibilities for Team Members People who belong to a team usually have a clear sense of their particular role or function on the team. As on a sports team, each team member has an understanding of how his or her job or responsibility helps the team achieve the goal. The roles and responsibilities of team members are explicitly discussed.[15] If one team member is absent, other team members know what needs to be done to accomplish that person's responsibilities. Sometimes team members may be trained to take on several roles just in case a team member is absent; this kind of training is called **cross-functional team-role training.** Team members' understanding other members' responsibilities helps the team to work more effectively.[16] In a group, the participants may perform specific roles and duties, but on a team, greater care must be devoted to explicitly ensuring that the individual roles and responsibilities are clear and are linked to a common goal or outcome. In fact, the key challenge in team development is to teach individuals who are used to performing individual tasks how to work together.

Teams Have Clearly Defined Rules for and Expectations about Team Operation A third difference between groups and teams is that teams develop specific operating systems to help them function well. A **rule** is a prescription for acceptable behavior. For example, a team may establish as a rule that all meetings will start and end on time. Another rule may be that if a team member is absent from a meeting, the absent member will contact the meeting leader after the meeting. Although expectations develop in groups, in a team those expectations, rules, and procedures are often overtly stated or written down. Team members know what the rules are and how those rules benefit the entire team.

Teams Have Coordinated and Collaborative Methods for Accomplishing the Work A fourth difference between groups and teams involves the methods team members use to accomplish their goals. Team members discuss how to collaborate and work together. Sports teams spend many hours practicing how to anticipate the moves of other team members so that, as in an intricate dance, all team members are moving to the same beat. Team members develop interdependent relationships; what happens to one affects everyone on the team. Of course, team members may be given individual assignments, but those assignments are clearly coordinated with other team members' duties so that all members are working together. Coordination and collaboration are the hallmark methods of a team. Although groups work together, they may accomplish their goal with less collaboration and coordination.

Even though we've made distinctions between groups and teams, we are not saying they are dramatically different entities. Think of these two concepts as existing on a continuum; some gatherings will have more elements of a group, whereas others will be closer to our description of a team. Keep in mind also that all teams are small groups, which means that throughout the book when we refer to a team we will also be referring to a small group. And the principles and practices of effective small group communication will thus also apply to teams.

REVIEW

COMPARING GROUPS AND TEAMS

	GROUPS	TEAMS
Goals	Goals may be discussed in general terms.	Clear, elevating goals drive all aspects of team accomplishment.
Roles and responsibilities	Roles and responsibilities may be discussed but are not always explicitly defined or developed.	Roles and responsibilities are explicitly developed and discussed.
Rules	Rules and expectations are often not formally developed and evolve according to the group's needs.	Rules and operating procedures are clearly discussed and developed to help the team work together.
Methods	Group members interact, and work may be divided among group members.	Team members collaborate and explicitly discuss how to coordinate their efforts and work together. Teams work together interdependently.

Characteristics of an Effective Team

Several researchers have been interested in studying how to make teams function better. One study found that team members need work schedules compatible with those of their colleagues, adequate resources to obtain the information needed to do the work, leadership skills, and help from the organization to get the job done.[17] Another study concluded that it's not how smart team members are, but how well they communicate that improves teamwork.[18] Using studies of several real-life teams (such as NASA, McDonald's, and sports teams), Carl Larson and Frank LaFasto identified eight hallmarks of an effective team. The more of these characteristics a team has, the more likely it is that the team will be effective.[19]

A Clear, Elevating Goal   Having a common, well-defined goal is the single most important attribute of an effective team.[20] But having a goal is not enough; the goal should be elevating and important—it should excite team members and motivate them to make sacrifices for the good of the team. Sports teams use the elevating goal of winning the game or the championship. Corporate teams also need an exciting goal that all team members believe is important.

A Results-Driven Structure   Teams need an efficient system or method of organizing how they work together. Team structure is the way in which a team is organized to process information and achieve the goal.[21] Explicit statements of who reports to whom and who does what are key elements of team structure. It is useful, therefore, for teams to develop a clear sense of the roles and responsibilities of each team member. A team needs individuals who perform task roles (getting the job done) and individuals who perform maintenance roles (managing the team process) to be high performing. A structure that is not results-driven, one that tolerates ineffective meetings, off-task talk, busywork, and "administrivia," always detracts from team effectiveness.

Competent Team Members   Team members need to know not only *what* their assignment is but also *how* to perform their job. Team members need to be trained and educated so they know what to do and when to do it. Without adequate training in both teamwork skills and job skills, the team will likely flounder.[22]

Unified Commitment   The motto of the Three Musketeers—"all for one and one for all"—serves as an accurate statement of the attitude team members should have when working together to achieve a clear, elevating goal. Team members need to feel united by their commitment and dedication to achieve the task.

A Collaborative Climate   Effective teams foster a positive group climate and the skills and principles needed to achieve their goal. Effective teams operate in a climate of support rather than defensiveness. Team members should confirm one another, support one another, and listen to one another as they perform their work. In Chapter 5 we will identify strategies for enhancing team climate.

Standards of Excellence   A team is more likely to achieve its potential if it establishes high standards and believes it can achieve its goals.[23] Goals that cause the team to stretch a bit can serve to galvanize a team into action. Unobtainable or unrealistic goals, however, can result in team frustration. If the entire team is involved in setting goals, the team is more likely to feel a sense of ownership of the standards it has established.

External Support and Recognition   Teams in any organization do not operate in isolation. They need support from outside the team to help acquire the information and materials needed to do the job. Team members also need to be recognized and rewarded for their efforts by others outside the team. Positive, reinforcing feedback enhances team performance and feelings of team importance.[24] There's evidence that less positive support from others discourages some team members from giving their full effort; negative feedback causes more group members to not give their full effort.[25] Most coaches acknowledge the "home-field advantage" that flows from the enthusiastic support and accolades of team followers. Corporate teams, too, need external support and recognition to help them function at maximum effectiveness.

Principled Leadership   Teams need effective leaders. This is not to say that a team requires an authoritarian leader to dictate who should do what. On the contrary, teams usually function more effectively when they adopt shared approaches to leadership. In most effective teams, leadership responsibilities are spread throughout the team. We will discuss leadership principles in more detail in Chapter 12.

Characteristics of Effective Team Members

Now that you have a sense of what a team is, you may still wonder, "What do effective team members do?" Several communication researchers have sought to answer that question by asking experienced team members what they consider to be the characteristics of outstanding team members.[26] Here's what they found.

Experience   Effective team members have practical experience in managing the problems and issues they face; they've "been there, done that." Less-experienced team members tend not to see the big picture and may lack the technical background needed to accomplish the task.

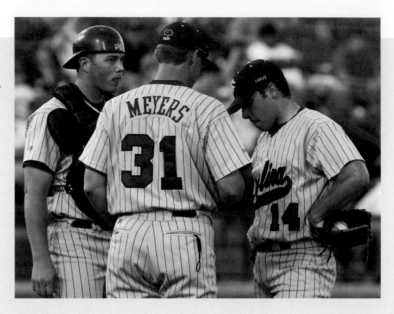

Experience, problem-solving ability, and supportiveness are key characteristics for effective teams. What characteristics make a baseball team effective?

Problem-Solving Ability   Analyzing information and issues while staying focused on the problem and possible solutions are characteristics of effective team members. Lack of focus on the team problem and indecisiveness have a negative impact on team success.

Openness   Openness is a basic ingredient for team success; having team members who are straightforward and willing to appropriately discuss delicate issues is a predictor of team success. Team members who are not open to new ideas and who participate less are perceived as less valuable to the team.

Supportiveness   Supportive team members listen to others, are willing to pitch in and accomplish the job, and have an optimistic outlook about team success. Nonsupportive members try to control team members and focus on their individual interests rather than on team interests.

Action Oriented   Team members who focus on "strategic doing" as well as on "strategic thinking" are vital for team success. Effective team members respond when action needs to be taken. Procrastinating and being slow to take action reduce team effectiveness.[27]

Positive Personal Style   Effective team members are motivated, patient, enthusiastic, friendly, and well liked.[28] In contrast, being competitive, argumentative, and impatient are perceived as hindrances to team success.

Positive Overall Team Perceptions   Effective team members believe they have the skills and resources to accomplish their task.[29] Teams members who think they will be less effective are, in fact, less effective.[30] And team members who are more effective think they will have more positive results because of the self-perceived quality of the team.[31] Are team members effective because of a self-fulfilling prophecy (expecting to be effective causes them to act effectively)? Or do team members think they are effective because they really are outstanding? We're not quite sure what the precise cause-and-effect relationship is between self-perceptions of being effective and effective performance. Perhaps team members who are optimistic about their success also work better with others and are cooperative. The bottom line is: Team member optimism appears to enhance team effectiveness.

Enhancing Team Effectiveness

Once you understand the characteristics of an effective team, the challenge—either as team facilitator or team participant—is to ensure that the team achieves its potential. The following strategies may prove useful in helping you develop team strengths.[32]

1. *Clarify group expectations and set team ground rules.* Teams function better if team members explicitly discuss how the team should operate. This is especially important if you are interacting via e-mail or the Internet.[33] Most team-building sessions include an opportunity for team members to develop a common vision of how the team will function. Discussing such issues as the value of being on time for meetings, reaching consensus, and having everyone's input on all ideas helps participants learn how to work together.

2. *Learn the strengths of each team member.* Before making team assignments, a coach usually takes time to learn about the players.[34] Team members have different strengths and talents. Learning about team members' abilities helps establish individual roles and responsibilities. Research by a team of scholars found that one of the most important factors in team success was ensuring that each team member knew what he or she was supposed to do. These same researchers found that this was a skill that could be taught to team members with positive results; teams who had training in how to clarify their individual roles were more successful than teams that did not have such training.[35] Effective teams do not operate as a "star system," where only a few members are hailed for their effectiveness.[36]

3. *Identify barriers that may keep the team from achieving its goal.* Gathering information, reviewing the issues under consideration, and analyzing the current situation are useful steps that help teams identify and overcome difficulties as they proceed.

4. *Develop a plan and put it into action.* Just as most sports teams have a playbook, any team needs a plan to accomplish a goal. A plan should be designed to help the group overcome obstacles that are keeping it from achieving its goal. Yet planning and plotting strategy alone will not get the job done. Teams need to go to work to implement strategy ideas and suggestions. Often the most efficient way is to divide the plan into small, manageable tasks while coordinating the work with other team members.[37]

DILBERT. © Scott Adams/Distributed by United Features Syndicate, Inc.

5. *Evaluate the plan and team procedures.* As the team works together, it needs to evaluate how things are going, stopping to assess whether the group's approach is achieving the desired results. Like football coaches who look at films of last week's game, the team needs to replay its procedures and examine whether they are appropriate.

WHAT ARE THE ADVANTAGES AND DISADVANTAGES OF WORKING IN GROUPS AND TEAMS?

There is no question about it: You *will* find yourself working in groups and teams. Collaborative projects are becoming the mainstay method of accomplishing work in all organizations. Students from kindergarten through graduate school are frequently called on to work on group projects.

How do you feel about working in groups and teams? Maybe you dread attending group meetings. Perhaps you agree with the observation that a committee is a group that keeps minutes but wastes hours. You may believe that groups bumble and stumble along until they reach some sort of compromise—a compromise with which no one is pleased. "To be effective," said one observer, "a committee should be made up of three people. But to get anything done, one member should be sick and another absent."

By understanding both the advantages and the potential pitfalls of working collaboratively, you will form more realistic expectations while capitalizing on the virtues of group work and minimizing the obstacles to success.[38] First, we'll identify advantages of group collaboration and then we'll present potential disadvantages.

Advantages

Groups and Teams Have More Information Than Individuals Do   Because of the variety of backgrounds and experiences that individuals bring to a group, the group as a whole has more information and ideas from which to seek solutions to a problem than one person would have alone. Research clearly documents that a group with diverse backgrounds, including ethnic diversity, comes up with better-quality ideas.[39] With more information available, the group is more likely to discuss all sides of an issue and is also more likely to arrive at a better solution.[40] Although group and team members tend to start out by discussing what group members already know, groups still have the advantage of having greater potential information to share with other group members.[41]

Groups and Teams Stimulate Creativity   Research on groups generally supports the maxim that "two heads are better than one" when it comes to solving problems.[42] Groups usually make better decisions than individuals working alone, because groups have more approaches to or methods of solving a specific problem. A group of people with various backgrounds, experiences, and resources can more creatively consider ways to solve a problem than one person can.

You Remember What You Discuss   Working in groups and teams fosters improved learning and comprehension, because you are actively involved rather than passive. Imagine that your history professor announces that the final exam is going to be comprehensive. History is not your best subject. You realize you need help. What do you do? You may form a study group with other classmates. Your decision to study with a group of people is wise;

education theorists claim that when you take an active role in the learning process, your comprehension of information is improved. If you studied for the exam by yourself, you would not have the benefit of asking and answering questions of other study group members. By discussing a subject with a group, you learn more and improve your comprehension of the subject.

You Are More Likely to Be Satisfied with a Decision You Help Make   Group problem solving provides an opportunity for group members to participate in making decisions and achieving the group goal. Individuals who help solve problems in a group are more committed to the solution and better satisfied with their participation in the group than if they weren't involved in the discussion.

You Gain a Better Understanding of Yourself   Working in groups helps you gain a more accurate picture of how others see you. The feedback you receive makes you aware of personal characteristics that you may be unaware of but that others perceive. By becoming sensitive to feedback, you can understand yourself better (or at least better understand how others perceive you) than you would if you worked alone. Group interaction and feedback can be useful in helping you examine your interpersonal behavior and in deciding whether you want to change your communication style.

Why do these advantages occur? One explanation is called social facilitation.[43] **Social facilitation** is the tendency for people to work harder simply because there are other people present.[44] Why does this happen? Some researchers suggest that the increased effort may occur because people need and expect positive evaluations from others; some people want to be liked and they work harder when others are around so that they gain more positive strokes. Social facilitation seems to occur with greater consistency if the group task is simple rather than complex.

Disadvantages

Although working in small groups and teams can produce positive results, problems sometimes occur when people congregate. Consider some of the disadvantages of working in groups. Identifying these potential problems can help you avoid them.

Group Members May Pressure Others to Conform to the Majority Opinion in Order to Avoid Conflict   Most people do not like conflict; they generally try to avoid it. Some people avoid conflict because they believe that in an effective group, members readily reach agreement. But this tendency to avoid controversy in relationships can affect the quality of

DILBERT: © Scott Adams/Distributed by United Features Syndicate, Inc.

a group decision. What is wrong with group members reaching agreement? Nothing, unless they are agreeing to conform to the majority opinion or even to the leader's opinion just to avoid conflict. Social psychologist Irving Janis calls this phenomenon *groupthink*—when groups agree primarily in order to avoid conflict.[45] Chapter 7 discusses conflict in small groups, talks about groupthink in more detail, and suggests how to avoid it.

An Individual Group or Team Member May Dominate the Discussion   In some groups it seems as if one person must run the show. That member wants to make the decisions and insists that his or her position on the issue is the best one. "Well," you might say, "if this person wants to do all the work, that's fine with me. I won't complain. It sure will be a lot easier for me." Yes, if you permit a member or two to dominate the group, you may do less work yourself, but then you forfeit the greater fund of knowledge and more creative approaches that come with full participation. Other members may not feel satisfied because they feel alienated from the decision making.

Try to use the domineering member's enthusiasm to the group's advantage. If an individual tries to monopolize the discussion, other group members should channel that interest more constructively. The talkative member, for example, could be given a special research assignment. Of course, if the domineering member continues to monopolize the discussion, other group members may have to confront that person and suggest that others be given an opportunity to present their views.

Some Group Members May Rely Too Much on Others to Get the Job Done   One potential problem of working in groups is that individuals may be tempted to rely too much on others rather than pitch in and help. The name for this problem is **social loafing**. Some group members hold back on their contributions (loaf), assuming others will do the work. They can get away with this because in a group or team, no one will be able to pin the lack of work on a single group member. There is less accountability for who does what.[46] Working together distributes the responsibility of accomplishing a task. Spreading the responsibility among all group members should be an advantage of group work. However, when some group members allow others to carry the workload, problems can develop. Just because you are part of a group does not mean that you can get lost in the crowd. Your input is needed. Do not abdicate your responsibility to another group member.[47]

To avoid this problem, encourage less-talkative group members to contribute to the discussion. Also, make sure each person knows the goals and objectives of the group. Encouraging each member to attend every meeting helps, too. Poor attendance at group meetings is a sure sign that members are falling into the "Let someone else do it" syndrome. Finally, see that each person knows and fulfills his or her specific responsibilities to the group.

Working with Others in a Group or Team Takes Longer Than Working Alone   For many people, one of the major frustrations about group work is the time it takes to accomplish tasks. Not only does a group have to find a time and place where everyone can meet (sometimes a serious problem in itself), but a group simply requires more time to define, analyze, research, and solve problems than do individuals working alone. It takes time for people to talk and listen to others. And, as you've heard, time is money! One researcher estimates that one 2-hour meeting attended by 20 executives would cost the equivalent of a week's salary for one of them.[48] Still, talking and listening in a group usually result in a better solution.

REVIEW

ADVANTAGES AND DISADVANTAGES OF WORKING IN GROUPS AND TEAMS

Advantages

Groups have more information.

Groups are often more creative.

Working in groups improves learning.

Group members are more satisfied if they participate in the process.

Group members learn about themselves.

Disadvantages

Group members may pressure others to conform.

One person may dominate the discussion.

Members may rely too much on others and not do their part.

Group work takes more time than working individually.

When Not to Collaborate

Although we've noted significant advantages to working in groups and teams, our discussion of the disadvantages of groups and teams suggests there may be situations when it's best *not* to collaborate. What situations call for individual work? Read on.

When the Group or Team Has Limited Time   If a decision must be made quickly, it may sometimes be better to delegate the decision to an expert. In the heat of battle, commanders usually do not call for a committee meeting of all their troops to decide when to strike. True, the troops may be better satisfied with a decision that they have participated in making, but the obvious need for a quick decision overrides any advantages that may be gained from meeting as a group.

When an Expert Already Has the Answer   If you want to know what it's like to be president of a university, you don't need to form a committee to answer that question; go ask some university presidents what they do. Or, if you want to know mathematical formulas, scientific theories, or other information that an expert could readily tell you, go ask the expert rather than forming a fact-finding committee. Creating a group to gather information that an expert already knows wastes time.

When the Information Is Readily Available from Research Sources   In this information age, a wealth of information is available with a click of a mouse. It may not be necessary to form a committee to chase after information that already exists. It may be helpful to put together a group or team if the information needed is extensive and several people are needed to conduct an exhaustive search. But if names, facts, dates, or other pieces of information can be quickly found in an encyclopedia or on the Internet, use those methods rather than making a simple task more complex by forming a group to get the information.[49]

When Group Members Are Involved in Unmanageable Conflict and Contention

Although both of your authors are optimists, sometimes bringing people together for discussion and dialogue is premature. When conflict clearly may explode into something worse, it may be best to first try other communication formats before putting warring parties in a group to discuss. What may be needed instead of group discussion is more structured communication, such as mediation or negotiation with a leader or facilitator. Or, if group members have discussed an issue and just can't reach a decision, they may decide to let someone else make the decision for them. The judicial system is used when people can't or won't work things out in a rational, logical discussion.

However, don't avoid forming or participating in groups just because of conflict. As you will learn in Chapter 7, conflict is virtually always present in groups; disagreements can challenge a group to develop a better solution. But if the conflict is intractable, another method of making the decision may be best.

Me versus We

Regardless of whether you are communicating using e-mail, via telephone, or face to face, the personal pronouns *I, me,* and *my* represent a primary stumbling block to collaboration

To work together effectively, individuals must develop common goals and a collective focus rather than pursuing only individual goals. Why might some cultures find this easier to achieve than others?

with others in small groups and to achieving the advantages of working together. Most North Americans value individual achievement over collective group or team accomplishment. Researchers describe our tendency to focus on individual accomplishment as individualism. According to Geert Hofstede, individualism is the "emotional independence from groups, organizations, or other collectivities."[50] Individualistic cultures value individual recognition more than group or team recognition. They encourage *self-actualization*—the achievement of one's potential *as an individual.* The United States, Britain, and Australia usually top the list of countries in which individual rights and accomplishment are valued over collective achievement.

By contrast, collectivistic cultures value group or team achievement more than individual achievement. People from Asian countries such as Japan, China, and Taiwan typically value collaboration and collective achievement more than do those from individualistic cultures. Venezuela, Colombia, and Pakistan are other countries in which people score high on a collective approach to work methods.[51] In collective cultures, *we* is more important than *me.* Collectivistic cultures usually think of a group as the primary unit in society, whereas individualistic cultures think about the individual.[52]

As you might guess, people from individualistic cultures tend to find it more challenging to collaborate in group projects than do people from collectivistic cultures. Table 1.1 contrasts individualistic and collectivistic assumptions about working in small groups.

TABLE 1.1   Individualism and Collectivism in Small Groups

Individualistic Assumptions	Collectivistic Assumptions
The most effective decisions are made by individuals.	The most effective decisions are made by teams.
Planning should be centralized and done by the leaders.	Planning is best done by all concerned.
Individuals should be rewarded.	Groups or teams should be rewarded.
Individuals work primarily for themselves.	Individuals work primarily for the team.
Healthy competition between colleagues is more important than teamwork.	Teamwork is more important than competition.
Meetings are mainly for sharing information with individuals.	Meetings are mainly for making group or team decisions.
To get something accomplished, you should work with individuals.	To get something accomplished, you should work with the whole group or team.
A key objective in group meetings is to advance your own ideas.	A key objective in group meetings is to reach consensus or agreement.
Team meetings should be controlled by the leader or chair.	Team meetings should be a place for all team members to bring up what they want.
Group or team meetings are often a waste of time.	Group or team meetings are the best way to achieve a goal.

Source: Adapted from John Mole, *Mind Your Manners: Managing Business Cultures in Europe* (London: Nicholas Brealey, 1995).

WHAT ARE THE DIFFERENT TYPES OF SMALL GROUPS?

To give you an idea of the variety and purposes of groups, we will discuss the role of both primary and secondary groups.

Primary Groups

A **primary group** is a group whose main purpose is to give people a way to fulfill their basic need to associate with others. Your family provides one of the best illustrations of a primary group. In his poem "The Death of the Hired Man," Robert Frost mused, "Home is the place where, when you have to go there / They have to take you in." Family communication usually does not follow a structured agenda; family conversation is informal. Conversation is also informal within other primary groups, such as informal cliques of friends or workers who interact over an extended period of time. Primary-group members associate with one another for the joy of community—to fulfill the basic human need to be social.

The main task of the primary group is to perpetuate the group so that members can continue to enjoy one another's companionship. Primary groups do not meet regularly to make decisions unless a meeting is necessary to perpetuate the social patterns of the group. As with any group, some members may assert more influence than others. The key reward of belonging to a primary group, however, is simply the satisfaction of being a member.

Secondary Groups

Secondary groups exist to accomplish a task or achieve a goal. Most of the groups you belong to at work or school are secondary groups. You are not involved in a committee or a class group assignment just for fun or to meet your social need for belonging (even though you may enjoy the group and make friends with other group members). The main reason you join secondary groups is to get something done.[53] There are several kinds of secondary groups to which you may belong at some point in your life.

Problem-Solving Groups   A **problem-solving group** exists to overcome some unsatisfactory situation or obstacles to achieving a goal. Many, if not most, groups in business and industry are problem-solving groups. The most common problem that any organization faces (whether it's a for-profit business or a nonprofit group) is finding a way to make more money. Chapters 9 and 10 will review principles and suggestions for improving your group problem-solving ability

Decision-Making Groups   The task of a **decision-making group** is to make a choice from among several alternatives. The group must identify what the possible choices are, discuss the consequences of the choices, and then select the alternative that best meets a need or achieves the goal of the group or parent organization.[54] A committee that screens applicants for a job has the task of making a decision. The group must select one person from among the many who apply.

As we will discuss in Chapter 9, decision making is usually a part of the problem-solving process. Groups that have a problem to solve usually must identify several possible solutions and decide on the one that best solves the problem. Although all group problem solving involves making decisions, not all group decision making solves a problem.

In small groups individuals have access to more information and resources to use in solving a problem than they would have working alone. What types of small groups would be helpful for teachers?

Study Groups As a student, you are no doubt familiar with **study groups.** The main goal of these groups is to gather information and learn new ideas. We have already noted that one advantage of participating in a group is that you learn by being involved in a discussion. A study group also has the advantage of having access to more information and a wider variety of ideas through the contribution of different individuals.

Therapy Groups A **therapy group**, also called an *encounter group, support group,* or *T-group,* helps group members work on personal problems or provides encouragement and support to help manage stress. Such groups are led by professionals who are trained to help members overcome, or at least manage, individual problems in a group setting. Group therapy takes advantage of the self-understanding that members gain as they communicate with one another. Members also learn how they are perceived by others. By participating in a therapy group, people with similar problems can benefit by learning how others have learned to cope. Groups such as Weight Watchers and Alcoholics Anonymous also provide positive reinforcement when members have achieved their goals. By experiencing therapy with others, members take advantage of the greater knowledge and information available to the group.

Committees A **committee** is a group of people who are elected or appointed for a specific task. Some committees are formed to solve problems. Others are appointed to make a decision or simply to gather information so that another group, team, or committee can make a decision. A committee may be either a **standing committee** (one that remains active for an extended time period) or an **ad hoc committee** (one that disbands when its special task has been completed). Like many other people, you may react negatively to serving on a committee. Committee work is often regarded as time-consuming, tedious, and ineffective—except in increasing the sale of aspirin! Perhaps you have heard that "a committee is a way of postponing a decision," or "a committee is a group of people who individually can do nothing and who collectively decide nothing can be done." Although frustration with committees is commonplace, you are not doomed to have a negative experience when working with others on a committee. Throughout this book we review principles and skills of group communication that can help you enhance the quality of committee meetings. In Appendix A we will provide specific tips for chairing and participating in meetings.

Quality Circles   A **quality circle** is a group of from three to fifteen employees who meet regularly to examine work processes with the goal of improving productivity, morale, and overall work quality. Employees trained to work in quality circles receive basic information about the group communication principles and practices that we discuss in this book, such as how to reach agreement, make decisions, solve problems, and develop a cohesive work team.

Focus Groups   A **focus group** is a small group of people who are asked to focus on a particular topic or issue so that others can better understand the group's responses to the topic or issue presented. One person usually serves as moderator, and this person asks open-ended questions and then simply listens to the responses of the group members. Many advertising agencies show new advertising campaigns to focus groups and then listen to the response of the group members to assess the impact or effectiveness of the campaign.

WHAT IS VIRTUAL SMALL GROUP COMMUNICATION?

Most of what is known about groups and teams is based on research that was conducted with groups of people who met face to face, because until relatively recently, most collaborative work occurred live, in real time, and in a single setting. However, collaborative work is increasingly being performed using e-mail, fax machines, video conferences, and other technologies.[55] With today's technological advances, people can work together even when they are physically in different locations. **Virtual small group communication** (also called electronically mediated communication) is communication among group members who are not together in the same physical location. People who are communicating in a virtual group are connected by a phone line, fiber optic cable, wireless signal, satellite signal, or other technology.

Electronic technology makes it possible for you to use virtual methods of communication under four conditions: (1) same time/same place; (2) same time/different place; (3) different time/same place; and (4) different time/different place.[56] Different types of technology make virtual communication possible. Let's take a closer look at these various technologies.

Telephone Conferences

The telephone conference call—one of the first uses of technology to support group and team meetings—involves a group of people agreeing to "meet" at a certain time by phone. To hold a conference call you need a special telephone service, available from most telephone companies, so that several people in different locations can be connected at the same time.

One of the obvious disadvantages of telephone conferencing is that you miss many nonverbal cues. Yes, you still can detect emotions from vocal cues, but without being able to see facial expressions, posture, and gestures, it's possible that you may not accurately understand the meaning of messages.[57] As we will discuss in Chapter 6, nonverbal cues help regulate communication interaction. Have you ever had the experience of talking over someone else's words on the phone? Without the nonverbal regulatory cues, it's trickier to know when to start and stop talking. This problem of regulating communication becomes worse if there are several people on a conference call.

Electronic Mail (E-Mail)

Electronic mail—**e-mail**—is one of the most prevalent technological methods used to send and receive messages in organizations. If you're typical, you regularly send and receive e-mail about personal and work-related topics.

Communicating via e-mail can be effective for the discussion of routine business. There is some evidence, however, that groups that make decisions by e-mail are less likely to reach agreement.[58] Other research, pointing to the value of e-mail meetings, suggests that electronic correspondence minimizes status differences that may be present if people meet face to face.[59] Yet another research team found that groups that use e-mail while solving problems are more likely to do a better job of analyzing the problem than groups that interact face to face.[60] The research on group use of e-mail, however, is still in its early stages.[61]

E-mail users can participate in what is called **synchronous communication**—communication interaction that is taking place in real time. This is what happens when you talk to someone on the telephone—you talk and another person responds immediately to what you've said. A real-time e-mail "conversation" is clearly not as immediate as a face-to-face discussion. Even instant messages and chat room visits are not as immediate as live-and-in-person interaction.

Asynchronous communication is interaction in which e-mail correspondents reply to messages after a time delay—somewhat like posting a message on a bulletin board and waiting for someone to read it and respond to it later. The advantage of asynchronous communication is that you do not have to be logged on to a chat room at the same time as your communication partners. You can post a message and then check back later to see how others have responded, like sending a memo to someone and then waiting for a response. Of course, you lose the immediate feedback, and it takes more time to get work accomplished because you don't get instant responses from others.

As with telephone conferencing, one disadvantage of e-mail and other forms of electronic communication is the loss of emotional information communicated by facial expression, vocal inflection, gestures, and body posture.[62] Some people use *emoticons*—keyboard symbols that are typed in certain visual arrangements expressing emotions—or just put their feelings into words: "I have a big grin on my face as I read what you sent me." Putting your e-mail message in all capital letters is another way to add emotional richness. But be careful using all capital letters: IT'S LIKE SHOUTING AT SOMEONE. Your readers may think you are rude if your message seems to scream at them.

Video Conferences

The **video conference**—a relatively media-rich use of technology—occurs when two or more individuals are linked by the Internet or by closed-circuit or satellite-linked TV. With the advent of mini-cameras, the Internet, and affordable software, it has become increasingly easy for groups to hold video conference meetings. The video conference has the

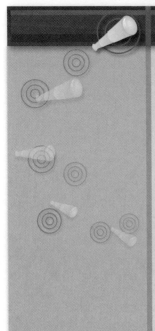

Cutting Edge Theory

MEDIA RICHNESS THEORY

Group and team members have a wealth of choices about how to communicate with each other. Today's technologies such as e-mail, instant messaging, and computer video streaming make it possible for people to collaborate without meeting face to face. One interesting theory with real-life applications is called **media richness theory.** It helps explain why certain types of technologies are effective and others are not. When is it best to meet face to face, and when is it acceptable to share information in a memo? It depends on the richness of the medium selected for the message.

A medium, or method, of communication is said to be *rich* if it has the following four characteristics:

1. Potential for instant feedback
2. Several verbal and nonverbal cues that can be processed by senders and receivers
3. Natural rather than formal language
4. A focus on individuals rather than on a mass of people.

Face-to-face meetings and in-person conferences are media-rich; a memo or an announcement posted on a bulletin board is media-lean. The facing page shows a continuum of media-rich and media-lean methods of communication.

Real-Life Applications

When should you choose media-rich channels of communication? According to Linda Trevino, Richard Daft, and Robert Lengel, the developers of media richness theory, select a media-rich channel (such as meeting face to face) when

- Your message is ambiguous.
- You think your message may be misunderstood.
- Your message is complicated and complex.

Select a media-lean channel (e-mail or memo) when

- Your message describes routine information.

obvious advantage of permitting people to interact over long distances when it may be very expensive to have all members travel to one destination. And the video conference has an advantage over a conference phone call because nonverbal behaviors such as facial expressions, eye contact, and posture—which allow the transmission of relational messages—can be seen. Several studies have found that a video meeting is more likely to be successful if group members have met one another prior to the video meeting.[63] Another study found that video conferences are better than face-to-face meetings when participants are involved in more structured discussion.[64] Group members also seem to prepare better for a video

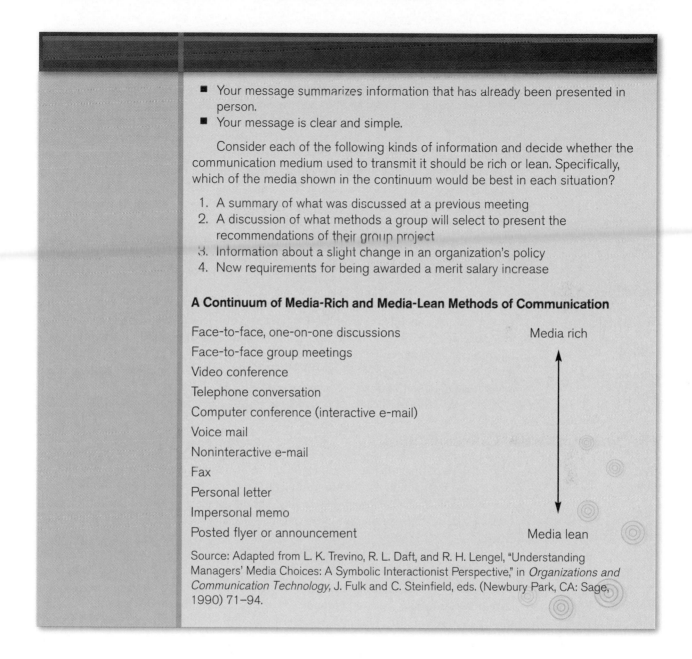

- Your message summarizes information that has already been presented in person.
- Your message is clear and simple.

Consider each of the following kinds of information and decide whether the communication medium used to transmit it should be rich or lean. Specifically, which of the media shown in the continuum would be best in each situation?

1. A summary of what was discussed at a previous meeting
2. A discussion of what methods a group will select to present the recommendations of their group project
3. Information about a slight change in an organization's policy
4. New requirements for being awarded a merit salary increase

A Continuum of Media-Rich and Media-Lean Methods of Communication

Face-to-face, one-on-one discussions   Media rich

Face-to-face group meetings

Video conference

Telephone conversation

Computer conference (interactive e-mail)

Voice mail

Noninteractive e-mail

Fax

Personal letter

Impersonal memo

Posted flyer or announcement   Media lean

Source: Adapted from L. K. Trevino, R. L. Daft, and R. H. Lengel, "Understanding Managers' Media Choices: A Symbolic Interactionist Perspective," in *Organizations and Communication Technology*, J. Fulk and C. Steinfield, eds. (Newbury Park, CA: Sage, 1990) 71–94.

conference than for a face-to-face meeting; perhaps group members view a video conference as more important than an ordinary meeting.

Electronic Meeting Systems

Electronic meeting systems (EMS) consist of both computer hardware and software programs that help group members do their work when they are not meeting face to face.[65] Sometimes this technology is called group decision support systems (GDSS) or group support systems (GSS). Whatever the name and abbreviation, EMS, GDSS, and GSS and other systems like them are all based on similar principles.

EMS systems can be used by people who are sitting at computer keyboards in the same room at the same time. What people type is shown on a large screen where all group members can see what each member has written. Sometimes the meeting participants talk to each other directly, just as they would in any face-to-face meeting; at other times they can make contributions via their keyboards. Group members can brainstorm ideas, vote, outline their ideas, or expand on the ideas of others using their computer keyboards. When sharing information electronically, people can make comments anonymously and thus be more creative and less concerned about what others may think of the ideas they share.

EMS systems can also be used when people are not in the same room at the same time. They can be used synchronously (when each group member is connected at the same time) or asynchrononously (when people are not working together at the same time).

Web Pages

Group and team members can collaborate in the same electronic space using a common Web page that functions as an electronic bulletin board. Members can go to the Web page for information and may be permitted to change or delete information. Each member has access to what others have gathered and shared. Group members could also post calendars and schedules on the Web page to help organize the work.

The Quality of Virtual Communication

There has been much debate about the quality of virtual communication compared with face-to-face interaction. A common complaint is the loss of nonverbal cues in electronic collaboration, which can slow understanding. The differences between virtual communication and face-to-face communication are still being discovered. However, some patterns are emerging.

Communication researcher Joseph Walther and his colleagues have developed a **social information-processing theory** that explains how you can develop quality relationships with others via e-mail and other electronic means.[66] According to this theory, a key difference between face-to-face and computer-mediated communication is the rate at which information reaches you. During live, in-person communication, you process a lot of information quickly; you process a myriad of nonverbal cues you see (facial expression and body posture) and hear (tone of voice and use of pauses). During e-mail interactions, there is less information to process, so it takes a bit longer for a relationship to develop—but it does develop as you learn more about your e-mail partner's likes, dislikes, and feelings.

A study by Lisa Tidwell and Joseph Walther extended the application of social information-processing theory. These researchers investigated how computer-mediated communication affects how much information people reveal about themselves, how quickly they reveal it, and the overall impressions people get of one another. In comparing computer-mediated exchanges with face-to-face conversations, Tidwell and Walther found that people in computer-mediated "conversations" asked more direct questions, which resulted in people revealing more, not less, information about themselves when online.

Also, if you expect to communicate with your electronic partner again, there is evidence that you will pay more attention to the relationship cues that develop. In one study, Joseph Walther and Judee Burgoon found that the development of relationships between people who meet face to face differed little from those between people who had computer-mediated interactions.[67] In fact, they found that many computer-mediated groups actually developed more satisfying relationships than the face-to-face groups.

HOW CAN YOU BECOME A COMPETENT SMALL GROUP COMMUNICATOR?

In the chapters ahead, we discuss principles and skills designed to enhance your competence as a member of a small group. You may be wondering "precisely what does a competent communicator do?" A **competent group communicator** is a person who is able to interact appropriately and effectively with others in small groups and teams. Communication researcher Michael Mayer found that the two most important behaviors of group members were (1) fully participating in the discussion, especially when analyzing a problem, and (2) offering encouraging, supportive comments to others.[68] Stated succinctly: Participate and be nice.

As a prelude to this book's discussion of the ideas and strategies that enhance communication in small groups, we will first introduce a more specific definition of competence and then present nine core small group communication competencies.

The Essence of Communication Competence

Researchers who have studied how to enhance communication competence suggest that three elements are involved in becoming a truly competent communicator: (1) you must be motivated, (2) you must have appropriate knowledge, and (3) you must have the skill to act appropriately.[69]

Motivation   **Motivation** is an internal drive to achieve a goal. To be motivated means you have a strong desire to do your best, even during inevitable periods of fatigue and frustration. If you are motivated to become a competent small group communicator, you probably have an understanding of the benefits or advantages of working with others in groups.

Knowledge   **Knowledge** is the information you need to competently do what needs to be done. One key purpose of this book is to give you knowledge that can help you become a more competent communicator in groups, on teams, and during the many meetings you will undoubtedly attend in the future.

Skill   A **skill** is an effective behavior that can be repeated when appropriate. Just having the desire to be effective (motivation) or being able to rattle off lists of principles and theories (knowledge) doesn't ensure that you will be competent; you have to have the skill to put the principles into practice. The subtitle of this book—*Principles and Practices*—emphasizes the importance of being able to translate into action what you know and think.

Research supports the commonsense conclusion that practicing group communication skills, especially when you practice the skills in a group or team setting, enhances your group performance.[70]

Case Study

It is the first meeting of the mayor's blue ribbon Tourism Task Force. The town of Walnut Springs, with a population of almost 45,000 people, was once a bustling tourist destination. The town used to have a small amusement park called Aquaworld, built near the springs, that was popular during the 1960s and 1970s. (Its claim to fame was a swimming pig that would take a swim across the springs each hour.) But attendance at Aquaworld dropped dramatically when a more modern theme park, Whale World, opened in a nearby city. Aquaworld has now closed and is operated as a small fish museum; only a few people come to look at a few tanks of fish. The town also has a large outlet mall that brings in tourists by the busload—or at least it used to. Because of competition from two new outlet malls built in other towns, the customer traffic at the mall is steadily dropping.

Members of the Tourism Task Force are to identify strategies that would again make Walnut Springs a thriving tourist destination. A related goal is to suggest tourism ideas that would create jobs and add to the tax base of the community.

You can see the bewilderment and uncertainty on the faces of the seven members of the task force as they assemble in the conference room in City Hall. The group has a leader appointed by the mayor, but they don't really have a clue about how to begin their work. The task force members are busy people. A few members suggest that they should hold several of their meetings by e-mail or have phone conferences rather than meeting in person. One member of the group, Arnold Thornton, suggests that the group doesn't really need to meet at all. Arnold thinks that most of the information the group needs is already available on the Internet. He thinks the task force leader should

just search the Web for ideas developed by other communities and report those to the mayor. "Why reinvent the wheel?" asks Arnold.

What should they do first? What information do they need? How should they go about developing their recommendations? Do they really need to meet together? These are just some of the questions on their minds.

Practice in Applying Principles

1. Where would you place the task force on a continuum between being a group and being a team, using a scale of 1 to 10 (1 = being a group; 5 = somewhere in the middle; 10 = being a team)? If you think the task force is closer to the definition of a small group, how does the definition of a small group on page 5 apply to the task force? If you think the task force is closer to being a team, apply the description of a team on page 6.
2. What could the task force leader do to further enhance teamwork among group members?
3. Based on the description of different types of groups on pages 18–20, what type of group or team is the task force?
4. Does this group really need to meet? Review the information about when not to collaborate on pages 15–16 to help you develop your answer.
5. Should the task force meet in person or become a virtual group, as suggested by a few members? Support your answer based on information on pages 20–25.
6. Which of the small group problem-solving competencies described on pages 27–28 will be most important at their first meeting?

THE NINE CORE SMALL GROUP COMMUNICATION COMPETENCIES

Although we've described the personal qualities of competent group or team members, you may still be wondering, "What specifically do effective group members do?" Following is an overview of some of the competencies that are essential for members of problem-solving groups. It's important to emphasize that this overview targets *problem-solving* discussion. To solve a problem or to achieve a goal you must seek to overcome an obstacle. There is more communication research about how to solve problems and make effective decisions in small groups and teams than on any other topic. The overview presented here sketches some of the core competencies that can result in more effective group outcomes. We will expand on this overview of these competencies in the chapters ahead.

The nine competencies are grouped into four categories. **Problem-oriented competencies** focus on defining and analyzing a problem. **Solution-oriented competencies** concern identifying solution criteria, generating solutions, and evaluating solutions. **Discussion-management competencies** help the group stay focused on the task and manage the interaction. Finally, **relational competencies** are concerned with managing conflict and maintaining a positive group climate. These competencies were identified after examining several bodies of research and consulting with several instructors of small group communication.[71]

Problem-Oriented Competencies

1. *Define the problem.* Effective group members clearly and appropriately define or describe the problem to be solved and the obstacles to be overcome. Ineffective group members either define the problem inaccurately or make little or no attempt to clarify the problem or issues confronting the group.
2. *Analyze the problem.* Effective group members offer statements that clearly and appropriately examine the causes, history, symptoms, and significance of the problem to be solved. Ineffective members either don't analyze the problem or they do so inaccurately or inappropriately.

Solution-Oriented Competencies

1. *Identify criteria.* Effective group members offer clear and appropriate comments that identify the goal the group is attempting to achieve or identify specific criteria (or standards) for an acceptable solution or outcome for the problem facing the group. Ineffective group members don't clarify the goal or establish criteria for solving the problem. Ineffective groups aren't sure what they are looking for in a solution or outcome.
2. *Generate solutions.* Effective group members offer several possible solutions or strategies to overcome obstacles or decision options regarding the issues confronting the group. Ineffective group members offer fewer solutions, or they rush to make a decision without considering other options or before defining and analyzing the problem.
3. *Evaluate solutions.* Effective group members systematically evaluate the pros and cons of the solutions that are proposed. Ineffective group members examine neither the positive and negative consequences nor the benefits and potential costs of a solution or decision.

Discussion-Management Competencies

1. *Maintain task focus.* Effective group members stay on track and keep their focus on the task at hand. Although almost every group wanders off track from time to time, the most effective groups are mindful of their goal and sensitive to completing the work before them. Effective group members also summarize what the group is discussing to keep the group oriented. Ineffective group members have difficulty staying on track and frequently digress from the issues at hand. They also seldom summarize what the group has done, which means that group members aren't quite sure what they are accomplishing.

2. *Manage interaction.* Effective group members don't monopolize the conversation; rather, they actively look for ways to draw quieter members into the discussion. Neither are they too quiet; they contribute their fair share of information and look for ways to keep the discussion from becoming a series of monologues; they encourage on-task, supportive dialogue. Ineffective group members either rarely contribute to the discussion or monopolize the discussion by talking too much. They also make little effort to draw others into the conversation and are not sensitive to the need for balanced interaction among group members.

Relational Competencies

1. *Manage conflict.* Conflict occurs in the best of groups. Effective group members are sensitive to differences of opinion and personal conflict, and they actively seek to manage the conflict by focusing on issues, information, and evidence rather than on personalities. Ineffective group members deal with conflict by making it personal; they are insensitive to the feelings of others and generally focus on personalities at the expense of issues.

2. *Maintain climate.* Effective group members look for opportunities to support and encourage other group members.[72] Although they may not agree with all comments made, they actively seek ways to improve the climate and maintain positive relationships with other group members through both verbal and nonverbal expressions of support. Ineffective group members do just the opposite: They are critical of others, and their frowning faces and strident voices nonverbally cast a gloomy pall over the group. Ineffective members rarely use appropriate humor to lessen any tension between members.

Communicating effectively in small groups and teams involves a variety of competencies. Even as we present these nine competencies, we are not suggesting that these are the *only* things you need to learn; instead, we present them as a practical beginning to learning the essentials of communicating in small group problem solving and decision making.

A competent communicator has not only knowledge and skill but also the motivation to work well with others. In his book *All I Really Need to Know I Learned in Kindergarten,* Robert Fulghum suggested that while he was in kindergarten he mastered the basics of getting along with others and accomplishing tasks effectively. This book is designed to add to what you learned in kindergarten and later, so you can become a valued member of the groups to which you belong.

Each of the nine group communication competencies is founded on the assumption that to be a competent communicator, you must be an ethical communicator. **Ethics** are the beliefs, values, and moral principles by which we determine what is right and what is wrong. Ethical principles are the basis for many of the decisions we make in our personal and professional lives. Throughout the book we will

www.CartoonStock.com

Collaborating Ethically: What Would You Do?

Your underlying ethical principles are like your computer's operating system, which always activates when you are working with other programs on your computer. How you interact with others is based on your underlying assumptions and beliefs about appropriate and inappropriate ways to treat others.

Suppose you found yourself in the following situation. Your group communication instructor has assigned all students to small groups to work on a semester-long group project. One member of your group has a friend who took the course last semester with a different instructor. He suggests that your group select the same discussion topic that his friend had so that the group could benefit from the research already gathered by his friend's group. Your group can also do some original research to build on the previous group's research, but you will rely heavily on the information already collected. Is it ethical to use the work of another group in this situation? Are there any conditions that would make it more ethical to use the work of the previous group? Even if the group you're in gathers additional research, is it appropriate to "borrow" heavily from the work already completed by others, especially if the goal is to learn how to conduct original research?

What would you do?

be spotlighting the importance of being an ethical group communicator in a feature we call Collaborating Ethically: What Would You Do? Each of these poses an ethical question or dilemma and then invites you to consider the most ethical course of action to take. The first one appears above.

Putting Principles into Practice

Groups and teams are integral parts of any society. This chapter has explained the importance of studying small group communication. To apply some of the principles of groups, consider the suggestions in the following sections.

Remember Some Essential Principles

- Work in small groups to benefit from the knowledge and information of others.

- Work in small groups to take advantage of other members' creative approaches to problem solving and decision making.
- Learn to recognize the key elements that make a team effective: a clear, elevating goal; a results-driven structure; competent team members; unified commitment; a collaborative climate; standards of excellence; external support and recognition; principled leadership.

- Cultivate those characteristics of individual team members that enhance team effectiveness: experience; problem-solving ability; openness; supportiveness; action-oriented approach; positive personal style.
- Form a discussion group and talk about a topic with others when you want to improve your understanding of a subject or issue.
- Work in small groups so that you can participate in making decisions that affect you. You will be more likely to support a decision if you have contributed to the discussion.
- Try to learn something new about yourself when you work with others in small groups.
- Do not let others pressure you to conform to the group's majority opinion just for the sake of agreement.
- Do not let one or two members of a small group dominate the discussion. If they do, you lose many of the advantages of working in a group.
- Avoid the trap of relying too much on other group members. Assume your fair share of the responsibility for getting things done.

- Avoid frustration by accepting the fact that groups take more time to accomplish tasks than do individuals.

Become a Competent Group Communicator

- Focus on the specific competencies needed to participate effectively in a small group so that you can employ them more efficiently.
- Help your group accomplish a task by defining and analyzing the problem, identifying criteria, generating solutions, evaluating solutions, and maintaining task focus.

Use Technology Wisely

- Use more media-rich methods when communicating information that may be misunderstood.
- Consider using telephone conferences, e-mail, video conferences, electronic meeting systems, or Web pages to share information between face-to-face meetings.

*P*RACTICE

Agree-Disagree Statements

Read each statement once. Mark whether you agree (A) or disagree (D) with each statement. Take five or six minutes to do this.[73]

1. _____ A primary concern of all group members should be to establish an atmosphere in which all feel free to express their opinions.
2. _____ In a group with a strong leader, an individual is able to feel more personal security than in a leaderless group.
3. _____ Individuals who are part of working groups should do what they think is right, regardless of what the groups decide to do.
4. _____ It is sometimes necessary to use autocratic methods to obtain democratic objectives.
5. _____ Sometimes it is necessary to push people in the direction you think is right, even if they object.
6. _____ It is sometimes necessary to ignore the feelings of others in order to reach a group decision.
7. _____ One should not openly criticize or find fault with leaders who are doing their best.
8. _____ Democracy has no place in a military organization such as an air task force or an infantry squad, when it is engaged in battle.
9. _____ When everybody in the group has to be considered before making a decision, much time is wasted talking.
10. _____ Almost any job that can be done by a committee can be done better by giving one individual responsibility for the job.

11. _____ By the time most people reach maturity, it is almost impossible for them to increase their skills in group participation.

After you have marked the statements, form small groups and try to agree or disagree unanimously with each statement. Try especially to find reasons for differences of opinion. If your group cannot reach agreement or disagreement, you may change the wording in any statement to promote unanimity.

Get-Acquainted Scavenger Hunt

Your instructor will ask you to find people in your class or your group who match as many of the following descriptions as possible. When you meet someone who matches a particular description, write his or her name on the line opposite it. Use this as a way of getting better acquainted with people with whom you will be working or studying.[74]

1. Someone with your eye color _____
2. Someone born in the same state you were _____
3. Someone whose astrological sign is the same as yours _____
4. Someone who likes the same sport you do _____
5. Someone who likes your favorite food _____
6. Someone who has the same number of letters in his or her name _____
7. Someone who feels it is okay to cry in public _____
8. Someone who is the youngest in the family _____
9. Someone who would like to write a book _____
10. Someone who has seen the same movie at least three times _____

11. Someone who has traveled outside the United States _____
12. Someone who likes to ski _____
13. Someone who is an only child _____
14. Someone who can speak two languages _____
15. Someone who likes to cook _____

Rating Your Team

Use the following assessment scale to rate a team you are part of. For each characteristic described, rate your team on a scale from 1 (not very effective) to 10 (exceptional). The higher the score (out of a possible 80 points), the more likely it is that your team is a high-performing team. These eight team characteristics are based on the work of Carl Larson and Frank LaFasto, as described in their book *Teamwork: What Must Go Right/What Can Go Wrong* and discussed on pages 8–9.

1. Our team clearly states its goals and mission. Each team member knows the primary task, product, or service that we are responsible for. Our clear, elevating (exciting) goal is written down and referred to often in our discussions.

   1   2   3   4   5   6   7   8   9   10

2. Our team is well organized. Each team member knows what his or her task or assignment is. We have a results-driven structure. We are not often distracted by "busy work" and tasks that do not relate to our primary mission.

   1   2   3   4   5   6   7   8   9   10

3. Our team has highly competent and skilled members. They are among the best possible team members available to achieve our goal.

   1   2   3   4   5   6   7   8   9   10

4. Our team is unified. We are all committed to achieving a common goal. We are a cohesive team. We talk about the importance of reaching group agreement and team consensus.

   1   2   3   4   5   6   7   8   9   10

5. Our team has a supportive work climate. We give each other praise. We manage our conflicts in a positive, supportive way. We work well together.

   1   2   3   4   5   6   7   8   9   10

6. Our team has high standards of excellence. We talk about the importance of doing a high-quality job. Doing a job well is important to all team members.

   1   2   3   4   5   6   7   8   9   10

7. We are rewarded for our good work. We reward each other, and we are rewarded in meaningful ways by others in this organization. We receive support and recognition for our high-quality work.

   1   2   3   4   5   6   7   8   9   10

8. Our team has good leaders to help us do our work. Our leaders are skilled and knowledgeable. Our leaders are sensitive to other team members' needs.

   1   2   3   4   5   6   7   8   9   10

Group Communication Journal

Keep a journal in which you describe, analyze, and evaluate your interactions with others in small groups during the semester. After each group activity, assignment, or case study, record your analysis of the group interaction. Consider organizing your journal entries this way:

1. *Describe what happened.* Make brief notes identifying what occurred during your group meeting.
2. *Analyze what happened.* Cite principles and research from your text to help you interpret why your group behaved as it did.
3. *Evaluate what happened.* What did the group do well? What could your group have done to improve its performance? What could you have done to improve the group?

Your instructor may collect your journal from time to time to assess your ability to describe, analyze, and evaluate your group experiences.

CHAPTER TWO

Small Group Communication Theory

"To despise theory is to have the excessively vain pretension to do without knowing what one does, and to speak without knowing what one says."

—*Bernard le Bovier de Fontenelle*

CHAPTER OUTLINE

The Nature of Theory and the Theory-Building Process

Theory: A Practical Approach to Group Communication

The Purpose of Communication in Small Groups: Making Sense

Theoretical Perspectives for the Study of Group and Team Communication

Case Study

Describing Elements of Group and Team Communication

Putting Principles into Practice

Practice

OBJECTIVES

After studying this chapter, you will be able to:

- Discuss the nature and functions of theory and theory construction.
- Explain the relevance of theory to the study of small group communication.
- Discuss five general theories that apply to small group communication.
- Explain the model of small group communication presented in this chapter.
- Identify some of the components of small group communication.

THEORY. *It is a word people encounter almost daily in their casual conversations, in classrooms, and on news broadcasts. They discuss and evaluate theories of evolution, the theory of relativity, and quantum theory. Fictitious criminal investigators on television develop theories about what took place at a crime scene. Psychologists and parents create theories of personality development and theories of childrearing (in fact, there are practically as many theories of childrearing as there are parents). In short, theories abound— some are simple, some complex; some are formal, some informal; some are scientific, some unscientific. Yet few people take the time to think about what theories are. Where do they come from? How are they built? What do people do with them after they've got them?*

The word theory *intimidates many people. To them, studying theory is an esoteric activity that has no relevance except for the scientist or the academician. Today's students are interested in relevant, practical kinds of knowledge, and sometimes they assume that theory is neither relevant nor practical. But theory is very practical. Theorizing helps to explain or predict the events in people's lives; Dance and Larson claim that "theorizing is a very basic form of human activity."[1] People theorize on a rudimentary level when they reflect on their past experiences and make decisions based on these experiences.* **Theory,** *then, has two basic functions: to explain and to predict. We discuss these functions more fully later in the chapter.*

This chapter examines some of the central issues of group communication theory. First, we discuss the nature of theory and the theory-building process. Second, we turn our attention to the relevance and practicality of theory in the study of small group communication. Third, we discuss five theoretical perspectives for the study of small groups. Finally, we present a theoretical model of small group communication.

THE NATURE OF THEORY AND THE THEORY-BUILDING PROCESS

As mentioned above, theories are very practical. Suppose, for example, that you do your weekly grocery shopping every Thursday after your late afternoon class. When you arrive at the store, you are pleased to see that several checkout lanes are open, with no one waiting at any of them. "Ah," you say, "I'll be out of here in short order." You proceed up one aisle and down the next. To your dismay, you notice that each time you pass the checkout lanes, the lines have grown. By the time you fill your cart, at least six people are waiting in each lane. You now have a 20-minute wait at the checkout.

If the situation just described were to occur once, you would probably curse your luck or chalk it up to fate. If you find, however, that the same events occur each time you visit the market, you begin to see a consistency in your observations that goes beyond luck or fate. In noticing this consistency, you take the first step in building a theory. You have observed a *phenomenon*. You have witnessed a *repeated pattern* of events for which you feel there must be some *explanation*. So you ponder the situation. In your mind you organize all the facts available to you: the time of your arrival, the condition of the checkout lanes when you enter the store each time, and the length of the lines when you complete your shopping. Lo and behold, you discover that you arrive at the store at approximately 4:45 each afternoon and reach the checkout lanes about 25 minutes later. You conclude that between the time you arrive and the time you depart, thousands of workers head for home, some of them stopping off at the store on the way. *Voilà*—you have a theory. You have organized your information to explain the phenomenon.

Assuming that your theory is accurate, it is now very useful for you. Having *explained* the phenomenon, you may now reasonably *predict* that under the same set of circumstances, the phenomenon will recur. In other words, if you continue to do your weekly shopping after your late class on Thursday, you will repeatedly be faced with long checkout lines. Given this knowledge, you can adapt your behavior accordingly, perhaps by doing your shopping earlier or later in the day.

On a more personal level, your theory about yourself—your **self-concept**—influences the choices you make throughout the day. You tend to do things that you see as being consistent (predictable) with your self-concept. In essence, this self-concept, or "self-theory," serves to explain you to yourself, thereby allowing you to predict your behavior and to successfully select realistic goals. This is theory at its most personal and pervasive.

Theory building is a common, natural process of human communication. You notice consistencies in your experience and examine relationships among the consistencies. You then build an explanation of the phenomena that allows you to predict future events and, in some cases, to exercise some control over situations. Some theories, of course, are very elaborate and formal, but even in these the fundamental features of explanation and prediction can be seen. George Kelly's definition of theory refers to these features:

> A theory may be considered as a way of binding together a multitude of facts so that one may comprehend them all at once. When the theory enables us to make reasonably precise predictions, one may call it scientific.[2]

Theory is crucial to the study of group and team communication. The explanatory power of good theory helps make sense of the processes involved when people interact with others in a group. The predictive precision of theory allows people to anticipate probable outcomes of various types of communicative behavior in the group. Armed with this type of knowledge, people can adjust their own communicative behavior to help make group work more effective and rewarding.

*T*HEORY: A PRACTICAL APPROACH TO GROUP COMMUNICATION

Theory, both formal and informal, helps people make intelligent decisions about how to conduct themselves. Working in small groups is no exception. Everyone brings a set of theories to small group meetings—theories about oneself, about other group members, and about groups in general. Once in the group, people regulate their behavior according to these theories. They behave in ways consistent with their self-concepts. They deal with others in the group according to their previous impressions (theories) of them. If they believe (theorize) that groups are essentially ineffectual, that "a camel is a horse designed by committee" or that "if you really want something done, do it yourself," then they probably will act accordingly and reinforce their belief. If, in contrast, they come to the group convinced that groups are capable of working effectively, and if they know how to make the group work, they will behave very differently and contribute much more to the group's effectiveness.

Explanatory Function

To be practical, theories of small group communication must suggest ways in which participants can make group discussion more efficient and rewarding. The **explanatory function** of theory is important in this regard. If people understand why some groups are effective while others are not, or why certain styles of leadership are appropriate in some situations but not in others, then they are better prepared to diagnose the needs of their own groups.

Predictive Function

In medicine, a diagnosis is useless unless it suggests some course of treatment. Nevertheless, diagnosis—explanation—is a necessary first step. *Understanding* the process leads toward

Collaborating Ethically: What Would You Do?

Ethical principles help people decide what's right or wrong. They are theoretical constructs that help people *explain* situations in which they find themselves, *predict* possible outcomes from a set of potential actions, and *control* their behavior to achieve desired effects. Sometimes people are unaware of their own ethical principles until confronted with specific situations that require ethical judgments.

What would you do in the following situation?

You and your three roommates see an advertisement for a $2,500 high-definition, flat-screen LCD television. You currently have a small TV in your apartment, and on your limited budgets, you can't really afford a new one. The ad says you may try out the TV in your home for six months with no obligation to buy. If not completely satisfied, you can return the set with no questions asked. If you decide to keep the set, you begin making monthly payments at that time. Will you try out the TV, knowing that there is no way you can keep it longer than six months? Or will you pass on the offer?

You may think there is clearly a right answer, but others may hold the opposite view and see it just as clearly. Our theories of ourselves (self-concepts) include ethical beliefs and principles. Can you identify the ethical principle that explains your decision in this case?

ways of *improving* the process, and herein lies the usefulness of the **predictive function** of theory. By understanding a specific group and group communication in general, and by being aware of possible alternative behaviors, you can use theory to select behaviors that will help you achieve the goal of your group. In other words, if you can reasonably predict that certain outcomes will follow certain types of communication, you can regulate your behavior to achieve the most desirable results. For example, consider this bit of theoretical knowledge about prediction and group communication: Predictions about time—such as how much time a task will take—that are made through group discussion tend to be more optimistic than predictions made by individuals in the group, probably because of the assumption that "many hands make light work." This tendency may lead to unrealistic time estimates and failure to meet deadlines. If you are a leader or member of a group or team facing such a situation, knowledge of this tendency can help you to moderate its effect by alerting the group and suggesting a little more time for the project at hand.[3]

Some theories presented in this book explain group and team phenomena. These theories are referred to as **process theories.** Other theories, called **method theories,** take a prescriptive approach to small group communication. These how-to theories are particularly useful in establishing formats for solving problems and resolving conflicts in a group. Both types of theories add to the knowledge and skills that can make you a more effective communicator. Central to your effectiveness as a communicator is the ability to use words, which is the subject of the next section.

THE PURPOSE OF COMMUNICATION IN SMALL GROUPS: MAKING SENSE

A group cannot function without words; communication is the vehicle that allows a group to move toward its goals. A verbal description of an idea for a new product at a manufacturing company's board meeting creates a vision of that product for board members. Presented effectively, the description may result in new or changed attitudes and behaviors; the idea may be adopted. Words, then, have the power to create new realities and change attitudes; they are immensely powerful tools. Although this may seem obvious, it is a truth that often goes unnoticed. We spend so much of each day speaking, listening, reading, and writing that language seems commonplace to us. It is not. Through language we unravel the immense complexity that is our world. With language, we build the theories that explain the world to ourselves and others.

In Chapter 1 we defined human communication as a transactive process by which we make sense out of the world and share that sense with others. Communication organizes and makes sense out of all the sights, sounds, odors, tastes, and sensations in the environment. As communication scholar Dean Barnlund states, "Communication occurs any time meaning is assigned to an internal or external stimulus."[4] Thus, when people arrive at a meeting room and begin to shiver, the sensation brings to their minds the word *cold.* Within themselves, or on an *intrapersonal level,* they have reduced uncertainty about the nature of an experience. The room is too cold. Giving verbal expression to an experience organizes and clarifies that experience.

At the *interpersonal level* of communication, the sense-making process is even more clearly evident. As you get to know someone, you progressively discover what makes that person unique. By developing an explanation of that person's behavior, you can predict how he or she is likely to respond to future communication and events. You base your predictions on what you know about the person's beliefs, attitudes, values, and personality. In

"Where are you going with this, Wingate?"

essence, you build a theory that allows you to explain another person's behavior, to predict that person's future responses, and to control your own communicative behavior accordingly. Theories help people make sense of others.

Complexity

Getting to know someone is a process of progressively reducing uncertainty—and a lot of uncertainty exists, especially at the outset of working with others in groups and teams. Think back to your first day at college or to your first day in group communication class. You were probably surrounded by many unfamiliar faces. At times such as these, you may feel tentative or uncertain and think "What am I doing here?" and "Who are all of these other people?" In the cafeteria line you encounter a person you find attractive. You say, "Hi! Are you new? What do you think of school so far?" This takes a bit of courage because you don't know what kind of response you will get. So you hesitate. You make small talk and look for signs in the other person's behavior that might indicate whether that person desires further communication. You communicate, observe the response, and base further communication on your interpretation of that response. This is a complex process, particularly because both you and another person must communicate, observe, respond, and interpret simultaneously!

The complexity of the process creates uncertainty—a sense of not being able to predict what will happen in the future. The presence of other people creates uncertainty because you don't know what they will do or say. Many communication theorists have noted that whenever an individual communicates with another person at least six people are involved: (1) who you think you are, (2) who you think the other person is, (3) who you think the other person thinks you are, (4) who the other person thinks he or she is, (5) who the other person thinks you are, and (6) who the other person thinks you think he or she is. All six of these people influence and are influenced by the communication—a very complex matter indeed.

TABLE 2.1	Increase in Potential Relationships with an Increase in Group Size
Size of Group	Number of Relationships
2	1
3	6
4	25
5	90
6	301
7	966

Source: From William M. Kephart, "A Quantitative Analysis of Intragroup Relationships," *American Journal of Sociology* 60 (1950). Reprinted by permission of the University of Chicago Press.

Small Groups: More Complexity

Table 2.1 shows dramatically how complexity increases with group size, even when one relationship involves two, not six, people. When eight people interact, literally thousands of factors influence communication and are influenced by it—factors such as "who I think Ted thinks Rosa thinks Amit is" or "who I think Lourdes thinks Tom thinks I am."

Fortunately, people don't think consciously about all these factors all the time. They would be horribly debilitated if they did so. Nevertheless, these dynamics subtly influence people whenever they interact.

THEORETICAL PERSPECTIVES FOR THE STUDY OF GROUP AND TEAM COMMUNICATION

Thus far, we have discussed the nature of theory and its relationship to effective small group communication. Uncertainty and complexity are pervasive characteristics of small groups, while communication is the driving force that moves groups toward their goals.

Small group communication theory attempts to explain and predict group and team phenomena. Given the complexity of the process and the number of variables that affect small group communication, no single theory can account for all the variables involved, nor can one theory systematically relate the variables to one another. Therefore, a number of approaches to group communication theory have emerged in recent years. Each seeks to explain and predict group behavior while focusing on different facets of the group process. We will briefly describe five of these theoretical perspectives: (1) systems theory, (2) social exchange theory, (3) symbolic convergence theory, (4) structuration theory, and (5) functional theory.

Systems Theory

Perhaps the most prevalent and promising approach to small group communication is **systems theory,** because it is flexible enough to encompass the vast array of variables that influence group and team interaction.

One way to approach the concept of a system is to think of your own body. The various organs make up systems (digestive, nervous, circulatory) that, in turn, make up the larger system: your body. Each organ depends on the proper functioning of other organs: A change in one part of the system causes changes in the rest of the system. Furthermore, the physiological system cannot be isolated from the environment that surrounds it; to maintain the proper functioning of your physiological systems, you must adjust to changes outside your body. A decrease in oxygen at a higher elevation will cause you to breathe more rapidly, a rise in temperature will make you perspire, and so forth. In other words, your body is an *open* system composed of interdependent elements. It receives *input* from the environment (food, air, water), *processes* that input (digestion and oxygenation), and yields an *output* (writing poetry, building cathedrals, cooking a fabulous dinner). Like the human body, a small group is an open **system**, composed of interdependent variables, that receives input, processes the input, and yields an output. The system also exhibits the properties of synergy, entropy, and equifinality.

Openness to Environment   A group does not operate in isolation; it is continually affected by interactions with its environment. New members may join and former members may leave; demands from other organizations may alter the group's goals. Even the climate may affect the group's ability to work.

Interdependence   The various components of the group process are interrelated in such a way that a change in one component will alter the relationships among all other components. A shift in cohesiveness can change the group's productivity level. The loss of a group member or the addition of a new member causes a change felt throughout the system. **Interdependence** in the small group makes the study of small group communication fascinating and difficult: None of the variables involved may be understood properly in isolation.[5]

Input Variables   By viewing them as parts of subsystems, we can categorize the variables of small group communication according to the systems-theory concept of input, process, and output. Input variables in the small group system include such things as group members and group resources, among them funds, tools, knowledge, purposes, relationships to other groups or organizations, and the physical environment.[6]

Process Variables   Process variables relate to the procedures that the group follows to reach its goals. Many of these variables are represented in Figure 2.1, discussed in the next section.

Output Variables   Output variables—the outcomes of the group process—range from solutions and decisions to personal growth and satisfaction.

Synergy   Just as you are more than a composite of your various parts (you are *you,* after all), groups must be seen as more than the sum of their elements. **Synergy** is present when the whole is greater than the sum of its parts. When individuals form groups, they create something—the group—that didn't exist before; the group is more than the individuals who compose it.

Entropy   The measure of randomness or chaos in a system is called **entropy.** Systems tend to decay (gain entropy) if not balanced by some countervailing force. For example, interpersonal relationships separated by distance tend to cool rapidly, unless maintained actively through visits, letters, phone calls, and e-mails. So, too, groups and teams experience entropy when they don't meet together regularly.

Equifinality   The principle of **equifinality** states that a system's final state may be reached by multiple paths and from different initial states; there is more than one way to reach the goal. This is an inherent characteristic of open systems. Conversely, systems (or groups and teams) that share the same initial conditions can reach very different end states.

Although systems theory does not explain small group phenomena, it serves as a useful organizational strategy. It also reminds us that a full understanding of group communication involves the broader contexts or environments in which groups operate. All the theories identified in this section are incomplete pictures of human behavior. Each does, however, provide insight into the maze of forces that affect small group communication.

Social Exchange Theory

Social exchange theory is a simple but powerful attempt to explain human behavior in terms that sound like a blend of behavioral psychology and economic theory. According to this theory, relationships can be described in terms of their rewards and costs, profits and losses. Rewards are pleasurable outcomes associated with particular behaviors; costs include such things as mental effort, anxiety, or even embarrassment.[7] Profit equals rewards minus costs; as long as rewards exceed costs, a relationship remains attractive.

Rewards and costs can take many forms in a group. As we will see more clearly in Chapter 3, fellowship, job satisfaction, achievement, status, and meeting personal needs and goals are all rewards that groups provide. However, group work takes time and effort and may be frustrating—all forms of cost. In one community theatre group, participants identified meeting people and the opportunity to perform as the primary rewards, while they saw disorganization, lack of coordination, and time issues as costs.[8] Social exchange theory predicts that as long as rewards exceed costs—that is, as long as group membership is

Small groups can be viewed as open systems comprising different interdependent variables. What input and output variables might there be for the group in this photograph?

profitable—group membership will continue to be attractive. Small group variables such as cohesiveness and productivity are directly related to how rewarding the group experience is to its members.

The basics of social exchange theory are useful in their descriptiveness. Keep them in mind as you read the remaining chapters and as you observe working groups.

Symbolic Convergence Theory

Symbolic convergence theory describes how groups' identities develop through shared fantasies. If you consider your closest interpersonal relationships, you can probably remember a point at which each relationship took on a life of its own. For example, when two acquaintances become friends, the relationship takes on an identity based on your experiences together and your shared stories and visions of those experiences. Perhaps you develop "inside," or private, jokes that have meaning only for the two of you.

Communication scholar Ernest Bormann notes that groups take on this kind of shared personality as well. The **symbolic convergence theory** of communication explains how certain types of communication shape a group's identity and culture, which in turn influence other dynamics such as norms, roles, and decision making. Over time groups develop a collective consciousness with shared emotions, motives, and meanings.[9]

This group consciousness, Bormann says, evolves as group members share group fantasies or stories. Within this theory, **fantasy** does not mean what it usually does—something not grounded in reality. Rather, it has a technical meaning: Fantasy is the creative and imaginative shared interpretation of events that fulfills a group's need to make sense of its experience and to anticipate its future.[10] A fantasy is usually introduced as a story that captures the imagination of the group and momentarily takes the group away from the specific issue under discussion. A group fantasy usually deals with real-life people and situations.

Theories reduce uncertainty and guide our behavior in groups. How could knowledge of group theory help contestants on the TV reality show *Survivor*?

Case Study

The dean of student affairs at your college has become sensitive about reports from students that the activities scheduled for orientation week each year are silly. Specifically, students have been reacting to two of the dean's favorite activities at the first orientation mixer: a pass-the-orange-under-your-chin race and a find-your-own-shoes-in-the-middle-of-the-room relay race. Students claim to feel undignified during these activities. They feel they are being treated more as children than as adults. Bewildered, the dean remembers how much the class of 1981 enjoyed these activities and is at a loss about what to do. Therefore, the dean appoints a group of students to rethink the matter. You are one of those students.

The committee is composed mostly of juniors and seniors. The dean thinks they have been around long enough to "know the ropes." As president-elect of next year's sophomore class, you are the youngest of the six committee members. The chairperson is a graduating senior.

You arrive at the first meeting ready to work. The committee is to plan activities that are "more closely aligned with the needs of today's college men and women." You are excited about being a part of a decision-making process that will have a real effect. To your dismay, the other members of the group seem to disregard their task and spend the meeting discussing the prospects for the basketball team, hardly mentioning orientation-week activities for next fall. You leave the meeting confused but hopeful that the next meeting will be more fruitful. You resolve to take a more active role and to try to steer the meeting more toward the committee's task.

At the second meeting, you suggest that the committee discuss orientation week. Members concur, then make jokes about past orientation-week activities. When the chairperson makes no effort to keep the group on track, you feel overwhelmed and bewildered. You know that the dean expects a report within a week.

Practice in Applying Principles

1. First, begin by analyzing the situation. What are the important components? Differences of status among group members? Time constraints? The group's task? What else? How many can you identify? Which of these do you think will help you explain the situation, make predictions, and choose the most effective course of action?
2. Use the variables you identified above to write a one-paragraph explanation of the situation.
3. Review the section in this chapter on social exchange theory. What costs and rewards (real or potential) can you identify in this situation that might influence participants' behaviors?
4. Consider this group as a system: How would a change in one part of the system affect the other components? For instance, if the dean gives the group three additional months to complete the work, what is likely to happen?
5. If you were really in this situation, what would you do?

In groups, as in almost all forms of human endeavor, we can discern two levels of reality: (1) what actually happens and (2) our interpretations and beliefs about what happens. What remains in our memories and what guides our subsequent behavior is the latter. Suppose, for example, you are in a group discussing how to reduce cheating and other forms of academic dishonesty, and a group member says "Hey, did anyone see the *Tonight Show* last night? They had a guy who won the national lying championship. He was so funny. He talked his way into getting photographed with the president of the United States." Another group member chimes in and says, "Yeah, I saw that. I had an uncle who used to tell whoppers. He once convinced my aunt that he had won a million dollars in the lottery." Yet another group member says, "My brother always plays practical jokes on my mom." Before you know it, the pace of conversation quickens and other group members tell stories about people who love to play practical jokes. A **fantasy theme** consists of the common or related content of the stories the group tells. In addition, the fantasy of one group member leads to a **fantasy chain**—a string of connected stories that revolve around a common theme. These fantasy chains help the group develop a shared sense of identity, just as the unique stories and experiences you have with a close friend help give your relationship a unique identity. Usually a fantasy chain includes all the elements you would find in any well-told story: conflict, heroes, villains, and a plot that gives shape to the story.

By being mindful of the fantasies or stories that develop in a group, you can gain insight into what the group values. What may seem like "off task" behavior, such as talking about TV programs, movies, or events seemingly unrelated to the group's agenda, can be beneficial in giving the group a sense of identity. Noting the common themes of the group's fantasy (such as who the villains are in the stories or who wins or loses in the story) can also give you insight about a group's values and culture. And fantasies may be a way for groups to deal with sensitive issues in an indirect way.

By describing how people in groups come to share a common social reality, symbolic convergence theory explains how groups make decisions and make sense of the decision-making process.[11] It points out that groups, like individuals, have unique "personalities," cultures, or identities built on shared symbolic representations related to the group, and that these cultures evolve through the adoption of fantasy themes or group stories. Just as we try to understand someone's behavior by taking into account "what sort of person he or she is," we must do the same for groups. Reflecting on the stories a group tells, which may seem off the topic, can give you insight into a group's personality, culture, values, and identity.

Structuration Theory

Anthony Giddens offers another contemporary theoretical approach to help us understand how people behave in small groups.[12] The approach is further advanced by communication researcher Marshall Scott Poole and his colleagues.[13] **Structuration theory** provides a general framework that explains how people structure their groups by making active use of rules and resources. The theory focuses attention on individuals' *behaviors* in groups rather than on dynamics of groups *per se*.

At first glance this concept may seem complicated because of abstract terms;[14] however, we have already talked about two concepts that are important in structuration theory: rules and systems. A system, as you recall, is composed of many interdependent elements. Rules are explicit or implied prescriptions that affect how people behave in a group (system). "Don't talk while others are talking" and "Don't leave the meeting until the boss says everyone is dismissed" are examples of rules. These rules determine how the group structures itself and performs tasks, and how group members talk to one another.

Structuration theory suggests that when we join a new group we use rules we learned in other groups to structure our behavior. For example, when you walked into your first college class, you probably drew on your experiences as a high school student to know how to act. But groups also create their own rules and resources to determine what is appropriate and inappropriate. You learned that a college class is similar to but not exactly like a high school class. You also know that different classes have different rules or structure; some classes have informal rules; others have more formal ones. One teacher may deduct points for being absent; another teacher may not take roll at all. How communication rules are organized is based on factors both internal and external to the group. Structuration theory helps explain why and how groups develop the rules and behavior patterns they adopt. It can be especially useful for understanding group communication within broader organizational cultures,[15] such as how a group of jurors in a trial draws on rules each juror has observed from other juries and from dramatic depictions of jury deliberations.[16]

Functional Theory

Much of this book aims to help you identify and enact behaviors that will help your groups reach intended goals. The term **function** refers to the effect or consequence of a given behavior within a group system. For example, communication can help a group make decisions or manage conflict. Communication has an effect on the group; it has a function. Theories that concern themselves with group functions, then, are those that seek to identify and explain behaviors that help or allow a group to achieve its goals. Functional relationships exist within a group when an outcome occurs as a consequence of a specific behavior, which in turn was intended to produce the consequence.[17]

The functional theory developed by Dennis Gouran and Randy Hirokawa advances three propositions. These researchers suggest that effective group problem solving and decision making are most likely to occur when (1) group members attempt to satisfy task requirements (including understanding the issue to be resolved, the characteristics of acceptable solutions, and what constitute realistic alternatives; examining the alternatives; and selecting the alternative most likely to satisfy the requirements of the problem); (2) group members use communication to overcome constraints such as stress from deadlines, interpersonal conflict, or self-serving interaction; and (3) group members take the time to review the process through which they arrived at choices and, if necessary, reconsider their choice.[18]

*R*EVIEW

THEORETICAL PERSPECTIVES FOR THE STUDY OF SMALL GROUP COMMUNICATION

- Systems theory: The small group is an open system of interdependent elements, employing input variables and process variables to yield output.
- Social exchange theory: Groups remain attractive to their members so long as the rewards of group membership exceed the costs.
- Symbolic convergence theory: Group members develop a group consciousness and identity through the sharing of fantasies or stories, which are often chained together and have a common theme.
- Structuration theory: People use rules and resources to structure social interactions.
- Functional theory: Communication in groups functions to promote sound reasoning, prevent errors, and build productive relationships among members.

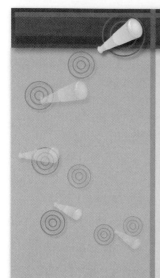

Cutting Edge Theory

STRUCTURATION AND THE EXERCISE OF FREE WILL

Throughout this book you learn many concepts and theories related to groups and teams. This chapter advances the proposition that concepts and theories are useful because they allow us to explain and predict group phenomena and thus give us a measure of control—over our own actions and, to an extent, over group processes and outcomes.

Structuration theory reminds us that groups are not simply the products of external factors; they are composed of individual human beings who think and act and who can intentionally change the course of the group. Forces such as status differences, norms, stress levels, and leadership styles are not absolute; they are mediated by the ways group members choose to react to them. This should be obvious, but it's an important point to emphasize. Armed with an understanding of these forces (provided by theories), you can use available rules and resources more effectively to achieve your goals and those of the group.

Real-Life Applications

The usefulness of any theory is in its application. Structuration theory deals with the power of each individual group member to change the behavior of a group by using rules and resources in interaction. Every action in a group structures subsequent actions. Consider the following:

- Remember that whenever you act, you are making choices, exercising your free will in a way that has consequences for, and that *structures*, subsequent group interaction.
- Also remember that our choices are somewhat constrained by external forces, existing group structures, and other members' behaviors. Try to be more aware of the choices—and constraints—before you.
- Work to identify the rules that are governing group members' behaviors. Are these rules contributing to the group's work or perhaps impeding it? You can call attention to dysfunctional rules and help the group to change them. You can sometimes change rules by violating them.
- Ask yourself what resources are available to you and to the rest of the group. Do you have particular knowledge or skills that are useful? Do others in the group have resources that you can help them tap into? Subtly bending group rules, sharing resources, and encouraging others to do the same are all ways to affect group processes and outcomes.

Rules and resources in interaction provide the structures that define your group's system. These systems can and do change over time—and sometimes suddenly—through the choices individual group members make. This book and the course you're taking are designed to arm you with an ever-greater understanding of the rules and resources available to you in group interaction.

In Chapter 1 we identified nine core competencies of effective group members, all of which were either group task competencies or group relationship competencies; in Chapter 4 we discuss task roles and maintenance roles; Chapters 9 and 12 introduce a *functional approach* to group problem solving and leadership. All these discussions are grounded in functional theories about how communication in groups promotes appropriate consequences—sound reasoning, critical thinking, the prevention of errors, and the building of productive relationships among group members.[19]

DESCRIBING ELEMENTS OF GROUP AND TEAM COMMUNICATION

A model that takes into account all the possible sender, receiver, and message variables in a small group would be hopelessly complicated, even before you added other variables central to the study of small group communication. Students must consequently settle for a less-comprehensive model but one that suggests the features and relationships critical to an understanding of small group communication.

Figure 2.1 represents such a descriptive model. This framework depicts small group communication as a constellation of variables, each related to every other. Communication establishes and maintains the relationships among these essential variables. This model thus reflects a systems approach to group and team communication. Chapters 3, 4, and 12 present in-depth discussions of these variables; for now, we'll consider each variable briefly.

Communication   Human communication is how you make sense out of the world and share that sense with others. Communication is what people say, how they say it, and to whom they say it. This process is the primary focus of study in small group communication research.

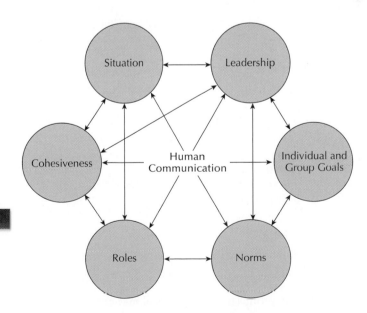

FIGURE 2.1

Constellation of Variables in Small Group Communication

Virtual Communication

The theories discussed in this chapter were developed with face-to-face interaction in mind. How do group dynamics change when communication is conducted in cyberspace?

- Research evidence suggests that computer-mediated groups react more negatively to events that are seen as "unfair," such as the arbitrary changing of a deadline or a budget reduction. Fair treatment from authorities appears to be highly important for these virtual groups, and this effect may even increase over time.[20]

- The costs and rewards identified by social exchange theory can clearly be related to virtual communication. The rewards of virtual communication include freedom from the constraints of time and space (and for some of us, the elimination of the need to make ourselves presentable for work!). Costs include the potential for misunderstanding when we are not able to see one another's facial expressions or hear tone of voice; when communicating virtually, you may need to work extra hard to express your feelings. Depending on the norms that develop in your group, consider the occasional use of emotional language ("I'm really getting frustrated") or use the growing vocabulary of emoticons to compensate.

- Group systems are patterns of relationships that group members form over time. The potential for "24/7" connection through cyberspace can alter these patterns and in many ways make the system more "open."

- Symbolic convergence theory suggests that groups develop their own identities through the development of fantasy chains and themes. These often begin with a group member's narrative, pun, or analogy that sends the group off in a direction seemingly unrelated to the group's stated goal. In cyberspace, the possibilities for visual, verbal, or aural communication can create new avenues for fantasy themes and group identity.

- Structuration theory points out that rules and resources are the "structures," or tools, with which group members interact. You can use computers, e-mail, and the Internet as resources that can expand the repertoire of structures available to group members.

- Functional theories explain how communication functions to accomplish tasks, overcome obstacles, and review procedures to maximize group effectiveness. You can use virtual group communication to enhance all of these areas of group interaction by extending opportunities for dialogue beyond the walls of the meeting room.

Leadership   Part of the definition of small group communication given in Chapter 1 concerned mutual influence. Leadership is behavior that exerts influence on the group.

Goals   All groups have goals. A goal may be to provide therapy for members, to complete some designated task, or simply to have a good time. Individual group members also have goals. Often individual goals complement the group goal; sometimes, though, they do not.

Norms   Norms are standards that establish which behaviors are normally permitted or encouraged within the group and which are forbidden or discouraged. Every group, from your family to the president's cabinet, develops and maintains norms. Some norms are formal, such as a rule about when a group must use parliamentary procedure. Formal, explicitly stated norms are rules that prescribe how group members should behave. Other norms are informal, such as the fact that your study group always meets 15 minutes late.

Roles   Roles are sets of expectations people hold for themselves and for others in a given context. People play different roles in different groups. Researchers have identified several roles that need to be filled in order for a small group to reach maximum satisfaction and productivity.

Cohesiveness   Cohesiveness is the degree of attraction group members feel toward one another and toward the group. Feelings of loyalty help unite the group.

Situation   The context in which group communication occurs is of paramount importance. The task is significant, but there are many other important situational variables, such as group size, the physical arrangement of group members, the location or setting, the group's purpose, even the amount of stress placed on the group by time constraints or other internal or external pressures. We will examine each of these situational variables later in the book.

The combined effect of these variables results in group outcomes. A group or team accomplishes something. Group and team outcomes include solving problems, making decisions, feeling satisfied, reaching agreement, or even making money. Small group communication theory seeks to explain the relationships among these and other variables and to make predictions about group outcomes. Thus, the theories presented in this book help explain most of the complexity and uncertainty that surface at every level of group and team interaction. A good theoretical understanding of small groups, coupled with an expanded repertoire of communicative behavior, is the recipe for developing group communication competence—the objective of this book.

Putting Principles into Practice

The theories discussed throughout this book explain consistencies in communicative behavior that researchers have observed within small groups. If you can attain a theoretical grasp of small group communication, you can more successfully predict and control behavior.

As you observe groups of which you are a member, keep the following in mind:

■ Theories provide explanations of behaviors that let us predict the likely consequences of various actions. Use the theories discussed in this chapter to help predict the probable consequences of various actions.

■ Systems theory can help you organize your observations and identify input variables, process variables, and output variables. Its primary application to small group communication is as an organizational strategy. Use systems theory to help you understand how your group's system relates to individual systems within it and the broader systems of which it is a part.

- Social exchange theory describes how satisfaction with a group relates to the relationship between the rewards and costs of group membership. Do a simple cost-benefit analysis to help you understand group members' behaviors.

- Symbolic convergence theory reminds us that groups, like individuals, have personalities that we must understand and adapt to in order to be most effective. Explore the ways in which your group's "personality" relates to other variables such as rules, roles, and decision making.

- Structuration theory helps reveal the power of rules and resources to structure interaction and outcomes. Identify existing rules and resources to enhance your influence in any group.

- Functional theories explain the connections between behaviors and their consequences in groups.

- Our general model of small group interaction includes seven variables: communication, leadership, goals, norms, roles, cohesiveness, and situation. Use these categories to help structure your thinking about groups.

As you read the rest of the book, continue to seek ways to apply what you're learning. The practicality of theories is measured only by how we can use them to be more effective group leaders, members, and scholars.

𝒫RACTICE

1. Make a list of informal theories you have about an ordinary day (for example, Professor X is boring, I'm afraid of speaking in class, etc.). On what basis did you formulate these theories? How do they affect your behavior? What might cause you to alter them?

2. Take a few minutes to reflect on rules that govern your behavior in groups. Express four or five of these rules as *if. . .then* (condition/action) statements (for example, "*if* someone in the group addresses me directly, *then* it is my responsibility to respond"). Share and discuss your rules with others in your group. See if others in your group agree with your list. How do these rules contribute or detract from effective group communication?

CHAPTER THREE

Group Formation

*"Coming together is a beginning;
keeping together is progress; working
together is success."*

—Henry Ford, Sr.

CHAPTER OUTLINE

OBJECTIVES

After studying this chapter, you will be able to:

- Discuss two classification systems of interpersonal needs and describe how they relate to group formation.
- Explain the potential conflict between individual goals and group goals.
- Suggest ways of establishing mutuality of concern in a work group.
- Identify and explain four factors that are elements of interpersonal attraction.
- Identify and describe three factors in group attraction.
- Facilitate a group's movement through the initial stages of its formation.
- Describe the importance of group expectations when changes in group membership cause group re-formation.
- Apply your knowledge of group formation toward greater effectiveness as a communicator.

ARE YOU CONSIDERING or being considered for membership in any particular group right now? A fraternity or sorority? A sports club? A political-action group? To which groups do you already belong? Can you identify a circle of friends you might refer to as "your group"? Do you belong to clubs? Teams?

From the moment you are born into your first group—your family—you belong to a succession of groups. Some are formally organized, some are loosely structured; some you choose, others you are assigned to. But membership in groups does not happen randomly. Groups meet specific needs and perform special functions. Thus, in order to understand group formation, you must examine the needs and functions around which groups form.

WHY DO PEOPLE JOIN GROUPS?

Understanding the many factors that draw people to groups can help explain the complexity of small group interaction. Groups are many things to many people. To one member of a committee, the group's problem is an exciting vehicle toward greater self-understanding. To another member, it is merely an uninteresting but necessary obstacle on the way to reaching a personal goal. To all human beings, the formation of groups—from families to teams to corporate boards—is part of a biological imperative that is simply part of our species; we are, all of us, social animals by nature.[1] Nevertheless, individuals differ in their motivation for joining a group and in their commitment and contribution to it. The answer to the question "Why do people join groups?" has many dimensions. The reasons can be placed into five broad categories: (1) **interpersonal needs,** (2) individual goals, (3) group and team goals, (4) interpersonal attraction, and (5) group attraction.

INTERPERSONAL NEEDS

Maslow's Theory

Abraham Maslow asserted that all humans have basic needs and that these needs can be arranged in a hierarchy; that is, people do not concern themselves with higher-level needs until lower-level needs are satisfied.[2] Figure 3.1 illustrates how interpersonal needs form a hierarchy.

Physiological Needs Maslow termed the first level of needs, at the bottom of the hierarchy, physiological needs. People have physiological needs for air, water, and food.

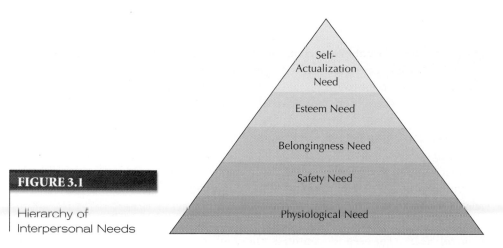

FIGURE 3.1

Hierarchy of
Interpersonal Needs

Safety Needs   Safety needs are for security and protection. Maslow called the first two levels of the hierarchy *survival needs;* satisfaction of these needs is necessary for basic human existence. During childhood years, the family satisfies these needs.

Once survival needs are fulfilled, the higher-level needs that Maslow called *psychological needs*—the need to belong, the need for esteem, and the need for self-actualization—become more important. These needs may affect people's group memberships throughout their lives.

Belongingness Need   People need to feel that they are a part of some group. Here again, the family provides a sense of belonging for children, but as they get older they begin to look outside the family to satisfy this need. Peer groups gain special importance during adolescence. At that time, people's need for affiliation is at its strongest.

Esteem Need   Once people have developed a sense of belonging, Maslow says that they have a need for respect or esteem. They need to feel not only that they are accepted but also that they are considered worthwhile and valued by others.

Self-Actualization Need   The need for self-actualization differs from the other four needs. The former needs Maslow calls *deficiency needs*, because individuals subconsciously perceive these needs as inner voids, which they fill by drawing on the resources of other people. Maslow called the need for self-actualization a *being* need. This need motivates people to try to fulfill their potential and live life to its fullest. They are ready to function as autonomous beings, operating independently in quest of their own full potential. They no longer need groups to take care of their deficiencies; instead, they need groups in which to find and express their wholeness. Although this need level is perhaps the most difficult to grasp conceptually, Maslow's hierarchy is consistent: People need groups to satisfy interpersonal needs. People also differ from one another in their motivations for joining groups. Their differing motivations may be reflected in their communicative behavior in a group. Those who simply want to belong may interact differently from those who need the group's esteem and respect. The higher we move up Maslow's hierarchy, the more important communication becomes in need satisfaction.[3]

Schutz's Theory

In an elaborate theory of interpersonal behavior, William Schutz suggested that three basic human needs influence individuals as they form and interact in groups: the need for **inclusion,** the need for **control,** and the need for **affection.**[4] Individuals' needs vary, but groups often provide settings in which such needs can be satisfied.

Inclusion Need   Just as Maslow postulated a belongingness need, Schutz said people join groups to fulfill their need for inclusion. They need to be recognized as unique individuals and to feel understood. When people try to understand someone, the implication is that the individual is worthy of their time and effort. In this respect, Schutz's inclusion need is also related to Maslow's esteem need.

Control Need   The need for control is a need for status and power. People need to have some control over themselves and others, and sometimes they need to give others some control over them, such as when they seek guidance and direction.

Affection Need   The need for affection drives people to give and receive emotional warmth and closeness.

In a broad sense, groups are more than collections of people with common goals; they are arenas in which individual needs are satisfied or frustrated. Schutz asserted that people's needs for inclusion, control, and affection influence group process throughout the life of the group. He observed that in the initial stages of group formation, communication aims primarily toward fulfilling members' inclusion needs. Group members are friendly but cautious as they try to evaluate one another and try to be accepted by other members. As the group develops, control needs become more evident; members contest issues and vie for leadership. Schutz observed that as conflicts resolve, people turn toward affection needs. Members characteristically express positive feelings in this phase. The progression, Schutz says, is cyclical.

Repeating Cycles of Group Process   From Schutz's perspective, group formation is a process not limited to the initial coming together of the group. Rather, formation patterns repeat themselves as the group develops over time. Group decision making involves a series of smaller decisions on the way toward achieving the group's primary goal. For example, a group of engineers planning a bridge must make decisions about the location and frequency of their meetings as well as the design and materials for the bridge. A group progresses through developmental phases throughout its life (as will be discussed in Chapter 9), and this cyclical pattern of formation and re-formation occurs whenever the group approaches a new meeting and a new decision. If this process could be visualized, it might look something akin to a large jellyfish moving through the water. The jellyfish floats in the water in a relatively aimless way until it needs to move forward. Then it organizes itself, contracts, and propels itself through the water, after which its movements again become less organized. Group process moves through a similar series of contractions until it reaches its ultimate goal.

A group is defined, in part, by a common purpose. Within that purpose are several smaller goals. As a group reaches each of these goals, it momentarily loses a bit of its definition until a new goal replaces the old. As people accomplish each new goal, they begin a new cycle of inclusion, control, and affection behaviors. The following example illustrates this point:

Harv: Well, it's been hard, but we've finally found a date for the banquet that we can all agree on.

Juanita: Yes, finally! For a while I thought we'd never agree, but I think we've made the best decision now.

Betsy: Yeah. We're over the major hurdle. Feels good, doesn't it?

Phil: Amen. We're organized now and ready to go for it! This is getting to be fun. (Laughter, followed by a pause)

Juanita: Well, here we are. What do we do next?

Phil: I guess we ought to talk about the theme and the speakers.

Harv: Hold on there! The speakers are irrelevant if no one is there to hear them. We've got to talk first about how we're going to publicize.

Phil: C'mon, Harv. How can we publicize if we don't even have a theme?

Betsy: Here we go again.

In this example you can see the end of one cycle and the beginning of the next. Members express positive feelings about the group and its accomplishments and halt a little in their conversation before regrouping for another attack on a new facet of their problem. The

"Somewhere along the line, our sewing circle took a strange turn."

People often form groups simply because they enjoy the same activities. What groups do you belong to for this reason?

sense of cohesiveness peaks during the affection phase and then falls off, only to rebuild around the next task. Like the jellyfish, which organizes its efforts around its task of propulsion, the small group does not end up back where it started. The whole process moves forward. To say that the phases are cyclical, then, is somewhat misleading. Certain types of communicative behaviors recur, but the whole process moves forward. Frank Dance captured the essence of this process when he described human communication as being like a helix.[5] A helix is both linear and circular. It turns in on itself and yet always moves forward. Seen in this light, group formation does not cease but pulses throughout the life of the group.

REVIEW

SCHUTZ'S THEORY

Individuals join groups in part to satisfy three needs:

- Inclusion: They want to be recognized and feel included. They also have needs to share and want to include others in their activities.
- Control: People have varying needs to control or to be controlled that groups can satisfy.
- Affection: Individuals satisfy their affection needs through giving and receiving emotional support in groups.

Groups pass through observable, cyclical phases of these needs.

INDIVIDUAL GOALS

Theories of psychological and interpersonal needs explain some of the bases for group formation. So, too, do individual goals. Goals have a more tangible and obvious effect on your selection of group memberships. What do you want out of life? Prestige? Status? Power? Anonymity? Recreation? Education? Personal growth? In other words, what goals do you have that exist apart from any particular group membership?

Individual goals are instrumental in determining which groups people join. Obviously, if people enjoy arranging flowers and wish to improve their skills, they'll join garden clubs. If personal growth is an aim, people will join support groups. If they desire status and power, they'll seek membership in elite social or professional groups. Sometimes the prestige associated with a particular group is enough to make membership attractive. This is often a motivation for joining a particular sorority or fraternity. Whatever their individual goals may be, people bring those goals with them when they join groups.

GROUP AND TEAM GOALS

Group and team goals are identifiable accomplishments that transcend the group members' individual goals. Accomplishment of team goals in the workplace is related to greater group attraction, individual satisfaction, and employee job satisfaction.[6] Certain professional and fraternal organizations serve community needs. For example, the Lions Club is well known for its sponsorship of research devoted to finding cures for eye diseases and preventing blindness. Individual members have many goals for joining the club: the chance to rub elbows with other professionals from the community, camaraderie and fellowship, the prestige of membership, the sense of belonging, or a genuine interest in serving the community. But though individual goals may vary, the group goal must take precedence over them. The many needs and goals that individuals bring to small groups may be incompatible with the group's goal. This is a potential source of problems in small group communication.

Needs and goals influence individuals' perceptions of group members and the group's task. If a group goal is the desired end result of a group, and an individual goal is the desired end result of an individual, then individual and group goals will likely overlap in any given group. Other individual goals will emerge from the group's focus. Differences between these goals may help or hinder the group. The conflict between individual and group goals is often the reason why some groups can't get off the ground. This is the paradox of group membership: We often join groups to help us reach personal goals—which must be set aside, in part, for the group to succeed.

If each group member pulls in a different direction, the results can be disastrous. The group may go nowhere, and, to make matters worse, each member may perceive the others as being uncooperative. For this reason, groups must question their members' mutuality of concern—the degree to which members share the same level of commitment to a group—during the initial stages of group formation.[7] Sometimes very high levels of commitment are required, as when members of a theater group must put their responsibilities to that group above their other group memberships for a short period around production time.

ℰSTABLISHING MUTUALITY OF CONCERN

When people join groups, they often assume that other group members share their commitment to the group's task. If a problem is to be solved, they take for granted that others view the problem in much the same way they do. However, each person brings a different perspective to a group. Some group members are invariably more conscientious than others. Studies have shown that the more dissimilar team members are in this respect, the less satisfied they are likely to be with their team.[8]

People also bring different levels of commitment or concern to groups. Suppose you have been appointed to a student-government group whose task is to recommend whether your college should institute a plus/minus grading system or continue with a traditional *A, B, C, D* grading policy. If you are a first- or second-year student, this policy change could have a direct effect on your grade-point average over your four years in college. If you are a graduating senior, a policy change would have little or no effect on you. Hence, the level of concern over the problem can vary from member to member. Once again, individual goals interact with a group goal. Those affected directly by the problem will probably become more active in the group than those who are not.

The degree to which members are concerned with the group's task needs to be clarified at the outset. All group members should clearly state their personal needs and goals regarding the topic area. Clarifying mutuality of concern can resolve a lot of misunderstanding and avoid needless conflict.

Although individual needs and goals may bring a group together in the first place, they can also break a group apart. The success or failure of a group depends, in part, on the degree to which its goal is assumed by individuals as their own. Unsatisfied or unclarified individual needs and goals can become **hidden agendas**—private goals toward which individuals work while seeming to work toward the group goal. Such hidden agendas can be extremely disruptive to the group. Establishing mutuality of concern can help reduce this negative influence.

Culture is another important factor in balancing individual and group needs and goals. The value placed on individuality or conformity varies widely from one culture to another. In Japan, China, Israel, and Russia, for example, individuals tend to acquiesce to the will of the group, as a high degree of conformity is expected. As we note in Chapter 1, North Americans and Europeans are thought to be more individualistic.[9] When we come to a group, our cultures—whatever they may be—come with us. These differing cultures, as well as individual differences, can contribute to a kind of tension in the group that communication scholars Kevin Barge and Lawrence Frey describe as "the product of two ideas being equally valid when considered alone, but contradictory when paired."[10] They give the following pairs of statements as examples:

I need to behave consistently in a group.

I need to adapt my behavior to changes in the group situation.

It is important to fit in with and be like other group members, even when doing so goes against my personal beliefs.

It is important to maintain my individuality when I am in a group.

Good group members defer their own needs to the larger needs of the group.

Good group members act independently within the group and pursue their personal agendas.[11]

Collaborating Ethically: What Would You Do?

We often join groups to satisfy personal needs or to accomplish personal goals. But is it ethical to join groups to promote personal objectives? Is it selfish? Imagine that you are part of an important team preparing to launch a new project. All of you know that the project will involve hard, time-consuming work, but if it succeeds, it will bring great benefits to your organization. A position opens up on your team because one of the members moves away. On several occasions one of your best friends has indicated that if a position on the team ever became available, she would like to be considered. You know that your friend is intelligent and capable and could make a contribution to the team's efforts if she can truly commit to it. The problem is, you know that she has already spread herself too thin. She is ambitious and has joined and taken leadership positions in several organizations, as she builds her résumé while applying to prestigious graduate schools. She says that appointment to your team would mean a lot to her and could make the difference in her graduate school acceptance. Do you recommend your friend for an appointment to the team?

In any given situation the interaction of individual and group needs will cause one of four possible outcomes:

1. Individual and group needs may be so diverse that they interfere with each other, with no positive effects accruing either to individuals within the group or to the group as a whole.
2. Group interaction may result in the realization of group goals, while individual needs are not met.
3. One or more group members may have their needs met, to the detriment or destruction of the group.
4. Individual and group needs may blend so completely that the needs realized by the group as a whole are the same needs individuals wish to realize.[12]

In the ideal, fully integrated group, this fourth alternative is realized. Mutuality of concern can merge individual and group needs and goals.

Aside from the relationships among interpersonal needs, personal goals, and group goals, two other factors have an influence on people's selection of groups: interpersonal attraction and group attraction.

INTERPERSONAL ATTRACTION

Often people are attracted to groups because they are attracted to the people in the groups. Of the many factors that influence interpersonal attraction, four are especially significant: similarity, complementarity, proximity/contact/interaction, and physical attractiveness.

Similarity

One of the strongest influences in interpersonal attraction is **similarity.** Remember your first day on campus? That feeling of being new and alone? You needed a friend, and with luck you found one. In looking for a friend, did you seek out someone you perceived to be very different from you? Probably not. As the principle of similarity in interpersonal attraction suggests, you probably looked for someone to talk to who appeared to be in the same situation—another lonely newcomer, or perhaps someone dressed like you were.

Who are your closest friends? Do you share many of the same attitudes, beliefs, and values? Do you enjoy the same activities? More than likely you do. People are often attracted to those they consider to be like them. A probable explanation for this is that similar backgrounds, beliefs, attitudes, and values make it easier to understand one another—and all people like to feel that others understand them. The converse of the similarity factor may also be true: People may be repelled by those whose attitudes differ from theirs.[13]

One danger of the similarity factor in group formation is that our tendency to be attracted to people like ourselves may result in a group that is too homogeneous to approach a complex task effectively. Indeed, research on classroom groups found that by a two-to-one margin, students reported their worst experiences occurred in groups they had formed themselves. Their best experiences occurred in groups to which professors had assigned them.[14]

Complementarity

In reading the previous section on similarity, some of you probably shook your heads and said, "No, that's not the way it is at all. My best friend and I are about as similar as an orchid and a fire hydrant!" No generalization is entirely true, and so it is with the principle of similarity. While birds of a feather flock together, it is also true that opposites attract. John Thibaut and Harold Kelley suggest that some interpersonal relationships are based primarily on similarity, whereas others are based on **complementarity.**[15] At times people may be attracted to others who exhibit qualities that they do not have but that they admire. For at least a partial explanation of attraction through complementarity, consider Schutz's theory of interpersonal needs, discussed earlier. According to this theory, a person who has a high need to control, for example, would be most compatible with a person who has a high need to be controlled. The same would be true of needs to express and to receive affection and the needs to feel included and to include others. These are complementary needs rather than similar needs.

Proximity, Contact, and Interaction

You tend to be attracted to people who are physically close to you, who live or work with you, and whom you see or communicate with often. If you know that you have to live or work close to another person, you may ignore that person's less desirable traits in order to minimize potential conflict. Furthermore, proximity, contact, and interaction breed familiarity, and familiarity has a positive influence on interpersonal attraction.[16] Interaction with another person helps you get to know that person, and through this process the two of you may uncover similarities and discover ways in which you can satisfy each other's interpersonal needs. The actual physical distance between people, then, does not influence attraction, but the interpersonal possibilities illuminated by proximity, contact, and interaction do.

Cutting Edge Theory

MUTUALITY OF CONCERN

People who join groups often assume that other group members share their commitment to the group's tasks. Individual needs and goals can bring a group together at the outset, but they can also break a group apart. For groups to succeed, the collective goal should transcend the goals of the individual group members.

The degrees to which members are concerned with the group's task need to be clarified at the outset. All group members should clearly state their own needs and goals regarding the task. They should also acknowledge constraints on their time or interest. Establishing realistic expectations among group members will help minimize misunderstandings and conflict.

Real-Life Applications

Communication scholar Michael Kramer studied a community theatre group to see how its members managed multiple group roles. A community theatre is a good example of a group that sometimes requires extraordinary commitment of time and effort over a limited period of time. Kramer found that members had to make their membership in the theatre group a priority over their membership in other groups until the production ended, after which they could again devote energy to their other commitments.

Members of the theatre group managed conflicts among their several group memberships in three ways. First, they auditioned for productions only if they thought conflicts would be minimal. Second, they negotiated conflicts (such as being required to attend regular meetings of other groups) in advance, so the theatre group could allow for such time conflicts in its planning. Third, they informed members of their other groups of their temporary conflicts.[17] While these strategies were noted in a particular context, they translate well to many types of groups and contexts. Consider the following:

- Try to avoid putting yourself in group situations if you don't have the time, energy, or interest to commit and do a good job.
- When you know you have conflicts and other interests that will compete for your time and attention, be "up front" with your group: Explain your situation and work to find acceptable solutions.
- When you accept new positions or assignments, explain the new demands on your time to those in groups you're already a part of; in other words, renegotiate your level of commitment to the groups of which you're a member.

Also, as you consider joining new groups and teams, keep the following practical questions in mind:

- How does participating in the group relate to your overall goals and objectives? Will it, for example, help you with your work or school goals, give your life more meaning or balance, or assist you in developing quality relationships with others?
- What will you have to give up if you participate in this group?
- How will your new group affect your existing obligations to your employer, colleagues, friends, or family members?

Physical Attractiveness

At least in the initial stages of interpersonal attraction, physical attractiveness influences people. If a person is physically beautiful, others tend to want to affiliate with him or her.[18] However, evidence indicates that this factor diminishes in importance over time and that— at least in North American cultures—physical beauty is more important to males than to females.[19]

In sum, people seem to be attracted to others who are similar to them and thus likely to understand them, who can fulfill their needs and complement their personalities, who are familiar to them because of repeated contact, and who are physically appealing. Those qualities in group members constitute a powerful influence on people's selection of groups.

GROUP ATTRACTION

Although individuals may be attracted to a group because of the members who compose it, they may also be attracted to the group itself. Such attraction usually focuses on the group's activities or goals, or simply on the desirability of group membership.

Group Activities

Although research is not extensive in this area, it seems fairly clear that people who are interested in the same activities tend to form groups.[20] People who enjoy intellectual pursuits may join literary discussion groups. Those who enjoy playing soccer join soccer teams. Beyond these obvious examples, people may be attracted to the activities of a group in a more general sense. Some may join groups simply because they enjoy going to regular meetings and joining in group discussions, regardless of the group's specific aims or goals. The structure and human contact provided by groups are potentially rewarding in and of themselves.

Group Goals

A group's goal is another factor that may attract people to the group. If, for example, people believe that the spread of coal-burning plants must be curtailed, they may join a group dedicated to changing national energy policy. If they believe in preserving and protecting the natural environment, they may join American Forests, the Sierra Club, the Audubon Society, or any organization that professes a similar goal.

Group Membership

Sometimes it is not a group's members, activities, or goals that attract people but membership itself. Potential members may perceive that membership in an exclusive club or honor society will bring them prestige, acceptance, or professional benefits outside of the group. For example, company officials may expect a young executive to belong to some civic group because such memberships provide good public relations for the firm.

The need for affiliation—Maslow's belongingness need and Schutz's inclusion need— is basic to human nature and can make group membership attractive. In addition to affiliation, group membership also fulfills people's needs for achievement and identity.[21] Indeed, a substantial body of research indicates that the satisfaction provided by group membership is important to people's happiness.[22]

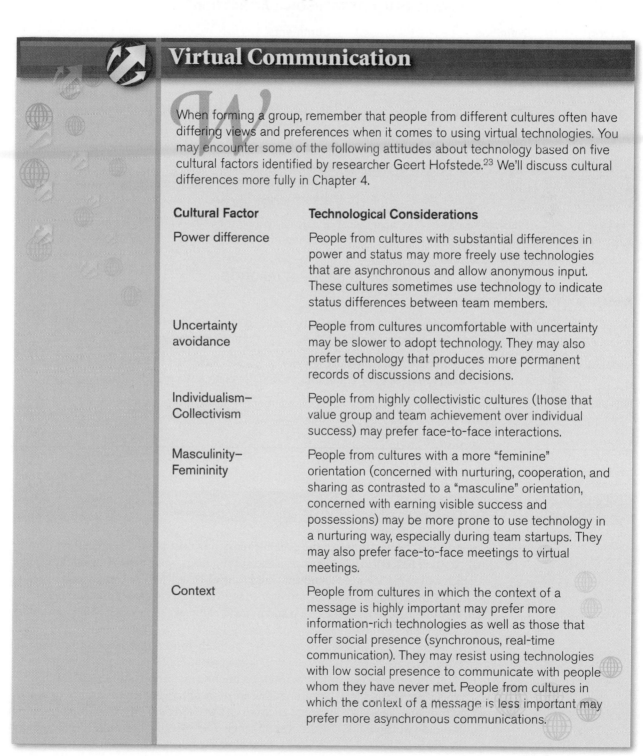

Virtual Communication

When forming a group, remember that people from different cultures often have differing views and preferences when it comes to using virtual technologies. You may encounter some of the following attitudes about technology based on five cultural factors identified by researcher Geert Hofstede.[23] We'll discuss cultural differences more fully in Chapter 4.

Cultural Factor	Technological Considerations
Power difference	People from cultures with substantial differences in power and status may more freely use technologies that are asynchronous and allow anonymous input. These cultures sometimes use technology to indicate status differences between team members.
Uncertainty avoidance	People from cultures uncomfortable with uncertainty may be slower to adopt technology. They may also prefer technology that produces more permanent records of discussions and decisions.
Individualism–Collectivism	People from highly collectivistic cultures (those that value group and team achievement over individual success) may prefer face-to-face interactions.
Masculinity–Femininity	People from cultures with a more "feminine" orientation (concerned with nurturing, cooperation, and sharing as contrasted to a "masculine" orientation, concerned with earning visible success and possessions) may be more prone to use technology in a nurturing way, especially during team startups. They may also prefer face-to-face meetings to virtual meetings.
Context	People from cultures in which the context of a message is highly important may prefer more information-rich technologies as well as those that offer social presence (synchronous, real-time communication). They may resist using technologies with low social presence to communicate with people whom they have never met. People from cultures in which the context of a message is less important may prefer more asynchronous communications.

REVIEW

FACTORS IN INTERPERSONAL ATTRACTION

Factors	Definition	Comments
Similarity	The degree to which two people are alike	You tend to like people who resemble you in their thinking and experiences; they are more likely than most to understand you.
Complementarity	The degree to which two people are compatibly different from each other	You tend to be attracted to people who possess qualities that you admire but do not yourself possess.
Proximity, contact, and interaction	The actual, physical availability of other people	Interacting with others reveals their similar and complementary traits and, thus, enhances their attractiveness to you.
Physical attractiveness	Physical beauty or handsomeness	Especially important in the early stages of a relationship; less important after you get to know someone.

FACTORS IN GROUP ATTRACTION

Factors	Comments
Group activities	People interested in the same activities tend to group together; for some people, simply the structure and human contact of group activities may provide rewards.
Group goals	People interested in particular goals join groups dedicated to those goals; civic groups, parent/teacher organizations, and environmental groups are examples.
Group membership	Some people seek the rewards of membership itself; group membership is often seen as having prestige or status.

HOMOGENEITY AND DIVERSITY IN GROUPS

Earlier in the chapter we noted the dynamic tension between individual goals and group goals. Each of us seeks to be independent and autonomous, while depending on the groups to which we belong. We need to influence and control, as well as being influenced and controlled by others. Even in the most homogeneous groups, varying levels of these needs coupled with differing views of the group and its goals can make for an interesting time and a fascinating field for study.

As we join or are assigned to groups, we are likely to find that those groups include increasing diversity. Research showing that women represent 59 percent and minorities 26 percent of the workforce in the United States is but one indication of this trend.[24]

What if we have a choice? Are groups that are more homogeneous in terms of race, gender, culture, and general ability more effective or less effective than more diverse groups? Which should we choose? Perhaps, not surprisingly, there are advantages and disadvantages to each. There is some evidence that over time diverse groups can be more effective because they include more potential in terms of skills and approaches to problems, as well as the ability to address the needs of an equally diverse base of clients or customers.[25] However, there is also evidence that differences in age and nationality often contribute to personality clashes, especially in newly formed teams. Such groups tend to fare better if they acknowledge their diversity at the outset and create a supportive climate tolerant of diverse opinions and personalities.[26]

When comparing homogeneous work groups with diverse work groups, researchers find that diverse work groups often have more trouble initially, but over time become more productive than homogeneous groups. This makes sense. We are more comfortable with people whom we think are similar to us. This makes for easier interaction in the initial stages of group formation. With a little effort, though, diverse groups can find the common ground to make interaction work; their diversity often produces more flexibility, more options, and more ways of looking at a problem.[27]

GROUP FORMATION OVER TIME

Once a group forms, it continues to grow and develop over time. Many researchers observe that group development follows fairly predictable stages. Perhaps the best-known scheme for these stages was advanced by Bruce Tuckman.[28] The initial stage is *forming*, a period characterized by anxiety and uncertainty about belonging to the group and a resulting cautiousness in behavior. In the second stage, *storming*, competition, individuality, and conflict emerge as group members try to satisfy their individual needs. *Norming*, the third stage, is characterized by attempts to resolve earlier conflicts, often by negotiating clear guidelines for the group. *Performing* is the fourth stage. Cooperation and productive work are the hallmarks of this stage. Although not all groups neatly cycle through these stages, you will probably be able to detect forming, storming, norming, and performing behaviors in many of the groups and teams in which you participate.

Remember these stages as you read this book. Developmental changes in the life of a group relate to many important group dynamics, including conflict management and leadership. We will revisit the phases of group development when we discuss a descriptive approach to group and team problem solving in Chapter 9.

GROUP RE-FORMATION

Over time, groups develop a "personality" of their own. Group or team members become oriented to one another, they set patterns of behavior and group norms, and they develop a shared collective experience—their own fantasy chains, rules, and systems. But what happens when a newcomer joins the team? Changes in membership alter the group's dynamics, sometimes profoundly. Continuing success depends on how well the new member adapts to particular group dynamics (is socialized) and how well the group adapts to the characteristics, abilities, and skills of the new member.

Successful socialization of a new group or team member depends largely on expectations: the newcomer's expectations of his or her own performance, as well as the group's expectations of the newcomer. The degree to which these expectations are compatible is the primary determinant of a successful transition. Just as a group should spend time establishing mutuality of concern at the beginning of its life, so it should revisit these considerations when group membership changes.

Case Study

The First Church of Roseville has a Building and Grounds committee. This committee, charged with overseeing the regular maintenance and upkeep of the church building and surrounding property, makes sure that the lawns are mowed, the hedges trimmed, the furnace maintained, the roof patched, and so forth.

The group convenes for its first monthly meeting. The church custodian has just resigned, and just before leaving, he reported that the roof of the church leaks. The group's goal is to maintain the building and grounds. All of the members are, to some degree, committed to the goal. However, this commitment means different things to different members.

The committee consists of the following members:

Roberto Bomblast. Roberto has been an accountant for a local firm for 23 years. He has never felt that his firm has given him a chance to show his true leadership ability. He sees the church committee, of which he is chair, as his big chance to prove himself and show the world what a truly fine administrator he is. He has another ulterior motive: He wants very much to be the new part-time business manager for the church when "Old George," the present manager, dies or retires. This committee, then, is Roberto's stepping-stone to greatness.

Marmalade. No one is sure of Marmalade's real name. He was found 10 years ago wandering around the sanctuary saying, "Wow . . . wow . . . wowwwww . . . ." The church members took him under their wing, and he has been sweeping floors and doing other odd jobs around the church since then. The pastor thought it would "do Marmalade some good" to get involved with a responsible committee, so he assigned him to this one.

Latasha Greene. Latasha is a young attorney who joined the church last year because she enjoys its outstanding music program. She has been dismayed, though, to find church governance dominated by white males. "What decade are we in?" she wonders "Don't they know it's a new century?" She is annoyed because Roberto Bomblast and Thurman Jester act as if they are in charge of everything.

Merry Placid. In all of her 47 years, Merry has not been outside of her home state. She loves her country, her state, her community, her home, and her family. She especially loves her church because of the sense of warmth and community she feels there. She has served on every committee in the church. Merry has a high need for inclusion. She is pleased to be on this committee.

Thurman Jester. Ever since his vacation trip to Dallas, Thurman wears a white belt and off-white shoes to work every day (and strongly urges his employees at the insurance office to do the same). He is committed to keeping up with the trendsetters, and Dallas, he feels, is where trends are set. Thurman was also impressed by a 40-foot neon cross he spotted outside a church in Dallas. Thurman is highly motivated by control needs.

Practice in Applying Principles

1. Analyze this situation. Where are the most likely sources of conflict? What do you predict will be the outcome of the committee's next meeting? What does the group need from its members in order to be successful?

2. This chapter discussed the importance of establishing mutuality of concern. Use a rating scale, from 1 to 10—10 being high concern for the group's task and 1 being low—to rate the level of concern of each of the characters in this case study. Does this help you identify potential conflicts?

3. Using Maslow's and Schutz's categories of interpersonal needs, identify the dominant needs of each of these individuals. What are their motivations for being in this group? How compatible are their individual goals with the group's goal? Which of these committee members do you expect to be most troublesome? Why?

4. If you were a member of this group, what suggestions would you make at your first meeting?

In many respects, the group is new each time its membership changes. This re-formation presents its own stages of development. The socialization of a newcomer actually begins with a period of *anticipation* prior to the first meeting at which the newcomer is present, in which the group formulates initial expectations. These expectations are modified or reinforced very quickly during the initial face-to-face *encounter* among team members. In the final phase of socialization, *adjustment*, newcomer and team members adjust to one another and team performance stabilizes.[29]

It is important to note here that positive team expectations for a new member enhance the probability of a successful outcome. Likewise, viewing changing team membership as beneficial will enhance the probability of a good outcome. Successful integration of new members is especially important in teams in which members have specialized roles and are highly interdependent.[30]

Putting Principles into Practice

The dynamic interrelatedness of all the variables that affect small group processes makes the study of small group communication challenging and exciting. As you continue through the rest of this book, it is important that you retain what you have previously learned. Only when you have fit all the puzzle pieces together can you see a clear picture of small group communication.

This chapter has highlighted one part of the puzzle: those needs and goals that motivate people to join groups and that influence their behavior within those groups. In the initial stages of group development, uncertainty—about the group, about its goals, and about each member's place in it—is at its peak. How you communicate at this sensitive stage of group development provides the basis for future interaction. As you join new groups, keep in mind the following:

- At the first meeting of any new group, you may feel anxious. You may be uncertain about who the other members are, what each person's role is to be, and what to say to whom. At this stage, share a little information about yourself and encourage others to do the same. Many group leaders ask participants to say a few words about themselves. This strategy breaks the ice and provides some familiarity on which to base further discussion. In short, it reduces people's uncertainty and helps them relax.

- Sometimes you do not choose the groups you belong to but are assigned to them, perhaps by a teacher, a supervisor, or an employer. When you are assigned to a group, look carefully at the group's goal. Then assess the resources that you can bring to accomplishing that goal. Evaluate the benefits you can derive from the experience. Begin establishing mutuality of concern.

- When you join a new group, ask yourself what attracts you to it: "Why am *I* a part of this group? What do *I* want to accomplish here? What are *my* goals? What do I want from these people . . . and what can I give to them?" Never assume that everyone in your group shares your level of commitment to the group and its task. Clarify this potential uncertainty by telling the group openly and honestly how you feel about the group and its task, with the clear expectation that others will do the same.

- You may find that you are attracted to a group only because you are attracted to its members. If that is so, think twice before you join. When a group is dedicated to a common purpose, its members will probably resent someone being there for purely social reasons.

- Once you have joined a group, work to facilitate its passage through developmental stages.
- Remember that diversity in a group's membership can provide real strength.
- When new members join a group, they must be socialized into the group. Help newcomers learn group norms and establish realistic expectations.

In sum, people are attracted to groups for different reasons and join groups to satisfy a variety of needs. An understanding of these factors in group formation should guide your communicative behavior in groups.

$\mathcal{P}$RACTICE

1. Select two groups in which you are an active member—a study group, a club, or your family, for example. For each group, indicate the importance to you of the various factors in group formation. Use a scale of 1 ("very important") to 5 ("not at all important to me").

	GROUP 1	GROUP 2
Interpersonal needs		
Inclusion	_____	_____
Control	_____	_____
Affection	_____	_____
Interpersonal attraction		
Similarity	_____	_____
Complementarity	_____	_____
Proximity	_____	_____
Physical attractiveness	_____	_____
Group attraction		
Group activities	_____	_____
Group goals	_____	_____
Group membership	_____	_____

    Compare your ratings of the two groups. Do you now have a better understanding of the roles these groups play in your life?

2. Make a list of the groups with which you are affiliated. Identify the members, activities, and goals of each. Then note your individual goals in regard to each group. Examine the results. What is your primary attraction to each group? Are your individual goals compatible with the group's goals? Do you have any hidden agendas? Do your answers to these questions explain any of your attitudes about or behaviors within these groups?

CHAPTER FOUR

Relating to Others in Groups and Teams

"No member of a crew is praised for the rugged individuality of his rowing."

—*Ralph Waldo Emerson*

OBJECTIVES

After studying this chapter, you will be able to:

- Describe how an individual develops and defines self-concept.
- Identify the task, maintenance, and individual roles that group members assume.
- Identify several group norms that often develop in small group discussions.
- Describe several effects of status differences on small group communication.
- Describe how five power bases affect relationships in small groups.
- Identify factors that foster trusting relationships with others.
- Apply guidelines for appropriate self-disclosure in small groups.
- Describe how relationships develop over time among group members.
- Recognize and adjust to cultural differences in group communication.

DO YOU CONSIDER YOURSELF *to be a leader or a follower in small group meetings? Do you usually talk a lot or a little when you serve on a committee? Perhaps your answers depend on the quality of your relationships with others in the group.*

Relationships are the ongoing connections you make with other people. In groups and teams, relationships are the feelings, roles, norms, status, and trust that both affect and reflect the quality of communication between you and others. Have you served on a committee with three or four other people who you felt were much better qualified than you? Your feeling of inferiority undoubtedly affected your relationship with the other group members. In small groups, and in other communication contexts as well, the quality of interpersonal relationships often determines what people say to one another.

Communication scholar Joann Keyton notes that

relational communication in groups refers to the verbal and nonverbal messages that create the social fabric of a group by promoting relationships between and among group members. It is the affective or expressive dimension of group communication as opposed to the instrumental, or task-oriented dimension.[1]

Relational communication theorists assert that every message people communicate to one another has both a content dimension and a relationship dimension. The content dimension of a message includes the specific information conveyed to someone. The relationship dimension involves message cues that provide hints about whether you like or dislike the person with whom you are communicating. Whether you give a public speech, talk with your spouse, or communicate with another member of a small group, you provide information about the feelings you have toward your listener as well as about ideas and thoughts.

This chapter will emphasize the relational elements that affect the quality of the relationships you establish with other group members. Specifically, it will concentrate on variables that have an important effect on the relationships you establish with others in small groups: (1) the roles you assume, (2) the norms or standards the group develops, (3) the status differences that affect the group's productivity, (4) the power some members wield, (5) the trust that improves group performance, and (6) the effects of cultural differences.

ROLES

Stop reading this chapter for just a moment, and reflect on the question "Who are you?" Now, write down ten different responses.

Who Are You?

1. *I am* _____
2. *I am* _____
3. *I am* _____
4. *I am* _____
5. *I am* _____
6. *I am* _____
7. *I am* _____
8. *I am* _____
9. *I am* _____
10. *I am* _____

As you relate to others in small groups, your concept of self—who you think you are—affects your communication and relationships with them. Your self-concept also has an impact on how others relate to you.

In trying to reduce the uncertainty that occurs when communicating in groups, people quickly assess the behaviors of others. They assign roles—sets of expectations—to others. In a small group, roles result from (1) people's expectations about their own behavior—their *self-concepts,* (2) the perceptions others have about individuals' positions in the group, and (3) people's actual behavior as they interact with others. Because their self-concepts largely determine the roles people assume in small groups, it is important to understand how self-concepts develop—how people come to learn who they think they are.

Self-Concept Development: Gender, Sexual Orientation, Culture, and Role

How do you know who you are? Why did you respond as you did when you were asked to consider the question "Who are you?" A number of factors influence your self-concept. First, other people influence who you think you are. Your parents gave you your name. Perhaps a teacher once told you that you were good in art, and consequently you think of yourself as artistic. Maybe somebody once told you that you cannot sing very well. Because you believed that person, you may now view yourself as not being very musically inclined. Thus, you listen to others, especially those whose opinions you respect, to help shape your self-concept.

One important part of everyone's self-concept is *gender.*[2] Whether you experience life as male or female affects your communication with others. While it is natural to assume that people's communication differs depending on their biological sex, recent research suggests that the psychological aspects of gender—how "feminine" or "masculine" a person is—may be at least as important a variable.[3] Research supports gender differences that "characterize women as using communication to connect with, support, and achieve closeness with others, and men as using communication to accomplish some task and to assert their individuality."[4] Sexual orientation may also affect a person's sense of self-concept, as well as how he or she relates to others.

Whether you approve or disapprove of another person's sexual orientation should not reduce your effectiveness when communicating in groups and teams. You already know that it is inappropriate to use racially charged terms that demean a person's race or ethnicity; it is equally important not to use derogatory terms or make jokes about a person's sexual orientation. Being sensitive to attitudes about sexual orientation is part of the role of an effective group communicator.

Another important component of self-concept is *culture of origin.* Different cultures foster different beliefs and attitudes about communication, status, nonverbal behavior, and all the interpersonal dynamics discussed throughout this book. The development of selfhood takes place differently from culture to culture. For example, Japanese and North American social lives flow from different premises. Many North Americans prize the image of the "rugged individualist"; many Japanese, in contrast, view this image as suggestive of egotism and insensitivity. For some Japanese, the line where self ends and others begin is far less clearly defined than it is for many North Americans.

Culture influences self-concept and thus such behaviors as the willingness to communicate in a group.[5] There is ample evidence that individuals from different cultures interpret situations and concepts very differently.[6] Therefore, understanding cultural differences is essential to understanding behavior in small groups.

The various groups with which one affiliates also help to define one's self-concept. If you attend college, you may describe yourself as a student. If you are a member of a fraternity or sorority, you may consider that association to set you apart from others. Your religious affiliation, your political party, and your membership in civic and social organizations all contribute to the way you perceive yourself.

You also learn who you are by simply observing and interpreting your own behavior. Just as before leaving your dorm or apartment you may look in the mirror to see how you look, so too do you try to see yourself as others will see you. You mentally watch your own behavior, almost as if you were looking at someone else, evaluating what you see and forming an impression of who you are. Of course, as both the observer and the observed, your impressions are subject to bias. You may be too critical of yourself. Your high expectations for your own behavior, when compared with your perceptions of your actions, may give you a distorted view.

Diversity of Roles in Small Groups

As a member of a small group, you bring your own perceptions and expectations, which are based on your experiences with other people. Your expectations thus provide a foundation for the roles you will assume in a group. Yet your role is also worked out between you and the other group members.[7] As you interact with others, they form impressions of you and your abilities. As they reward you for your actions in the group, you learn what abilities and behaviors they will reinforce. These abilities and behaviors may, in turn, become part of your self-concept.

People assume roles because of their interests and abilities and because of the needs and expectations of the rest of the group. Some roles, especially in teams, are formally assigned. When police officers arrive on the scene of an accident, bystanders do not generally question their assumption of leadership. In a task-oriented small group, a member may be assigned the role of secretary, which includes specific duties and responsibilities. A chairperson may be elected to coordinate the meeting and delegate responsibilities. Assigning responsibilities and specific roles reduces uncertainty. A group can sometimes get on with its task more efficiently if some roles are assigned. Of course, even if a person has been elected or assigned the role of chairperson, the group may reject his or her leadership in favor of that of another member who may better meet the needs of the group. In other words, roles can be assigned *formally* or can evolve *informally*.[8]

The kinds of roles discussed so far are **task roles**—they help accomplish a group's task. There are also two other kinds of roles. **Maintenance roles** define a group's social atmosphere. A member who tries to maintain a peaceful, harmonious group climate by mediating disagreements and resolving conflicts performs a maintenance function. **Individual roles** call attention to individual contributions and tend to be counterproductive to the overall group effort. Someone who is more interested in seeking personal recognition than in promoting the general benefit of the group is adopting an individual role.

Kenneth Benne and Paul Sheats have compiled a comprehensive list of possible informal roles that individual group members can assume.[9] Perhaps you can identify the various roles you have assumed while participating in small group discussions.

Group Task Roles

Initiator-contributor	Proposes new ideas or approaches to group problem solving; may suggest a different procedure or approach to organizing the problem-solving task
Information seeker	Asks for clarification of suggestions; also asks for facts or other information that may help the group deal with the issues at hand
Opinion seeker	Asks for a clarification of the values and opinions expressed by other group members
Information giver	Provides facts, examples, statistics, and other evidence that pertains to the problem the group is attempting to solve
Opinion giver	Offers beliefs or opinions about the ideas under discussion
Elaborator	Provides examples based on his or her experience or the experience of others that help to show how an idea or suggestion would work if the group accepted a particular course of action
Coordinator	Tries to clarify and note relationships among the ideas and suggestions that have been provided by others
Orienter	Attempts to summarize what has occurred and tries to keep the group focused on the task at hand
Evaluator-critic	Makes an effort to judge the evidence and conclusions that the group suggests
Energizer	Tries to spur the group to action and attempts to motivate and stimulate the group to greater productivity
Procedural technician	Helps the group achieve its goal by performing tasks such as distributing papers, rearranging the seating, or running errands for the group
Recorder	Writes down suggestions and ideas of others; makes a record of the group's progress

Group-Building and Maintenance Roles

Encourager	Offers praise, understanding, and acceptance of others' ideas and suggestions
Harmonizer	Mediates disagreements among group members
Compromiser	Attempts to resolve conflicts by trying to find an acceptable solution to disagreements among group members
Gatekeeper and expediter	Encourages less talkative group members to participate and tries to limit lengthy contributions of other group members
Standard setter	Helps to set standards and goals for the group
Group observer	Keeps records of the group's process and uses the information that is gathered to evaluate the group's procedures
Follower	Basically goes along with the suggestions and ideas of other group members; serves as an audience in group discussions and decision making

Individual Roles

Aggressor	Destroys or deflates the status of other group members; may try to take credit for someone else's contribution
Blocker	Is generally negative, stubborn, and disagreeable without apparent reason
Recognition seeker	Seeks the spotlight by boasting and reporting on his or her personal achievements
Self-confessor	Uses the group as an audience to report personal feelings, insights, and observations
Joker	Reflects a lack of involvement in the group's process by telling stories and jokes that do not help the group; lack of interest may result in cynicism, nonchalance, or other behaviors that indicate lack of enthusiasm for the group and a focus on himself or herself
Dominator	Makes an effort to assert authority by manipulating group members or attempting to take over the entire group; may use flattery or assertive behavior to dominate the discussion
Help seeker	Tries to evoke a sympathetic response from others; often expresses insecurity or feelings of low self-worth
Special-interest pleader	Works to serve an individual need; speaks for a special group or organization that best fits his or her own biases

In looking at the preceding list of roles, you may have recognized yourself—for instance, as a harmonizer or a follower—and said, "Yes, that's me. That's the role I usually take." You may also have tried to classify other members of some group into these categories. Although identifying the characteristics of roles may help you understand their nature and function in small group communication, stereotyping individuals can lock them into roles.

Both group task roles and group-building and maintenance roles are important to a group's success. What roles do you usually take in a group?

Ernest Bormann has extensively studied role behavior in groups and notes that, when asked to analyze group roles, group members often categorize and label other members, based on the roles they are perceived to fill.[10] As you identify the roles adopted by group members, be flexible in your classifications. Realize that you and other members can assume several roles during a group discussion. In fact, a group member rarely serves only as an "encourager," "opinion seeker," or "follower." Roles are dynamic; they change as perceptions, experiences, and expectations change. An individual can assume leadership responsibilities at one meeting and play a supporting role at the next.

Because a role is worked out jointly between you and the group, you will no doubt find yourself assuming different roles in different groups. Perhaps a committee you belong to needs someone to serve as a procedural leader to keep the meeting in order. Because you recognize this need and no one else keeps the group organized, you may find yourself steering the group back on to the topic, making sure all members have a chance to participate. In another committee, where others serve as procedural leaders, you may be the person who generates new ideas. Whether consciously or not, you develop a role unique to your talents and the needs of the group. Your role, then, changes from group to group.

Roles in groups and teams can be either *informal*, as we've discussed, or *formal*. In the case of teams, roles are likely to be more formally defined. For example, one team member may have primary responsibility for communicating with the supervisor or with other teams and departments. Another may head up project planning. When roles within a team are formally established, it is important that these roles be clearly defined and coordinated with one another.[11]

If you understand how group roles form and how various roles function, you will be better able to help a group achieve its purpose. For example, groups need members to perform both maintenance and task functions. Task functions help the group get the job done, and maintenance functions help the group run smoothly. If no one is performing maintenance functions, you could point this out to the group, or assume some responsibility for them. If you notice individuals hindering the group's progress because they have adopted individual roles (blocker, aggressor, recognition seeker, etc.), you could bring this to the attention of the offending group member. Explain that individual roles can make the group less efficient and can lead to conflict among members. Although you cannot assume complete responsibility for distributing roles within your group, your insights can help solve some of the group's potential problems. Understanding group roles—and when to use them—is an important part of becoming a competent group communicator.

NORMS

You have undoubtedly seen a movie or television show about the Old West in which townspeople feared villains who had no respect for the law. According to the way movies depict history, people such as Wyatt Earp were among the first to enforce the law and restore peace and order. As in the Old West, in groups and teams standards of acceptable behavior are necessary to keep peace and order. Although a small group or team does not need a Wyatt Earp to enforce order, it probably does need certain norms to help its members feel comfortable with their roles and their relationships.

Identifying Group Norms

Norms are rules or standards that determine what is appropriate and inappropriate behavior in a group. They establish expectations of how group members should behave. Norms reduce some of the uncertainty that occurs when people congregate. People's speech, the clothes they wear, or do not wear, and how and where they sit are all influenced group norms. Group norms also affect group-member relationships and the quality of group decisions.[12]

If you recently joined a group, how do you know what the group's norms are? One way to identify norms is to observe any repeated behavior patterns. Note, for example, any consistencies in the way people talk or dress. In identifying normative behavior in a group, consider the following questions:

- How do group members dress?
- What are group members' attitudes toward time? (Do group meetings begin and end on time? Are members often late to meetings?)
- What type of language is used by most group members? (Is swearing acceptable? Is the language formal?)
- Do group members use humor to relieve tension?
- Do group members address the group leader formally?
- Is it proper to address group members by their first names?

Answering these questions will help you identify a group's norms. Some groups even develop norms for developing norms. For example, members may discuss the type of clothing that will be worn to meetings or talk about how tardiness or absenteeism should be handled.

Noting when someone breaks a rule can also reveal group norms. If a member arrives late and other members frown or grimace at that person, they probably do not approve of the violation of the norm. If, after a member uses obscene words, another member says, "I wish you wouldn't use words like that," you can be certain that for at least one person a norm has been broken. Thus, punishment indicates violated norms. Often the severity of the punishment corresponds to the significance of the norm.[13] Punishment can range from subtle nonverbal expressions of disapproval (which may not even be noticed by the person expressing them) to death. The hangman's noose was commonly the ultimate punishment for those who violated the norms or laws of the Old West.

How Do Norms Develop?

Have you noticed that in some classes it is okay to say something without raising your hand, but in others the instructor must call on you before you speak? Raising your hand is a norm. How did different norms develop in two similar situations? There are at least two key reasons: (1) People develop norms in new groups based on those of previous groups they have belonged to, and (2) norms develop based on what happens early in a group's existence.

Marshall Scott Poole suggests that a group organizes itself based, in part, on norms that members encountered in previous groups,[14] As we noted in Chapter 2, Giddens and Poole call this process *structuration*. Groups do things (become structured) based on the ways those things were done in other groups. If many of your classmates previously had classes in which they had to raise their hands before speaking, then they will probably introduce

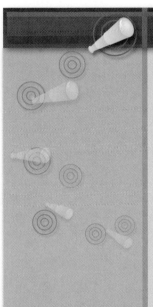

Cutting Edge Theory

ESTABLISHING GROUP NORMS

Norms are the rules or standards that tell us what is acceptable and unacceptable behavior in a group. Structuration theory tells us that groups are structured by members' use of the rules and resources they bring with them into the group. A group's norms, then, are established, in part, by members' previous experiences. Group members interact with one another to establish new group norms.

Real-Life Applications

You can leave the development of group norms to chance and relatively random group interaction, or you can approach the establishment of group norms intentionally. Often, spending some time to establish norms when a group is first formed can save time and conflict later on. Just as establishing mutuality of concern among group members is important, as we suggested in Chapter 3, so too is consciously setting some ground rules.

You might suggest discussing the ground rules for the group along with the usual discussions about how frequently and where you'll meet. What is acceptable and unacceptable behavior? Is it OK to show up late to a meeting or to miss one altogether? What will happen if you do? If you have to miss a meeting, how will you let the others know? What provisions will the group establish for bringing a member who has missed a meeting up to date?

In the long run, a clear mutual understanding of a group's norms frees group members to focus their attention on the actual work of the group. Your own reflections on your experience with group norms and your leadership in helping the groups you are part of adopt norms that facilitate their work can be important resources that you provide your groups.

that behavior into other groups. If enough people accept it, a norm is born—or, more accurately, a norm is reborn.

Norms also develop from the kinds of behavior that occur early in a group's development. Because of member uncertainty about how to behave when a group first meets, members are eager to learn acceptable behavior. If, for example, on the first day of class, a student raises his or her hand to respond to the instructor, and another student does the same, that norm is likely to stick. However, if several students respond without raising a hand, chances are that raising hands will not become a norm in the class.

Conforming to Group Norms

What influences how quickly and rigidly people conform to the rules and standards of a group? According to Harold Reitan and Marvin Shaw, at least five factors affect conformity to group norms.[15]

1. *The individual characteristics of the group members: In summarizing the research on conformity, Shaw makes the following observation:*

   > More intelligent persons are less likely to conform than less intelligent persons; women usually conform more than men, at least on traditional tasks; there is a curvilinear relationship between age and conformity; persons who generally blame themselves for what happens to them conform more than those low on self-blame; and authoritarians conform more than nonauthoritarians.[16]

   Thus, group members' past experiences and unique personality characteristics influence how they conform to established norms.

2. *The clarity of the norm and the certainty of punishment for breaking it:* The more ambiguous a group norm, the less likely it is that members will conform to it. The military spells out behavior rules clearly so that little if any ambiguity remains. A new recruit is drilled on how to talk, march, salute, and eat. Failure to abide by the rules results in swift and sure corrective sanctions. Thus, the recruit quickly learns to conform. In small groups, as soon as rules become clear and norms are established, members will usually conform.

3. *The number of people who have already conformed to the norm:* Imagine walking into a room with five or six other people, as participants once did in a study by Solomon Asch.[17] Three lines have been drawn on a blackboard. One line is clearly shorter than the other two. One by one, each person is asked which line is shortest, and each says that all the lines are the same length. Finally, it is your turn to judge which of the lines is shortest. You are perplexed because your eyes tell you that one line is definitely shorter. Yet can all the other members of your group be wrong? You answer that all of the lines are the same length— you conform. You do not want to appear odd to the other group members. Factors such as the size of a group, the number of people who agree with a certain policy, and the status of those who conform contribute to the pressure for conformity in a group.

4. *The quality of the interpersonal relationships that have developed in the group:* A group whose members like one another and respect one another's opinions is more likely to support conformity than is a less cohesive group. Employees who like their jobs, bosses, and coworkers and take pride in their work are more likely to support group norms than those who have negative or frustrating relationships with their employers or colleagues.

5. *The sense of group identification that members have developed:* If group members can readily identify with the goals of the group, they are more likely to conform to stan-

"Damn it, Hopkins, didn't you get yesterday's memo?"

dards of behavior. For example, church members who support the doctrine of a church are probably going to conform to the wishes of those in leadership positions. In addition, group members who feel they will be a part of a group for some time are more likely to conform to group norms.

Conforming to group norms requires participants to be aware of both *general norms* and more specific *operationalized norms*. Groups often adopt general norms very quickly. For example, "We all need to communicate with one another frequently" would be a common general group norm. But while there may be clear consensus around this general norm, it may mean different things to different people. For one person, *frequently* might mean "weekly," whereas another team member may be thinking in "daily" terms. Thus, norms tend to evolve from the general to the operational (what the norms mean in terms of actual behaviors) over time as the specifics are negotiated. As always, communication about norms is key.[18]

Although violating a group norm usually results in group disapproval and perhaps chastisement, such a violation can occasionally benefit a group. Just because members conform unanimously to a rule does not mean that the rule is beneficial. For example, in some situations the opinion of group members may matter more to decision making than the facts they exchange.[19] When most group members, especially those of higher status, are in

Collaborating Ethically: What Would You Do?

Relational communication is the process of building relationships between and among group members. But what happens when you see another group member behaving unethically?

Suppose that in the final semester of your senior year, you and a classmate are student interns for a not-for-profit organization that raises funds and develops programs to help children who have suffered abuse. Each of you receives a small stipend for your work on the organization's programming team, as well as three college credits (assuming successful completion of the internship and a favorable review by your supervisors).

It has come to your attention that your friend has been taking office supplies for personal use. At first it was small packages of sticky notes, but now your friend has gone home with 500 sheets of printer paper, an ink cartridge, several rolls of cellophane tape, a tape dispenser, and a stapler.

What would you do?

agreement, it is tempting for other group members to disregard contradictory evidence or facts and to go along with the majority. Such disregard for facts and evidence can lead to unfortunate consequences, as we'll discuss in Chapter 7 when we consider groupthink.

Establishing Ground Rules and a Mission Statement

Norms often develop in a group without anyone explicitly identifying what is or is not acceptable behavior. A group or team may decide to develop more precise rules to help accomplish its task. According to communication researcher Susan Shimanoff, a rule is "a followable prescription that indicates what behavior is obligated, preferred, or prohibited in certain contexts."[20] Group or team **ground rules** are explicit, agreed-on prescriptions for acceptable and appropriate behavior. Undoubtedly your school has rules about what constitutes appropriate behavior: Don't cheat on a test, plagiarize a paper, carry a gun to campus, or consume alcohol in class—these are typical college and university rules. Rules help keep order so that meaningful work can be accomplished. Rules also state what the group or organization values. Honesty, fairness, freedom of speech, and personal safety are typical values embedded in rules.

Because teams are usually more structured and coordinated than a typical group discussion, most training sessions that teach people how to become an effective team stress that a high-performing team needs clear ground rules.[21]

How does a team develop ground rules? The team leader may facilitate a discussion to establish the ground rules. If a group has no designated leader, any team member can say, "To help us stay organized and get our work done, let's establish some ground rules." Groups and teams operate better if members develop their own ground rules rather than having them imposed from "on high" or from the leader.

To help your group or team develop ground rules, consider the following questions:

- How long should our meetings last?
- Should we have a standard meeting place and time?
- What should a member do if he or she can't attend a meeting?
- How will we follow up to ensure that each member is doing his or her assigned work?
- Who is going to organize the agenda for our meetings?
- How will we manage conflict?
- How will we make our decisions—by majority vote or consensus?
- What kind of climate do we want in our meetings?
- What other kinds of guidelines do we need to develop?

Typical team ground rules include:

- Everyone will attend all meetings.
- Meetings will start on time.
- Each team member will follow through on individual assignments.
- Each team member will be prepared for every meeting.
- We will make decisions by consensus rather than majority vote.
- We will work together to manage conflict when it arises.

Another component related to team ground rules that is usually taught in team training is that each team should develop a mission statement. A team **mission statement** is a concise description of the goals or desired outcomes of the team. A mission statement not only helps you to accomplish your task but also lets you know when you've completed your task. Your work is finished when you've accomplished your mission. As author Stephen Covey suggests, begin with the end in mind.[22] A well-worded team mission statement should be (1) specific—it should be brief and clearly describe what the team should accomplish; (2) measurable—the team must be able to determine whether the mission was achieved; (3) attainable—the mission should be realistic; (4) relevant—whatever the mission, it should be appropriate to the larger organization and the overall purpose of the team; (5) time bound—the team should set a deadline or time frame for achieving the mission; and (6) a bit of a challenge, so as to stretch the team—if the mission is too simple, it won't inspire the team to do its best work. As we noted in Chapter 1, a team should have a "clear and elevating goal." A good team mission statement should pass the SMARTS test—it should be Specific, Measurable, Attainable, Relevant, Time bound, and should Stretch the team.[23]

Often teams are given their "marching orders" by someone from outside the group. Even when the team is given its goal, sometimes called a **charge**—the purpose of the team, group, or committee—the team should take some time to discuss the mission so that each person clearly understands and agrees to it. Also, discuss whether it passes the SMARTS test.

*R*EVIEW

Conformity to group norms depends on ...

- The individual characteristics of group members
- The clarity of the norm and the certainty of punishment for breaking it
- The number of people who already conform to the norm
- The quality of interpersonal relationships in the group
- The sense of group identification that members have developed

*S*TATUS

"My dad can run faster than your dad."

"Oh, yeah? Well, my dad is smarter than your dad."

"No, he's not!"

"Oh, yes he is!"

"Says who?"

"Says me. Wanna make something of it?"

Children, as well as adults, are concerned about status—who is better, brighter, and more beautiful. **Status** is an individual's importance. People with higher social status generally have more prestige and command more respect than do people of lower status. People want to talk to and talk about, see and be seen with those of high status.

Privileges Accorded to High-Status Group Members

Most people like to be perceived as enjoying some status within a group. Because occupying a position of status fulfills a need for attention, it also builds self-respect and self-esteem. Bormann explains why high-status positions are pleasant:

> The group makes a high-status person feel important and influential. They show him deference, listen to him, ask his advice, and often reward him with a greater share of the group's goods. He gets a bigger office, more secretaries, better furniture, more salary, a bigger car, and so forth. Even in communication-class discussion groups, the high-status members receive considerable gratification of their social and esteem needs. One of the most powerful forces drawing people into groups is the attraction of high status.[24]

Perhaps you have participated in small groups in which the status of an individual afforded him or her certain privileges that were not available to the rest of the group. The chairperson of the board may have a private dining room or an executive washroom, while other members must eat in the company cafeteria and use public washrooms.

Effects of Status Differences

In groups and teams, members' status exerts a significant effect on interpersonal relationships. Status affects who talks to whom and how often a member speaks. The status or reputation an individual has before joining a group certainly affects the role he or she assumes. In addition, norms that help groups determine how they will deal with status differences and what privileges they should allow those with greater prestige develop quickly. Several researchers have observed how status differences affect the relationships among members of a small group. Consider the following research conclusions:

- High-status group members talk more than low-status members.[25]
- High-status group members communicate more with other high-status members than they do with those of lower status.[26]
- Low-status group members tend to direct their conversation to high-status group members rather than to those of lower or equal status.[27]
- Low-status group members communicate more positive messages to high-status members than they do to those of equal or lower status.[28]
- High perceived status and expertise increase a group member's tendencies to participate actively and to generate positive self-evaluations of his or her own input into the group's task.[29]
- High-status group members usually abide by the norms of the group more than do low-status group members. (The exception to this research finding occurs when high-status members realize that they can violate group norms and receive less punishment than low-status group members would receive; thus, depending on the situation, they may violate certain group norms.)[30]
- Group members are more likely to ignore the comments and suggestions made by low-status members than those made by high-status members.[31]
- Low-status group members communicate more irrelevant information than do high-status members.[32]
- High-status members are less likely than low-status members to complain about their jobs or their responsibilities.[33]

- Communication with high-status group members can replace the need for the upward movement of low-status members in the group's status hierarchy.[34]
- High-status group members tend to talk to the entire group more than members of lower status do.[35]
- The leader of a small group is usually the member with the highest status. (The exception to this conclusion occurs when the leader emerges because of capability and competence and not necessarily because of popularity. That kind of leader holds a lower status than does a more popular and well-liked group member.)[36]

EFFECTS OF STATUS DIFFERENCES IN GROUPS

Group members with high status:

Talk more
Communicate more often with other high-status members
Have more influence
Generally abide by group norms
Are less likely to be ignored
Are less likely to complain about their responsibilities
Talk to the entire group
Are likely to serve in leadership roles

Group members with low status:

Direct conversation to high-status rather than low-status members
Communicate more positive messages to high-status members
Are more likely to have their comments ignored
Communicate more irrelevant information
Talk to high-status members as a substitute for climbing the social hierarchy in the group

Observing Status Differences to Predict Group Dynamics

Knowing how status affects the relationships among group members helps you predict who will talk with whom. If you can perceive status differences, you can also predict the type of messages communicated in a small group discussion. These research conclusions suggest that the social hierarchy of a group affects group cohesiveness, group satisfaction, and even the quality of a group's solution. One of the benefits of increased status within a group is the relative increase in the group member's influence or power.

Sociologist Robert Bierstedt once observed that in the "entire lexicon of sociological concepts, none is more troublesome than the concept of *power*. We may say about it in general only what St. Augustine said about time, that we all know perfectly well what it is—until someone asks us."[37] Although scholars debate definitions of power as well as its relationship

Virtual Communication

Technology development is not neutral, but reflects the values of the cultures in which it develops. A team of researchers at the University of California at Santa Barbara analyzed the structure of the Internet to determine the social impact of that technology. They found that the primary use (70%) of the Internet is information dissemination and gathering. Its decentralized structure makes government regulation of the medium extremely difficult and encourages open communication. According to the authors, these democratic values implicit in the technology reflect a North American cultural influence that will most certainly drive the future development of the Internet.

These democratic values may also reflect the fact that communication on a computer screen minimizes status differences that are far more influential in face-to-face situations. Students and faculty members who use online chat rooms or threaded discussions in their classes report an interesting finding that supports this notion. Those who participate most actively in online discussions are often not the same students who participate most actively in face-to-face classroom discussions. Some students are simply more comfortable in an environment where they can choose their words more carefully and less publicly; it suits their personalities better. As you add virtual group communication to your group communication repertoire, keep in mind these tips:

- Online discussions may seem more democratic because of the factors noted above. However, status differences don't disappear when we no longer can see the other person. Remember to adapt your messages to your audience—friend, peer, colleague, professor, supervisor, CEO—as appropriate.
- The disembodied messages of virtual communication can be easily misinterpreted without attending nonverbal signals. Be sure you understand the sender's meaning before you react.
- Resist the tendency to communicate solely online in lieu of face to face. Convenience and effectiveness are often competing values.

Educators know that active engagement in the learning process and time on task are the best predictors of student academic success. It follows, then, that given the different personalities of group members and the democratic value of participation, a combination of face-to-face interaction and virtual communication may reduce the effects of status differences, maximize the contributions of each group member, and consequently maximize the effectiveness of your group.

For more information, see Andrew Flanigan and Wendy Jo Mayard Farinola, "The Technical Code of the Internet/World Wide Web," *Critical Studies in Media Communication* 17 (2000): 409–28. Also see Merlyna Lim and Mark E. Kann, "Democratic Deliberation and Mobilization on the Internet," Networked Publics—Annenberg Center for Communication (2005–2006). http://netpublics.annenberg.edu/about_netpublics/democratic_deliberation_and_mobilization_on_the_internet to other variables such as status and authority, they generally agree that **power,** at its core, involves the ability of one person to control or influence some other person or decision.[38] Power in a small group, then, is reflected in an individual's ability to get other members to conform to his or her wishes. Power is about influence.

Certain group members may have more power in the group than others. Sometimes the sources of their power are clear to members, such as in groups with large status differences; but in other cases, the sources of power are not so clear. In order to map out the territory of social power in small groups, you need to look at power bases and the effects of power on group processes.

Power Bases

Your power base in a group is the sum of the resources that you can use to control or influence others. Because no two group members have exactly the same resources, each member operates from a different power base. What are some of these power bases? John French and Bertram Raven identified five power bases in their study of small groups: (1) legitimate power, (2) referent power, (3) expert power, (4) reward power, and (5) coercive power.[39]

Legitimate power stems from a group member's ability to influence others because of being elected, appointed, or selected to exert control over a group. Legitimate power comes from occupying a position of responsibility. The principal of a school has the legitimate power to control school policy; the senators from your state have legitimate power to represent their constituents. Many of the privileges enjoyed by high-status group members reflect this kind of power base. A small group member who has been elected chairperson is given legitimate power to influence the group's procedures.

Referent power is the power of interpersonal attraction. Recall from Chapter 3 that people are attracted to others whom they admire and want to emulate. Put simply, people we like have more power over us than those people we do not like.

Expert power stems from a group member's ability to influence others based on the knowledge and information the member possesses. As the saying goes, knowledge is power. Suppose you are a member of a group studying ways to improve the environment of the river in your community. If one of your group members has a Ph.D. in aquatic plant life, that person's knowledge and access to information give him or her expert power. More than likely, that person can influence the group. However, just because a group member has knowledge does not mean that he or she will exert more influence in the group. The group must find the knowledge credible and useful.

Reward power is based on a person's ability to reward behaviors. If you are in a position to help another member gain money, status, power, acceptance, or other rewards, you will have power over that person. Of course, group members are motivated by different needs and goals. What is rewarding to one may not be rewarding to others. Reward power is effective only if a person finds the reward satisfying or valuable. Others must also believe that a person actually has the power and resources to bestow the reward.

Coercive power, the negative side of reward power, is based on the perception that another can punish you for acting or not acting in a certain way. The ability to demote others, reduce their salaries or benefits, force them to work overtime hours, or fire them are examples of resources that can make up this power base. Even though coercive power may achieve a desired effect, group members usually resent threats of punishment intended to make them conform. Punished group members often try to dominate in other interactions or escape from heavy-handed efforts to accomplish a group goal.

Effects of Power on Group Process

Members who have power influence the group process. Whether their influence will be positive or negative depends on how wisely the members use their influence. The following principles summarize the impact of power on group deliberations:

- A struggle for power among group members can result in poor group decisions and less group cohesion.
- Members who overtly seek dominance and control over a group often focus attention on themselves rather than on achieving group goals. They typically serve as aggressors, blockers, recognition seekers, dominators, or special-interest pleaders (roles discussed earlier in this chapter).
- Group members with little power often talk less frequently in a group.
- Charles Berger observed that "persons who talk most frequently and for the longest periods of time are assumed to be the most dominant group members. In addition, persons receiving the most communication are assumed to be most powerful."[40] While not all powerful members dominate group conversations, there is a relationship between verbal contributions to the group and influence. The exceptions to this principle are members who talk so frequently that they are ignored by the group. Cultural variations can influence this dynamic as well.
- Group members can lose power if other members think they use power for personal gain or to keep a group from achieving its goals.
- Group members usually expect individuals with greater power to have high-status privileges. However, if members believe that powerful members are having a detrimental effect on the group, their credibility and influence are likely to diminish. Too many perks and privileges given to some members sap a group's ability to do its job and can result in challenges to the influential group members.

A person's power base in a group is the sum of the resources that person can use to control or influence others. What types of power do you think Donald Trump exercises over his employees?

- Too much power in one individual can lead to less group decision making and more autocratic decision making. Autocratic decision making occurs when one person with several power bases (for example, one who can reward and punish, has needed information, is well liked, and has been appointed to lead) makes a decision alone rather than with the group as a whole. Group members may not speak their minds for fear of reprisals.
- Increasing your level of activity in a group can increase your power and influence.
- Groups with equal power distribution show higher quality group communication than do groups with unequal power distribution.[41]
- In corporate work teams, individual power is related to the fact that group members must depend on each other.[42]

If you participate in a group and sense that your influence is diminishing, try to participate more and to take an active role in helping the group achieve its goal. Volunteering to help with tasks and increasing your knowledge about group problems, issues, or decisions can also enhance your influence. If you see other group members losing influence, you can give them (or suggest that they take responsibility for) specific tasks that will bring them back into the group's mainstream (assuming that they are willing to accept the responsibility).

$\mathcal{R}$EVIEW

POWER BASES

Type of Power	Source of Influence
Legitimate	Being elected, appointed, or selected to lead the group
Referent	Being well liked
Expert	A member's knowledge and information
Reward	The ability to provide rewards for desired behavior
Coercive	The ability to punish others

Power and Gender

Stereotypes portray women as being more easily influenced than men and as having less power over others than their male counterparts. However, although results are mixed, research tends to dispel these illusions.[43] In one study, when women were placed in positions of power, they were just as likely as men to use strategies associated with power. Because men typically occupy roles of higher power in society, the opportunity for them to use power strategies is greater than for women. This observation led the researcher to conclude that the unequal distribution of power results in the illusion of gender differences, which are really the result of women's and men's relative social status. Thus, apparent gender differences must be understood within a context of status and power.[44]

Clearly there are inequities in the workplace. But social and organizational expectations for men and women have changed and will continue to do so. Indeed, there is evidence that more and more firms value diversity in the ranks of management and believe that such diversity provides a competitive advantage. As these changes unfold, more and more women managers will likely feel free to "be themselves" without compromising their organizational image.[45]

Status and Power: A Cultural Footnote

It is important to remember that status is primarily in the eye of the beholder. Frequently status becomes meaningless when someone crosses a cultural boundary; a Ph.D. will not be revered in a country-and-western bar. Communication scholar Marshall Singer offers this observation:

> The Ph.D. holder and the famous athlete have acquired high status and the ability to influence their respective "constituents." Because high status—whether ascribed or acquired—depends so much on its being perceived as such, it may be the least transferable, across cultural barriers, of all the components of power we are discussing.[46]

Cultural differences in perceptions of status are revealed pointedly in the following letter. On June 17, 1744, commissioners from Maryland and Virginia negotiated a treaty with the Native American members of the Six Nations at Lancaster, Pennsylvania. The Native Americans were invited to send young men to William and Mary College. The next day they declined the offer, as the letter explains.

> We know that you highly esteem the kind of learning taught in those Colleges, and that the Maintenance of our young Men, while with you, would be very expensive to you. We are convinced, that you mean to do us Good by your Proposal; and we thank you heartily. But you, who are wise must know that different Nations have different Conceptions of things and you will therefore not take it amiss, if our ideas of this kind of Education happen not to be the same as yours. We have had some Experience of it. Several of our young People were formerly brought up at the Colleges of the Northern Provinces: They were instructed in all your Sciences; but, when they came back to us, they were bad Runners, ignorant of every means of living in the woods . . . neither fit for Hunters, Warriors, nor Counsellors, they were totally good for nothing.
>
> We are, however, not the less oblig'd by your kind Offer, tho' we decline accepting it; and, to show our grateful Sense of it, if the Gentlemen of Virginia will send us a Dozen of their Sons, we will take Care of their Education, instruct them in all we know, and make Men of them.[47]

TRUST

What do used-car salespeople, politicians, and insurance agents have in common? They are often stereotyped as people whose credibility is suspect. The untrustworthy images of such people are not always justified; but when they want something from you, whether it is money or a vote, you are often suspicious of the promises they make. When you trust people, you have faith that they will not try to take advantage of you and that they will be mindful of your best interests. In small groups, the degree of trust you have in others affects your developing interpersonal relationships with them. The following sections consider how trust in relationships affects group members and suggests how you can elicit more trust as you interact with others.

Developing Trusting Relationships

Why do you trust some people more than others? What is it about your closest friend that enables you to confide your most private feelings? How can group members develop trusting relationships? First, developing trusting relationships in a group takes time. Just as assuming a role in a group discussion requires time, so does developing confidence in others. Second, you base trust on the previous experiences you have had with others. You probably would not give a stranger your bank account number. You would, however, more than likely trust this number to your spouse or to a friend you have known for many years. As you communicate with other people, you gradually learn whether you can trust them. First you observe how they complete various tasks and responsibilities. Then you decide whether you can rely on them to get things done.

Trust, then, develops when you can predict how another person will behave under certain circumstances. Put another way, trust helps you reduce uncertainty as you form expectations of others. As you participate in a group, you trust those who, because of their actions and support in the past, have given you reason to believe that they will support you in the future. Group members establish trusting relationships as they develop mutual respect and as the group becomes more cohesive. One interesting piece of research shows that in computer-mediated teams, levels of trust among group members start lower than in face-to-face groups. But over time, trust increases to a level comparable to that in face-to-face teams.[48]

However, even time and experience cannot guarantee trust. A certain amount of risk is always involved whenever you trust another person. As Richard Reichert suggests, "Trust is always a risk, a kind of leap in the dark. It is not based on any solid proof that the other person will not hurt you … trust is always a gamble."[49] Sometimes the gamble does not pay off. And if you have worked in a small group with several people who proved untrustworthy, you may be reluctant to trust others in future groups. Thus, your good and bad experiences in past groups affect the way in which you relate to people in future groups.

Self-Disclosure

One of the most important ways to establish and maintain trusting relationships with others is through **self-disclosure**—the deliberate communication of information about yourself to others. Self-disclosure, like trust, involves risk. When you reveal personal, private information, you open yourself to the possibility that others might reject you. John Powell, in his book *Why Am I Afraid To Tell You Who I Am?*, says that people hesitate to disclose much about themselves because "if I tell you who I am, you may not like who I am, and it's all that I have."[50]

Self-disclosure should be timed to suit the occasion and the expectations of the individuals involved. Telling all too soon may violate what the other person expects. In Western cultures, it would not be appropriate to talk about the intimate aspects of your life (for example, your financial net worth or your romantic endeavors) when you first introduce yourself to someone. The other person would likely feel uncomfortable and might want to terminate the relationship. Thus, when you first meet someone, you usually reveal information that is not too personal. As you establish a trusting relationship with an individual, you may feel more comfortable about discussing private feelings and concerns. Powell notes that the information you reveal about yourself often progresses through several predictable levels:

Level 5:   *Cliché communication.* Standard phrases such as "Hi, how are you?", "Nice to see you," "Beautiful weather, isn't it?," and "How's it going?" signal the desire to initiate a relationship.

Level 4:   *Facts and biographical information.* You reveal nonthreatening information about yourself, such as your name, hometown, or occupation.

Level 3:   *Personal attitudes and ideas.* After introducing yourself and beginning discussion of whatever task brings you together, you respond to various ideas and issues, noting where you agree and disagree with others.

Level 2:   *Personal feelings.* Talking about your personal feelings makes you more vulnerable than discussing attitudes and ideas does, particularly when you reveal feelings about yourself or others.

Level 1:   *Peak communication.* People seldom reach this level. Only with your closest friends or people you have known for some time will you share personal insights that may result in rejection. This level of self-disclosure takes much time and trust to develop.[51]

These five levels are merely a means of describing the self-disclosure process, so do not try to classify all your personal communication with others into one of these categories. Such thinking may detract from an otherwise spontaneous conversation. Although self-disclosure should not be used as a tool to manipulate others into trusting relationships, you should develop greater awareness of the self-disclosure process to help evaluate your relationships with others in small groups.

One researcher describes five characteristics of appropriate self-disclosure.[52]

1. *Self-disclosure is a function of the ongoing relationship.* This means that self-disclosure is not something you do just once; you continually share information about yourself with others.
2. *Self-disclosure is reciprocal.* When you disclose something to another person, that person will probably disclose something to you—at least, if you give him or her an opportunity. If you rarely give others a chance to talk, they probably will not respond to you. If you want to create a climate of trust in your group, you must be willing to share with others.
3. *Self-disclosure is timed to what is happening in your group.* For example, if your group is discussing where a new highway should be located, it would not be appropriate for you to talk about how much you enjoy playing with your cat. In other words, do not disclose just for the sake of disclosing. Your comments should be relevant to the discussion at hand.
4. *Self-disclosure should deal with what is happening among the people present.* Not only should your self-disclosure be appropriate to an occasion, it should also be appropriate for the people in your group. You need not talk about a troubled relationship if it clearly is of no concern to the others present. You may find someone who will listen to you, but if the others present have no interest in your confessions, keep them to yourself.
5. *Self-disclosure usually moves by small increments (it takes time).* Establishing trusting relationships with others cannot be rushed. If a group of people will meet for only two or three sessions, do not feel compelled to disclose personal information. Furthermore, if you ask others to disclose personal information too quickly, group members may interpret your efforts to establish trust as prying into their personal lives. Although you should not disclose too much too soon, you should persevere in trying to get to know other group members. Self-disclosure is a useful way to improve relationships.

THE DEVELOPMENT OF GROUP RELATIONSHIPS OVER TIME

We noted in Chapter 3 that group formation takes place over time. It takes time for relationships to develop. You experience some tension and anxiety the first time you participate in a small group. You may be uncertain of your role, and the group may not have met long enough for norms to develop. True, in some groups, certain standards of behavior already exist because of the common culture that group members share, but these expectations provide only skeletal guidance for behavior. Status differences among group members can also create tension. Bormann has defined this initial uneasiness as **primary tension**, or the social unease and stiffness that accompanies getting acquainted. Students placed in a discussion group with strangers will experience these tensions most strongly during the opening minutes of their first meetings. The earmarks of primary tensions are extreme politeness, apparent boredom or tiredness, and considerable sighing or yawning. When members show primary tension, they speak softly and tentatively. Frequently they can think of nothing to say, and many long pauses result.[53]

Expect to find some primary tension during initial meetings. It is a normal part of group development. A group leader can minimize this tension, however, by helping members get to know one another, perhaps through get-acquainted exercises or brief statements of introduction. While members of groups that meet only once might deem getting to know one another impractical, using a few minutes to break the ice and reduce some of the primary tension can help create more satisfying relationships among group members.

Case Study

Your university has a Strategic Planning Committee composed of the following people:

The Dean of the College

The Vice President for Finance

The Vice President for Development (fundraising)

A representative from the Board of Trustees

The Director of Admissions

The Director of Planning and Institutional Research

Three elected faculty members

Two students selected by the Student Government Association

An alumni representative

Some committee members (administrators) are appointed to the committee permanently. Others (faculty members and students) are appointed to one-year terms. The committee's charge is to make recommendations to the president about new goals and objectives for the Strategic Plan. To do this, the committee has been asked first to review the University's Mission Statement, as well as the Institutional Goals for Graduates and how they relate to the Mission.

Then the committee is asked to evaluate progress made toward these goals since establishment of the previous Strategic Plan. The committee then must facilitate and coordinate the annual update of the Plan before finally making their recommendations.

Practice in Applying Principles

1. Consider the membership of this group. What source(s) of power can you identify for each member based on the member's title or affiliation?
2. Review the list of group roles on pages 73–74. Can you predict which group members are most likely to enact certain group roles? Which members and which roles? Why do you think this?
3. Rank-order committee members by their status. What is the basis for your rankings?
4. This is a committee that has relatively permanent members (dean, vice presidents, and directors), as well as members who are more short term (representatives from trustees, alumni, students, faculty). How will this affect the establishment of group norms from year to year?

After a group resolves primary tension and its members become more comfortable with one another, another type of tension develops. **Secondary tension,** according to Bormann, occurs as conflicts arise and differences of opinion emerge. Whether recognized as a personality conflict or simply as a disagreement, secondary tension surfaces when members try to solve the problem or accomplish the task facing the group. Secondary tension also results from power struggles, and it usually establishes group norms. Joking or laughing often helps manage secondary tension. But no matter how cohesive a group may be, some conflict over procedure will normally develop as relationships among members form. Chapter 7 will consider some suggestions for managing the conflict and controversy that result from secondary tension, and Chapter 9 will discuss the phases of a group's growth and development in more detail.

$\mathcal{R}$EVIEW

GROUP TENSION

Primary tension:	Uneasiness and discomfort in getting acquainted and managing initial group uncertainty about the group task and group relationships
Secondary tension:	Tension that occurs as group members struggle for influence, develop roles and norms, and explore differences in approaching the group task

$\mathcal{C}$ULTURE

We now turn our attention to an always present but often unseen variable that affects our interactions with others: culture. **Culture** is a learned system of knowledge, behavior, attitudes, beliefs, values, and norms that is shared by a group of people.[54] We often think of cultural differences as existing between ethnic groups or nations, but they can also exist between families, organizations, or even different parts of the same country or state. It is not surprising that when individuals of different cultures interact, cultural differences can interfere with effective communication. Culture is a difference that *makes* a difference in how we relate to others.

One obvious aspect of culture is language—it would be challenging indeed to participate in a group without a common language! But it can also be challenging to work with others with whom you have nonverbal cultural differences. Differences in how people from different cultures respond to context and their attitudes toward personal contact have a direct bearing on communication in small groups.

Individualism and Collectivism

Groups often have difficulty establishing norms and roles because of cultural variations in individualism among group members. As we discussed in Chapter 1, in some cultures (such as among Americans), individual autonomy and initiative are valued; in others (the Japanese, for instance), collective well-being takes precedence over individual achievement. People from collectivist cultures are therefore more likely to view assertive individualists as self-centered, while individualists may interpret their collectivist counterparts as weak. Collectivists are more likely to conform to group norms and to value group decisions highly.[55] We caution you, though, against overgeneralization. Although different cultures clearly foster different orientations, there is also ample evidence that there are vast differences among people *within* any culture. Thus, it is nearly impossible to predict with certainty an individual or collectivist orientation based on culture alone.[56]

Although differences in individualism always exist in groups, these differences can be extreme if group members are culturally diverse, and extreme differences can result in low group satisfaction and productivity. To establish and maintain norms with which all members can feel comfortable, groups need to understand and be sensitive to the cultural expectations of all participants.

High-Context and Low-Context Cultures

In some cultures the surrounding context of an interaction or the unspoken, nonverbal message plays a greater role than in others.[57] A **high-context culture** is one in which more emphasis is placed on nonverbal communication. We will discuss the power and importance of nonverbal messages in more detail in Chapter 6. In high-context cultures, the physical environment is important in helping communicators interpret the message. The environment, the situation, and the communicator's mood are especially significant in decoding messages. A **low-context culture** places more emphasis on verbal expression. Figure 4.1 shows cultures arranged along a continuum from high to low context.

FIGURE 4.1

Where Different Cultures Fall on the Context Scale

Source: Adapted from Donald W. Klopf and James McCroskey, *International Encounters: An Introduction to Intercultural Communication* (Boston: Allyn & Bacon, 2006).

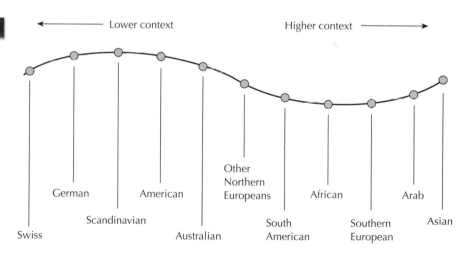

← Lower context   Higher context →

Swiss
German
Scandinavian
American
Australian
Other Northern Europeans
South American
African
Southern European
Arab
Asian

Low-context cultures: Information must be provided explicitly, usually in words. Members of such cultures

- Are less aware of nonverbal cues, environment, and situation
- Lack well-developed networks
- Need detailed background information
- Tend to segment and compartmentalize information
- Control information on a "need to know" basis
- Prefer explicit and careful directions from someone who "knows"
- View knowledge as a commodity

High-context cultures: Much information drawn from surroundings. Very little must be explicitly transferred. Members

- Respond to nonverbal cues
- Share information freely
- Rely on physical context for information
- Take environment, situation, gestures, and mood into account
- Maintain extensive information networks

People from high-context cultures may be more skilled in interpreting nonverbal information than people from low-context cultures. Individuals from high-context cultures may also use fewer words to express themselves. Because individuals from low-context cultures place greater emphasis on speech, they may talk more than those from high-context cultures. People from a low-context culture typically are less sensitive to the nonverbal cues in the environment and the situation in interpreting the messages of others.[58]

In a small group, high- or low-context orientation can play a role in the amount of time a person talks and his or her sensitivity in responding to unspoken dynamics of a group's climate. Sometimes people from a high-context culture will find those from a low-context culture less credible or trustworthy. Someone from a low-context culture may be more likely to make explicit requests for information by saying, "Talk to me," "Give it to me straight," or "Tell it like it is." In contrast, a person from a high-context culture expects communication to be more indirect and to rely on more implicit cues.

High-Contact and Low-Contact Cultures

In some cultures, people are more comfortable being touched or being physically close to others; these are said to be **high-contact cultures.** Individuals from **low-contact cultures** tend to prefer more personal space, typically make less eye contact with others, and are much more uncomfortable with being touched or approached by others.[59]

Whether group members are from high- or low-contact cultures can affect preferred seating arrangements and other aspects of small group ecology. For example, people from some cultural groups, such as the Chinese, prefer sitting side by side rather than directly across from one another.[60] Fathi Yousef and Nancy Briggs found that in Middle Eastern countries it is appropriate to stand close enough to someone to smell their breath.[61] North Americans usually prefer more space around them than do Latin Americans, Arabs, and Greeks.[62] Cultural differences can also be found among ethnic groups within the same country.

Cultural differences and similarities influence nonverbal interaction when people communicate. How would you manage cultural differences in a group?

It may be tempting to make stereotypical inferences about all people within a given culture based on some of the research conclusions we cite. But Robert Shuter cautions against making broad, sweeping generalizations about a specific culture.[63] His research found significant variations in nonverbal behavior *within* cultures. Our discussion has been intended simply to document the existence of cultural differences and to warn that such differences may hamper effective communication in small groups.

No list of simple suggestions or techniques will help you manage the cultural differences that you will encounter in groups. However, a basic principle can help: *When interacting with people from a culture other than your own, note differences you think may be culture-based and adapt accordingly. Become other-oriented.* We are not suggesting that you abandon your cultural norms, traditions, and expectations—only that you become more flexible, thereby minimizing the communication distortion that cultural differences may cause. Carley Dodd suggests that if you think you have offended someone or acted inappropriately, you can ask the other person if you have, and if so, find out what exactly you did wrong.[64] Being aware of and responding to cultural differences in small groups can enhance your ability to interact with others.

Gender and Communication

Deborah Tannen's best-selling book *You Just Don't Understand* struck a responsive chord by identifying gender differences in verbal communication. Her work popularized a research conclusion that most of us already knew: Both within a given culture and from one culture to another, men and women have different communication patterns. Evidence indicates that men and women sometimes use language differently and that they also interpret nonverbal behavior differently. Clara Mayo and Nancy Henley[65] as well as Diana Ivy and Phil Backlund[66] are among the scholars who provide excellent comparisons of how males and females use and respond to nonverbal cues. Note some of the following conclusions about gender differences in sending and receiving nonverbal messages:

People of both sexes tend to move closer to women than to men.[67]

Women tend to move closer to others than men do.[68]

Men tend to maintain less eye contact with others than women do.[69]

Women seem to use more expressive facial expressions than men do.[70]

Men tend to use more gestures than women do.[71]

Men initiate touch more often than women do.[72]

Women speak with less volume than men do.[73]

Besides differing in their use of nonverbal behaviors, there is evidence that women tend to receive and interpret nonverbal messages more accurately. Why are there differences in the way males and females use and respond to nonverbal messages? Some theorize that the answer lies in physiological differences between men and women. But the leading explanation focuses on how men and women are socialized into society. Women typically are socialized to value interpersonal relationships and to respond to others' emotions, which are largely expressed nonverbally. Also, men typically have higher status in North American culture and in many other cultures throughout the world. And as we noted earlier, those of higher status are typically talked to more; receiving verbal information from others may lessen men's need to interpret nonverbal messages.

The research conclusions reviewed here can help explain some of the differences in the way that men and women communicate in groups and teams. We emphasize, however, that these are research generalizations; do not expect all men and all women to exhibit these differences. In your group deliberations, be cautious about always expecting to see these differences. But knowing that there can be gender differences in both verbal and nonverbal behavior may help you become both more flexible and tolerant when communicating with others in groups.

Conversational Style

Conversational norms vary by culture.[74] If not understood, these differences can cause misunderstanding, anxiety, and group conflict.

The white middle-class North American norm that leads one group member to quietly await a turn to speak may cause him or her to wait a very long time when those from other cultures do not share that norm. People from some cultures love a good argument, whereas others revere harmony and the ability to assimilate differences to build consensus.[75] Some cultures are put off by North Americans' frankness and relative lack of inhibition about sharing negative information. In Western cultures, control is exerted through speaking; in Eastern cultures, control is expressed through silence and in the outward show of reticence.[76]

The topics we address and our willingness to talk about personal matters vary by culture. Whereas Mexicans may talk about a person's soul or spirit, such talk may make North Americans uncomfortable. Persons from Hispanic cultures often begin conversations with inquiries about one's family, even with casual acquaintances or in a business meeting. Many North Americans view family matters as too personal to be discussed casually.[77]

Time

Thomas Fitzgerald recounts an anecdote that illustrates cultural differences in the temporal dimension. While interviewing a group of Brazilian students, Fitzgerald asked them how they felt about a person who was consistently late. He was surprised to find that the students viewed such a person as probably more successful than those who were on time. A person of status, they reasoned, is *expected* to be late.[78]

Some people are **monochronic.** They are most comfortable doing only one thing at a time, like to concentrate on the job at hand, are more serious and sensitive to deadlines and schedules, like to plan how to use their time, and stress the importance of starting and ending meetings on time.[79] Other people are **polychronic.** Such individuals can do many things at once, are less influenced by deadlines and schedules, feel that relationships are more important than producing volumes of work, frequently change plans, and are less concerned about punctuality than are monochronic individuals.

Communication researchers Dawna Ballard and David Seibold confirmed what scholars have suspected: Groups have different approaches to how they use time. Ballard and Seibold found that groups they investigated had three general approaches to time: (1) flexible, (2) separation, and (3) concurrency.[80] Groups with a flexible approach to time set fewer deadlines and provided group members more autonomy. Groups with a separation approach to time preferred literally to separate themselves from others when working on a group task; they were more likely to keep the door closed and get away from others. Concurrency groups were more likely to attempt to do several things at once (multitask); they would look for ways to combine projects and activities. Being aware of how groups and teams in which you participate use time can help you better understand why your group behaves as it does. If you're in a flexible group, you may need to monitor deadlines more closely. Separation groups may need to ensure they don't separate themselves so far from the organization that they lose sight of the overall organizational goal. Because concurrency groups have a tendency to do several things at once, such groups may need added structure and a system to keep track of the various projects undertaken.

The use of time and expectations about time can cause conflict and frustration if group members have widely differing perspectives. Time use and expectations vary from culture to culture.[81] People from the United States and Northern Europe tend to be more monochronic; attention to deadlines and punctuality are important. Latin Americans, Southern Europeans, and Middle Easterners are more often polychronic; they give less attention to deadlines and schedules. Western cultures tend to approach problems in a linear, step-by-step fashion. How events are structured and sequenced is important. Eastern cultures (Chinese and Japanese) approach time with a less-structured perspective. The observations of several researchers have been summarized in Table 4.1.[82]

Even if your group does not have members from widely different cultures, you may notice that people have different approaches to time. Groups develop their own norms about time. It may be useful to explicitly discuss and clarify norms, such as the importance of deadlines, expectations for group productivity, and general attitudes about punctuality, in order to manage any uncertainty about time that may exist.

Whether a group is struggling with cultural differences or differences in role expectations, norms, status, perceived power, or trust, it's important to remember that through effective and appropriate communication, we can bridge differences and develop productive relationships with others. In the next chapter we examine those communication variables that can contribute to a positive group climate.

TABLE 4.1   **Cultural Differences in the Use of Time**

In Western Cultures	In Eastern Cultures
Time is something to be manipulated.	Time simply exists.
The present is a way-station between the past and the future.	The present is more important than the past or the future.
Time is a resource that can be saved, spent, or wasted.	Time is a limitless pool.
Time is an aspect of history rather than part of an immediate experience.	Events occur in time; they cause ripples, and the ripples subside.

Source: Adapted from Donald W. Klopf and James McCroskey, *International Encounters: An Introduction to Intercultural Communication* (Boston: Allyn & Bacon, 2006).

Putting Principles into Practice

Six variables affect and reflect relationships among members of small groups: (1) roles, (2) norms, (3) status, (4) power, (5) trust, and (6) culture. An understanding of how these variables affect your performance and the performance of other group members will help you explain and predict the types and quality of relationships that form in small groups. As you attempt to apply the information presented in this chapter, consider these suggestions:

Roles

- Roles grow out of self-concept, which is based on a composite of life experiences. These experiences are influenced by gender, sexual orientation, and culture, as well as by the significant groups to which we have belonged. Work to understand your own self-concept; doing so will help you understand your role in small groups.
- If no one performs important group roles, point this out to the group or assume the responsibility for performing them yourself.
- If you observe a group member hindering the progress of your group because he or she has adopted an individual group role (blocker, aggressor, recognition seeker, etc.), bring this to the attention of the group or the offending group member.
- Do not try to limit yourself (or other group members) to just one or two group roles. Group members can assume several roles during the course of a discussion.

Norms

- Identify group norms by noting repeated patterns of behavior.
- Another way to identify group norms is by noting what kind of offenses group members punish.
- Consider the individual characteristics of group members, the clarity of norms and the certainty of punishment for breaking them, the number of people who have broken norms, the quality of rela-

tionships among group members, and the sense of group identification to help determine whether members will conform to the group norms.

Status

- Identify the status of group members by the privileges that high-status group members receive.
- If you can spot status differences in small groups, you can predict who talks to whom.
- If you are aware of status differences, you can communicate more effectively and with greater influence.

Power

- People develop power in a group because they can provide information, expertise, rewards, or punishment; because they have been elected or appointed; or because they are well liked or have status in the group.
- Consider the possible sources of power in your group to help you understand patterns of influence.
- Work to maximize the positive sources of power for all group members.

Trust

- Don't expect group members to form trusting relationships early—it takes time for trust to develop.
- Self-disclosure is an important factor in developing trusting relationships with others. Self-disclosure and trust involve risk. Taking these risks with others helps them to do the same with you.

Culture

Culturally diverse groups often have difficulty establishing satisfactory roles and norms because of differences in cultural expectations. Such groups require extra effort in group building and maintenance.

When group members do not share a common native language, some additional tactics may be necessary:[83]

- *Slow down* communication.
- *Repeat* or paraphrase when nonverbal expressions suggest that listeners do not understand.
- *Verify* common understanding by having others restate the argument or idea.
- If necessary (and possible), encourage *restatement* in the listener's native language.

Remember that cultures vary widely in conversational style as well as the appropriateness assigned to topics of conversation. Do not make the mistake of attributing such differences to impoliteness or insensitivity.

Self-Disclosure

- Do not think that self-disclosure just happens once when the group first gets together; it is a function of ongoing group relationships.
- Do not talk solely about yourself without giving other people a chance to talk about themselves.
- Appropriate self-disclosure should deal with what is happening among the people present. Your revelations should be relevant to the discussion at hand.
- Take your time self-disclosing; appropriate self-disclosure moves by small increments.
- Consider using get-acquainted exercises or brief statements of introduction during the first group meeting to help manage primary tension.

PRACTICE

Group Roles and Problem-Solving Competencies

In Chapter 1 we discussed seven task-focused and two relationship-focused problem-solving competencies that are essential skills for effective group interaction in certain settings. In this chapter we introduced group roles—patterns of behavior that can move a group toward, and sometimes away from, its goal. Compare the lists on pages 27–28 and pages 73–74. Work with others in your group to reach consensus on which roles from Chapter 4 fit with the competencies from Chapter 1. Do any of the roles not fit into this scheme? If so, how do you explain that? Be prepared to report your results to the class.

Group-Role Inventory

When you see yourself differently from the way others see you, or when your expectations of people cloud your perceptions of them, there is a potential for uncertainty, confusion, frustration, and conflict in the group. The following inventory was designed to help members become more aware of the roles they play and of how others perceive those roles. It is time-consuming (it takes at least 45 minutes) but worth the time and effort,

particularly when a group is having trouble establishing norms. The group-role inventory can also be an effective means of dealing with one or two problem members by bringing everyone's role expectations into the discussion rather than by ganging up on the troublemakers.

Objectives: To become aware of the roles you play in your group and of how others perceive your roles

Materials: Group-role inventory sheet

Time: 45 minutes

Procedure:

1. Fill out group-role inventory sheet.
2. Go over the list and check the role you would like to have performed but did not perform.
3. Go over the list again and star (*) the role you performed but would rather not have performed.
4. Discuss results with your group.

Group-Role Inventory Sheet

Who in your group, including yourself, is most likely to do the following:

1. Take initiative, propose ideas, get things started?
2. Sit back and wait passively for others to lead?
3. Express feelings most freely, frankly, openly?
4. Keep feelings hidden, reserved, unexpressed?
5. Show understanding of other members' feelings?
6. Be wrapped up in personal concerns and not very responsive to others?
7. Interrupt others when they are speaking?
8. Daydream, become lost in private thoughts during group sessions, be "far away"?
9. Give you a feeling of encouragement, warmth, friendly interest, support?
10. Converse privately with someone else while another member is speaking to the group?
11. Talk of trivial things, engage in superficial chitchat?
12. Criticize, put people on their guard?
13. Feel superior to other members?
14. Be listened to by everyone while speaking?
15. Act inferior to other members?
16. Contribute good ideas?
17. Contradict, disagree, argue, raise objections?
18. Sulk or withdraw when displeased with the group?
19. Be the one you would like to have on your side if a conflict arose in the group?
20. Agree or conform with whatever is said?
21. Be missed, if absent, more than any other member?

CHAPTER FIVE

Improving Group Climate

"All for one, and one for all."

—*Alexander Dumas*

OBJECTIVES

After studying this chapter, you will be able to:

■ Observe a group discussion and identify behaviors that contribute to a defensive or supportive group climate.

■ Identify examples of confirming and disconfirming interpersonal responses.

■ Observe, identify, and describe at least four factors in group cohesiveness.

■ Explain communication networks and their effects on group climate and individual satisfaction.

■ Describe the relationships among group size, composition, climate, and productivity.

■ Communicate in ways that are more likely to improve group climate.

WHAT DOES THE WORD climate *call to mind? If you've taken a course in geography or meteorology or have studied weather patterns, you may think of temperature gradients, barometric pressure, and how bodies of water, latitude, ocean currents, and mountains affect the weather of a particular region. Look out your window. What about today's weather? Does it make you want to curl up indoors with a book? Go to the beach? Go skiing? How do you feel about spending a cold, snowy night in front of a roaring fire in a cozy room? Would you say that climate affects your desire to engage in certain activities?*

Group climate is roughly analogous to geographic climate. A variety of factors interact to create a group feeling or atmosphere. How group members communicate, with whom they communicate, and how often they communicate influence their satisfaction as well as their productivity. This chapter examines how people communicate in ways that help a group or team establish a positive climate.

DEFENSIVE AND SUPPORTIVE CLIMATES

Think about two or three groups or teams you've participated in recently. How did you feel during meetings? Energized? Tense? Did you look forward to meetings or did you hope they'd be cancelled? In other words, what was the group's climate?

How team members communicate with one another is a primary determinant of climate. In some groups we feel supported; in others, we may feel defensive. For several years social psychologist Jack Gibb observed the communicative behavior of people in groups and identified the categories of behaviors that contribute to defensive climates and supportive climates. Gibb suggests that a defensive climate is counterproductive in any group.

> The person who behaves defensively, even though he also gives some attention to the common task, devotes an appreciable portion of his energy to defending himself. Besides talking about the topic, he thinks about how he appears to others, how he may be seen more favorably, how he may win, dominate, impress, or escape punishment, and/or how he may avoid or mitigate a perceived or an anticipated attack.[1]

More recent research reinforces the relationship of a supportive climate to productivity.[2] Indeed, supportive communication in the workplace has been found to reduce stress and burnout for many employees. Supportive communication provides links among employees or group members characterized by self-disclosure (see Chapter 4) and a shared definition of the relationship. Often, the key to building a supportive climate lies not only in *what* we communicate but in *how* we communicate it.[3] A message can be delivered in ways that evoke support or defense. Consider some examples based on Gibb's categories.

Evaluation versus Description

Problem solving in small groups involves generating and evaluating ideas. Unfortunately, not all ideas are perfect, and the group needs to discover this if it is to reach the most effective decision. When someone puts forth a less-than-perfect idea, you can respond by saying, "You idiot, that's the most ridiculous idea I've heard in a decade," or you can say, "As I think through that idea and apply it to our problem, I run up against some other problems. Am I missing something?" Imagine yourself on the receiving end of the first comment. How do you feel? You have just been put down and are likely to be defensive. This is an example of evaluation (albeit an extreme one). The second response, an example of description, is much more effective and supportive. Your idea may, in fact, be terrible, but at least the second response allows you to save face. It also keeps the door open for further discussion of your idea. Quite possibly, further investigation into your bad idea may lead to a better idea.

In a nutshell, *evaluation* is "you" language: It directs itself to the worth of the other person or of that person's ideas. As a result, it can provoke defensiveness. *Description*, in contrast, is "I" language: It describes the speaker's thoughts about the person or idea. This type of response leads to more trust and cohesiveness in groups.

Control versus Problem Orientation

Communicative behavior that aims at controlling others can produce defensiveness in group members. This pattern characterizes many aggressive salespeople who, quite intentionally, manipulate others into answering trivial questions that lead up to the final question of whether or not they want to buy a product. Various persuasive tactics aim at controlling behavior (as any student of television commercials can observe). Implicit in attempts to control lies the assumption of the controller—the "I know what's good for you" assumption. When people become aware of this attitude, they frequently get defensive.

In a group, maintaining a *problem orientation* is a more effective approach. If others perceive you as a person who genuinely strives for a solution that will benefit all concerned (rather than just yourself), this perception will contribute to a supportive climate, greater cohesiveness, and increased productivity.

LITZLER

"...AND THEN, APPARENTLY THEY STONED THE COMMITTEE CHAIRMAN."

© Mark Litzler.

Strategy versus Spontaneity

Like controlling behavior, strategy suggests manipulation because it implies preplanned communication. Such strategies range from "pitching a fit" and acting upset to withholding information, acting mysterious, or pouting. This sort of behavior places the self before the group and does not lead to the most effective solutions to group problems.

If others perceive you as a person who acts *spontaneously* (that is, not from hidden motivations or agendas) and as a person who immediately and honestly responds to the present situation, you are likely to create a more supportive climate.

Neutrality versus Empathy

If you behave in a detached, uncaring fashion, as if the people in your group and the outcome of the group's process do not concern you in the least, your behavior will probably arouse defensiveness. Involvement and concern for the group task and for other group members are perceived as supportive.

Superiority versus Equality

If you feel superior, a small group meeting is not the place to show it. You probably know people who approach you in class after tests have been returned and ask, "What'd ya get?" Frequently these students use this question merely as a preface to showing you their superior grade. Most people think such behavior is obnoxious. It makes them feel defensive. In groups, some people preface their remarks with words such as "obviously" or point out their greater knowledge, experience, or some other attribute that makes them superior to other members. Most likely, their behavior will meet with some resistance. People create more supportive climates when they indicate a willingness to enter into participative planning with mutual trust and respect.

Certainty versus Provisionalism

Do you know people who always have all the answers, whose ideas are truths to be defended, who are intolerant of those with the wrong (that is, different) attitudes? These highly dogmatic people are easily recognizable because of the defensiveness they produce in others.

Communication that is spontaneous is perceived as more supportive than communication that appears planned. Why might these office workers appreciate spontaneous communication?

The usual response is to want to prove them wrong. This behavior is counterproductive in groups. Individuals are likely to be more effective if their attitudes appear to be held provisionally; that is, if they appear flexible and genuinely committed to solving problems rather than to simply taking sides on issues. If people keep themselves open to new information and can admit that, from time to time, they may be wrong about something, they will be more effective group members and will help build more supportive group climates.

As a communicator, you control your own actions. Your knowledge of defensive and supportive behaviors will help you make your group work more effectively. Another area of research and application in group climate is interpersonal confirmation and disconfirmation. This research deals not with communicative behaviors that you initiate, but with the ways in which you respond to other group members.

*R*EVIEW

BEHAVIORS THAT FOSTER DEFENSIVE AND SUPPORTIVE CLIMATES

DEFENSIVE CLIMATE

Evaluation: Use of "you" language calls into question the worth of another person.

Control: Efforts to get others to do what you want them to do.

Strategy: Planned communication—for example, saying something nice before criticizing someone.

Neutrality: Emotional indifference—the unspoken attitude that "you'll get over it."

Superiority: Attitude that you're better than the other person.

Certainty: Taking dogmatic, rigid positions; "Don't bother me with facts, my mind is made up." Those who behave this way are usually more interested in winning an argument than in solving a problem.

SUPPORTIVE CLIMATE

Description: "I" language describes your own feelings and ideas.

Problem orientation: Communication aimed at solving problems: "Let's find a solution that works for both of us."

Spontaneity: Here-and-now orientation; being honest rather than planning how to manipulate.

Empathy: Emotional involvement; nonverbal behavior is important.

Equality: Communication based on mutual respect; "I'm okay, you're okay."

Provisionalism: Openness to receiving new information; showing some flexibility in the positions you take.

*I*NTERPERSONAL CONFIRMATION AND DISCONFIRMATION

Group process sometimes seems to go nowhere. Questions are left unanswered and ideas remain ignored. One of the most frequent complaints of group members is that communication in the group seems disconnected and disjointed, fostering vague feelings of uneasiness, as if the members are being disregarded.[4] Unfortunately, this is a common phenomenon that restricts the satisfaction of task, process, or individual needs. For example, while attending a series of committee meetings, one observer noted that hardly anyone directly acknowledged what anyone else said. Rather, the meetings proceeded as a series of soliloquies. Not surprisingly, most group members expressed dissatisfaction with the group's process and frustration with their inability to reach decisions.

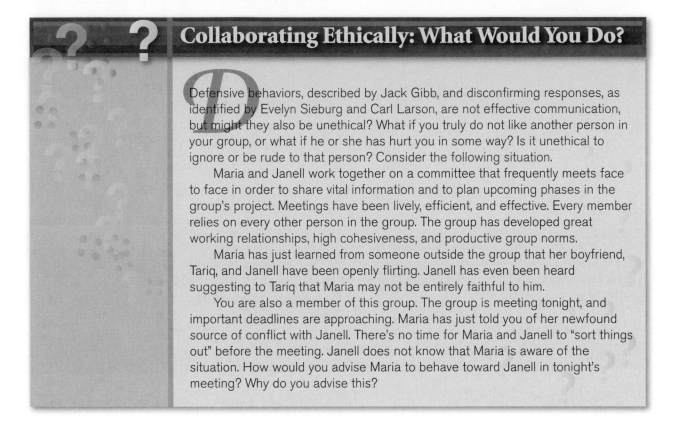

Collaborating Ethically: What Would You Do?

Defensive behaviors, described by Jack Gibb, and disconfirming responses, as identified by Evelyn Sieburg and Carl Larson, are not effective communication, but might they also be unethical? What if you truly do not like another person in your group, or what if he or she has hurt you in some way? Is it unethical to ignore or be rude to that person? Consider the following situation.

Maria and Janell work together on a committee that frequently meets face to face in order to share vital information and to plan upcoming phases in the group's project. Meetings have been lively, efficient, and effective. Every member relies on every other person in the group. The group has developed great working relationships, high cohesiveness, and productive group norms.

Maria has just learned from someone outside the group that her boyfriend, Tariq, and Janell have been openly flirting. Janell has even been heard suggesting to Tariq that Maria may not be entirely faithful to him.

You are also a member of this group. The group is meeting tonight, and important deadlines are approaching. Maria has just told you of her newfound source of conflict with Janell. There's no time for Maria and Janell to "sort things out" before the meeting. Janell does not know that Maria is aware of the situation. How would you advise Maria to behave toward Janell in tonight's meeting? Why do you advise this?

In an investigation of communication in effective and ineffective groups, Evelyn Sieburg examined how group members responded to the communicative acts of others. In this seminal study and in later work with Carl Larson, Sieburg identified several types of responses that she classified as *confirming* or *disconfirming*. Simply stated, **confirming responses** are those that cause people to value themselves more, while **disconfirming responses** are those that cause people to value themselves less.[5] Sieburg's identification of confirming and disconfirming responses has been one of the most important contributions to the understanding of group climate.

Some interpersonal responses are obvious examples of confirmation and disconfirmation—for example, when a person responds to another with overt praise or sharp criticism. However, group members disconfirm and confirm one another in more subtle ways. Alvin Goldberg and Carl Larson identify some of those behaviors, as follows.[6]

Disconfirming Responses

- *Impervious response:* One speaker fails to acknowledge, even minimally, another speaker's communicative attempt.
- *Interrupting response:* One speaker cuts another speaker short or begins while the other is still speaking.
- *Irrelevant response:* A speaker responds in a way that seems unrelated to what the other has been saying, or introduces a new topic without warning or returns to his or her earlier topic, apparently disregarding the intervening conversation.

- *Tangential response:* A speaker acknowledges another person's communication but immediately takes the conversation in another direction. Occasionally individuals exhibit what may appear to be direct responses to the other, such as "Yes, but ..." or "Well, you may be right, but ...," and then continue by discussing something very different from what preceded.
- *Impersonal response:* One speaker conducts a monologue, or exhibits speech behavior that appears intellectualized and impersonal, contains few first-person statements and many generalized "you" or "one" statements, or is heavily loaded with euphemisms or clichés.
- *Incoherent response:* A speaker responds with incomplete sentences; with rambling, difficult-to-follow statements; with sentences containing much retracing or rephrasing; or with interjections such as "you know" or "I mean."
- *Incongruous response:* A speaker engages in nonverbal behavior that seems inconsistent with the vocal content, which results in a response that may be called incongruous. For example, "Who's angry? I'm not angry!" (said in a tone and volume that strongly suggest anger), or "I'm really concerned about you" (said in a tone that suggests lack of interest or disdain).

Confirming Responses

- *Direct acknowledgment:* A speaker acknowledges another person's communication and reacts to it directly and verbally.
- *Agreement about content:* A speaker reinforces information expressed by another.
- *Supportive response:* A speaker expresses understanding of another person or tries to reassure or make the other feel better.
- *Clarifying response:* A speaker tries to clarify another person's message or feelings. A clarifying response may involve requesting more information, encouraging the other person to say more, or repeating what the other said and asking the person to confirm one's understanding.
- *Expression of positive feeling:* One speaker describes his or her own positive feelings related to what another person has said. For example, "Okay, now I understand what you are saying."

When you perceive others' behavior as threatening to your emotional security or position in a group, your uncertainty about your role in the group increases. Individual needs are elevated to a place equal to or even greater than the group's task and process needs. If you respond defensively, you are likely to evoke further defensiveness from the rest of the group. People who find themselves in a defensive, disconfirming climate do not trust one another. The realization that you cannot trust another suggests that that person's behavior is unpredictable—that you do not know for sure how he or she will respond. Such uncertainty is counterproductive in a problem-solving group. In contrast, in a supportive, confirming climate, where mutual respect and trust prevail, you are more certain of your own well-being. This security, in turn, allows you to increase your concentration on the task and the process needs of the group.

The implication of this research is this: By using confirming rather than disconfirming responses when communicating with other group members, people contribute toward a supportive, trustful climate and therefore promote greater group effectiveness and individual satisfaction.

Confirming responses cause us to value ourselves more. What responses from others make you feel good during your group activities?

GROUP COHESIVENESS

Historically, cohesiveness has been considered to be one of the most important small group variables.[7] If this were a textbook in introductory physics, it would define cohesion as the mutual attraction that holds together the elements of a body. Of course, this is a textbook on small group communication, but it offers a very similar definition of **group cohesiveness:** the degree of attraction members feel toward one another and the group. It is a feeling of deep loyalty, of "groupness," of *esprit de corps*, and the degree to which each individual has made the group's goal his or her own. It is a sense of belonging and a feeling of high morale.[8] Cohesiveness results from the interaction of a number of variables, including group composition, individual benefits derived from the group, task effectiveness, and, first and foremost, communication. The productivity of groups and teams is strongly related to their cohesiveness.[9]

Composition and Cohesiveness: Building a Team

As noted in Chapter 3, people often join groups because they feel an attraction toward the people in that group. Factors discussed earlier, such as the similarity of group members or the degree to which group members' needs complement one another, are influential in the development of group cohesiveness.

To borrow a metaphor from the sports world, the best team has the right players at the right positions—and good coaching. Based on their size, speed, aggressiveness, reaction time, and so forth, different players are suited for different positions. So it is with all groups and teams. For maximum effectiveness, they need participants with different talents that complement one another.

Cohesiveness develops around both the task and the relationship dimensions discussed in Chapter 4. Building a group solely on the basis of similarity in interpersonal attraction (Chapter 3) is likely to lead to strong cohesiveness based on relationships but mediocrity as a task group. This is why self-selected groups are often less cohesive—and less productive—than groups in which membership has been assigned carefully, with the group's task in mind. The characteristics we find most attractive in a friend may not be those best suited to help us do a job. Evidence from college classroom groups suggests strongly that self-selection is not the best policy, as we noted in Chapter 3. In one study, by a nearly two-to-one margin, students who formed their own groups reported that group as one of their worst group experiences.[10] However, extreme diversity within a group brings stimulating perspectives to problem solving but may strain the relational aspects of group process. Likewise, negative emotions such as envy can have a detrimental effect on cohesiveness and productivity.[11]

Most work groups today are culturally and racially diverse in addition to reflecting a range of talents and expertise. As we noted in Chapter 4, such diversity can be a source of strength because of the multiple perspectives it brings to problem solving, as long as the group can work together to minimize misunderstandings that can derive from that diversity.[12]

Individual Benefits and Cohesiveness

Cohesiveness is a combination of forces that holds people in groups. Depending on the nature of the group, its members can derive benefits of affiliation, power, affection, and prestige. People like to be with groups in which these needs are satisfied. For example, group members who experience relational satisfaction also tend to perceive their groups as more cohesive and as reaching consensus.[13] An important determinant of group cohesiveness, then, is the degree to which a particular group is capable of meeting members' needs in comparison to the ability of any other group to meet those same needs. If people perceive that they derive benefits from a group that no other group could provide, their attraction toward that group will strengthen considerably. This factor partially accounts for the intense attraction most people feel toward their families or closest friends.

Task Effectiveness and Cohesiveness

The relation of personal and interpersonal variables to group cohesiveness has already been discussed. The performance of the group as a whole has considerable influence as well; success fosters cohesiveness.[14] The mutuality of concern for the group's task, which provides the focal point for working toward that task, becomes socially rewarding when the task is completed successfully. Here is another example of the interrelatedness of the task and social dimensions: Reaching a particular goal provides a common, rewarding experience for all group members. This commonality, or shared experience, further sets a group apart from other groups.

Communication and Cohesiveness

None of the factors described so far is enough, in and of itself, to build a cohesive group. Rather, the interaction of these variables determines the degree of cohesiveness. Communication is the vehicle through which this interaction takes place. Through communication, individual needs are met and tasks are accomplished. In other words, "the communication networks and the messages that flow through them ultimately determine the attractiveness of the group for its members."[15]

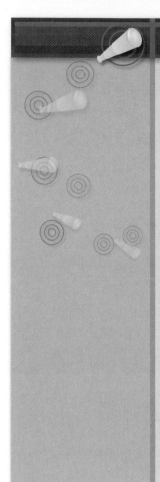

Cutting Edge Theory

COHESIVENESS AND PRODUCTIVITY AT HARLEY-DAVIDSON

Group cohesiveness and productivity are often strongly related. Cohesive groups possess the kind of bonds that foster trust, openness, and the ability to manage conflicting views productively (see Chapter 7 for more on this).

In the 1980s, the Harley-Davidson Motor Company experienced a widely celebrated turnaround that was achieved largely by replacing a "command-and-control" culture with a new culture that involved assembly employees' making important decisions in their work teams. Former Harley-Davidson CEO Rich Teerlink purposely delegated his authority to "lead" the company. The Public Broadcasting Service presented a video (*The Working Group*, 1999) highlighting the new Kansas City Harley-Davidson assembly plant as an "ideal workplace" where employees have "jobs of the future." At the Kansas City plant, there are no team leaders per se; instead, work teams—known at the plant as "natural work groups"—make consensus decisions. Plant workers reported that the absence of "bosses looking over my shoulder" and the trust in employees implied by this freedom from constant supervision were real strengths of the organizational structure.

Harley-Davidson's Kansas City plant provided a natural setting for researchers Phillip Chansler, Paul Swamidass, and Corlandt Cammann to study cohesiveness and productivity. Their studies found that much of the improvement in team cohesion that was evident after the reorganization at Harley-Davidson could be explained by two factors: employees' perception of plant leadership's fairness and employees' influence on team staffing and training decisions. The

Recall our discussion in Chapter 2 of the role of communication in creating symbolic convergence through which a cohesive group identity evolves. According to symbolic convergence theory, the group develops a unique identity through the sharing of fantasies or stories. A feeling of cohesiveness is likely to increase as group members share stories and other group members respond to those stories. A fantasy chain occurs when one story leads to another story, thus creating a bond among group members and the revelation of common fantasies.

The earlier discussion of defensive and supportive communication suggests some ways in which people can adjust their communicative behavior to improve group cohesiveness. Research shows that an "agreeable" style is positively related to team members' willingness to share their knowledge with their groups, which relates to job performance and to satisfaction with the group.[16] In addition to the quality of communication, the amount of communication in the group also affects cohesiveness. George Homans states that if "the frequency of interaction between two or more persons increases, the degree of their liking for one another will increase, and vice versa."[17] Free and open communication characterizes highly cohesive groups. The more people interact, the more they reveal themselves to each other. Through communication, people negotiate group roles, establish goals, reveal similarities and differences, resolve conflict, and express affection. It makes sense, then, that as researchers concluded that to improve cohesiveness within work teams, companies should do two things: (1) increase team members' influence over staffing and training and (2) treat employees with greater fairness and work to enhance perceptions of fairness.[18]

Real-Life Applications

In the groups and teams in which you participate, and especially those in which you serve as a leader, remember the lessons learned at Harley-Davidson:

- Encourage group members to take an active role in deciding who is responsible for performing specific tasks; don't dictate who should do what.
- Ask group members what training, information, and resources they need in order to accomplish their task.
- Be fair. One of the most corrosive behaviors of leaders and other members in groups and teams is treating other members unfairly. (Note, however, that being fair doesn't always mean treating everyone equally. It may be unfair, for example, to treat everyone the same if some group members have worked harder or contributed more to the group than others.)
- Don't let slackers get away with not doing their part; their low level of participation can hurt cohesiveness and productivity. How do you confront a slacker? At the very least, start with gentle questions and efforts to encourage the nonparticipant to do his or her share of the work. If gentle suggestions don't help, and more direct requests yield no results, you may need to seek help in engaging the low-performing group member from someone outside the group with greater authority or power.

the frequency of communication within a group increases, so does the group's cohesiveness. Communication is also the foundation for interpersonal trust within the group.

COMMUNICATION NETWORKS

Another influence on group climate is the **communication network**—the pattern of interaction within a group, or who talks to whom. If you think about the group meetings in which you participate, it may seem that although some people talk more than others, most of their communication is addressed to the group as a whole. Next time you are in a group, note who is talking to whom. You will find that people address relatively few comments to the group as a whole and that they direct most of what they say in groups toward specific persons. In some groups, communication tends to be distributed equally among group members. Figure 5.1 represents such a distribution. In other groups, members address most comments to one central person, perhaps the designated leader or chairperson. Figure 5.2 represents this type of communicative pattern.

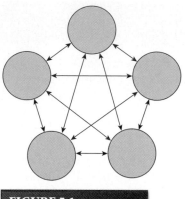

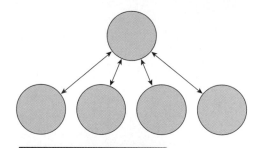

FIGURE 5.1

Equal Distribution of
Communication

FIGURE 5.2

Communication
Addressed to Leader

Other patterns may emerge. These include circular patterns, in which people talk primarily to those sitting next to them, or linear patterns, in which people communicate in a kind of chain reaction. These patterns may be built into the group from the outset, or they may emerge spontaneously. Either way, networks tend to stabilize over time. Once people establish channels of communication, they continue to use these same channels. This network of channels influences group climate, as well as group productivity.

A review of research suggests that, in general, "groups in which free communication is maximized are generally more accurate in their judgments, although they may take longer to reach a decision."[19] People also tend to feel more satisfied in groups in which they participate actively.[20] When interaction is stifled or discouraged, people have less opportunity to satisfy their needs through communication. Groups with centralized communication networks (see Figure 5.2) are certainly more efficient. That efficiency enhances group cohesiveness, but considerable evidence suggests that free and open communication networks that include everyone in the group (see Figure 5.1) are more likely to lead to more accurate group judgments, as well as to better goal attainment and task performance.[21]

GROUP SIZE

In a group, there is a positive relationship between the level of people's participation and the degree of their individual satisfaction. Obviously, as the size of a group increases, the opportunity to interact with other members decreases. What size should a group be in order to achieve maximum cohesiveness and productivity? Three heads are better than one, but are twenty heads better than three?

No one knows the precise number of people that will maximize the effectiveness of your group, but some observations may provide guidance. As a group's size increases, the principle of diminishing returns sets in. Imagine a long rope attached to a heavy weight. By yourself, using all your strength, you may not be able to move that weight. As more people join you in your effort, the weight begins to move and the task becomes easier. But as the

Virtual Communication

Trust among group members is important to a healthy group climate, open exchange of information, and effective decision making. But can trust exist in global virtual teams, given the lack of shared social context in such teams?

We discuss in Chapter 4 some of the factors that build trust in face-to-face groups. But when team members are in different locations, even scattered around the globe, they can't rely on the usual face-to-face nonverbal cues to gauge sincerity or effort. This "behavioral invisibility" adds risk to virtual groups and teams. Because of this, virtual teams experience considerably more conflict than do face-to-face teams. Occupational psychologists at the consulting firm Pearn Kandola studied effective business communication in virtual teams and have these suggestions for minimizing such conflict:

- Plan extra time for relationship and trust building in virtual teams.
- Facilitate cognitive trust building (acceptance of others' opinions and ideas) at the outset by sharing information about each team member's accomplishments, experience, competence, and integrity.
- Facilitate affective trust building (acceptance of others' feelings) using socialization strategies such as virtual coffee breaks via online chat rooms or social conferencing via video or telephone.
- Be aware of the negative effects of "silence"—explain unexpected delays in response; communicate your availability or unavailability to team members.
- Encourage team members to be explicit in communicating what they are thinking and doing.

Source: Pearn Kandola, "The Psychology of Effective Business Communications in Geographically Dispersed Teams," An Executive Summary of the Research Report, Cisco Systems Report, September 2006. A summary of the report can be found at http://newsroom.cisco.com/dlls/2006/prod_091906.html

group size increases, after a certain point each extra person makes little or no difference in moving the weight, and individuals use smaller and smaller percentages of their total strength. As group size increases, individual group members' efforts tend to decrease.[22] One study found that cohesiveness is positively related to the opportunity for interaction afforded by group size: As group size increases, the opportunity for interaction decreases.[23] What, then, is the optimum size?

Herbert Thelen has suggested the principle of "least group size." Clearly, people want groups small enough to encourage maximum participation yet large enough to generate the maximum number of ideas. Thelen says that "the group should be just large enough to include individuals with all the relevant skills for problem solutions."[24] Although this principle provides no firm rule about group size, it does at least provide a guideline. In small group communication, bigger is not necessarily better. Groups of five to seven members are just about the right size.

Case Study

Not long ago I received a mysterious telephone call from a good friend. He said that he and his wife had a business proposition for me and my wife, which they would like to discuss as soon as they could. No, he really didn't want to discuss any details over the phone. When could we meet? Tuesday evening? At our place? They'd see us then.

Our curiosity piqued, we eagerly awaited the Tuesday evening rendezvous. What could our friends possibly have up their sleeves? The appointed hour arrived. Right on time, the doorbell rang. ("Unusual," we thought, "they're usually a half-hour late.") Our next surprise was that our friend George was dressed in a three-piece suit, his wife Margaret in a tailored dress. My wife and I looked at each other in our jeans, bare feet, and T-shirts, then returned our gaze to George and Margaret and asked whether they had just returned from a funeral. They laughed nervously, marched past us, and began to set up a small demonstration board on our dining room table. Turning down our offer of wine, they asked if we could begin the meeting. This was becoming stranger by the moment. My wife, Nancy, and I began to feel as if we had invited insurance agents into our home—even though we had gone camping, hiking, canoeing, and spent many an evening with George and Margaret.

Something didn't fit, but our curiosity was aroused, so we decided to play along.

It wasn't long before the experience began to get frustrating. George and Margaret asked us what we wanted out of life. We suggested that they probably ought to have some idea of that by now—that most of our goals were inward, state-of-being kinds of goals, like having a greater awareness of ourselves and others, peace of mind, and so forth. This answer agitated our guests, who responded by suggesting that it might be nice if we never again had to worry about money. We agreed that it would, indeed, be pleasant. At this, they seemed to breathe a little more easily and proceeded to haul out charts, graphs, and illustrations which, they claimed, proved that we could double our present income in a little over a year—in our spare time, of course.

After an hour, George and Margaret still refused to tell us what it was we would have to sell (we'd figured out *that* much) or to whom we'd have to sell it. ("Please bear with us until the end," they said.) Something was definitely wrong. Here I was sitting in my own dining room with my wife, my friends, and a glass of wine, yet I felt as if I were back in middle school being asked to please hold all my questions until the end. I've had the same

GROUP CLIMATE AND PRODUCTIVITY

Thus far this chapter has discussed many variables that affect group climate—defensive behavior, confirming and disconfirming responses, group cohesiveness, group size—and has made some suggestions about how to improve the climate of groups. When communication is free and open and when everyone participates, people tend to feel more attraction toward the group and consequently receive more personal satisfaction. Another reason for developing and maintaining a positive group climate is that climate affects productivity. There is substantial evidence that factors such as strong work norms and cohesiveness interact in groups and teams to increase productivity.[25]

In computer-mediated groups, group members' familiarity with one another has a positive effect on the group's efficiency. As familiarity in these groups increases, the time it experience with life insurance agents and encyclopedia salespeople. George and Margaret were treating us not as people, but as faceless members of the great mass of consumers.

Finally they revealed the name of the company and its line of products and set about the task of showing how rapidly the company had grown as a result of its unique marketing concepts, fine products that sell themselves (of course), and so forth. It didn't matter, I had already decided not to do it. I felt dehumanized and abused by my friends. Why hadn't they simply told us that they were involved with the company (which we had heard of long before) and that they'd like to explore the possibilities of our becoming involved as well? With friends, it would be a much more effective approach—certainly a more honest one.

The formal part of the presentation ended. They asked for our comments and questions. I was ready. As a communication professor, I am well versed in the art of critiquing oral presentations and visual aids. I proceeded to evaluate their entire presentation, emphasizing their failure to adequately analyze their audience and to adapt their communication style accordingly. George and Margaret were shocked and hurt. They had not, they said, come into our home to be criticized. They

had come in good faith with an honest proposal from which we all stood to benefit. If they had offended us, they were sorry. No, they still did not care for a glass of wine. We'd get together again sometime soon.

Practice in Applying Principles

1. What previously existing group norms can you infer from this story? How were the norms violated? What were the consequences?
2. Which of Gibb's "defensive communication" behaviors can you identify? Do you see any evidence that anyone tried to use supportive communication?
3. What evidence of group cohesiveness can you identify?
4. What kinds of confirming and disconfirming responses can you identify?
5. This case study came from the actual experience of one of your authors. His relationship with "George" and "Margaret" suffered following this episode. What recommendations would you give George and Margaret for avoiding such trouble in the future? What advice do you have for your author and his wife?

takes to reach a decision decreases. However, group members report lower satisfaction with computer-mediated groups than with face-to-face groups. Furthermore, there is evidence that decision accuracy for computer-mediated groups is lower than for face-to-face groups.[26]

As we note in Chapter 4, trusting relationships are those in which we feel we can count on others to behave in certain ways and in which there is mutual respect. Communication scholars Judy Pearson and Paul Nelson note two kinds of trust that are relevant to small group communication:

Having trust regarding the task means members can count on each other to get things done. A common source of conflict for many groups is having a member who doesn't contribute a fair share of the work, so others have to pick up the slack. That makes members angry and the climate tense. Having interpersonal trust means that members believe the others are operating with the best interests of the group in mind and not from hidden agendas.[27]

When a group has a trusting, open atmosphere and a high level of cohesiveness, members "do not fear the effects that disagreement and conflict in the task dimension can have on their social fabric. *Cohesive groups have strong enough social bonds to tolerate conflict.*"[28] Chapters 7 and 9 explore the function of conflict in groups. Here it is enough to say that through constructive conflict, groups deal with the difficult issues confronting them. When there is no conflict, it is usually because people do not trust one another enough to assert their individuality. However, avoiding the issues does not lead to clarity about those issues. And an absence of clarity prevents the group from reaching the most effective solutions.

It is a mistake to think that positive group climate and group cohesiveness mean everyone is nice all the time. Quite the contrary. In a highly cohesive group, members know that they will not be rejected for their views and are therefore more willing to express them—even though expressing them may provoke disagreement. Ernest Bormann notes,

> At a point where someone in a cohesive group would say, "You're wrong!" or "I disagree!" an individual in a less cohesive group will say, "I don't understand," or "I'm confused." Members of groups with little cohesion have yet to create much of a common social reality.[29]

This "common social reality," which includes group roles and group norms, gives people the freedom to assert their individuality within a predictable context.

Another aspect of a common social reality is the degree to which group members make the group's goal their own. Members of a highly cohesive group personally commit themselves to the group's well-being and to accomplishing the group's task. In part, this personal commitment can be attributed to the feeling that this particular group meets people's needs better than any other group. When this is the case, as it often is in a cohesive group, people have a degree of *dependence* on the group. This dependence increases the *power* the group has over individuals. To put this in a less intimidating way: "There can be little doubt that members of a more cohesive group more readily exert influence on one another and are more readily influenced by one another."[30] These factors—personal commitment to the group, personal dependence on the group, group power over individuals within the group—come together in a positive group climate. The result is that cohesive groups work harder than groups with little cohesiveness, regardless of outside supervision.[31]

With few exceptions, building a group climate in which cohesiveness can grow leads to not only greater individual satisfaction but greater group productivity, as well.[32]

 Putting Principles into Practice

Chapters 4 and 5 focus on knowledge and skills associated with communication competence—communicative behavior that is both effective and appropriate in a given context. *Effectiveness,* says communication scholar Brian Spitzberg, is "the successful accomplishment of valued goals, objectives, or rewards relative to costs. *Appropriateness* means that the valued rules, norms, and expectancies of the relationship are not violated significantly."[33]

Successful group communication requires communication competence: "The competent communicator knows how and when to communicate (cognitive ability) and is able to do so (behavioral ability)."[34] This chapter provides principles that, when put into practice, can help you become a more competent communicator in groups.

■ To the extent that you engage in supportive—rather than defensive—communication, you will foster a positive group climate in which people are free to focus their attention on the group and its task.

■ If you can develop a sensitivity to your own confirming and disconfirming behaviors, you can become more confirming in your group behavior, thus contributing to a more positive group climate.

■ Cohesiveness is the result of the interaction of a number of variables, including the group's composition, individual benefits derived from the group, and task effectiveness and communication.

Be aware of these factors to help foster group cohesiveness.

■ If you are forming a group, include just enough people to ensure the presence of all the relevant skills for problem solving—and no more.

■ A positive group climate is essential if you are to reach your maximum potential as a working group. A trusting and open climate allows all members the freedom to be themselves: to agree or disagree, or to engage in conflict without fear of rejection. The ability of a group not only to withstand but to benefit from constructive conflict is crucial to a group's productivity. To build such a climate, learn to communicate more supportively and confirmingly: Avoid defensive, disconfirming behavior.

$\mathcal{P}$RACTICE

Confirmation/Disconfirmation

In your discussion group, stage a discussion in which group members attempt to use all of the disconfirming responses listed in this chapter. Choose a familiar topic about which everyone has something to say. Have observers keep a record of the number and type of disconfirming responses and the reactions (especially nonverbal reactions) to them. Now repeat the discussion, covering as many of the same topics as possible, but this time concentrate on using only confirming responses. Again, have observers keep records. When you have completed both rounds of discussion, have group members discuss their reactions and have observers report their findings.

Observing Communication Networks: Interaction Diagrams

Communication networks—who talks to whom—have an effect on group cohesiveness, leadership patterns, and group productivity. A few minutes spent observing small group interaction will show you clearly that members do not very often address the group as a whole; instead, they tend to address specific group members. An **interaction**

diagram can reveal a lot about the interaction patterns in your group. It tells you who is talking to whom and how often. You can identify the most active and the most reticent members. You can discover patterns in the relationships that form among group members. By combining an interaction diagram with a category system, such as the confirming and disconfirming responses described in this chapter, you can recognize the contributions each member makes to the group. Interaction diagrams are extremely useful tools. This is how to make one:

1. Draw a circle for each member of the group, arranging your circles in the same relative positions as those in which group members are seated (see the interaction diagram on the following page).
2. Refer to the interaction diagram. If Nancy were to open the meeting by asking Phil for the minutes from the last meeting, you would draw an arrow from Nancy's circle to Phil's, indicating the direction and destination of Nancy's communication. Each subsequent remark Nancy makes to Phil would then be indicated by a short crossmark at the base of the arrow.

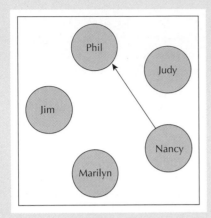

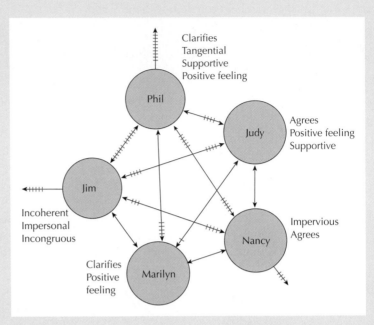

3. Repeat this process each time someone in the group addresses someone else. If Phil were to direct his reading of the minutes to Nancy, you would put an arrowhead at the other end of the line that connects the two.

4. Indicate communication addressed to the group as a whole with a line pointing away from the center of the group. Again, note subsequent remarks with crossmarks.

Above on the right is an example of how a completed interaction diagram might look. If you take a few moments to examine the diagram, which incorporates a category system, you will see some patterns. For example, Phil seems to be the most vocal member of the group. Furthermore, most members address their remarks to Phil, which suggests that they perceive Phil to be the group's leader. The frequency with which Phil addresses the group as a whole supports this observation. The amount of communication between Phil and Jim indicates a strong relationship there, perhaps that of a leader and his "lieutenant."

The interaction diagram is an easy way to describe graphically the interaction patterns in a

group. Also, this method of observation can be used without seriously disrupting the regular workings of the group. By updating the interaction diagram during several meetings, you can observe changes in group interaction. The addition of a category system to the interaction diagram renders this a most powerful descriptive tool.

Assessing Your Group's Cohesiveness

Invite each member of a group you participate in to use the classic Seashore Index of Group Cohesiveness to measure group cohesiveness. After each person has completed the scale, summarize the results and compare impressions about the degree of cohesiveness present in your group.

Seashore Index of Group Cohesiveness

Check one response for each question.

1. Do you feel that you are really a part of your work group?
   _____ Really a part of my work group
   _____ Included in most ways

_____ Included in some ways, but not in others
_____ Don't feel I really belong
_____ Don't work with any one group of people
_____ Not ascertained

2. If you had a chance to do the same kind of work for the same pay in another work group, how would you feel about moving?
   _____ Would want very much to move
   _____ Would rather move than stay where I am
   _____ Would make no difference to me
   _____ Would want very much to stay where I am
   _____ Not ascertained

3. How does your work group compare with other similar groups on each of the following points?

	Better than most	About the same as most	Not as good as most	Not ascertained
a. The way the members get along together	_____	_____	_____	_____
b. The way the members stick together	_____	_____	_____	_____
c. The way the members help each other on the job	_____	_____	_____	_____

Source: S. Seashore, _Group Cohesiveness in the Industrial Work Group_ (Ann Arbor: University of Michigan Institute for Social Research, 1954).

CHAPTER SIX

Enhancing Group and Team Communication Skills

"As I grow older, I pay less attention to what people say; I just watch what they do."

—*Andrew Carnegie*

CHAPTER OUTLINE

Verbal Dynamics in the Small Group

Listening

The Importance of Nonverbal Communication in Groups

Applications of Nonverbal Communication Research to Groups and Teams

Functions of Nonverbal Cues in Groups and Teams

Interpreting Nonverbal Communication

Case Study

Putting Principles into Practice

Practice

OBJECTIVES

After studying this chapter, you will be able to:

■ Describe three "word barriers" and how to avoid them.
■ Identify four listening styles.
■ Describe two major barriers to effective listening.
■ Listen more effectively.
■ Explain why nonverbal communication is important to the study of groups.
■ Apply research findings about nonverbal communication to groups and teams.
■ Describe how nonverbal cues should be interpreted in light of gender and cultural differences.
■ Identify guidelines for interpreting nonverbal communication in small groups.

ANDREW CARNEGIE'S WORDS *remind us that communication in small groups is not an abstraction; it is something that people actually do, something that can be observed. Chapter 2 asserts that good theory is the foundation for good practice; what we know should guide what we do. Communication effectiveness can be improved by good theory, but only if that theory manifests itself in good practice. Good communication takes skill.*

This chapter will help you understand and sharpen your communication skills by focusing on three essential abilities: using words accurately, listening, and communicating nonverbally.

VERBAL DYNAMICS IN THE SMALL GROUP

The most obvious yet elusive component of small group communication is the spoken word. Words lie at the very heart of who and what people are. Their ability to represent the world symbolically gives humans the capacity to foresee events, to reflect on past experiences, to plan, to make decisions, and to consciously control their own behavior.

Words as Barriers to Communication

Words are the tools with which people make sense of the world and share that sense with others. Although words can empower people and can influence attitudes and behaviors, they can also impede a process. Speech communication gives individuals access to the ideas and inner worlds of other group members, but it can also—intentionally or unintentionally—set up barriers to effective communication.

If you grew up in the United States, you can probably remember chanting defensively, "Sticks and stones can break my bones but names can never hurt me." Even as you uttered these lines you knew you were using a lie to protect yourself. People often unwittingly communicate in ways that threaten others and make them feel defensive. As noted in Chapter 5, when group members feel a need to protect themselves, they shift their attention from the group's goal to their own personal goal of self-protection, thus creating a barrier to effective group process. Some subtle but pervasive word barriers are (1) bypassing, (2) allness, and (3) fact-inference confusion.

Bypassing   The meanings of the words you use seem so obvious to you that you assume those words suggest the same meanings to others. Nothing could be further from the truth. **Bypassing** takes place when two people assign different meanings to the same word. Many words are open to an almost limitless number of interpretations—consider, for example, the words *love, respect,* and *communication.* Similarly, you may know precisely what you mean when you say that the department's account is "seriously overdrawn," but how are others to interpret that? How serious is "seriously"?

According to some estimates, the 500 most frequently used words in the English language have over 14,000 dictionary definitions. Considering that a dictionary definition reflects only a tiny percentage of all possible meanings for a word and that people from different cultures and with different experiences interpret words differently, it is amazing that people can understand one another at all.

In groups, the number of people involved compounds the problem; the possibility for multiple misunderstandings always exists. This possibility points to the importance of good feedback among group members. Feedback is any response by listeners that lets speakers know whether they have been understood accurately. To overcome word barriers, people must understand that words are subjective. They need to check that what they understand from others is really what those others intend.

Throughout our discussion of the power of verbal messages, we invite you to keep one important idea in mind: *You are not in charge of the meaning others derive from your messages.* Meaning is created in others.[1] You do not determine what other people think, and words do not have meaning in and of themselves.

Allness   **Allness statements** are simple but untrue generalizations. You have probably heard such allness statements as "Women are smarter than men," "Men can run faster than women," and "Football players are stupid." These statements are convenient, but they simply are not accurate. The danger of allness statements is that you may begin to believe them and to prejudge other people unfairly based on them. Therefore, be careful not to overgeneralize; remember that each individual is unique.

Fact-Inference Confusion   Statements of fact can be made only after direct observation. Inferences can be made at any time; no observation is necessary. **Fact-inference confusion** occurs when people respond to something as if they have actually observed it, when in reality, they have merely drawn a conclusion. The key distinction between a fact and an inference is that in statements of inference people can speculate about and interpret what they *think* occurred. Suppose, for example, that you hear someone comment, "Men are better than women at math." If this statement were true, it would mean that *all* men and women were tested and that the results indicated that men are better in math than women. The statement is, in reality, an inference. If the speaker is summarizing research that has investigated the issue, he or she should say, "Some studies have found that . . ." rather than "It's a fact that . . . ." The first statement more accurately describes reality than does the second. Like bypassing and allness statements, fact-inference confusion can lead to inaccuracy and misunderstanding.

*R*EVIEW

WORD BARRIERS AND HOW TO AVOID THEM

BARRIER	DESCRIPTION	APPROACH
Bypassing	Occurs when the same word is used to mean different things	Use specific language; be aware of multiple interpretations of what you say; clarify.
Allness statements	Simple but untrue generalizations	Don't overgeneralize; remember that all individuals are unique.
Fact-inference confusion	Mistaking a conclusion you have drawn for an observation	Clarify and analyze; learn to recognize the difference between fact and inference, and communicate the difference clearly.

Conversational Style

Another factor that can contribute to misunderstandings in groups and teams is differences in conversational styles. Sometimes barriers are not in words but in how they are delivered. If you watch two groups discussing a problem, you are likely to see different conversational styles in action. In one group, things may seem orderly. Participants politely await their turn, listening attentively. In another group, the process appears more chaotic; everyone seems to be talking at once. In Chapter 4 we observed that different cultures often exhibit different conversational styles. But even within the dominant cultures of North America, individuals may vary significantly in their conversational styles. Understanding these different styles can help you avoid needless conflict.

Each of us has assumptions about how and why conversations should take place. Some of these assumptions are associated with gender. Linguist Deborah Tannen observes that women and men use conversation differently. Women, says Tannen, are socialized to believe that "talk is the glue that holds relationships together"[2] and conversation is for the purpose of building a sense of community. For men, however, conversations are more likely to be competitive and to be undertaken as a way of gaining or conveying information. Tannen refers to these types of talk as "rapport talk" and "report talk."

The different assumptions we bring to conversations are not necessarily defined by our gender, but they do influence conversational styles. Tannen's rapport talk leads to an *overlapping style*. Her report talk leads to a *turn-taking style*. Neither of these styles is good or bad, and each can be productive, but each can lead to misunderstanding and conflict if those involved do not share assumptions. Consider how each style can appear to those who hold the opposite view about conversation, as shown in Table 6.1.

TABLE 6.1 **Disadvantages of Conversational Styles[3]**

Overlapping	Turn-Taking
Selfish, distracting interruptions	Selfish, serial monologues
Individual ideas lost or undervalued	Individual ideas not connected together
Incomplete thoughts	Repetition
Outcomes: frustration and domination	Outcomes: withdrawal and domination

To repeat, neither style is right or wrong. An overlapping style is associated with more intimate and trusting relationships. A turn-taking style is typically found with more formal group relationships, such as those found in a classroom or a courtroom. Awareness of the differences can lead to greater understanding and more productive group meetings.[4]

LISTENING

Good listening skills are an important component of being an effective group member or leader.[5] However, poor listening habits are one of the most common sources of defensiveness and discord. It is easier to be a poor listener in groups than it is in interpersonal situations, because often in a group you do not have to respond to the speaker. After all, the other group members can always pick up the conversation. However, groups cannot reach their maximum effectiveness unless all members listen actively to one another.

Listening is a skill that can be improved with practice. It is an active process through which people select, attend, understand, and remember. To listen effectively, people must actively select and attend to the messages they receive. This involves filtering out the other stimuli that compete for their attention: the hunger pangs they're starting to feel, mental lists of the groceries they need to pick up on the way home, curiosity about the attractive person nearby. Improving any skill takes knowledge and practice. This section will provide some knowledge. The practice is up to you. Are you listening?

Listening Styles

Do your ears perk up when you hear someone telling an interesting story, or would you be more interested in listening to data, facts, and details? There is evidence that different people have different listening styles.[6] Your **listening style** is your preferred way of making sense out of the spoken messages you hear.[7] Listening researchers have identified four overarching listening styles: people-oriented, action-oriented, content-oriented, and time-oriented.

What difference does it make to know your preferred listening style? In a small group, with multiple verbal messages coming at you from several people, you may find yourself focused more on one person's message than another's. We'll discuss each of the four listening styles so that you can identify your preferred style and develop strategies for listening that may not come naturally to you.

People-Oriented Listeners   People-oriented listeners are most comfortable listening to other people's feelings and emotions. They empathize with others and search for common areas of interest; they are other-oriented. When in a small group, people-oriented listeners will focus on the stories others tell and be good at developing relationships and fulfilling group maintenance roles.

Action-Oriented Listeners   Action-oriented listeners prefer information that is well organized, brief, and error free. While a people-oriented listener likes to hear longer stories about others, action-oriented listeners want others to get to the point so that they can figure out what to do with the information. Action-oriented listeners tend to be a bit more skeptical of what they hear; they are likely to focus on the underlying reasoning and evidence that supports the conclusions presented. Action-oriented listeners help a group stay focused on the task and assess the quality of information presented. They are more likely to assume task-oriented roles to achieve the group's goal.

Content-Oriented Listeners   Content-oriented listeners like information-rich content; they are more comfortable listening to complex, detailed information than are people with other listening styles. A content-oriented listener is likely to perk up when someone says, "Here are five things we should consider." If a message does not include enough supporting evidence and specific details, the content-oriented listener will be more likely to reject the message. A content-oriented listener would be a good person to take notes at group meetings and to help the group analyze the issues.

Time-Oriented Listeners   Time-oriented listeners prefer brief messages. They are busy and do not have time to listen to long, rambling talks. Time-oriented listeners remain constantly aware of the amount of time they have to listen. That is why it's good to have time-oriented listeners in a group—they will help the group keep on schedule and stay focused on the agenda.

There is no single best listening style for communicating in groups and teams. Each style has its advantages and disadvantages. If you were focused only on distilling from the speaker's words a brief and concise message (that is, if you were a time-oriented listener), you would not be as attuned to the relationships and feelings of others (people-oriented listeners). And although it's good to focus on details (as would a content-oriented listener) or on what the action steps are (as would an action-oriented listener), spending too much time on the task without being aware of relationships can also be detrimental to a group. Just as it's a good thing for groups to have people play a variety of roles, it's also useful for groups to have people with differing listening styles. If, for example, most of your group members are people-oriented listeners, then the group will have to be more mindful of focusing on facts, data, and evidence. On the other hand, a team composed entirely of content- or action-oriented listeners may need to ensure that they are managing the relational aspects of the group. Once you know your own preferred listening style, you can work to develop other styles, so you will be able to adapt your style to different situations.

Barriers to Effective Listening

Regardless of your listening style, you need to overcome the common obstacles to effective listening. There are many such barriers—outside distractions, an uncomfortable chair, a headache—but the focus here will be on two prevalent and serious barriers: prejudging and rehearsing.

Prejudging the Communicator or the Communication   Sometimes you simply dislike some people or always disagree with them. You anticipate that what these people will say will be offensive, and you begin to tune them out. An example of this is many people's tendency not to listen carefully to the speeches of politicians who hold political beliefs different from their own. In a group, you must overcome the temptation to ignore those you think are boring, pedantic, or offensive. Good ideas can come from anyone, even from people you do not like. Likewise, you should not prejudge certain topics as being too complex, boring, or controversial. This can be difficult, especially when a cherished belief is criticized or when others say things about you that you might not want to hear. These are precisely the times when communication needs to be clear, open, honest, and confirming. To communicate in that way, you need to listen.

Good listening skills are an important characteristic of a good group member.

It is especially important not to prejudge others on the basis of culture, ethnicity, or race. Despite continuing social progress, such prejudices linger.[8] In one study, college students indicated that racial stereotypes are alive and well. African Americans said that Whites were "demanding" and "manipulative," Whites reported that Blacks are "loud" and "ostentatious."[9] Such prejudices inhibit our ability to listen effectively and also foster defensiveness in groups.

Rehearsing a Response   Rehearsing is perhaps the more difficult barrier to overcome. It is the tendency people have to rehearse in their minds what they will say when the other person stops speaking. One of the reasons for this barrier is the difference between speech rate and thought rate. Most people speak at a rate of about 100 to 125 words per minute, but they have the capacity to think or listen at a rate of 400 or more words per minute! This gives them the time to wander off mentally while keeping one ear on the speaker. The thought-speech differential is better used, though, to attend fully to what the speaker is saying—and

DILBERT: © Scott Adams/Distributed by United Features Syndicate, Inc.

not saying. When people learn to do this, their responses can be more spontaneous, accurate, appropriate, confirming, and supportive.

A Guide to Active Listening

Supportive, confirming communication focuses not only on verbal messages but on the emotional content of the messages and on nonverbal behaviors as well. Learning to quiet one's own thoughts and to avoid prejudging others is a first step. Fully understanding others, though, involves considerable effort. Active listening is an attempt to clarify and understand another's thoughts and feelings. To listen actively involves several steps. These steps may seem like common sense, but they are far from common practice.

1. *Stop:* Before you can effectively tune in to what someone else may be feeling, you need to stop what you are doing, eliminate as many distractions as possible, and focus fully on the other person.[10] Two listening researchers conducted a study to identify the specific behaviors of good listeners.[11] What they discovered supports our admonition that the first thing you have to do to be a better listener is to stop focusing on your own mental messages and instead be other-oriented. Specifically, here are five actions you should take during what the researchers called the "pre-interaction phase" of listening:

   - Put your own thoughts aside.
   - Be there mentally, not only physically.
   - Make a conscious, mindful effort to listen.
   - Take adequate time to listen—don't rush the speaker; be patient.
   - Be open-minded.

2. *Look:* Now look for nonverbal clues that will help you identify how the other person is feeling. Most communication of emotion comes through nonverbal cues. The face provides important information about how a person is feeling, as do voice quality, pitch, rate, volume, and use of silence. Body movement and posture clearly indicate the intensity of a person's feelings. We will discuss the role of nonverbal messages in more detail later in the chapter.

3. *Listen:* Listen for what another person is telling you. Even though that person may not say exactly how he or she feels, look for cues. Match verbal with nonverbal cues to decipher both the content and the emotion of the person's message. In addition, ask yourself, "How would I feel if I were in that person's position?" Try to interpret the message according to the sender's code system rather than your own.

4. *Ask appropriate questions:* As you try to understand another person, you may need to ask some questions. Most of these will serve one of four purposes: (1) to obtain additional information ("How soon will you be ready to give your part of our presentation?"); (2) to find out how someone feels ("Are you feeling overwhelmed by this assignment?"); (3) to ask for clarification of a word or phrase ("What do you mean when you say you didn't realize what you were getting into?"); and (4) to verify your conclusion about your partner's meaning or feeling ("Are you saying that you can't complete the project without some additional staff assistance?").

5. *Paraphrase content:* Restate in your own words what you think another person is saying. Paraphrasing is different from parroting back everything that person has said. After all, you can repeat something perfectly without understanding what it means. Rather, from time to time, summarize the message another person has given you so far.

> *Emily:* I think this job is too much for me; I'm not qualified to do it.
>
> *Howard:* You think you lack the necessary skills.

Note that at this point Howard is dealing only with the content of Emily's message. The goal of active listening, though, is to understand both the feelings and the content of another person's message.

6. *Paraphrase feelings:* In the example just given, Howard could follow his paraphrase of the content of the message with a question such as "You're probably feeling pretty frustrated right now, aren't you?" Such a paraphrase would allow Emily either to agree with Howard's assessment or to clarify how she's feeling. For instance, she might respond, "No, I'm not frustrated. I'm just disappointed that the job's not working out."

Effective listening skills can contribute a great deal to building a supportive, cohesive group. Effective listening is also the cornerstone of critical thinking—the skill required to make decisions and solve problems effectively, as you'll learn in later chapters. For now, we turn our attention to the second step of active listening: looking for nonverbal communication.

THE IMPORTANCE OF NONVERBAL COMMUNICATION IN GROUPS

Nonverbal communication is communication behavior that does not rely on written or spoken words. This definition includes body posture and movement, eye contact, facial expression, seating arrangement, spatial relationships, personal appearance, use of time, and even tone of voice. Although the words someone utters are not classified as nonverbal communication, the pitch, quality, and intonation of the voice, the rate of speaking, and the use of silence can speak volumes; thus, vocal tone is considered part of nonverbal communication.

Every message contains both content and information about relationships. Nonverbal messages, particularly facial expression and vocal cues, are often the prime source of information about interpersonal relationships. Thus, they play important functions in meta-communication—which literally means communication about communication. The nonverbal aspects of a message communicate information about its verbal aspects.

You have undoubtedly participated in group and team meetings that were dull and boring. Although not all unexciting group discussion results from poor or inappropriate nonverbal communication, group members' posture, facial expression, tone of voice, and unspoken enthusiasm (or lack of enthusiasm) dramatically affect a group's climate and members' attitudes toward the group. We'll examine three reasons why nonverbal communication variables are important to group discussion.

More Time Is Spent Communicating Nonverbally Than Verbally

In a group or team discussion, usually only one person speaks at a time. The rest of the members can, however, emit a host of nonverbal cues that influence the deliberations. (Some cues are controlled consciously, others are emitted less intentionally.) Eye contact, facial expression, body posture, and movement occur even when only one person is speaking. Because group members are usually within just a few feet of one another, they can easily observe most nonverbal cues. In other words, it is safe to say that "you cannot not communicate."

Emotions and Feelings Are Typically Expressed Nonverbally Rather Than Verbally

In the past several chapters we identified factors that influence the climate of a group, what it feels like to be a group member. If a group member is frustrated with the group or disenchanted with the discussion, more than likely you will detect those feelings by observing that person's nonverbal behavior—even before he or she verbalizes any frustration. If a member seems genuinely interested in the discussion and pleased with the group's progress, this, too, can be observed through nonverbal behavior. Albert Mehrabian and some of his colleagues devised a formula that suggests how much of the total emotional meaning of a message is based on verbal components and how much on nonverbal components.[12] According to this research, only 7 percent of the emotional meaning of a message is communicated through its verbal content. About 38 percent of the emotional content is derived from the voice (its pitch, quality, and volume and the rate of speech). The largest source of emotional meaning, 55 percent, is a speaker's facial expression. Thus, approximately 93 percent of the emotional portion of a message is communicated nonverbally. Although these percentages cannot be applied to all situations, Mehrabian's research suggests that when inconsistencies exist between people's verbalized emotional states and their true emotions, expressed nonverbally, nonverbal cues carry more clout in determining how receivers interpret speakers' emotions.

Vincent Brown and his colleagues suggest that the expression of feelings and emotions during group discussion can have a negative effect on group members' brainstorming ideas.[13] During a freewheeling brainstorming session, group members are not supposed to evaluate others' ideas; yet because of nonverbal expression of feelings, it's almost impossible not to let true positive or negative feelings leak out.

Nonverbal Messages Are Usually More Believable Than Verbal Messages

Nonverbal communication affects how others interpret our messages. Nonverbal cues are so important to communication that when a verbal message (either spoken or written) contradicts a nonverbal message, people are more inclined to believe the nonverbal message. The group member who sighs and, with a sarcastic edge, says, "Oh, what a great group this is going to be," communicates just the opposite meaning of that verbal message. One researcher suggests that as much as 65 percent of the way we convey meaning in our messages is through nonverbal channels.[14]

An understanding of nonverbal communication, then, is vital to even a superficial understanding of communication in general and of group communication in particular. As you become a more skillful observer of nonverbal behavior, you will understand more thoroughly the way people interact in small groups.

APPLICATIONS OF NONVERBAL COMMUNICATION RESEARCH TO GROUPS AND TEAMS

Relatively few research studies have investigated nonverbal behavior in groups. Despite the undoubted importance of nonverbal group dynamics to group discussion, researchers have found this aspect of communication difficult to observe and investigate. When group members simultaneously emit a myriad of nonverbal behaviors, it is difficult to systematically observe and interpret them. In addition, nonverbal messages are considerably more ambiguous than verbal messages. No dictionary has definitive meanings for nonverbal behaviors. We suggest that you exercise caution, then, when you attempt to interpret the nonverbal behavior of other group members.

The following sections describe some research that should help you become more sensitive to your own nonverbal behavior and to the role nonverbal communication plays in group discussions. Specifically, the sections discuss research on the following aspects of nonverbal communication in small groups: (1) physical posture, movement, and gestures, (2) eye contact, (3) facial expressions, (4) vocal cues, (5) personal space, (6) territoriality, (7) seating arrangement, (8) personal appearance, and (9) the communication environment.[15]

Posture, Movement, and Gestures

To observe and analyze movement, posture, and gestures, Paul Ekman and Wallace Friesen have identified five major types of nonverbal behavior: (1) emblems, (2) illustrators, (3) affect displays, (4) regulators, and (5) adaptors.[16]

Emblems are nonverbal cues that have specific verbal counterparts and are shared by all group members. Emblems often take the place of spoken words, letters, or numbers. Group leaders who place index fingers vertically in front of their lips use a nonverbal emblem to take the place of the words "Shhhh, let's be quiet now." A hitchhiker's raised thumb and a soldier's salute are other examples of emblems. Group members who point to their watches to indicate that the group should get on with it because time is running out, or who use their index fingers and thumbs to signify all is okay, also depend on nonverbal emblems to communicate their messages.

Illustrators are nonverbal behaviors that add meaning to accompanying verbal messages. For example, a group member who emphasizes a spoken message while jabbing a raised index finger in the air with each word illustrates conviction and determination. Several researchers have observed that people synchronize many of their body movements to their speech.[17] A blink of the eyes, a nod of the head, or a shift in body posture can accent spoken messages.

An **affect display** is a nonverbal cue that communicates emotion. As mentioned before, the face is the primary *source* of emotional display, but research suggests that the body indicates the *intensity* of the emotion, or affect, that is being expressed. For example, the faces of group members may indicate that they are bored. If they are also slouched in their chairs, they are probably more than just moderately apathetic about the discussion.

Regulators are nonverbal behaviors that help a group control the flow of communication. They are very important to small group discussions because people rely on them to know when they should talk and when they should listen. Regulators also provide cues to indicate when other group members want to contribute to the discussion. Eye contact, posture, gestures, facial expression, and body position all help regulate communication in a group discussion. Generally, large groups operate with a rather formal set of regulators; for example, participants raise their hands so that the chairperson will recognize them before they speak. In a less formal discussion, group members rely on direct eye contact (to indicate that a communication channel is open), facial expression (raised eyebrows often signify a desire to talk), and gestures (such as a raised index finger) as cues to regulate the flow of communication. When nonverbal regulators are absent, such as during electronic collaboration when team members are not in the same physical location, team members have a more difficult time coordinating their conversation.

Eye contact, posture, facial expression, and vocal clues tell other people how involved or uninvolved you are in the discussion. What nonverbal cues are evident here, and what do they tell you about the people in the photo?

Adaptors are nonverbal acts that satisfy personal needs and help people adapt to their immediate environment. Adaptors are also important for learning to get along with others and for responding to certain situations. Generally, people are not aware of most of their adaptive nonverbal behavior. Self-adaptors, for example, are things people do to their own bodies, such as scratching, biting their nails, or twirling their hair. Researchers have noted that when people become nervous, anxious, or upset, they frequently display more self-adaptive behaviors.[18]

$\mathcal{R}$EVIEW

CATEGORIES OF NONVERBAL COMMUNICATION

Category	Description	Example
Emblems	Movements and gestures that replace spoken messages	Group members shake their heads to communicate "no"
Illustrators	Nonverbal behaviors that add meaning to accompany verbal communication	A group member holds her hands 3 feet apart while saying "We'll need about a yard of fabric."
Affect displays	Expressions of feeling	Frowning, smiling, grimacing, smirking
Regulators	Nonverbal behaviors that control the flow of communication within a group	Eye contact, raising a hand or a finger to signal you want to talk
Adaptors	Nonverbal acts that satisfy personal needs and help group members adapt to their environment	Scratching, yawning, adjusting your glasses

Eye Contact

Have you ever felt uncomfortable because the person you were talking to seemed reluctant to establish eye contact? Maybe you've wondered, "Why doesn't she look at me when she's talking to me?" Perhaps you've had just the opposite experience—the person you were talking to would not stop staring at you. You become uneasy in these situations because they violate norms of eye contact. Although you may think that you do a pretty good job of establishing eye contact with others, researchers estimate that most people look at others only between 30 and 60 percent of the time.[19] Eye contact usually lasts less than 10 seconds.

Researchers have identified several factors that determine when you look at another person:[20] You are listening rather than talking; you like the other person; you want to persuade or influence someone; you have a high need for approval or affiliation; you seek a response from someone.

Other circumstances will dictate when you are less likely to have eye contact with someone: You are from a culture in which people tend not to look directly at others; you are embarrassed; you do not want to talk or participate in the discussion; you don't like someone; you are shy or introverted; you have a low need for approval.

When eye contact does occur in a small group setting, it may serve one or more important functions: (1) cognitive, (2) monitoring, (3) regulatory, and (4) expressive.[21]

Cognitive Function   The cognitive function of eye contact (or lack of it) is to indicate thought processes. For example, some people look away when they are thinking of just the right word to say. Others look away before they speak so they won't be distracted by the person to whom they are talking.

Monitoring Function   Monitoring is the way you seek feedback from others when communicating with them. You make eye contact in order to monitor how your message is being received. For example, if you say something that other members disagree with, you may observe a change in facial expressions, body posture, or restless movement. Because you've monitored their nonverbal expression, you may then decide that you need to spend more time explaining your point.

Regulatory Function   Eye contact plays a vital role in regulating the back-and-forth flow of communication; it signals when the communication channel is open or closed. You can invite interaction simply by looking at others. If the chair of a committee asks for volunteers and you don't want to participate, you are unlikely to establish eye contact. Nonverbally this says, "I don't want to talk; I don't want to participate."

Expressive Function   Although eyes generally do not provide clues about specific emotions, the areas of the face immediately around the eyes provide quite a bit of information about feelings, emotions, and attitudes.

Eye contact or lack of it thus reveals information about thought processes, provides feedback, regulates communication channels, and expresses emotions. Eye contact also provides clues about status and leadership roles in small groups. One researcher has documented that group members who talk more receive more eye contact.[22] In addition, research suggests that eye contact is the predominant cue that regulates when you want to speak and when you want to stop speaking during group discussion.[23] In the next small group meeting you attend, determine who receives the most eye contact in the group. Where do group members look for information and guidance? They probably look at the group leader. If, as in many groups, several members share leadership, participants may look toward any of those leaders, depending on the specific problem or level of uncertainty facing the group.

REVIEW

FUNCTIONS OF EYE CONTACT

Cognitive function: Provides cues about thought processes

Monitoring function: Allows feedback from others

Regulatory function: Signals when the communication channel is open and closed

Expressive function: Provides information about feelings, emotions, and attitudes

---

Facial Expressions

As discussed before, the face is the most important revealer of emotions. Sometimes you can mask your emotional expressions, but the face is usually the first place you look to determine someone else's emotional state. Facial expressions are particularly significant in interpersonal and small group communication because of the close proximity of communicators to one another. You can readily detect emotions displayed on a person's face. Even though some researchers estimate that the face can produce thousands of different expressions, Ekman and Friesen have identified six primary emotions displayed on it: happiness, anger, surprise, sadness, disgust, and fear.[24]

Ekman and his colleagues have also developed a method of identifying which areas of the face play the most important roles in communicating emotion.[25] According to this research, people communicate happiness with the area around their eyes and with smiles and raised cheeks. They reveal disgust with raised upper lips, wrinkled noses, lowered eyelids, and lowered brows. They communicate fear with the area around their eyes, but their mouths are also usually open when they are fearful. When they are angry, people are likely to lower their eyebrows and stare intensely. They communicate surprise with raised eyebrows, wide-open eyes, and often open mouths. They communicate sadness in the area around the eyes and mouth.

Facial expressions are important sources of information about a group's emotional climate, particularly if several members express similar emotions. Their faces may suggest that they are bored with the discussion or that they are interested and pleased. Remember that group members may attempt to mask their facial expressions in an effort to conceal their true feelings.

Vocal Cues

"John," remarked a group discussion member, obviously upset, "it's not that I object to what you said; it's just the way you said it." The pitch, rate, volume, and quality of your voice (also

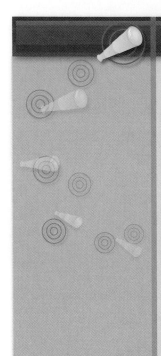

Cutting Edge Theory

NONVERBAL VIRTUAL COMMUNICATION

If you have been reading the Virtual Communication feature in each chapter thus far, you should be aware that technology can facilitate communication by eliminating the constraints of time and space, but it brings with it liabilities as well. The difficulty of communicating emotion is one of those liabilities, because people rely so much on tone of voice and visual cues to ascertain others' feelings and reactions.

Researcher Gary Baker studied the performance of 64 virtual teams using four modes of technological collaboration: text-only, audio-only, text and video, and audio and video. The study found no significant difference in the quality of strategic decisions made by teams using text-only communication versus those using audio-only communication. But when video was added to audio communication, there was significant improvement in team decisions.[26]

Real-Life Applications

Baker's study leads to some recommendations about nonverbal communication in virtual groups. Consider the following:

- Whenever possible, groups and teams should meet face to face. There is no substitute for the "full picture" we get when in the presence of another human being.
- Especially in the formative stages of group interaction, meeting face to face is critical to getting to know one another and building predictability and trust. When face-to-face communication is not possible, video conferencing can improve the quality of a group's work.
- When face-to-face or video communication is not possible and you are limited to text or audio interaction, pay extra attention to emotional cues. Hearing a sigh, a yawn, or a nervous giggle, or seeing the word *sigh* or an emoticon :-) in the text on your screen will help you interpret verbal messages.

called **paralanguage**) are important in determining the meanings of messages. From a speaker's paralanguage cues you can make inferences about how that person feels toward you. You may also base inferences about a person's competence and personality on vocal cues. A speaker who mispronounces words and uses "uhs" and "ums" will probably be perceived as less credible than a speaker who is more articulate.[27] In addition to determining how speech affects a speaker's credibility, researchers have studied the communication of emotion via vocal cues.[28]

At times you can distinguish emotional states from vocal cues, but as a group member you should beware of drawing improper inferences and labeling someone negatively just because of vocal cues.[29] As this chapter has emphasized, nonverbal cues do not operate in isolation. They should be evaluated in the context of other communicative behaviors.

Personal Space

The next time you are sitting in class, note the seat you select. Even though no one instructed you to do so, chances are that you tend to sit in about the same general area, if not in the same seat, during each class. Perhaps in your family each person sits at a certain place at the dinner table. If someone sits in your chair, you feel your territory has been invaded and you may try to reclaim your seat. Human behavior with respect to personal space and territoriality reflects competition between the need for affiliation with others and the need for privacy.[30]

Research pioneer Edward T. Hall investigated the silent language of how we use the personal space around us. His investigation of **proxemics**, the study of how close or far away we choose to be to other people and objects, helps us better understand how our use of personal space gives us clues about the relationships we have with others.[31] Hall identified four spatial zones that people in Western cultures typically use, depending on the activity and nature of the relationship they have with those around them. Figure 6.1 illustrates each of these zones.

- **Intimate zone:** Between 0 and 1½ feet. This is the zone in which our most personal and intimate conversation occurs. It would be unusual in a group to have someone this close to you unless you are whispering something confidential in his or her ear.
- **Personal zone:** Between 1½ and 4 feet. Most conversations with family and friends occur in this zone. Group members may sit within this zone, but even at 4 feet we may feel that the other person is too close.
- **Social zone:** Between 4 and 12 feet. Most group interaction happens within this zone. This is also the zone in which interaction with colleagues and other professionals occurs.

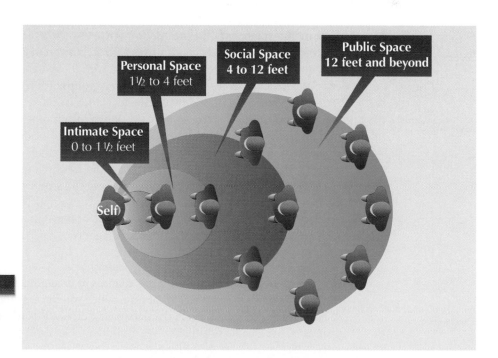

FIGURE 6.1

Edward T. Hall's Four Zones of Space

■ **Public zone:** 12 feet and beyond. Teachers and public speakers typically communicate with at least 12 feet between speaker and listener.

Of course, not every person you'll meet will interact with you using these zones; these are just estimates of typical interactions with others.

Territoriality

Territoriality is a term used in the study of animal behavior to refer to how animals stake out and defend given areas. Humans, too, exhibit this behavior. Understanding territoriality may help you understand certain group behaviors. For example, the readiness of group members to defend personal territory may provide insights about their attitudes toward the group and toward individual members. At the next meeting you attend, observe how members attempt to stake out territories. If the group is seated around a table, do members place objects in front of and around themselves to signify that they are claiming territory? Higher-status individuals generally attempt to claim more territory.[32] Notice how group members manipulate their posture and gestures if their space is invaded. Lower-status individuals generally permit greater territorial invasion. Note, too, how individuals claim their territory by leaving markers—such as books, papers, or a pencil—when they have to leave the group but expect to return shortly.

Seating Arrangement

The area of study known as **small group ecology** examines the consistent way in which people arrange themselves in small groups. Understanding the effects of seating arrangement can give you insights as to who is likely to talk to whom, who may emerge as a leader, and the overall effects of seating arrangement on the communication climate in the group.

Seating Arrangement and Interaction Patterns   Where you sit in a group can have an effect on who you are likely to talk to. Bernard Steinzor found that when group members are seated in a circle, they are more likely to talk with those across from them than to those on either side.[33] Another research team observed groups of three people in snack bars, restaurants, and lounges and found that individuals who are more centrally located and most visible in a group usually receive more eye contact from others.[34] They also tend to initiate more communication than those who are less centrally located in the group. Furthermore, when other group members speak, they tend to direct their comments more to these centrally located members in the group. Yet another research team came to a similar conclusion: Group members who were in the center of the group spoke most often.[35] Because of where people sit, their eye contact with others is an important factor in determining who speaks, who listens, and who has the greatest opportunity to dominate a conversation. Figure 6.2 illustrates some typical interaction patterns determined by seating arrangement.

Seating Arrangement and Leadership Emergence   There is evidence that where you sit in a group or team can influence your chances of emerging as a leader. If you like to lead others, you may typically select a seat from which you can see other people in the group and maximize your eye contact with them. In their study, Lloyd Howells and Selwyn Becker had groups of five people seat themselves around a table; three people sat on one side of the

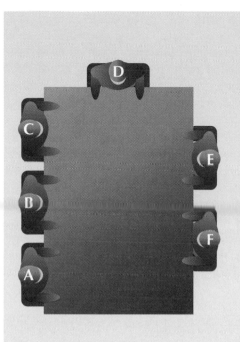

Person A:
A person sitting at a corner seat often contributes less to the group; the person is farther away from the "power seat" (person D).

Person D:
The person seated at the head of a rectangular table is often perceived as being seated in the "leadership seat."

Persons E and F:
The person who selects a seat that maximizes eye contact with others typically has greater control over the group's interaction; eye contact is a key variable that regulates who talks and who listens.

FIGURE 6.2

Group Interaction Patterns Are Influenced by Seating Arrangement

table; the other two sat opposite them.[36] The researchers discovered that participants had a greater probability of becoming leaders if they sat on the side of the table facing the three discussion members. The ability to make direct eye contact with more group members, which can subsequently result in greater control of verbal communication, may explain why the two individuals who faced the other three emerged as leaders.

There is also evidence that a person who likes to assume a leadership role will select a seat to maximize his or her interaction with others. One researcher found clear evidence that the dominant group member tends to select a seat at the head of a rectangular table or one that maximizes the opportunity to communicate with others.[37] In contrast, people who sit at the corners of tables generally contribute the least to a discussion and are less likely to emerge as leaders. Again, eye contact coupled with seating arrangement seems to be a major predictor of leadership emergence. In addition, people who have higher status in a group tend to have more space around them.

Seating Arrangement and Stress   Some people prefer greater personal space when they are under stress.[38] If, as a group or team leader, you know that an upcoming discussion will probably produce anxiety, hold the meeting in a room that permits members to have more freedom of movement. This will allow them to find their preferred personal distance from other group members. Or, if you know that an upcoming meeting may produce conflict, arrange the chairs so that there is more space around each participant. Crowding people together can amplify whatever emotions group members may feel.

Seating Arrangement and Gender   There is evidence that in North America, women tend to sit closer to others than men do (whether those others are men or women). Men generally prefer greater personal space when sitting next to other men.[39] We're not suggesting that you use this research conclusion to measure the distance between seats in an upcoming meeting; simply realize that there may be differences in how much space men and women prefer to have around them. Where possible, let group members adjust their own seating distance from other members.

Seating Arrangement and Personality   People who are extroverts, those who are outgoing and like to talk with others, are more likely to sit across from other people than are introverts, those who are less willing to initiate conversation with others.[40] Introverts generally prefer more distance between themselves and others. Of course, you may not know who is an introvert and who is an extrovert before a meeting. Again, it's best to let group members determine their comfort zones for interacting with others.

Collectively, the research conclusions just highlighted suggest that people do arrange themselves with some consistency in small group discussions. A discussion leader who

SMALL GROUP ECOLOGY

Interaction Patterns

- Who you have eye contact with during group discussions usually affects who you talk with.
- People who are more centrally located in a group often receive more oral messages from other group members than do people who are less central.
- You are more likely to talk with people seated directly across from you than with those next to you.

Leadership

- We often expect the person seated at the head of a rectangular table to be the leader.
- More outspoken, dominant individuals often choose to sit at the head of the table.
- People who sit at the corner of a rectangular table often contribute less to the discussion and consequently may have less influence in the group.
- People who are perceived to have high status are given more personal space around them.

Stress

- During times of stress or conflict, people prefer more space around them.

Gender

- Women generally sit a bit closer to others than men do.
- Men tend to prefer greater personal space when sitting next to other men.

Personality

- Extroverts (people who are outgoing) tend to sit across from others.
- Introverts (people who are less outgoing) prefer more distance between themselves and others.

understands seating preferences will be able to provide a comfortable climate for small group discussion.

Personal Appearance

How long does it take to determine whether you like someone? Some researchers claim that within seconds after meeting another person you make an initial judgment about whether to continue to communicate with him or her or try to excuse yourself from the conversation. You base many of your initial impressions of others primarily on personal appearance. The way people dress, their hairstyles, weight, and height affect your communication with them.

Research suggests that women who are thought attractive are more effective in changing attitudes than are women thought less attractive.[41] In addition, more attractive individuals are often thought by others to be more credible than less attractive people. They are also perceived to be happier, more popular, more sociable, and more successful than are those rated as being less attractive.

It is important to note we are *not* advocating making stereotypical judgments of others based on personal appearance. We *are* suggesting, however, that your personal appearance may affect how others perceive you. And yes, you may be influenced by others' personal appearance. Therefore, you should try to monitor not only how your appearance may be affecting others' perceptions, but also how you may inappropriately dismiss others because their appearance distracted you.

Communication Environment

Five students have been assigned to work together on a project for their group communication class. Their task is to formulate a policy question and solutions to it. Their first problem is finding a place to meet. Apparently, the only available place is a small, vacant office in Smythe Hall, the oldest building on campus. Although the students are relieved to have found a place to meet, no one seems happy about holding meetings in the old office. When they arrive for their first meeting, they find a dirty, musty room with peeling paint, only three hard wooden chairs, and a gray metal desk. The ventilation is poor, and half of the light bulbs are burned out. Such a dismal environment will undoubtedly affect the group's ability to work.

People can generally comprehend information and solve problems better in a more attractive environment. Research does not suggest, however, that one environment is best for all group communication situations. The optimal environment for any group depends on its specific task, as well as the needs and expectations of its members. Some students need absolute quiet to read or study, while others can be productive while listening to music. Group members or leaders should attempt to find the best environments for their group based on the group's needs and the types of tasks confronting it. Group leaders could ask members which type of environment they prefer. If a group must solve problems that require considerable thought, energy, and creativity, it might work best in a quiet, comfortable room.

SOURCES OF NONVERBAL CUES

Posture, movement, and gestures	Provide information regarding status, intensity of attitude, warmth, approval seeking, group climate, immediacy, deception
Eye contact	Serves cognitive, monitoring, regulatory, and expressive functions
Facial expression	Communicates emotion, especially happiness, anger, surprise, sadness, disgust, and fear
Vocal cues	The pitch, rate, volume, and quality of the voice communicate emotion, credibility, and personality perceptions
Personal space, territoriality, and seating arrangement	People in Western cultures use four zones of personal space, depending on their interpersonal relationships. They arrange themselves in consistent ways in groups and stake out space to reflect status, roles, stress levels, leadership, and personality traits
Personal appearance	Clothing, body shape, and general attractiveness influence others' perceptions and reactions
Communication environment	The general attractiveness or unattractiveness of a physical space contributes to the group's productivity and overall group climate

FUNCTIONS OF NONVERBAL CUES IN GROUPS AND TEAMS

Now that we've seen how specific cues contribute to understanding messages in group discussion, you may still be wondering about some of the more general effects or functions of nonverbal messages. Unspoken messages play a significant role in how leaders are perceived, group members are persuaded, body posture and movement are synchronized, and lying is detected.

Nonverbal Messages Influence Perceived Leadership

To lead is to influence. Nonverbal cues have a major effect on how leaders are perceived in groups and teams. Communication researcher John O'Connor discovered that one person's frequent gesturing was highly correlated with other members' perception that the person was a leader in the group.[42] In a follow-up study, John Baird found that group members who other members thought of as leaders used shoulder and arm gestures more often.[43] Although leaders may gesture more frequently than do followers, this does not mean that frequent gesturing causes a person to emerge as a leader. The evidence does not suggest a cause-and-effect relationship. It simply suggests that people in leadership roles may use more nonverbal gestures, perhaps to coordinate or regulate message flow.

Nonverbal Messages Influence Persuasion Skills

Do individuals in small groups use certain nonverbal cues during their attempts to persuade others? One study found that when a person "mirrors," or imitates, the nonverbal behavior of other group members, they are more likely to see that person as more confident and persuasive. [44] Albert Mehrabian and Martin Williams found that persuasive communicators exhibit more animated facial expressions, use more gestures to emphasize their points, and nod their heads more than do those who are less persuasive.[45] Another team of researchers found that people trying to project warm, friendly images will be more likely to smile, less likely to fidget with their hands, and more likely to shift their postures toward others. [46]

One team of researchers found that we rely extensively on nonverbal cues to signal when we want to speak or change topics. Typically, a group member signals topic change by leaning forward, smiling, making a head nod, shifting posture, having a foot make contact with the floor, or breaking eye contact to signal a change in the direction of thought.[47]

Nonverbal Messages Help Synchronize Interaction

An excellent book by Judee Burgoon and her colleagues reports that nonverbal cues play a central role in adapting and relating to others.[48] We tend to mirror the posture and behavior of others; it seems to get us "in sync" with those with whom we interact. At your next group meeting, note how one member tends to unconsciously mirror the posture of another. This is especially true of members seated across from each other or within each other's line of vision. You may find, for example, that a person sitting across from someone with folded arms may assume a similar posture. Like partners in an intricate dance, people constantly reflect each other's movements, eye contact, gestures, and other nonverbal cues as they respond and adapt.

We respond not only to physical posture and movement but also to the rhythm and sound of human speech. William Condon and others, using slow-motion films, documented a distinct relationship between facial expressions and head movements and speech.[49] Adam Kendon observed that people may shift their body positions in response to verbal messages.[50] Davida Navarre and Catherine Emihovich report similar evidence that group members may respond in synchrony to the movements and postures of others.[51] These authors suggest that during group interactions people may adopt poses similar to those of others they like or agree with. Thus, coalitions of group members may be identified not only by their verbal agreement but also by their synchronized nonverbal behavior. It is probably more than just coincidence that group members consistently fold their arms and cross their legs in the same way. Just as religious services use singing and group litanies to establish unity and a commonality of purpose, small groups may unwittingly use common nonverbal behaviors to foster cohesiveness. Counselors report that they can help clients self-disclose by adopting body postures similar to those of their clients. By synchronizing body position, counselors believe they can better empathize and establish rapport with their clients. In your small group discussions, observe the similarity and dissimilarity of members' postures, positions, and gestures. Such cues may provoke interesting insights about group climate, leadership, and cohesiveness.

In one of the few studies that examined nonverbal behavior in groups, Edward Mabry sought to discover whether group members' nonverbal behavior changes from one meeting to the next. After observing a group that met five times, he found that during the second and third meetings, group members were more likely to show the palms of their hands. Group members also tended to lean back more in the first and fifth sessions of their deliberations. Participants also made more direct eye contact with one another after they had met together once. What do these differences mean? Mabry's study suggests that group members' nonverbal behavior changes from one group meeting to the next. Groups do not develop a static way of behaving nonverbally; nonverbal communication may depend on the topic and how group members feel toward one another as they become more comfortable after meeting together over several sessions.[52]

Nonverbal Messages Provide Information About Perceived Honesty or Dishonesty

In addition to categorizing movement, posture, and gestures, researchers have studied whether nonverbal behavior provides clues to whether someone is lying. Sigmund Freud said, "He that has eyes to see and ears to hear may convince himself that no mortal can keep a secret. If his lips are silent, he chatters with his fingertips; betrayal oozes out of him at every pore." Ekman and Friesen found that feet and legs often reveal people's true feelings.[53] They theorized that while people consciously manipulate their facial expressions to hide deception, they are not so likely to monitor their feet. One team of researchers suggested that the following nonverbal behaviors, listed in order from most to least important, can provide clues as to whether someone is lying.[54]

> Greater time lag in response to a question
>
> Reduced eye contact
>
> Increased shifts in posture
>
> More hand/shrug emblems
>
> More adaptors
>
> Unfilled pauses
>
> Less smiling
>
> Slower speech
>
> Higher pitch in voice
>
> More deliberate pronunciation and articulation

Of course, simply because a group member exhibits one or more of these nonverbal behaviors does not mean that he or she is lying. Although a person trying to hide something or lie may exhibit some of the cues listed above, not everyone who displays such behavior is deceptive. The ambiguity of nonverbal cues prevents you from drawing such definitive conclusions about the motives of other people based on nonverbal cues alone.

INTERPRETING NONVERBAL COMMUNICATION

Nonverbal cues do not create meaning independently of other communication cues (such as message content, language style, and message organization). Also, there is much we still do not know about nonverbal communication. After reading the research conclusions reported here, you may be tempted to interpret someone else's body language, but you should remember several principles when ascribing meaning to the posture and movement of others.

Interpret Nonverbal Communication in Context   Just as you can misunderstand the meaning of a sentence taken out of context, so can you make an inaccurate inference about

Virtual Communication

If you've participated in an online chat room, you know that it's sometimes difficult to catch the subtle meaning of messages, because nonverbal cues are not available. Electronic meetings and other e-collaborations have both positive and negative consequences. The lack of nonverbal cues, especially emotional and relational cues, can result in missed meaning. On the positive side, however, electronic collaboration often results in more equal participation. If you aren't worried about seeing someone frown or grimace, you may be more likely to offer your ideas to the group. Electronic collaborators are also more honest, because often their contributions are anonymous.[55] There is usually more expressed disagreement in face-to-face group and team deliberations than in electronic discussion. Why? Because the nonverbal reactions in face-to-face group meetings result in increased verbal expressions of conflict and disagreement. If there is unresolved conflict and expressions of disagreement, such emotional displays can have a negative impact on a group.[56]

You should work to overcome the limitations of the virtual environment by making a special point to communicate to group members how you *feel* about the topic as well as what you *think*. Sometimes, clear verbal expression of your feelings is most appropriate. At other times, the use of emoticons and acronyms will help.

Most people today know how to use emoticons—a smiley face such as :-) or a frowning face :-(, or any of the many other emoticons that can be created with keystrokes. In fact, most contemporary word processing and e-mail software programs now include graphic emoticons to make it easy to communicate emotions explicitly. Another way to express your emotions is to use acronyms such as LOL, which means "laughing out loud," or J/K, which is shorthand for "just kidding."

Even without visual nonverbal cues, it's possible to express emotions when using e-mail or text messages. It just may take communication partners a bit longer to discern the emotional or relational messages embedded in a text message.

a nonverbal behavior when it is interpreted out of context. Simply because a group member sits with crossed legs and folded arms does not necessarily mean that person does not want to communicate with others. Other variables in the communication system may be affecting the person's posture and position.

Look for Clusters of Cues   Look for a pattern of cues to help you interpret what a specific behavior means rather than considering only one gesture, expression, or use of personal space. Seek corroborating cues that can help you reach a more accurate conclusion about what a specific behavior means. Besides noting whether someone makes eye contact, also note whether vocal cues, posture, and gestures confirm your conclusion.

Collaborating Ethically: What Would You Do?

An understanding of nonverbal communication and small group ecology can be used strategically to influence group interaction and group outcomes. For example, one of our friends has been seated twice on trial juries. In each case, when the jury moved to the jury room to deliberate, our friend walked confidently to the head of the table, put his hands on the table while intently surveying the faces of his fellow jurors, and said "Well, the first thing we need to do is to elect a foreman." He was elected unanimously in both cases.

Imagine that you have been assigned to a task group with no designated leader. For a variety of reasons, you believe that you should be elected leader. The information you've learned in this chapter has given you insight into how you can manage the group's impression of you and of your competence through strategic use of nonverbal behaviors and group ecology principles. Is it ethical for you to use what you know to get elected? Or does doing so amount to unfairly manipulating the group?

Recognize That People Respond Differently to Different Stimuli   Not all people express emotions in the same manner. It may take considerable time before you can understand the unique, idiosyncratic meaning underlying another person's specific nonverbal behaviors.

Consider Cultural and Gender Differences   Keep the person's cultural background or gender in mind when you draw an inference from his or her nonverbal behavior. No nonverbal behavior has a generally accepted universal meaning. Even though some evidence indicates that facial expressions can be interpreted across several cultures with up to 92 percent accuracy, there are subtle as well as dramatic differences in the way nonverbal behaviors may be interpreted. In small group interactions, it is especially interesting to observe cultural differences in how people use space and territory. In Chapter 9, we'll offer additional tips for being sensitive to cultural differences.

Consider Your Past Experience with Someone When Interpreting Nonverbal Cues   As you spend time working with group members, chances are you will learn how to interpret their nonverbal cues. For example, when you first met Lee you weren't sure why he seemed so distant and aloof. His lack of eye contact suggested that he was not interested in being a productive member of the group. After you had spent several meetings getting to know him better, you realized that Lee is simply shy. He has good ideas but needs to be drawn out. Working with him convinces you that you should not make snap judgments of other group members. First impressions are not always accurate.

Look for Cues That Communicate Liking, Power, and Responsiveness   Albert Mehrabian has developed a three-dimensional model that identifies how people respond to nonverbal messages. Even though this framework was not designed exclusively for small groups, his research can be useful in helping to interpret the meaning of messages. His conclusions cannot be applied universally, but they do reflect the way many North Americans interpret nonverbal messages. His research suggests that people derive meaning from nonverbal behavior based on (1) immediacy or liking, (2) power, and (3) responsiveness.[57]

1. *Immediacy: behaviors that communicate liking and disliking.* As defined by Mehrabian, immediacy refers to whether people like or dislike others. The immediacy principle states that "people are drawn toward persons and things they like, evaluate highly, and prefer; and they avoid or move away from things they dislike, evaluate negatively, or do not prefer." According to Mehrabian, such nonverbal behaviors as touching, leaning forward, reducing distance and personal space, and maintaining direct eye contact can communicate liking or positive feelings. Based on the immediacy principle, group members who consistently sit closer to you, establish more eye contact with you, and, in general, are drawn to you probably like you more than group members who generally do not look at you and who regularly select seats away from you.

2. *Power: behaviors that communicate influence and status.* People of higher status generally determine the degree of closeness permitted in their interactions. A person of higher status and influence, for example, usually is surrounded by more space. A boss who sits at the head of the table is more likely to have empty chairs around him or her; subordinates are more likely to give the boss more space. A person of higher status generally has a more relaxed body posture when interacting with a person of lower status. High status members also tend to have less eye contact with others, to use a louder voice, to make more expansive movements and postures, and may reflect their status in the way they dress.

3. *Responsiveness: behaviors that communicate interest and attention.* Body movements, facial expressions, and variation of vocal cues (such as pitch, rate, volume, and tone) all contribute to our perceptions of others as responsive or unresponsive. A group member who communicates energy and enthusiasm would be rated highly responsive.

*R*EVIEW

DIMENSIONS OF NONVERBAL MEANING

Dimension	Definition	Nonverbal Cues
Immediacy	Behaviors that signal liking, attraction, and interest	Touching, forward leaning, close personal space, eye contact
Power	Behaviors that communicate power, status, and influence	Protected space, increased distance, relaxed posture
Responsiveness	Behaviors that communicate active interactions and attention	Eye contact, varied vocal cues, animated facial expression

Develop the Skill of Perception Checking   People judge you by your behavior, not by your intent. You judge others the same way—by what you see, not by what they are thinking. Unless you are a mind reader, the only way to check your perception of others' nonverbal behavior is to ask them. **Perception checking** is the skill of asking someone whether your interpretation of his or her unspoken message is accurate. There are three steps to using this skill. First, observe the nonverbal cues we have discussed. Next, mentally draw a conclusion about what the nonverbal behavior may mean. Finally, ask the other person if your inference was accurate.

Suppose you offer a solution to a problem your group has been discussing. After you announce your proposal, the group is silent, your colleagues break eye contact, and you see one person frown. To find out whether their nonverbal response means that your proposal has been rejected, you could ask, "Does your silence mean you don't like my idea?" You could also add, "From the look on your face, you don't seem to be pleased with my suggestion." Your colleagues may say, "Oh, no. Your idea is a good one. We just need some time to think about how we could put your suggestion into action."

We recommend that you not overuse perception checking. Stopping to seek confirmation of every facial expression or vocal tone would irritate others. Do, however, consider perception checking when you genuinely do not understand a group member's response.

These principles point to a key conclusion: Nonverbal messages are considerably more ambiguous than verbal messages. No dictionary has definitive meanings for nonverbal behaviors. Exercise caution, then, when you attempt to interpret the nonverbal behavior of other group members.

Case Study

Scene One

Meg: Nice outfit . . . . Did you make it yourself?

Nancy: No, my grandmother made it for me.

Meg: I was just wondering; it has such a "homespun" look.

Scene Two

She: Do these jeans make me look fat?

He: Uhhhhh . . . .

Scene Three

She: Dear, it's been a long time since we went out dancing on a Saturday night.

He: Sure has.

Scene Four

Boss: Thanks for coming in, Jean. I know it's short notice and you're pretty overloaded, but we have to get this contract done and back to the client first thing Monday morning. I'm looking for someone who can work over the weekend. Do you have any suggestions?

Jean: Let me check my calendar, Mr. Jefferson. Maybe I can do it.

Scene Five

She: Honey, I'm working on a guest list for our party. Did the Ronnings invite us to their open house last fall?

He: Beats me . . . .

Practice in Applying Principles

1. The brief scenes above provide examples of indirect communication—the words convey a surface meaning that, with further analysis, may reveal deeper, unspoken meanings. Rewrite each scene using dialogue that is more direct.
2. If you were the recipient of the indirect communication in each case, what additional information would you need to verify whether your interpretation of the comment was correct? What nonverbal cues would you look for to help you interpret the comment in each case?
3. What emotions (if any) do you associate with these dialogues? Why? What nonverbal cues would you look for to identify these emotions?
4. What perception-checking responses might you use in similar situations?

REVIEW

PERCEPTION CHECKING

Steps	Factors to Consider
1. Observe someone's nonverbal behavior.	What is his or her facial expression?
	Does he or she make eye contact?
	What is his or her posture?
	What is his or her tone of voice?
2. Think about what the behavior may mean.	Does he or she appear to be angry, sad, depressed?
	Is the nonverbal message contradicting the verbal message?
3. Check your perception by asking whether your interpretation is accurate.	"The expression on your face suggests you may be upset. Are you?"

Putting Principles into Practice

This chapter has discussed three important communication skills: overcoming language barriers, listening, and understanding nonverbal communication. Consider the following suggestions, derived from the research discussed in the chapter.

Verbal Dynamics and Word Barriers

- Use specific language; be aware of multiple interpretations. Clarify.
- Don't overgeneralize. Remember that all individuals are unique.
- Analyze. Learn to recognize the difference between a fact and an inference.
- Identify your own assumptions about conversational style. Work to adapt your style in ways that are most appropriate to situations.

Listening

- Be aware of your listening style.
- When listening, do so actively. Stop what you're doing; avoid doing anything that distracts you from listening.

- Look for nonverbal cues that help you interpret what you're hearing. Listen with your eyes, as well as with your ears.
- Listen for feelings; ask yourself how you would feel if you were in the other's situation.
- Ask questions to clarify.
- Paraphrase content and feelings to confirm with the other person that you're understanding correctly.

Body Posture, Movement, and Gestures

- You may be more effective in persuading others when you use eye contact, maintain a direct body orientation, and remain physically close to others.
- You can often identify high-status group members (or at least those who perceive themselves as having high status) by such nonverbal cues as relaxed postures, loud voices, territorial dominance, expansive movements, and, sometimes, their keeping themselves at a distance from others.

- Someone who is lying may speak with a higher-pitched voice, use less eye contact, show less enthusiasm, shrug more often, nod less, speak more slowly and with more errors, and adopt a less immediate posture.
- Group leaders may gesture more than followers.
- Observing the similarity of group members' posture and gestures can reveal insights about group climate, leadership, and cohesiveness.

Eye Contact

- People sometimes interrupt eye contact with others because they are trying to think of the right words to say, not because they are uninterested.
- When talking with others in a small group, be sure to look at all members so that you can respond to the feedback they provide.
- You sometimes can draw a person into the conversation just by establishing direct eye contact.
- Because eye contact signals whether a communication channel is open or closed, you may be able to quiet an extremely talkative member by avoiding eye contact.
- By noting who looks at whom in a small group, you can get a good idea of who the leader is. Group members usually look at their leader more than they look at any other member (assuming that they respect their leader's ideas and opinions).

Facial Expression

- Look at group members' facial expressions to find out the emotional climate in the group.

Vocal Cues

- You may find that you dislike a group member not because of what he or she says but because of that person's vocal quality, pitch, or rate of speech. People's vocal cues affect your perceptions of them.

Personal Space and Territoriality

- Members typically stake out their territory or personal space early on in group gatherings.
- When group members' territories are invaded, they often respond nonverbally (via posture or territorial markers) to defend their territories.

- Because people prefer greater personal space when they are under stress, make sure that group members have plenty of territory when you know that a meeting is going to be stressful.

Seating Arrangement

- If you want to increase your interaction with a group member, sit directly across from him or her.
- If you know that a group member generally monopolizes the conversation, try to get that person to select a corner seat rather than one at the head of a conference table.
- You are more likely to emerge as a group leader if you sit so that you can establish eye contact and a direct body orientation with shoulders squared toward most of the group members.

Personal Appearance

- Your personal appearance will affect the way other group members perceive you. It can also influence your ability to persuade others.

Communication Environment

- Make sure that the physical environment for a group meeting is as comfortable and attractive as possible to enhance satisfaction and productivity.

Functions of Nonverbal Communication in Groups and Teams

- *Leadership function:* Nonverbal messages influence who is perceived as group or team leader.
- *Persuasion function:* Skilled persuaders use animated facial expressions and frequent gestures, smile, are less likely to fidget with their hands, and lean forward when communicating.
- *Synchronization function:* Nonverbal cues help synchronize our communication with others.
- *Honesty function:* Nonverbal behavior often provides cues about whether the communicator is honest or dishonest; dishonest communicators often speak slowly and more distinctly with a higher pitch and have more pauses and hesitations, have less eye contact, and evidence more shrugs and postural shifts.

Interpreting Nonverbal Behavior

- Consider the context when making inferences about what a specific behavior may mean.
- Look for clusters of cues rather than focusing on just one nonverbal behavior when interpreting unspoken messages.
- Because not all people have the same reaction to a given situation, avoid interpreting one person's nonverbal expression in the same way as the identical expression displayed by another person.
- Factor in cultural and gender expectations of others when interpreting nonverbal messages.
- You will likely be more successful in interpreting nonverbal messages of people you know or have worked with over a long period of time. Therefore, be cautious when drawing a conclusion about a new acquaintance's nonverbal behavior.
- Others' eye contact, posture, touch, and personal space will help you determine whether they like or dislike you.
- Use posture, appearance, personal space, and relaxation cues to help you interpret someone's perception of his or her power and influence.
- Use eye contact, vocal cues, movement, and facial expressions to help interpret someone's interest in and responsiveness to you.
- To check your interpretation of someone's nonverbal behavior, ask the person whether your understanding of his or her unspoken message is accurate.

PRACTICE

Receiving Nonverbal Reinforcement

Pair up with another student and take turns telling each other about a personally important idea, feeling, or experience. The partner should give no nonverbal indications that he or she is paying attention while the other speaks: no smiles, nods of the head, "um-hums," postural orientation, facial expressions. After each of you has talked for three to five minutes, discuss what it felt like (1) to receive no nonverbal attention and (2) to give no nonverbal attention. After you discuss the importance of nonverbal communication, again take turns talking and listening to each other—this time with genuine nonverbal feedback. With the rest of the class, discuss the experience of receiving and not receiving nonverbal reinforcement.

Nonverbal Group Observation

Videotape any small group working on a project or a case study. Play the videotape with the sound turned off so you can focus on group members' actions, not their words. (If you don't have access to video equipment, simply observe a group from a distance so you are less able to hear their conversation.)

- Notice group members' use of emblems, illustrators, affect displays, regulators, and adaptors.
- Observe how nonverbal cues regulate the flow of communication.
- How do body posture and movement communicate members' status and attitudes?
- Try to identify the four functions of eye contact in the group.
- Do group members communicate much emotion with their faces?
- Note relationships among territorial behavior, seating arrangement, leadership, status, and verbal interaction in the group.
- If this is a group you are ordinarily a member of, and it met in a special room for the videotaping, do you detect any changes in nonverbal behavior that may be a result of the change in environment?

Redesign Your Meeting Room

Working with a group of others, discuss how you would redesign your classroom. Or, if you're working on a small group project and you have a regular meeting place, discuss how you would redesign that space for maximum meeting effectiveness. As you brainstorm suggestions, consider the architecture, lighting, colors, furniture, sounds, and any other features that would enhance the room's functional design for group deliberations.

CHAPTER SEVEN

Managing Conflict

"When we all think alike, then no one is thinking."

—Walter Lippman

OBJECTIVES

After studying this chapter, you will be able to:

■ Explain why conflict occurs in small groups.
■ Describe the negative impact of conflict on group communication.
■ List three misconceptions about conflict.
■ Describe five conflict-management styles.
■ Identify strategies for managing different types of conflict.
■ Describe four conflict-management principles.
■ Define groupthink.
■ Identify six symptoms of groupthink.
■ Apply techniques for reducing groupthink.
■ Define consensus.
■ Apply techniques for managing conflict and reaching consensus in small groups.

CONFLICT HAPPENS. *Social psychologists and communication researchers say that people inevitably disagree when they interact.[1] Throughout history, people have been involved in conflicts ranging from family feuds to world wars. Whether groups are involved in negotiating international trade agreements or deciding how to repave a parking lot, their members experience conflict.*

This chapter gives you some ideas about the causes of conflict and presents some strategies for managing it in groups and teams. You will learn not how to eliminate group conflict but how to understand it and its importance in your group deliberations.

Despite the prevalence of conflict in group and team deliberations, communication researchers Steven Farmer and Jonelle Rothe note that much of what we know about group conflict has been generalized from research that has investigated interpersonal conflict.[2] The prime objective of this chapter is to help you understand how conflict in groups and teams can be both useful and detrimental to collaborative decision making.

WHAT IS CONFLICT?

Conflict is about disagreement. Communication experts William Wilmot and Joyce Hocker define conflict as including the following four elements: (1) an expressed struggle (2) between at least two interdependent people (3) who perceive incompatible goals, scarce resources, and interference from others, (4) to achieve specific goals.[3]

- *Expressed struggle*: A conflict becomes a concern to a group when the disagreement is expressed verbally or, more often, nonverbally. Early signs of conflict include furrowed brows, grimacing facial expressions, and flashes of frustration evident in the voice. If the conflict persists, words are usually exchanged and unmanaged tempers may flare.
- *Between at least two interdependent people*: From a systems theory perspective, people in a group are *interdependent*; what happens to one person has an impact on others in the group. A conflict between even just two people in a group of five will undoubtedly have an impact on the dynamics of the entire group.
- *Incompatible goals, scarce resources, and interference*: Conflict often occurs because two or more people want the same thing, yet both can't have it. If resources are scarce or if something or someone is blocking what others want, conflict is likely.
- *Achieving a goal*: People in conflict want something. Understanding what the people in conflict want is an important step toward finding a way to manage the conflict.

If a group experienced no conflict, it would have little to discuss. One value of conflict is that it makes a group test and challenge ideas. Conflict can, however, be detrimental to group interaction and group decision making. Conflict has a negative impact on a group

151

when it (1) keeps the group from completing its task, (2) interferes with the quality of the group's decision or productivity, or (3) threatens the existence of the group.[4]

Causes of Conflict

What causes conflict in groups and teams? Conflict results from differences between group members—differences in personality, perception, information, culture, and power or influence. Differences in group members' tolerance for taking risks also contributes to group conflict; some people are comfortable with risk, others aren't.[5] Because people are unique, their different attitudes, beliefs, and values will inevitably surface and cause conflict. No matter how much they try to empathize with others, people still have individual perspectives on the world. People also differ in the amount of knowledge they have on various topics. In groups, they soon realize that some members are more experienced or more widely read than others. This difference in information contributes to different attitudes. People also have different levels of power, status, and influence over others—differences that can increase conflict. People with power often try to use that power to influence others, and most do not like to be told what to do or think.

Conflict does not just "happen." You can often discern phases or stages of conflict development. Communication scholar B. Aubrey Fisher found that group deliberations can be organized around four phases: orientation, conflict, emergence, and reinforcement.[6] Several researchers have discovered that the conflict phase in groups often emerges in predictable stages.[7]

Conflict in groups can be directed toward people (interpersonal conflict), ideas (task conflict), or both people and ideas.[8] One research team found that conflict often occurs because of perceived inequity; if we think someone has more resources or is getting more than his or her fair share, conflict often results.[9] When the conflict is directed toward people, we may first try to manage the conflict by avoiding the individual or the topic of conflict. If the conflict is more task-centered, we usually first try more integrative approaches by seeking solutions that are agreeable to all parties. One of the prime effects of conflict and discord that occurs in groups is that the seeming lack of progress toward the group's goals results in a lack of motivation to keep working at a solution to resolve the conflict.[10] Two of the biggest triggers of conflict occur when people believe they haven't been treated fairly or that they are entitled to something that they didn't receive.

Misconceptions about Conflict

People often have misconceptions about the role of conflict in groups, because they think that conflict is bad and should be avoided. With higher rates of divorce, crime, and international political tensions, it is understandable that people view conflict negatively. The following discussion of myths will examine some of the feelings you may have about conflict and point out how a different attitude might improve the quality of your group discussions.[11]

Misconception 1: In Group Discussions, Conflict Should Be Avoided at All Costs   Conflict is a natural byproduct of communication; unless participants in your group share the same attitudes, beliefs, and values (an unlikely situation), there will be some conflict. Several researchers have discovered that conflict is an important, indeed useful, part of group communication.[12] Members who believe that conflict is unhealthy become frustrated when conflict erupts in a group. They should realize that conflict probably will occur and that it is a natural and healthy part of group communication.

Research suggests that when conflict occurs, group members are often challenged to research issues in greater detail and learn more about the issues under discussion.[13] In the end, conflict can enhance learning and spur more in-depth analysis.

Misconception 2: All Conflict Occurs Because People Do Not Understand One Another   Have you ever been in a heated disagreement with someone and found yourself blurting out "You just don't understand me!"? You easily assume that conflict occurs because another person does not understand your position. Not all conflict occurs because of misunderstandings, however. You may believe that if others really understood you, they would agree with you. Sometimes, however, conflict occurs because you *have* communicated your position clearly, it's just that others disagree with that position.[14] Yes, of course conflict can result from not understanding what someone says, but some conflicts intensify when a person clarifies his or her point.

Misconception 3: All Conflict Can Be Resolved   Perhaps you consider yourself an optimist. You like to think that problems can be solved. You may also feel that if a conflict arises, a compromise will resolve it. However, you should realize that not all conflicts can be resolved. Many disagreements are not simple. For example, fundamental differences between those who oppose abortion and those who support it can obviously not be resolved easily, if at all. Some ideologies are so far apart that resolving conflicts between them is unlikely. This does not mean that whenever a conflict arises in your group, you should despair and say, "Oh, well, no use trying to solve this disagreement." That position also oversimplifies the conflict-management process. Because some conflicts cannot be resolved, group members may have to focus on differences on which they *can* most likely reach agreement.

*T*YPES OF CONFLICT

Communication scholars Gerald Miller and Mark Steinberg identify three classic types of interpersonal conflict: (1) pseudo-conflict, (2) simple conflict, and (3) ego conflict.[15] They suggest that by identifying the type of conflict in a group, you will be better able to manage it. The following sections look at these three types of conflict in the context of a small group.

Pseudo-Conflict: When People Misunderstand One Another

Some conflict occurs because of misunderstandings. **Pseudo-conflict** occurs when individuals agree, but, because of poor communication, they believe that they disagree. *Pseudo* means fake or false. Thus, pseudo-conflict is conflict between people who really agree on issues but who do not understand that their differences are caused by misunderstandings or misinterpretations. "Oh, I see," said Mark after several minutes of heatedly defending a position he had suggested to the group. "I just misunderstood you. I guess we really agree."

To manage pseudo-conflict, consider these strategies:

■ Ask others what they mean by terms or phrases they use.
■ Establish a supportive rather than a defensive climate if misunderstandings occur.

Groups must find ways of managing conflict and channeling energy constructively. How might conflict be healthy?

■ Become an active listener by using the skills we discussed in Chapter 6:

Stop: Tune in to what your partner says rather than to your own thoughts.

Look: Pay attention to unspoken messages and monitor the emotional climate.

Listen: Focus on key details and link them to major ideas.

Question: Ask appropriate questions about information or ideas that are unclear to you.

Paraphrase content: To test your understanding, summarize your conception of what your partner says.

Paraphrase feelings: When appropriate, check your perception of your partner's feelings.

Research clearly supports the importance of good listening skills in small groups and teams.[16]

Simple Conflict: When People Disagree about Issues

Simple conflict occurs when two people's goals or ideas are mutually exclusive or incompatible. "Simple conflict involves one person saying, 'I want to do X,' and another saying, 'I want to do Y,' when X and Y are incompatible forms of behavior."[17] Although the conflict may seem far from simple, it's called "simple conflict" because the issues are clear and each party understands the problem. For example, in a corporation with only a limited amount of money to invest, one board member may want to invest in real estate and another may want to make capital improvements. The issue is clear; the individuals simply believe the company should take different courses of action.

When you understand what someone says but simply disagree with his or her point, consider using these skills:

■ Clarify your perception and your partner's perception of the message.

■ Keep the discussion focused on issues, not personalities.

- Use facts that support your point rather than opinions or emotional arguments.
- Use a structured problem-solving approach to organize the discussion: Define, analyze, identify several solutions, evaluate the solutions, select the best one.
- When appropriate, look for ways to compromise.
- Make the conflict a group concern rather than a conflict between just two people; ask others for information and data.
- If there are several issues, decide which issues are the most important, and then tackle them one at a time.
- Find areas of agreement.
- If possible, postpone decisions until additional research can be conducted. Such a delay may also lessen tensions.

Ego Conflict: When Personalities Clash

Of the types of conflict under discussion, the third is the most difficult to manage. **Ego conflict** occurs when individuals become defensive about their positions because they think they are being personally attacked. Ego conflicts are charged with emotion, and defensiveness in one individual often causes defensiveness in others. Underlying many ego conflicts are power struggles.[18] "Just because you're the chair of the group doesn't give *you* the right to railroad decision making," snaps Frank. "Well, you're just jealous. You think you should have been elected chairperson," retorts Ed. Based on his study of small group communication, Dennis Devine suggests that a disagreement about issues (simple conflict) can quickly evolve into a more emotionally charged discussion that becomes personal (ego conflict) unless group members consciously monitor how they interact with one another.[19]

If you are trying to mediate an ego conflict, find issues the disagreeing parties can agree on. Identify and emphasize the common ground between them, and encourage them to describe the sequence of events that created the conflict. A key immediate concern when ego conflict flares up in a group is to permit the disagreement to be verbalized without heightening the emotional tension. Just venting anger and irritation won't lessen tensions, nor will simply ignoring the conflict make the tension go away. Research clearly documents that the emotional climate in a group shapes how effectively the conflict will be managed.[20]

Here are additional strategies that may help manage the clash of egos:

- Encourage active listening.
- Return the discussion to the key issues under discussion.
- Try to turn the discussion into a problem to be solved rather than a conflict someone has to win.
- Seek to cool the emotional climate by lowering your voice and speaking more calmly, not in a patronizing way but in a way that signals your interest in dialogue rather than emotional argument.
- Be descriptive rather than evaluative or judgmental when discussing the issues of contention.
- Develop rules or procedures that permit differences of opinion.
- Unless the disagreement is central to the nature of the group, agree to disagree and return to areas of agreement.

EVIEW

SUMMARY OF THREE CONFLICT TYPES

SOURCE OF CONFLICT

Pseudo Conflict

Individuals misunderstanding each other's perceptions of a problem.

Simple Conflict

Disagreement over a course of action, idea, policy, or procedure.

Ego Conflict

Defense of ego: Individual believes he or she is being attacked personally.

SUGGESTIONS FOR MANAGING CONFLICT

Pseudo Conflict

1. Ask for clarification of perceptions.
2. Establish a supportive rather than a defensive climate.
3. Employ active listening:
   - *Stop*
   - *Look*
   - *Listen*
   - *Question*
   - *Paraphrase content*
   - *Paraphrase feelings*

Simple Conflict

1. Listen and clarify perceptions.
2. Make sure issues are clear to all group members.
3. Use a problem-solving approach to manage differences of opinion.
4. Keep discussion focused on the issues.
5. Use facts rather than opinions as evidence.
6. Look for alternatives or compromise positions.
7. Make the conflict a group concern rather than an individual concern.
8. Determine which conflicts are the most important to resolve.
9. If appropriate, postpone the decision while additional research is conducted. This delay also helps relieve tensions.

Ego Conflict

1. Let members express their concerns, but do not permit personal attacks.
2. Employ active listening.
3. Call for a cooling-off period.
4. Try to keep discussion focused on issues (simple conflict).
5. Encourage parties to be descriptive rather than evaluative and judgmental.
6. Use a problem-solving approach to manage differences of opinion.
7. Speak slowly and calmly.
8. Agree to disagree.

CONFLICT AND DIVERSITY IN SMALL GROUPS

At the root of most conflicts are differences—differences in understanding, perception, attitudes, or preferred action. Yet one of the key advantages of working in groups and teams is the opportunity to capitalize on the different perspectives that group and team members have. As the saying goes, if both of us agree, then one of us is irrelevant. The challenge is to use group diversity without becoming locked in intractable conflict. Although we've emphasized that not all conflict is bad and not all of it should be avoided, entrenched conflict decreases a group's effectiveness. The key to understanding how differences lead to conflict is understanding how group members communicate with one another when conflict occurs. Effective communication helps manage the conflict.[21] Two frameworks for describing cultural differences shed light on how some conflicts develop and fester.

Approaches to Conflict in Individualistic and Collectivistic Cultures

In Chapter 1 we noted that some cultures expect and nurture a team or collective approach to working with others; more individualistic cultures, such as that of the United States, place greater value on individual achievement.[22] This culturally learned difference can explain why individuals who place different values on the role of the individual or the team manage conflict as they do. Stella Ting-Toomey suggests that people in individualistic cultures are more likely to use direct, confrontational methods of managing disagreements than people who value a collective or team approach to group work.[23] She also suggests that people from collectivistic cultures, especially cultures that place considerable stock in nonverbal messages, are more comfortable with nonconfrontational and indirect methods of resolving differences. She suspects this difference may be because people from individualistic cultures tend to approach problem solving from a linear, step-by-step perspective, whereas people from collectivistic cultures often use a more intuitive problem-solving process. Ting-Toomey finds that people from individualistic cultures are more likely to use facts or principles as a basis for approaching conflict, negotiation, or persuasion situations.[24] People from collectivistic cultures adopt more relationship-based messages to manage differences. It is important for people from collectivistic cultures to save face by not being perceived as having lost a confrontation.

Approaches to Conflict in High-Context and Low-Context Cultures

In Chapter 4 we noted that a high-context culture is one in which considerable weight is given to the context of unspoken messages. In a low-context culture, such as that of the United States, more emphasis is placed on words and their explicit meaning than on implicit, nonverbal cues.[25] Researchers have found that people in low-context cultures give greater importance to task or instrumental issues than do people in high-context cultures.[26] In high-context cultures, the expressive or emotional aspects of managing conflict take on special importance. In expressive conflict, the goal is often to express feelings and release tension.[27] Keeping the relationship in balance, maintaining the friendship, and managing the emotional climate often take a higher priority in a high-context culture than achieving a particular outcome. Here again, saving face and avoiding embarrassment for all parties are more important in high-context cultures than in low-context cultures.

A similar conclusion has been put forward about differences between the way men and women manage disagreements in North America. Women tend to emphasize expressive goals in conflict, whereas men emphasize instrumental or task objectives.[28] Such a generalization needs to be tempered by considering each individual as unique, even though some gender patterns in conflict-management styles have been observed.

In your group deliberations, knowing that culture and gender differences exist can help you decide which strategies will be more effective than others. We caution you, however, to avoid stereotyping others by cultural, national, ethnic, or gender differences alone. For example, it would be most inappropriate to draw a stereotyped conclusion that all Asians will emphasize expressive rather than instrumental objectives in conflict. Similarly, taking an egocentric view (that is, assuming your perspective is correct) or an ethnocentric view

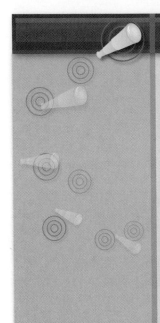

Cutting Edge Theory

MANAGING CONFLICT IN DIVERSE GROUPS

One of the most interesting questions that group communication researchers have explored is, how does diversity in group membership affect group performance? Although one of the benefits of working in groups is learning from diverse perspectives, do differences in race, ethnicity, culture, age, and gender enhance group quality? And how does the diversity of group members affect the conflict-management process?

Communication researcher Ralph Rodriguez suggests that it's not differences in such demographic characteristics as race, ethnicity, culture, age, or gender that affect group performance, but rather, differences in underlying values or approaches to problems.[29] But Leonard Karakowsky and Jacob Siegel offer a different explanation of how issues of diversity influence group discussion: They suggest that it's not the racial, ethnic, cultural makeup of the group, but the number or proportion of members of a particular minority who are present; if there are only a few of them, those in the minority may feel isolated and may thus be less likely to contribute to the discussion.[30] But if there is a sizable number of members of a particular minority in a group, then there is less likelihood that the minority opinion will be ignored. From a conflict-management perspective, those in the minority will be more likely to use an accommodating conflict-management style rather than a competing style.

Some research clearly suggests that group diversity can decrease team performance because of the potential for conflict and misunderstanding.[31] In small group interactions, your cultural expectations about how conflict should be managed may clash with those of someone from another culture who has different fundamental assumptions about managing or resolving differences. Other studies, however, suggest that racial, ethnic, cultural, gender, and age diversity enhance group performance because of the presence of a variety of viewpoints.[32]

(assuming your cultural methods of managing conflict are superior to those used by others) can be detrimental to effective communication.

CONFLICT-MANAGEMENT STYLES

Regardless of our cultural backgrounds or the types of conflict we experience, research suggests that each of us behaves in predictable ways to manage disagreements with others. What is your conflict-management style? Do you tackle conflict head-on or seek ways to remove yourself from the fray? Although these are not the only options available for managing conflict, reduced to its essence, conflict-management style often boils down to fight or flight.

Real-Life Applications

What are the best strategies for managing conflict that may stem from differing cultural, racial, ethnic, or gender- or age-based points of view? Consider the following suggestions.

If you are in the minority in a group:

■ Make sure that you tactfully yet assertively express your ideas, opinions, facts, and information to the group.
■ Ask the group to consider an alternative point of view. Your worldview is your fundamental outlook on reality. Help the group understand that those with a different life experience or racial, ethnic, or cultural worldview may see the issue differently.

If you are in the majority in the group:

■ Don't monopolize the conversation; be a gatekeeper by inviting those who have not spoken up to participate in the conversation.
■ Encourage people to share ideas and information via e-mail. Some quieter group members may be more likely to participate this way than voicing their opinion in person.
■ Be cautious of making sweeping generalizations about those who are from a culture different from your own. Each person's opinions and ideas are unique and may not necessarily be shared by others in the same racial or ethnic group.
■ Don't expect a person from a minority group to be a spokesperson for others in the same racial group. Don't, for example, turn to an African American student and say, "So, what do Blacks think about this topic?" You can ask what an individual may think or believe, but don't ask someone to speak for a particular group.

Ralph Kilmann and Kenneth Thomas suggest that your conflict-management style is based on two factors: (1) how concerned you are for other people and (2) how concerned you are for yourself.[33] These two factors, or dimensions, result in five conflict-management styles, shown in Figure 7.1. The five styles are (1) avoidance, (2) accommodation, (3) competition, (4) compromise, and (5) collaboration. The following sections examine each style in some detail.

Avoidance

Some people just don't like to deal with conflict, so they avoid it. The **avoidance** conflict-management style is one in which a person attempts to ignore disagreements. Why do people sometimes avoid conflict? People who sidestep conflict may not like the hassle of dealing

© 1999 Ted Goff

"And should there be a sudden loss of consciousness during this meeting, oxygen masks will drop from the ceiling."

with a difficult, uncomfortable situation, or they may be unassertive and afraid of standing up for their rights. At other times people avoid conflict because they don't want to hurt someone's feelings.

There are disadvantages to ignoring conflict. If people avoid directly addressing the conflict, the cause of the conflict may remain and emotions may escalate, making the conflict worse. Avoiding conflict may also signal to others that you simply don't care about the needs and interests of others in your group.

When may it be advantageous to avoid conflict? Taking a break from addressing a difficult, conflict-producing issue may be just what a group needs in some circumstances. Avoiding conflict could give the group time to cool off or to simply think about the issues that are the source of the conflict. If the conflict is about something trivial or unimportant, it may not be worth the time and effort to manage the conflict.

Accommodation

Some people simply give in to avoid a major blow-up or controversy. The **accommodation** style is another approach used to try to make conflict go away by giving in to the wishes of others. This style is sometimes called a "lose-win" approach. People may accommodate for several reasons. Perhaps they have a high need for approval, and they want others to like them. Or they may want to reduce threats to their sense of self-worth, so they decide to give in rather than defend their own views on the issue. Some people who accommodate appear to maintain their cool, doing what others want them to do, but in reality they are using accommodation to serve their own needs—to get other people to like them.

There may be times when it's disadvantageous to accommodate to others during conflict. Giving in too quickly to what others want may cause the group to make a bad decision because the issues underlying the conflict have not been thoroughly examined. Remember, conflict is not inherently bad; it is normal and to be expected. If several people quickly accommodate, then the group has lost a key advantage of using different points of view to hash out the best solution or decision.

FIGURE 7.1

Conflict-Management Styles. The five conflict management styles in relation to concern for others and concern for self.

Concern for Self

Competition

Collaboration

Compromise

Avoidance

Accommodation

Concern for Others

But there are also advantages to accommodating to the views of others. To agree with others can indicate that you are reasonable and that you want to help. If the issue is a trivial matter, it may be best to let it slide. If you realize that your position is wrong, then by all means go ahead and agree with others. If you admit your errors, then others may be more likely to admit their mistakes as well, which can help create a climate of trust. Stubbornly clinging to your position, even when you realize it's wrong, creates a defensive climate. Research suggests that one way to break an upward spiral of conflict is to find something about which members can agree.[34] So, accommodating can help the group develop a supportive climate; just don't make a habit of *always* accommodating quickly to squelch *all* disagreement.

Competition

People who have power or want more power often seek to compete with others so that others will accept their point of view as the best position. The **competition** conflict-management style occurs when people stress winning a conflict at the expense of one or more other people. Think of the competition style of conflict management as an arm wrestling match: One person tries to win so that the other person will lose. Winning is often about power, and power is about exerting control over others. Group members who seek power and position are often the ones who talk the most.[35]

There are several disadvantages to creating a group climate built on competition. The competitive style may result in greater defensiveness, messages that blame others, and efforts to control other group members. We've stressed that it's important for group and team members to have a common goal and to work toward the common good. If some group members seek to promote their own interests over the group interests, then the undue competition diminishes the overall power of the group.

It is not always wrong to compete: If you are certain that you have accurate information and that your insights and experiences can help the group achieve its goal, then stick to your position and seek to persuade others. Likewise, if some group members advocate a course of action that is immoral or illegal or that violates your personal instincts of what is right and wrong, it's appropriate to advocate a different course of action.

But competing with others can be a problem if you try to control without being sensitive to their needs or rights. To compete can also be detrimental if your method of competition is simply to outlast or out-shout others, threaten them, or use unethical means of persuasion, such as knowingly using false information to win. When assertiveness crosses the line into aggression (trying to force others to support your point), most group members find that the competition style becomes tiresome over the course of several group meetings.

Compromise

Often when people give up some of what they hope to achieve, no one gets precisely what they want. The **compromise** style of conflict management attempts to find a middle ground—a solution that somewhat meets the needs of all concerned. The word *somewhat* is important. Although on the surface a compromise can look like a "win-win" approach, it can also create a lose-lose result if nobody gets what he or she actually wants or needs. When trying to reach a compromise, you're really expected to lose something and win something simultaneously; you also expect others to lose and win. As shown in Figure 7.1, when you compromise, you have some concern for others, as well as some concern for yourself.

Although compromise sounds good in principle, it may not be best in practice. If, for example, no one feels that the compromise solution is a good one, then it probably isn't the best solution. If group members quickly try to reach a compromise without hashing out why they disagree, the group may lose some of its power to develop the best solution or decision. Compromise can be tempting because it seemingly gives in to each position. An old joke says that a camel is a horse designed by a committee. When groups compromise, the final product may not quite be what anyone had in mind, and it may not really solve the problem.

Although we've cautioned against too quickly reaching a compromise to manage conflict, there are obvious advantages to crafting a compromise solution. If a decision is needed quickly and a compromise can be achieved to meet the time demands of the situation, then compromise may be best. Compromise may help everyone save face, especially after a long, contentious conflict. Compromise may also maintain the balance of power in a group. A compromise on one issue can create a climate of cooperation and support that will serve the group well as it faces other challenges and disagreements.

Collaboration

When group members work side-by-side, rather then jostling for power and supremacy, the result may be a win-win outcome.[36] To **collaborate** is to have a high concern for both yourself and others. Group members who use a collaboration style of conflict management view conflict as a problem to be solved rather than as a game in which some people win and others lose. In the long run, groups that take the time to collaborate have better results.[37] Several research studies have found that when there are cultural differences among group members, a collaborative approach to conflict management works best.[38] Essential elements of a collaborative style include leaving personal grievances out of the discussion and describing problems without being judgmental or evaluative of other people. To compromise is to realize that each person loses something, as well as wins something; to collaborate is to take the time to find a solution in which all parties are comfortable with the outcome rather than harboring a sense of loss and sacrifice.

The main disadvantage of a collaboration style is the time, energy, and skill it takes to collaborate. Collaboration requires patience. If your group needs a quick decision, group members may find that taking time to reach a truly "win-win" outcome is more trouble than the issue at hand is worth. Additionally, some people may use the appearance of collaboration as a pretense to compete: A person who is skilled in negotiation and who uses words well can manipulate a collaborative effort and ultimately "win."

The obvious advantage to investing time and energy in collaboration is the prospect of both a better solution to issues facing the group and more satisfied group members. Collaboration is also advantageous when the group needs fresh, new ideas because the old approaches of trying to hammer out a solution simply haven't worked. Working to develop a true consensus on a solution that all individuals support is a good goal for most groups to consider.

It may sound like the collaborative approach is always the best conflict-management style to use. And we do think it's worth pursuing in many, if not most, cases. But the best conflict-management style depends on a variety of factors. Research suggests that most people find three things about conflict uncomfortable: (1) the participants fail to reach a clear solution, (2) the conflict is managed poorly, and (3) the participants avoid discussing the key issues and true sources of the conflict.[39] There is no specific conflict-management style that "works" in all situations. However, we will discuss research conclusions that identify specific strategies and practices for collaboration that increase the likelihood that all individuals involved in a conflict will be satisfied.

COLLABORATIVE CONFLICT MANAGEMENT: PRINCIPLES AND SKILLS

What principles and strategies can help a group manage conflict collaboratively? No simple checklist of techniques will miraculously resolve or manage group differences. Research supports the principle that focusing on shared interests and developing a collaborative conflict-management style are usually preferred over more combative conflict-management styles.[40] However, based on several studies of what works and what does not work when managing conflict, Roger Fisher and William Ury identified the four conflict-management principles discussed in the following sections.[41]

Separating the People from the Problem

When conflict becomes personal and egos become involved, it is very difficult to develop a positive climate in which differences can be managed. As we discussed in Chapter 5, if people feel they are being evaluated and strategically manipulated, they will respond with defensiveness. Separating the person from the problem means valuing the other individual as a person, treating her or him as an equal, and empathizing with her or his feelings. A key to valuing others is to use good listening skills. It is also useful to acknowledge the other person's feelings. Emotion is the fuel of conflict. Several scholars agree that efforts to manage our feelings facilitate the conflict-management process.[42]

One strategy for constructively expressing how you feel toward others in conflict is to use the approach John Gottman and his colleagues call the **X-Y-Z formula.**[43] According to this method, you say "When you do X, in situation Y, I feel Z." Here's an example: "When you are 15 minutes late to our staff meetings, I feel like you don't care about us or our meetings."

When you are the recipient of someone's wrath, you could use the X-Y-Z formula to explain how being yelled at makes it difficult for you to listen effectively. Trying to understand and manage your own and others' feelings helps separate personal issues from issues of substance. Joyce Hocker and William Wilmot suggest that when you are the receiver of someone's emotional outburst, you could consider the following actions.[44]

1. *Acknowledge the person's feelings.*
2. *Determine what specific behavior is causing the intense feelings.*
3. *Assess the intensity and importance of the issue.*
4. *Invite the other person to join you in working toward solutions.*
5. *Make a positive relational statement.*

Research also supports the value of using well-crafted arguments rather than emotion-laden opinions to help those in conflict sort through periods of contention.[45] No technique or simple formula exists to help you manage the challenging task of separating personal from substantive issues. Using good listening skills, acknowledging how others feel, and expressing your own feelings (without ranting and raving) make a good start toward mediating challenging conflict situations.

Focusing on Shared Interests

The words to one old song begin with the advice "Accentuate the positive. Eliminate the negative." A collaborative style focuses on areas of agreement and what all parties have in common.[46] If, for example, you are in a group debating whether public schools should distribute condoms, group members are more likely to have a productive discussion if they verbalize the goals and values they hold in common. A comment such as "We all agree that we want to reduce the spread of AIDS" might be a good place to start such a discussion.

Conflict is goal-driven. The individuals embroiled in the conflict want something. Unless goals are clear to everyone, it will be difficult to manage the conflict well. If you are involved in conflict, determine what your goals are. Then, identify your partner's goals. Finally, identify where goals overlap and where there are differences.

Do not confuse a goal with the strategy for achieving what you and a feuding group member want. For example, you may ask the group to make fewer copies on the copy machine. Your goal is to save money, because you are in charge of managing the office. Asking that your colleagues make fewer copies is a strategy that you have suggested for achieving your goal. Clarifying the underlying goal rather than only debating the merits of one strategy for achieving it should help unravel clashes over issues or personalities.

Generating Many Options to Solve Problems

During negotiation, group members who adamantly hold to only one solution create a competitive climate. Collaborative conflict managers are more likely to use brainstorming or the nominal-group technique (strategies we will discuss in Chapter 11) or other strategies for identifying a variety of options to manage the disagreement; they seek several solutions to overcome obstacles. Research by Shaila Miranda suggests that using e-mail or other electronic support systems to generate and evaluate ideas can also be a productive way of increasing the number of options a group or team might consider.[47] Sometimes feuding group members become fixated on only one approach to their goal. When conflict management degenerates into a verbal arm-wrestling match, where combatants perceive only one way to win, the conflict is less likely to be managed successfully.

Basing Decisions on Objective Criteria

Criteria are the standards for an acceptable solution to a problem. Typical criteria are such things as a limit to how much the solution can cost or a deadline by which a solution must be implemented. If, for example, group members agree that a solution must decrease the spread of AIDS but also not cost more than $1 million to implement, the group is using criteria to help identify an acceptable solution.

WHEN PEOPLE ARE NOT COOPERATIVE: DEALING WITH DIFFICULT GROUP MEMBERS

Evidence suggests that managers spend up to 25 percent of their time dealing with conflict.[48] One author boldly claims that 98 percent of the problems we face are "people problems."[49] Scholars call them "group deviants"; you may call them a pain in the neck. Even though we hope that you will not have to deal with difficult or cantankerous group members, we are

Case Study

The Department of Music faculty at a small Midwestern college received a gift of several thousand dollars to refurbish their faculty lounge, which was in need of updating. The old furniture, bare walls, and painted cement floor gave the lounge a cold and austere character. The department chair appointed a four-person committee to decide how to spend the money to refurbish the lounge. Committee members generally agreed about the overall color scheme, furniture style, and other redecorating decisions, with one notable exception: Two members wanted to carpet the floor and two wanted to tile it. The two carpet proponents thought that carpet would add warmth and texture to the room. The two in favor of tile thought tile would add a sleek, contemporary ambiance to the room; they thought it would also maintain the fine acoustics in the room—an important consideration, because the vocal faculty sometimes holds choir rehearsals in the lounge.

At first, the committee members remained polite yet firm in their positions. Luciano Povance and Rene Flambe, the two singers on the faculty, favored the tile. Joshua Chang and Sarah Bell, both violinists, wanted carpet. However, what at first seemed like a polite disagreement about floor covering choices began to deteriorate into more personal attacks.

Luciano and Rene accused the two violin faculty members of harboring a grudge against the vocal faculty. Joshua and Sarah felt a need not only to press for carpet but to defend the other string musicians on the faculty, who they felt were being attacked by the two vocalists. Although deciding between carpet and tile appeared to be a trivial issue, the conflict soon escalated to become less a conversation about tile versus carpet and more about the importance of vocal musicians versus string musicians.

Luciano, preferring to avoid conflict, withdrew from the conversation. Rene, on the other hand, felt quite strongly about the need for tile and pushed hard for her solution. Joshua thought maybe part of the room could be tile and part could be carpet, but when he saw how strongly Sarah felt about the importance of carpet, he withdrew his suggestion and continued to press for carpet.

The group appeared to be getting nowhere, and other department members became aware of the disagreement. Before long the feud about tile versus carpet spilled over into the rest of the faculty, and everyone started to take sides.

Practice in Applying Principles

1. Using the descriptions on pages 153–155 of different types of conflict, determine whether this is primarily a pseudo-conflict, a simple conflict, or an ego conflict.
2. Based on your analysis of the type of conflict, what specific strategies discussed on pages 153–155 should group members use to help manage their differences?
3. What hints of different conflict-management styles are present in the group? How do those differences in style affect the dynamics of the conflict?
4. If you were the department chair and heard about the deadlocked group, what would you do to help manage the disagreement? What specific strategies described on pages 176–179 could be used to help the group develop consensus?
5. Identify an example from your own group experience in which a topic that seemed on the surface to be trivial became a larger issue that symbolized deep differences within the group.

not naive. Not all group members will separate people from the problem, focus on shared interests, be eager to search for more alternatives, or base decisions on objective criteria. Our individualistic cultural traditions often make it challenging to develop collaborative groups and teams. It sometimes takes special "people skills" to deal with some group members. Drawing on the principles and skills of the collaborative conflict-management style, we offer the following tips for dealing with the more difficult group members.

Manage Your Emotions

When we are emotionally charged, we may find it difficult to practice rational, logical methods of managing conflict. One researcher offers this description of what happens to our bodies when we become upset:

> Our adrenaline flows faster and our strength increases by about 20 percent. . . . The veins become enlarged and the cortical centers where thinking takes place do not perform nearly as well. . . . the blood supply to the problem-solving part of the brain is severely decreased because, under stress, a greater portion of blood is diverted to the body's extremities.[50]

It's normal to feel angry when someone seems constantly to say or do things that make you feel judged or evaluated. In that situation, you may say or do something you later regret. Although some people advocate expressing anger, to "clear the air," expressing uncensored emotions can make matters worse. On the other hand, communication researchers Barbara Gayle and Raymond Preiss confirmed what most of us intuitively know: Unresolved conflict is a breeding ground for emotional upheaval in groups and organizations.[51] Although it's been said that time heals all wounds, there are instances when ignoring hurt feelings can make the conflict escalate. Leaders and team members need to recognize when to be active in addressing emotional volatility.[52]

Consider the following five strategies for managing your emotions during conflict.

1. *Be aware of your anger level.* Candidates for anger management programs don't monitor their emotions well; before they know it, their emotions boil over. Uncensored emotional outbursts rarely enhance the quality of communication. An emotional purge may make you feel empowered momentarily, but it usually only escalates conflict and tension.

2. *Breathe.* It may sound too simple, but it works. As you become aware of your increased emotional arousal, take a slow, deep breath. A deep breath can help calm you and manage the physiological changes that adrenaline creates. A slow, deep breath can help soothe your spirit and give you another focus besides lashing out at others.

3. *Use self-talk.* Your thoughts are linked to your feelings. You can affect your emotional state by first being aware that you are becoming upset and then telling yourself to calm down and stay focused on the issues at hand. Eleanor Roosevelt's observation that "no one can make you feel inferior without your consent" is an acknowledgment of the power of self-talk to affect your emotional response to what others say and do.

4. *Monitor your nonverbal messages.* Emotions are usually communicated nonverbally rather than verbally. Monitoring your emotional signals (such as noting whether your voice gets louder, your facial expression less friendly, and your gestures more dramatic or emphatic) can help de-escalate an emotionally charged situation before it erupts. Speaking more slowly and calmly, maintaining direct eye contact, and adopting a neutral facial expression can help ensure a climate of civility and decorum. We're not suggesting that you manipulate your nonverbal behavior so that you feel inauthentic or that you speak in a patronizing tone. However, being aware of how your nonverbal

messages contribute to the emotional climate can help bring the emotional temperature down a degree or two.

5. *Avoid personal attacks.* When conflict gets personal (ego conflict) it becomes more difficult to manage. Calling people names and hurling negative personal messages at others usually adds to a deteriorating emotional group climate.

Don't **gunny-sack**. Gunny-sacking is dredging up old problems and issues from the past, like pulling them out of an old bag, or gunny sack, to use against your partner. Bringing up old problems that can't be changed now only serves to make matters worse, especially when emotions are raw. Focus on the present and what can be discussed now and changed in the future, rather than reliving past problems.

Describe What Is Upsetting You

Try to avoid lashing back at the offending person. Use a descriptive "I" message to explain to the other person how you are feeling; for example, "I find it difficult to listen to you when you raise your voice at me," or "I notice that is the fourth time you have interrupted me when I was trying to explain my point." Keep in mind that the goal is not to increase the conflict. "You shouldn't yell at me" or "You shouldn't interrupt me" are examples of "you" statements. Such statements are evaluative and are likely to increase resentment and anger.

Disclose Your Feelings

After describing the behavior that offends or irritates you, disclose how you feel when the behavior occurs: "When I'm interrupted, I feel that my opinion isn't valued" or "I become increasingly frustrated when I try to contribute to our meeting but I don't feel you are listening." When disclosing your feelings, try to avoid emotional overstatement such as "I've

Collaborating Ethically: What Would You Do?

What would you do in the following situation? You've been assigned by your boss to be the project leader on a major new company initiative. One of the members of your group clearly is not happy with your leadership (in fact, he wanted to be assigned project leader) and has loudly and consistently voiced his objections to many of your decisions. At the last meeting, he directly attacked your credibility by saying, "You have no idea what you're talking about. You haven't done your homework. Your actions will make a mess of this entire project." The project is almost finished. You only have two more weeks of meetings. How do you handle this situation? Do you just go on with your work and ignore the bluster and insulting comments, since the project is about over (avoidance style)? Do you assertively seek to put a stop to the comments (competitive style)? Or do you try to have a heart-to-heart conversation and seek a positive resolution to the tension (collaborative style)?

What would you do?

never been so upset in all my life." Such hyperbole raises the emotional stakes and can trigger a new volley of retorts.

Two researchers have found that simply prefacing a statement with the word "I," as we suggested you do when using "I" language, may sometimes be too subtle to help defuse a conflict.[53] You may need to add a longer justification when you provide negative, emotional information to another group member. We call this using *extended "I" language*, which is a brief preface to a feedback statement. You might begin by saying something like "I don't want you to take this the wrong way. I really do care about you and I need to share something with you," or "I don't think this is completely your fault. Yet I find myself becoming more frustrated when I hear that you've talked to others about me." These extended comments may have a better chance of taking the sting out of a negative message than simply beginning a sentence with the word *I* instead of the word *you*. There are no magic words that will de-escalate conflict. Being sensitive and thoughtful about how others may respond to your messages can help you express your ideas in ways that are more likely to be heard rather than immediately rejected.

Return to the Issue of Contention

The only way to return to a collaborative style is to get back to the issue that is fueling the disagreement. Avoiding the issue will not resolve the issue.[54] Sometimes one of those in conflict has a hidden agenda that makes it difficult to confront the key issues. A wise person once said, "Often what we fight about is not what we fight about." Although an argument may seem on the surface to be about a substantive issue—such as which solution to adopt or whose research to use—the underlying issue may be about power and control. Only if the underlying issue is exposed and addressed will the conflict be managed.

These general suggestions provide basic principles for dealing with difficult group members, but you may need more specific strategies for managing such people. Table 7.1 offers several specific ways to deal with group members who perform such self-focused roles as dominator and blocker or who are irresponsible or unethically aggressive. Remember: *No one can change the behavior of another person*. But competent communicators have the knowledge, skill, and motivation to respond appropriately and effectively to others' behavior, even when that behavior is difficult, self-serving, or unethical.

GROUPTHINK: CONFLICT AVOIDANCE

Groupthink is the illusion of agreement[55]—a type of thinking that occurs when a group strives to minimize conflict, maximize cohesiveness, and reach a consensus without critically testing, analyzing, and evaluating ideas. Columnist William Safire notes that the term *groupthink* first appeared in a 1952 *Fortune* magazine article by William H. Whyte, Jr.[56] When a group reaches decisions too quickly, it does not properly consider the implications of its decisions. Groupthink results in an ineffective consensus; too little conflict often lowers the quality of group decisions. When a group does not take time to examine the positive and negative consequences of alternative decisions, the quality of its decision is likely to suffer.[57]

Sociologist Irving Janis believes that many poor decisions and policies are the result of groupthink.[58] In 1999, eleven students at Texas A&M University were tragically killed when the traditional pre-football-game bonfire they were building collapsed; many other students

TABLE 7.1   **How to Deal with Difficult Group Members**

What the Group Member Does	Options for Managing the Problem
Dominates: Tries to tell people what to do without seeking permission from the group; tells rather than asks; monopolizes the conversation	1. Use gatekeeping skills to invite other group members to participate; explicitly state that you'd like to hear what others have to say. 2. In private, ask the dominating group member to be less domineering and to give others an opportunity to participate. 3. Channel the dominator's energy by giving him or her a specific task to accomplish, such as recording the minutes of the meeting or periodically summarizing the group's progress. 4. The group or team may collectively decide to confront the domineering member, clearly describe the behavior that the group perceives as inappropriate.
Blocks Progress: Has a negative attitude. Is often stubborn and disagreeable without a clear reason. When the group is making progress, the blocker seems to keep the group from achieving its goal.	1. Ask for specific evidence as to why the blocker does not support the group's position. 2. Calmly confront the blocker and explain how consistently being negative creates a negative group climate. 3. Use humor to help defuse the tension that the blocker creates. 4. Assign the blocker the role of devil's advocate before the group makes a decision; giving the blocker permission to be negative at certain times can help the group avoid groupthink.
Is Irresponsible: Does not carry through with assignments; is often absent from or late to meetings	1. Speak to the offending group member privately and convince him or her to pull his or her own weight. Explain how his or her irresponsibility is hurting other group members and the overall success of the group. 2. Assign a mentor. Call the person or send an e-mail to remind him or her to attend the meeting. Ask for a progress report on the status of assigned work. Work one-on-one trying to help the irresponsible member see how his or her behavior hurts the group. Provide more structure. 3. If confronting the offending group member first privately and then collectively does not get results, ask for help from a supervisor or instructor. 4. Clarify who will get the credit. To minimize social loafing, tell the offending member that when the final product is complete, the group will clearly indicate her or his lack of participation.
Is Unethically Aggressive: Is verbally abusive toward other group members or purposefully disconfirms others. Tries to take credit for the work of others	1. Do not accept unethical behavior in silence. Immediately describe the offensive behavior to the aggressor, and indicate its negative effect on individuals or the entire group. 2. Several group members may confront the offending group member collectively. The group as a whole should not tolerate mean-spirited actions toward others. 3. Become an advocate for other group members; support those who are attacked or singled out. 4. Seek help from an instructor or supervisor or from someone in authority outside the group to stop the unethical, offending behavior. Sometimes a bully only responds to a person of greater power.

were injured. Investigators found that a structural engineering professor had for years tried to warn university officials that the bonfire's design was unsafe; other engineering faculty members who also thought the bonfire was a disaster waiting to happen finally stopped trying to influence the university because no one would listen.[59] The decision to launch the flawed space shuttle *Challenger* on that unforgettable January morning in 1986 was also tinged by groupthink.[60] Corporate executives and others did not challenge assumptions in the construction and launch procedures; disaster resulted. The pressure for consensus resulted in groupthink. In hindsight, one contributing cause of the 2002 *Columbia* shuttle disaster was believed to have been groupthink as well.

Yet another example: The Congressional 9/11 commission, investigating why U.S. intelligence organizations were not as vigilant as they should have been in anticipating the terrorists attacks on September 11, 2001, concluded that groupthink was a contributing factor. The commission found that leaders and analysts in intelligence organizations reached conclusions about the presence of weapons of mass destruction in Iraq that were based on unchallenged assumptions and unverified information.[61]

The Texas A&M bonfire tragedy, the *Challenger* and *Columbia* shuttle disasters, and the terrorist attacks of September 11 are dramatic examples of how groupthink has contributed to faulty decision making. The groups and teams in which you participate are equally susceptible to this illusion of agreement.

Groups with highly esteemed leaders are most prone to groupthink. Because these leaders' ideas are often viewed as sacrosanct, few members disagree with them. A group may also suffer from groupthink if its members consider themselves highly cohesive and take pride in getting along well with one another and providing support and encouragement for members' ideas.

One research study found that groupthink is most likely to occur when (1) the group is apathetic about the task, (2) group members have low expectations about their ability to be successful, (3) there is at least one highly qualified, credible group member, (4) one group member is exceptionally persuasive, and (5) there is a norm that group members should conform rather than express negative opinions.[62]

Although some small group communication scholars question the theoretical soundness of the theory of groupthink, it continues to serve as a useful and practical way of helping groups understand why they make poor decisions.[63]

Symptoms of Groupthink

Can you identify groupthink when it occurs in groups to which you belong? Here are some of the common symptoms of groupthink.[64]

Critical Thinking Is Not Encouraged or Rewarded   If you are working in a group that considers disagreement or controversy counterproductive, chances are that groupthink is alive and well in that group. One advantage of working in groups is having an opportunity to evaluate ideas so that you can select the best possible solution. If group members seem proud that peace and harmony prevail at their meetings, they may suffer from groupthink.

Members Believe That Their Group Can Do No Wrong   During the 1972 presidential election, members of the committee to reelect President Nixon did not consider that they might fail to obtain information from Democratic headquarters. They thought their group was invulnerable. But the burglary of the Watergate office and the subsequent coverup ultimately led to the resignation of President Nixon. This sense of invulnerability is a classic symptom of groupthink. Another symptom is that members dismiss potential threats to the group as minor problems. If your group is consistently overconfident in dealing with problems that may interfere with its goals, it may suffer from groupthink.[65]

Members Are Too Concerned About Justifying Their Actions Members of highly cohesive groups like to feel that they are acting in their group's best interests. Therefore, groups that experience groupthink like to rationalize their positions on issues. A group susceptible to groupthink is too concerned about convincing itself that it has made proper decisions in the past and will make good decisions in the future.

Members Apply Pressure to Those Who Do Not Support the Group Have you ever voiced an opinion contrary to the majority opinion and quickly realized that other members were trying to pressure you into going along with the rest of the group? Groups prone to groupthink have a low tolerance for members who do not "go along." They see controversy and conflict injected by a dissenting member as a threat to *esprit de corps*. Therefore, a person voicing an idea different from the group's position is often punished.[66]

Sometimes pressure is subtle, taking the form of frowns or grimaces. Group members may not socialize with the dissenting member, or they may not listen attentively to the dissident. Usually their first response is to try to convince this member to reconsider his or her position. But if the member still does not agree with the others, he or she may be expelled from the group. Of course, if a group member is just being stubborn, the others should try to reason with the dissenter. Do not, however, be too quick to label someone as a troublemaker simply because he or she has an opinion different from that of other group members.

Members Often Believe That They Have Reached a True Consensus A significant problem in groups that suffer from groupthink is that members are not aware of the phenomenon. They think they have reached genuine consensus. For example, suppose you and your friends are trying to decide which movie to rent on Friday night. Someone suggests *The Lord of the Rings.* Even though you've already seen the movie, you don't want to be contentious, so you agree with the suggestion. Other group members also agree.

After your group has seen the movie, you overhear another one of your friends say, "I enjoyed the movie better when I saw it the first time." After a quick poll of the group, you discover that most of your friends had already seen the movie! They agreed to see it only because they did not want to hurt anyone's feelings. They thought everyone else was in agreement. Although the group appeared to reach consensus, only a few people actually agreed with the decision. Therefore, even if you think that the rest of the group agrees and that you are the only dissenter, your group could still be experiencing groupthink. Just because your group seems to have reached a consensus does not necessarily mean that all the members truly agree.

Members Are Too Concerned About Reinforcing the Leader's Beliefs Leaders of small groups often emerge because they suggest some of the best ideas, motivate group members, or devote themselves to group goals more than others do. If group members place too much emphasis on the credibility or infallibility of their leader, groupthink may occur. Leaders who like to be surrounded by yes people (who always agree with their ideas) lose the advantage of having their ideas tested. Most people do not like criticism and do not like to be told that their ideas are inept or inappropriate. Therefore, group leaders are understandably attracted to those who agree with them. Leaders sensitive to the problem of groupthink will solicit and tolerate all viewpoints because testing the quality of solutions requires different opinions.

One researcher has found empirical support for the symptoms of groupthink. Rebecca Cline found that groups exhibiting groupthink do express more agreement without clarification and also use simpler and fewer substantiated agreements than groups that avoid groupthink.[67] She also found that groups that experience groupthink spend about 10 percent more of their discussion time making statements of agreement or disagreement than other groups. Groups that experience groupthink perpetuate the illusion of agreement by sprinkling in frequent comments such as "Yeah, I see what you're saying," "That's right," or "Sure."

*R*EVIEW

SYMPTOMS OF GROUPTHINK

- Critical thinking is not encouraged or rewarded.
- Members think their group can do no wrong.
- Members are too concerned about justifying their actions.
- Members apply pressure to those who do not support the group.
- Members often believe that they have reached a true consensus.
- Members are too concerned about reinforcing the leader's beliefs.

Suggestions for Reducing Groupthink

How can you reduce the chances of groupthink occurring in your group? Consider the following specific suggestions, based on Janis's initial observations, as well as on the theories and the research of several small group communication researchers.

Encourage Critical, Independent Thinking   The leader should make clear that he or she does not want the group to reach agreement until each member has critically evaluated the

Technicians examine debris from the space shuttle *Columbia* at Cape Canaveral. Some blame the disaster, in part, on groupthink at NASA.

issues. Most group leaders want to command the respect of their groups, but a leader's insistence that the group always agree with him or her does not encourage respect; instead, it may demonstrate a fear of disagreement. Thus, if you find yourself a leader in a small group, you should encourage disagreement—not just for the sake of argument, but to eliminate groupthink. Even if you are not a leader, you can encourage a healthy discussion by voicing any objections you have to the ideas being discussed. Do not permit instant, uncritical agreement in your group.

Be Sensitive to Status Differences That May Affect Decision Making   Group members should not yield to status differences when evaluating ideas, issues, and solutions to problems. Instead, they should consider the merits of suggestions, weigh evidence, and make decisions about the validity of ideas without being too concerned about the status of those making suggestions. Of course, this is easier said than done.

Numerous studies suggest that a person with more status is going to be more persuasive.[68] Cereal companies know this when they hire famous athletes to sell breakfast food. The implied message is "Don't worry about the quality of the product. If this Olympic gold-medal winner eats this stuff, you'll like it too." The athlete's fame and status do not necessarily make the cereal good; however, you still might buy the cereal, making a decision based on emotion rather than fact. Group members sometimes make decisions this way, too. Avoid agreeing with a decision just because of the status or credibility of the person making it. Evaluate the quality of the solution on its own merits.

Invite Someone from Outside the Group to Evaluate the Group's Decision-Making Process   Sometimes an objective point of view from outside the group can identify unproductive group norms more readily than group members can and thereby help prevent groupthink.[69] Many large companies hire consultants to evaluate organizational decision making, but you do not have to be part of a multinational corporation to ask someone to analyze your group's decision-making process. Ask someone from outside your group to sit in on one of your meetings. At the end of the meeting, ask the observer to summarize his or her observations and evaluations of the group. An outside observer may make some members uncomfortable, but if you explain why the visitor is there, the group will probably accept the visitor and eagerly await objective observations.

Assign a Group Member the Role of Devil's Advocate   If no disagreement develops in a group, members may enjoy getting along and never realize that their group suffers from groupthink. If you find yourself in a group of pacifists, play devil's advocate by trying to raise objections and potential problems. Assign someone to consider the negative aspects of a suggestion before it is implemented. It could save the group from groupthink and enhance the quality of the decision.

Ask Group Members to Subdivide into Small Groups to Consider Potential Problems with the Suggested Solutions   In large groups, not all members will be able to voice their objections and reservations. The U.S. Congress does most of its work in small committees. Members of Congress realize that in order to hear and thoroughly evaluate bills and resolutions, small groups of representatives must work together in committees. If you are working in a group too large for everyone to discuss the issues, suggest breaking into groups of two or three, with each group composing a list of objections to the proposals. The lists could be forwarded to the group secretary, who then could weed out duplicate objections and identify common points of contention. Even in a group of seven or eight, two subcommittees could evaluate the recommendations of the group. Group members should be able to

Virtual Communication

Whether you're communicating in person or via the Internet, the same factors that contribute to conflict can arise. But the fact that virtual team members work with words and usually do not see or hear nonverbal communication may have an effect on how they manage conflict.

One research group found that when groups attempt to negotiate differences in computer-mediated settings, the use of forcing behavior decreases as the conflict escalates.[70] These researchers also found that as conflict increases in virtual communication situations, the negotiators tend to avoid the conflict. During face-to-face conflict negotiations, there is greater use of controlling behavior than in computer-mediated situations. And in face-to-face settings there is more of a reciprocal, tit-for-tat escalation of conflict than in mediated settings.

Another study found that when attempting to brainstorm and generate ideas, members of computer-mediated groups experience more negative conflict management behaviors than those in face-to-face groups; the computer-mediated groups are less effective in managing conflict.[71] The results of this study suggest that it may be more challenging to manage conflict in a productive way in computer-mediated groups than in face-to-face groups.

Research by Mitzi Montoya-Weiss, Anne Massey, and Michael Song explored the effects on conflict-management styles of participating in virtual teams—whether team members are avoidant, competitive, or collaborative.[72] The researchers made several observations:

- It's not a good idea to suppress ideas and suggestions that are in conflict with those of other virtual team members. Avoiding conflict had a significantly negative effect on team performance. Confronting conflict directly typically resulted in a more positive team outcome.
- Team members' attempts to accommodate or express agreement as a means of avoiding conflict had no major effects. The researchers thought that in the absence of nonverbal cues, it may not have been clear whether group members were actively trying to accommodate one another. Nonverbal messages are important in conveying relational messages of agreement and accommodation.
- Without the accompanying nonverbal cues, team members' attempts to negatively evaluate others had less of a sting. It seems that expressing negative ideas may sometimes be more acceptable to virtual team members communicating via the Internet because nonverbal messages are not reinforcing the negative messages.
- Collaboration is perceived as a positive strategy in both virtual teams and face-to-face teams.
- Attempting to reach a compromise, especially an early compromise before team members have a chance to discuss the issues, is not as productive in virtual groups as it is in face-to-face groups.

In summary, virtual groups should closely monitor their approaches to managing disagreement. Because of the absence of the relationship cues that are usually available in face-to-face meetings, the conflict-management styles used in face-to-face settings may have different outcomes when used in virtual teams.

participate frequently and evaluate the issues carefully. Individuals could also write down their objections to the proposed recommendations and then present them to the group.

One technique that may reduce groupthink is to have groups divide into two teams to debate an issue. The principle is simple: Develop a group structure that encourages critical thinking. Vigilant thinking fosters quality decisions.

Consider Using Technology to Help Your Group Gather and Evaluate Ideas   One study found that having group members share and test ideas and evidence through the use of computerized group decision support system (GDSS) rather than always meeting face to face may facilitate more extensive testing of ideas and opinions.[73] Some of the groups you participate in may not have access to such systems. Considerable research, however, suggests that the quality of group decisions can be enhanced if group members contribute ideas by using e-mail or other software programs to help gather and evaluate ideas.[74] Research also suggests, though, that being separated from other group members geographically can increase the likelihood of conflict.[75] One advantage to using GDSS methods in reducing groupthink is that ideas can be presented anonymously. Certain software programs let group members share ideas without revealing whether a member is the boss or the new intern. GDSS technology also helps separate the process of generating ideas from evaluating ideas.

Identifying and correcting groupthink should help improve the quality of your group's decisions by capitalizing on opposing viewpoints. A textbook summary of suggestions for dealing with groupthink may lead you to think that this problem can be corrected easily. It cannot. Because many people think that conflict should be avoided, they need specific guidelines for identifying and avoiding groupthink. In essence, be critical of ideas, not people. Remember that some controversy is useful. A decision-making group uses conflict to seek the best decision everyone can agree on—it seeks consensus. The last section of this chapter discusses managing conflict in the search for consensus.

*R*EVIEW

SUGGESTIONS FOR REDUCING GROUPTHINK

- Encourage critical, independent thinking.
- Be sensitive to status differences that may affect decision making.
- Invite someone from outside the group to evaluate the group's decision-making process.
- Assign a group member the role of devil's advocate.
- Ask group members to subdivide into small groups (or to work individually) to consider potential problems with suggested solutions.
- Use e-mail and other electronic technology to permit people to make anonymous contributions; this will reduce the effects of group member status differences.

*C*ONSENSUS: REACHING AGREEMENT THROUGH COMMUNICATION

Some conflict is inevitable in groups, but this does not mean that all group discussions are doomed to end in disagreement. Conflict can be managed. **Consensus** occurs when all group members support and are committed to a decision. Even if a group does not reach consensus on key issues, it is not necessarily a failure. Good decisions can certainly emerge from groups whose members do not all completely agree on decisions. The U.S. Congress, for example, rarely achieves consensus; that does not mean, however, that its legislative process is ineffective.

Although conflict and controversy can improve the quality of group decision making, it is worthwhile to aim for consensus.[76] A few words about consensus may help you form more realistic expectations about working in small groups. The following sections also suggest some specific ways to help your group reach agreement.

The Nature of Consensus

Consensus should not come too quickly. If it does, your group is probably a victim of groupthink. Nor does consensus usually come easily. Sometimes group agreement is built on agreements on minor points raised during the discussion. To achieve consensus, group members should try to emphasize these areas of agreement. This can be a time-consuming process, and some members may lose patience before they reach agreement. Regardless of how long a group takes to reach consensus, consensus generally results from careful and thoughtful communication between members of the group.

Is taking the time to reach consensus worth the effort? Groups that reach consensus (not groupthink) and also effectively use good discussion methods, such as testing and challenging evidence and ideas, achieve a better quality decision.[77] Evidence also suggests that groups that achieve consensus are likely to maintain agreement even after several weeks.[78]

To achieve consensus, some personal preferences must be surrendered for the overall well-being of the group. Group members must decide, both individually and collectively, whether they can achieve consensus. If two or three members refuse to change their minds on their positions, the rest of the group may decide that reaching consensus is not worth the extra time. Some group communication theorists suggest that groups might do better to postpone a decision if consensus cannot be reached, particularly if the group making the decision will also implement it. If several group members oppose the solution, they will be less eager to put it into practice. Ultimately, if consensus cannot be reached, a group should generally abide by the decision of the majority.

Suggestions for Reaching Consensus

Communication researchers agree that group members usually go through considerable effort before reaching consensus. Using specific communication strategies may help members more readily foster consensus in group and team meetings.[79]

We suggest you keep three key pieces of advice in mind when striving for group consensus.

1. Because groups have a tendency to get off track, help keep the group oriented toward its goal. Groups and teams often fail to reach agreement because they engage in discussion that is not relevant to the issue at hand—groups digress.

2. Be other-oriented and sensitive to the ideas and feelings of others. Listen without interrupting. Make an honest effort to set aside your own ideas and seek to understand the ideas of others.

3. Promote honest interaction and dialogue. Genuine consensus is more likely to occur if group and team members honestly express their thoughts and feelings; withholding ideas and suggestions may lead to groupthink.

How to Orient the Group Toward Its Goal   The following strategies can help your group reach consensus by staying focused and on task.

- *Use metadiscussional phrases:* **Metadiscussion** literally means discussion about discussion. In other words, a metadiscussional statement focuses on the discussion process rather than on the topic under consideration.[80] Metadiscussional statements include "Aren't we getting a little off the subject?" or "John, we haven't heard from you yet. What do you think?" or "Let's summarize our areas of agreement." These statements contain information and advice about the problem-solving process rather than about the issue at hand. Several studies show that groups whose members help orient the group toward its goal by (1) relying on facts rather than opinions, (2) making useful, constructive suggestions, and (3) trying to resolve conflict are more likely to reach agreement than groups whose members do not try to keep the group focused on its goal.[81]

  One of the essential task competencies identified in Chapter 1 is to maintain a focus on the group's task. Metadiscussional phrases help to keep the group or team focused on the task or meeting agenda. This is an exceptionally powerful and useful skill to learn because you can offer metadiscussional statements even if you are not the designated leader of the group.

- *Keep the focus on the group's goal rather than on specific strategies to achieve the goal:* Focusing on shared interests and reminding the group what the goals are can help the group move on from debating only one or two strategies to achieve the goal. Group members sometimes fall in love with an idea or strategy and won't let go of it. In order to move forward, explicitly and frequently remind the group of the overarching goal you are trying to achieve.

- *Display known facts for all group members to see:* Consider using a chalkboard, Power-Point, flipchart, or overhead projector to display what is really known about the issues confronting the group. When group members cannot agree, they often retreat to restating opinions rather than advocating an idea based on hard evidence. If all group members can be reminded of what is known, consensus may be more easily obtained.

  One way to display facts is to use the is/is not technique. Draw a line down the middle of the chalkboard or flip chart. On one side of the line, note what is known about the present issue. On the other side, identify what is unknown or is mere speculation. Separating facts from speculation can help group members focus on data rather than unproven inferences.[82]

- *Do not wait until the very end of the deliberations to suggest solutions:* Research suggests that groups that delay identifying specific solutions until the very end of the discussion are less likely to reach consensus than those groups that think about solutions earlier in the deliberations.[83] Of course, before jumping to solutions, groups need to analyze and assess the present situation.

How to Be Other-Oriented: Listen to the Ideas of Others   What follows are tips and suggestions to help manage the relational tension that usually occurs when groups can't reach consensus.

- *Give your idea to the group:* People often defend a solution or suggestion just because it is theirs. Here is a suggestion that may help you develop a more objective point of view: If you find yourself becoming defensive over an idea you suggest, assume that your idea has become the property of the group; it no longer belongs to you. Present your position as clearly as possible, then listen to other members' reactions and consider them carefully before you push for your point. Just because people disagree with your idea does not necessarily mean they respect you less.

- *Do not assume that someone must win and someone must lose:* When discussion becomes deadlocked, try not to view the discussion in terms of "us" versus "them" or "me" versus "the group." Try not to view communication as a game that someone wins and others lose. Be willing to compromise and modify your original position. Of course, if compromising means finding a solution that is marginally acceptable to everyone but does not really solve a problem, then seek a better solution.

- *Use group-oriented rather than self-oriented pronouns:* Harry likes to talk about the problem as *he* sees it. He often begins sentences with phrases such as "I think this is a good idea" or "My suggestion is to. ..." Studies suggest that groups that reach consensus generally use more pronouns like *we, us,* and *our,* while groups that do not reach consensus use more pronouns like *I, me, my,* and *mine.*[84] Using group-oriented words can foster cohesiveness.

- *Avoid opinionated statements that indicate a closed mind:* Communication scholars consistently find that opinionated statements and low tolerance for dissenting points of view inhibit agreement. This is especially apparent when the opinionated person is the discussion leader. A group with a less opinionated leader is more likely to reach agreement. Remember that using facts and relying on information obtained by direct observation are probably the best ways to avoid making opinionated statements.

- *Clarify misunderstandings:* Although not all disagreements arise because conflicting parties fail to understand one another, misunderstanding another's meaning sometimes creates conflict and adversely affects group consensus. Dealing with misunderstanding is simple. Ask a group member to explain a particular word or statement that you do not understand. Constantly solicit feedback from your listeners. During periods of disagreement, consider repeating the previous speaker's point and ask if you've got it right before you state your position on an issue. This procedure can become time-consuming and stilted if overused, but it can help when misunderstandings about meanings arise. It may also be helpful for you to remember that meanings are conveyed through people, not words. Stated another way, the meaning of a word comes from a person's unique perspective, perception, and experience.

- *Emphasize areas of agreement:* When the group gets bogged down in conflict and disagreement, it may prove useful to stop and identify the issues and information on which group members *do* agree. One study found that groups whose members were able to keep refocusing the group on areas of agreement, particularly following episodes of disagreement, were more likely to reach consensus than groups that continued to accentuate the negative.[85]

How to Promote Honest Interaction and Dialogue   To help groups and teams avoid a false consensus (groupthink) and to share ideas in a climate of openness and honesty, consider these suggestions.

- *Do not change your mind too quickly just to avoid conflict:* Although you may have to compromise to reach agreement, beware of changing your mind too quickly just to reach consensus. Groupthink occurs when group members do not test and challenge the ideas of others. When agreement seems to come too fast and too easily, be suspicious. Make certain that you have explored other alternatives and that everyone accepts the solution for basically the same reasons. Of course, you should not create conflict just for the sake of conflict, but do not be upset if disagreements arise. Reaching consensus takes time and often requires compromise. Be patient.

■ *Avoid easy techniques that reduce conflict:* You may be tempted to flip a coin or to take a simple majority vote when you cannot resolve a disagreement. Resist that temptation, especially early in your deliberation. If possible, avoid making a decision until the entire group can agree. Of course, at times, a majority vote is the only way to resolve a conflict. Just be certain that the group explores other alternatives before it makes a hasty decision to avoid conflict. When time permits, gaining consensus through communication is best.

■ *Seek out differences of opinion:* Remember that disagreements may improve the quality of a group's decision. With a variety of opinions and information, a group has a better chance of finding a good solution. Also remember that complex problems seldom have just one solution. Perhaps more than one of the suggestions offered will work. Actively recruit opposing viewpoints if everyone seems to be agreeing without much discussion.[86] Or, appoint someone to play the role of devil's advocate. Of course, do not belabor the point if you think that group members genuinely agree after considerable discussion.

■ *Involve everyone in the discussion; frequently contribute to the group:* Again, the more varied the suggestions, solutions, and information, the greater the chance that a group will reach quality solutions and achieve consensus. Encourage less-talkative members to contribute to the group. Several studies suggest that members will be more satisfied with a solution if they have had an opportunity to express their opinions and to offer suggestions.[87] Remember not to dominate the discussion. Good listening is important, too, and you may need to encourage others to speak out and assert themselves.

■ *Use a variety of methods to reach agreement:* One researcher has found that groups are more likely to reach agreement if members try several approaches to resolve a deadlocked situation rather than using just one method of achieving consensus.[88] Consider (1) combining two or more ideas into one solution; (2) building, changing, or extending existing ideas; (3) using effective persuasion skills to convince others to agree; and (4) developing new ideas to move the discussion forward rather than just rehashing old ideas.

■ *Expand the number of ideas and alternatives:* One reason a group may not agree is because none of the ideas or solutions being discussed are good ones. Each solution on the table may have flaws. If that is the case, the task should change from trying to reach agreement on the alternatives in front of the group to generating more alternatives.[89] Switching from a debate to brainstorming may help pry group members away from a foolish adherence to existing solutions. Consider using one of the techniques discussed in Chapter 10 as a structured way to set more ideas on the table when the group seems stuck.

Are there differences between the ways face-to-face groups reach consensus and the ways virtual groups that interact online do? As we noted earlier in the chapter, one research study found that virtual groups use more negative conflict management behaviors.[90] Negative behaviors include taking a quick vote rather than discussing issues, suppressing

SUGGESTIONS FOR REACHING CONSENSUS

Orient the Group Toward Its Goal

EFFECTIVE GROUP MEMBERS

- Talk about the discussion process using metadiscussional phrases.
- Help keep the group focused on the goal.
- Display known facts for all members in the group to see.
- Suggest possible solutions throughout the group's deliberation.

INEFFECTIVE GROUP MEMBERS

- Do little to help clarify group discussion.
- Go off on tangents and do not stay focused on the agenda.
- Fail to provide summaries of issues or facts about which members agree or rely only on oral summaries.
- Wait until time is about to run out before suggesting solutions.

Be Other-Oriented: Listen to the Ideas of Others

EFFECTIVE GROUP MEMBERS

- Give their ideas to the group.
- Approach conflict as a problem to be solved rather than a win/lose situation.
- Use group-oriented pronouns to talk about the group.
- Avoid opinionated statements that are not based on facts or evidence.
- Clarify misunderstandings.
- Emphasize areas of agreement.

INEFFECTIVE GROUP MEMBERS

- Argue for an idea because it is their own.
- Assume that someone will win and someone will lose an argument.
- Talk about individual accomplishments rather than group accomplishments.
- Are closed-minded and inflexible.
- Do not clarify misunderstandings or check to see whether their message is understood.
- Ignore areas of agreement.

Promote Honest Interaction and Dialogue

EFFECTIVE GROUP MEMBERS

- Do not change their minds quickly just to avoid conflict.
- Avoid easy conflict-reducing techniques.
- Seek out differences of opinion.
- Try to involve everyone in the discussion and make frequent, meaningful contributions to the group.
- Use a variety of methods to reach agreement.
- Expand the number of ideas and alternatives using various techniques.

INEFFECTIVE GROUP MEMBERS

- Give in to the opinion of group members just to avoid conflict.
- Find easy ways to reduce the conflict, such as taking a quick vote without holding a discussion.
- Do not recruit a variety of viewpoints.
- Permit one person to monopolize the discussion or fail to draw out quiet group members.
- Use only one or two approaches to reach agreement.
- Seek a limited number of options or solutions.

differences of opinions, and assuming an "I-must-win-you-must-lose" approach to managing differences. Both online and in person, it's best to encourage honest conversation and dialogue and avoid squelching opposing viewpoints.

In summary, research suggests that groups that search for areas of agreement while critically testing ideas and reducing ambiguity are more likely to reach consensus than groups that don't do these things. Also, one research team found that groups that strive for unanimous agreement ultimately are more likely to at least reach consensus than groups that are seeking only minimal consensus.[91] As you strive for consensus, rather than just saying, "No, you're wrong," identify specific issues that need to be clarified. Groups that focus on disagreement about procedures rather than on substantive issues are less likely to reach consensus. Building consensus takes time and skill and is not necessarily the goal of the group, but if it can be achieved, consensus may result in a better quality decision.

Putting Principles into Practice

Conflict can have both positive and negative effects on a group. Conflict occurs because people are different, because they have their own ways of doing things. These differences affect the way people perceive and approach problem solving.

Collaborative Conflict-Management Principles

- Separate the people from the problem.
- Focus on shared interests.
- Generate many options to solve problems.
- Base decisions on objective criteria.

Groupthink

The absence of conflict or a false sense of agreement is called groupthink. It occurs when group members are reluctant to voice their feelings and objections to issues. To help reduce the likelihood of groupthink, review the following suggestions:

- If you are the group leader, encourage critical, independent thinking.
- Be sensitive to status differences that may affect decision making.
- Invite someone from outside the group to evaluate the group's decision making.
- Assign a group member the role of devil's advocate.
- Ask members to subdivide into small groups to consider potential problems and suggested solutions.

Consensus

Consider applying the following suggestions to help reach consensus and to help manage the conflicts and disagreements that arise in groups.

- Keep the group oriented toward its goal.
- Be other-oriented: Listen to the ideas of others.
- Promote honest interaction and dialogue.

PRACTICE

Agree/Disagree Statements about Conflict

Read each statement once, and mark whether you agree (A) or disagree (D) with it. Take five or six minutes to do this.

1. Most people find an argument interesting and exciting.
2. In most conflicts someone must win and someone must lose. That's the way conflict is.
3. The best way to handle a conflict is simply to let everyone cool off.
4. Most people get upset with a person who disagrees with them.
5. Most hidden agendas are probably best kept hidden to ensure a positive social climate.
6. If people spend enough time together, they will find something to disagree about and will eventually become upset with one another.
7. Conflicts can be solved if people just take the time to listen to one another.
8. Conflict hinders a group's work.
9. If you disagree with someone in a group, it is usually better to keep quiet than to get the group off track with your personal difference of opinion.
10. When a group cannot reach a decision, members should abide by the decision of the group leader if he or she is qualified and competent.
11. To compromise is to take the easy way out of conflict.
12. Some people produce more conflict and tension than others. These people should be restricted from decision-making groups.

After you have marked the statements, break up into small groups and try to agree or disagree unanimously with each statement. Try in particular to find reasons for differences of opinion. If your group cannot reach a unanimous opinion on a given statement, you may change the wording in the statement to promote consensus. Assign one group member to observe your group interactions.

After your group has attempted to reach consensus, the observer should report how effectively the group used the guidelines suggested in this chapter.

Assessing Groupthink in Your Group

Complete the following groupthink assessment scale to determine whether a group you are part of avoids groupthink. For each statement, circle a number between 1 (if your group *never* does what the statement describes) and 10 (if your group *always* does what the statement describes). The higher your score, the better your group does in avoiding groupthink; a perfect score is 60.

1. Members of our group encourage and reward other group members for evaluating evidence and using good reasoning skills.
   1   2   3   4   5   6   7   8   9   10
2. Members of our group periodically ask whether we are making accurate, high-quality decisions.
   1   2   3   4   5   6   7   8   9   10
3. Members of our group sometimes admit they made a mistake or acknowledge that they reached an inaccurate conclusion.
   1   2   3   4   5   6   7   8   9   10
4. Members of our group let other group members make up their minds without pressuring them to agree with what others think.
   1   2   3   4   5   6   7   8   9   10
5. Members of our group periodically check to make sure that decisions the group has made continue to be supported by other group members.
   1   2   3   4   5   6   7   8   9   10
6. Members of our group voice their honest opinions and do not just agree with what the group leader or dominant or most vocal group members suggest.
   1   2   3   4   5   6   7   8   9   10

Win as Much as You Can

This activity is designed to explore the effects of trust and conflict on communication.[92] You will be paired with a partner. There will be four partner teams working in a cluster.

4 Xs:	Lose $1 each
3 Xs:	Win $1 each
1 Y:	Lose $3
2 Xs:	Win $2 each
2 Ys:	Lose $2 each
1 X:	Win $3
3 Ys:	Lose $1 each
4 Ys:	Win $1 each

Directions: Your instructor will provide detailed instructions for playing this game. For ten successive rounds, you and your partner will choose either an X or a Y. Your instructor will tell all partner teams to reveal their choices at the same time. Each round's payoff will depend on the decision made by others in your cluster. For example, according to the scoring chart above, if all four partner teams choose X for round one of this game, each partner team loses $1. You are to confer with your partner on each round to make a joint decision. Before rounds 5, 8, and 10, your instructor will permit you to confer with the other pairs in your cluster; in these three rounds, what you win or lose will be multiplied by either 3, 5, or 10. Keep track of your choices and winnings on the score sheet below. When you finish the game, compare your cluster's results with those of others. Discuss the factors that affected your balances. There are three rules:

- Do not confer with the other members of your cluster unless you are given specific permission to do so. This applies to nonverbal and verbal communication.
- Each pair must agree on a single choice for each round.
- Make sure that the other members of your cluster do not know your pair's choice until you are instructed to reveal it.

Round	Time Allowed	Confer with	Choice	$ Won	$ Lost	$ Balance	
1	2 min.	Partner	___	___	___	___	
2	1 min.	Partner	___	___	___	___	
3	1 min.	Partner	___	___	___	___	
4	1 min.	Partner	___	___	___	___	
5	3 min.	Cluster	___	___	___	___	Bonus Round:
	1 min.	Partner	___	___	___	___	Pay × 3
6	1 min.	Partner	___	___	___	___	
7	1 min.	Partner	___	___	___	___	
8	3 min.	Cluster	___	___	___	___	
	1 min.	Partner	___	___	___	___	Pay × 5
9	1 min.	Partner	___	___	___	___	
10	3 min.	Cluster	___	___	___	___	
	1 min.	Partner	___	___	___	___	Pay × 10

CHAPTER EIGHT

Preparing to Collaborate

"To solve a problem it is necessary to think. It is necessary to think even to decide what facts to collect."

—Robert Maynard Hutchins

CHAPTER OUTLINE

Developing a Discussion Plan

Formulating Discussion Questions

Case Study

Using Logic and Reasoning

Evaluating Evidence in Group Discussion

Using Critical-Analysis Skills: Avoiding Reasoning Fallacies

Putting Principles into Practice

Practice

OBJECTIVES

After studying this chapter, you will be able to:

- Develop a plan in preparation for a group discussion.
- Formulate a question of fact, prediction, value, or policy for a group discussion.
- Identify three criteria for a well-phrased policy-discussion question.
- Use appropriate logic and reasoning to develop sound conclusions.
- Identify appropriate ways to use facts, examples, opinions, and statistics in group discussions.
- Identify appropriate methods for researching group discussion questions using the Internet.
- Avoid reasoning fallacies by critically analyzing the reasoning and evidence presented in group discussions.

THE PRIMARY MESSAGE *of this chapter can be summarized by the Boy Scout motto "Be prepared!" Have you ever spent an hour or two at a group or team meeting, only to find no one was ready to make a meaningful, informed contribution? Many wasted meetings boil down to the fact that group members just haven't done their homework. GIGO is the acronym that computer programmers use for the expression "Garbage in, garbage out." If you put poor information (garbage) into a computer program, you get poor results when you're finished. It works the same way in group discussion.[1] To achieve a quality decision, a group needs quality information gleaned from research as well as effective reasoning and critical-thinking skills.[2]*

With this chapter we shift the focus away from the relational dimension of group communication, which we've emphasized in the last four chapters, to the task dimension—we delve into the processes and procedures by which groups and teams accomplish their work and achieve their goals. We'll discuss how to prepare effectively for group discussion and how to use research and critical-thinking skills to enhance the quality of the work accomplished by group members.

The Greek philosopher Socrates believed that the primary goal of dialogue and discussion was the search for truth. Today, group discussion continues to be a trusted method of seeking answers to tough questions. Our legal system is based on the idea that a jury of adults, after hearing evidence and using their best critical-thinking and analysis skills, should be able to decide whether someone is guilty of a crime. In corporations, teams and task forces hammer out key decisions. Regardless of a group's composition, goal, or context, its discussion will be more productive if group members have prepared and if they know how to critically evaluate information used to reach reasoned conclusions.[3]

DEVELOPING A DISCUSSION PLAN

Imagine you've been assigned to a group or committee. Perhaps the instructor in your group communication class has assigned you to a group to make a recommendation, solve a problem, or make a decision. What should you do first? How do you develop a plan to get your work accomplished? What should you *not* do? It's tempting for groups to jump in with

Cutting Edge Theory

WHY DO WE SHARE WHAT WE KNOW?

One of the key reasons that groups often do a better job of solving problems and making decisions than individuals do is that in groups there are more people who can share information. Groups that have more information are more likely to arrive at a better solution or outcome.[4] But there's a problem: Group members sometimes don't share what they know. What factors make group members more willing to share their knowledge? According to one study, you are more likely to share information if (1) everyone in the group already knows the information—that is, there is a common core of information that group members talk about; (2) at least one person knows the same information you know; and (3) you are perceived to be an expert on the topic at hand.[5] You might also share information with others to enhance your position in the group. Group members share information, even information that everyone already knows, to confirm that they are "in the know" and part of the group's core of well-respected members.[6] Another study found that groups that begin their deliberations with conflict and contention especially need additional information to help them sort through their disagreements.[7]

Real-Life Applications

How can you ensure that members of groups in which you participate share all of the relevant information that group members need to know?

■ Make sure that group members feel positive about the group. Early in your conversations, discuss why accomplishing the group's task will result in benefits. Look for ways to offer sincere compliments and support to other group members. Group members who feel positive about the group's goal,

both feet and start deciding what to do without adequate research or preparation. The most effective groups develop a plan for accomplishing their goal. Groups are more likely to deliberate wisely and effectively if group members clarify their goals, have good discussion skills, and are motivated to do a good job.[10] Suggesting solutions or making final recommendations at your first meeting is not a good idea. Effective groups prepare for *discussion*. We'll outline the general parts of a discussion plan and then spend the rest of the chapter describing these strategies in detail.

Get Acquainted with Your Group Members

"Let's get down to business. What are we supposed to do? Get to the point" are typical statements heard at most first meetings of teams or groups. It's important, however, to take a few minutes to get better acquainted with group members before focusing on the task. A consistent conclusion from teamwork research is that is vital to ensure that group members as well as its members, are more likely to share information with other group members.[8]

- If the group gets off to a rocky start and experiences significant conflict, perhaps your group needs to make a conscious effort to do additional research so that new information can shed light on the conflict.

- Consider having each group member, one at a time, share the information and ideas they have.

- Assess the range of knowledge, education, and information among group members, as well as the group's cultural diversity. Research suggests that group members who have different levels of information and education are likely to share information among team members up to a certain point.[9] A highly educationally diverse group will tend to share *less* information among team members. Don't let differences in education, knowledge, or culture keep group members from sharing what they each know. Encourage group members in the cultural minority to share information with the entire group.

- Some group members are shy, while others are just apprehensive about speaking up in any situation. Ask group members to first jot down some of their information on a piece of paper and then take turns sharing what they have written. Having a written "script" may help quieter members speak up.

- Ask group members to first share their information via e-mail that goes to every group member. One study found that virtual groups that collaborate only via computer connections typically have access to more information. Use the structure provided by having information in written form (either on paper or via e-mail) to gently prod each group member to share what he or she knows. The more you are able to tap the expertise of your group members, the more likely it is that your group will develop a high-quality outcome.

know one another in order to develop appropriate roles and responsibilities.[11] In fact, often the most serious problems group and team members encounter are not caused by task issues; problems occur because people have difficulty relating to each other. Taking time to establish good working relationships and trust can help a group or team be more productive in the long run.

Do more than just announce your name to the group. Perhaps you can provide information about how much experience you have with the topic or, if no specific task has been articulated, you can talk about your experience in working on group and team projects. You may want to exchange phone numbers and e-mail addresses so that you can contact each other. You need not artificially prolong this initial orientation period, but it will be useful for group or team members to spend some time setting to know their fellow members.

In addition to taking time to get acquainted with group members, avoid the temptation to make quick decisions. Groups sometimes feel pressure to get something accomplished. One team of researchers found that some groups encounter a "speed trap" when group members focus too much on speed and not enough on quality.[12] In essence, the researchers found that an overemphasis on making fast decisions results in a group's getting caught in a spiral of emphasizing speed and efficiency over quality of decision making. Since norms are established early in the group's history, make sure the group doesn't make speed of decision making the goal.

Clarify the Goals of the Group

Once you've completed introductions, make sure you know what the group's purpose, goal, and assignment are. A key question to ask as the group begins focusing on the goal is, When do you know when you're finished with your task? When developing the group's goal, visualize what the completed project will look like. Is the goal to produce a written report or to deliver an oral presentation in which you will make recommendations? You should be able to summarize the group goal in your own words. Most work-group goals boil down to one of three tasks: (1) generating ideas, information, or options; (2) making a choice, often about how to solve a larger problem; and (3) putting an idea into action. Your team may be involved in only one of these tasks, or all three. Whatever the group goal, it should be expressed in the form of a question that the group will discuss. Later in this chapter, we suggest that you formulate a discussion question as either a fact (something did or did not happen), a prediction (something will happen), a value (something is better or worse than something else), or a policy (something should be done). Consider writing your question or group goal on a chalkboard or flipchart for all team members to see. When the group starts to wobble or get off track, point group members back to the central reason for the discussion—to achieve the goal of the group. As we noted in Chapter 1, having a clear, elevating goal is one of the essential requirements for an effective team. Leadership expert Stephen Covey suggests that to be successful you should "begin with the end in mind."[13]

Develop a Plan for Gathering Information and Analyzing Issues

Once you develop your discussion question and clarify your goal, you need to collect information and research conclusions to help answer your question. It's best to develop a coordinated plan for gathering research information.[14] Groups tend to be overly optimistic in judging their efficiency. It typically takes more, rather than less, time to accomplish group tasks than group members realize.[15] So be realistic in estimating how long it will take the group to complete its work. Developing a step-by-step plan that involves all group members will help your group work effectively and create a realistic time-table for accomplishing its goal.

But before you head out to the library or start surfing the Internet, find out what you and your group members already know about the topic and issues. Researchers have found that one of the most important things you can do early in a group's history is to identify who in your group has special skills or is an expert on the topic you're discussing.[16] Once you identify information experts, make sure that these information leaders contribute to the group's conversation.

After assessing your group's knowledge, figure out what kind of information you need. Identify who is most interested in specific aspects of your topic. Begin to "divide and conquer." Assign members—or ask for volunteers—to begin researching the topic. Coordinate your group's research efforts rather than having group members scatter and then plunge into the research process. Without coordination, you may needlessly duplicate your research efforts. Besides just divvying up the work, be sure to give yourselves specific deadlines when

© 1999 Ted Goff

"To ensure that we keep this meeting under thirty minutes, I'll just set this timer."

the information will be collected. Allow plenty of time for the group to discuss the information (rather than just compiling the facts and data) before you make final recommendations. Research suggests that groups that have more time to solve a problem tend to do a better job of sharing information among group members; this finding is especially true of virtual groups sharing information via the Internet.[17] The more time allotted to solve a problem, the greater the chance that group members will share what they know. So, in addition to making assignments, indicate when the information should be shared with the group. Develop a concrete plan for structuring the workload.

Especially if you have limited time, divvying up the research tasks is a good idea. With a longer time period and low levels of information, however, some research suggests it may be best to work collaboratively rather than independently to gather information.[18] What's important is to make sure that group members share the information they gather with other group members.

According to a research team led by communication researcher Charles Pavitt, once a group member shares information or a proposal with the group, all group members will join in the discussion and talk about the ideas presented.[19] However, evidence also suggests that some people may dominate the discussion, as indicated in a classic study by Robert Bales. He found that some group members can dominate at least 40 percent of the talk time.[20] To maximize the benefits of information sharing and group deliberation, avoid letting one person run the show. Seek balanced participation and sharing of ideas and information.

Follow a Structured Agenda to Accomplish the Task

Here's a powerful principle for effective group discussion: *Groups and teams need an agenda to help them organize their discussion.* An **agenda** is a thoughtfully prepared list of the issues, topics, and questions that the group will discuss. There is an art to preparing an agenda—it is not just a list of topics that come to mind. Appendix A presents principles and practices for developing meeting agendas, as well as strategies for facilitating meeting discussion.

A group needs not only an agenda for each meeting but also an overarching plan of how to accomplish the group's goal. If your group is solving a problem, then a straightforward problem-solving agenda should provide the necessary structure. In Chapter 9 we share several techniques and methods for organizing a problem-solving discussion. The most basic problem-solving structure includes these steps:

1. Identify and define the problem
2. Analyze the problem
3. Generate several possible solutions
4. Select the best solution or combination of solutions
5. Test and implement the solution

Organizing your overall work plan around these steps can help keep your group on track.

Use Critical-Thinking and Analysis Skills

As the group begins to analyze the information it has gathered and generate possible options or recommendations, examine the quality of the evidence you're using. In addition, test the validity of the logic and reasoning that you are using to reach your conclusions. There is evidence that the more complicated and vexing the problem, the more likely people are to agree with the advice of a so-called expert.[21] Even with the recommendations of an expert, be on guard against conclusions reached using poor reasoning. Examine the evidence and avoid reasoning fallacies. We present some of the most common reasoning errors that people make later in the chapter.

Be Supportive of Other Group Members

Because group norms develop early in a group's history, it's important that you encourage and support other group members during initial meetings. Doing so makes the group meetings more pleasant, and you will be more likely to reach better conclusions if group members have a positive, supportive communication style. Research has found that when group members feel positive about their group and other members, they are more likely to share information.[22] In groups, information is the fuel for good decisions.

Determine How to Present Your Information

Once you have developed your conclusions, you'll need to decide how best to present your information to others. Appendix B describes three common formats for doing this: (1) a panel discussion, (2) a symposium presentation, and (3) a forum presentation. In addition to presenting your conclusions orally, you may need to prepare a written report.

Consider organizing your written report around the problem-solving steps noted earlier (definition of the problem, analysis of the problem, possible solutions, best solution or solutions). Most written reports are prepared for a specific individual or group. Keep your reader in mind as you develop the written report. Follow any specific guidelines or structure prescribed for you.

In most groups, time for group discussion is limited. Developing a plan of action and talking about it with the entire group can be a productive way to take advantage of the variety of skills and talents in your group or team. The rest of this chapter presents specific details on developing discussion questions, conducting research, reaching logical conclusions from evidence, and avoiding reasoning fallacies.

*F*ORMULATING DISCUSSION QUESTIONS

Before most scientists begin an experiment or conduct research, they have some idea of what they are looking for. Some researchers start with a *hypothesis,* a guess based on previous theory and research about what they will find in their search for new knowledge. Other investigators formulate a research question that provides a direction for their research. Like scientific research, problem solving seeks answers to questions. It makes sense, then, for group members to formulate a question before searching for answers. By identifying a spe-

Virtual Communication

When working on a group or team project, it may be useful to distribute and share your initial research findings via e-mail. A study by Carol Saunders and Shaila Miranda concluded that virtual groups that collaborate only via e-mail typically have access to more information.[23] According to the research, although face-to-face group meetings result in the sharing of more information initially, over the long term, exchanging information via e-mail may ensure that more information is shared and that all members of the group receive the information. In addition to using e-mail, consider the following strategies to facilitate sharing information.

- Develop a group listserv through which any group member can send information to every other group member simultaneously.
- For an extensive group project, consider developing a group Web page where group members can add information and ideas. One group member could serve as Web Master to coordinate what appears on the site. The group might post minutes of previous meetings, the group work plan, and a time line for completing group projects, as well as other information related to the group project.

cific question they must answer, members can reduce some of the initial uncertainty accompanying their discussion.

A discussion question should be phrased with considerable care. This is an important part of initiating and organizing any group discussion, particularly problem-solving discussions, because the quality and specificity of a question usually determine the quality of the answer. The better a group prepares a discussion question, the more clearly articulated will be the group's goal, and the greater will be the chances for a productive and orderly discussion.

For some group discussions and conferences, the question has been predetermined. Government committees and juries exemplify such groups. But usually groups are faced with a problem or need and are responsible for formulating a specific question to guide their deliberations. There are basically four types of discussion questions: (1) questions of fact, (2) questions of prediction, (3) questions of value, and (4) questions of policy. To help you determine which type is most appropriate for your various group discussions, we discuss each in the following sections.[24]

Questions of Fact

Some **questions of fact** are phrased such that the answer to the question is either yes or no. Something either did or did not occur. (Although, of course, a yes or no response can be qualified in terms of the probability of its accuracy.) The question "Did the St. Louis Cardinals win the World Series in 2006?" is a question of fact—either they did or they did not.

Questions of fact like that can simply be looked up online or in library sources and probably don't require group deliberations. On the other hand, a group may be asked to investigate a question such as "Did John Smith violate our company ethics policy last year?"

Dennis Gouran suggests that one way to investigate a question of fact is to construct a story or narrative to answer the discussion question.[25] To determine, for example, if John Smith *did* violate an ethics policy, the group should reconstruct what John Smith did or did not do. The reconstruction involves developing a story with a beginning, a middle, and an end, to answer the question.

In trying to answer a question of fact, make sure that all group members understand the key words and phrases in the discussion question. For example, faced with the question "Are there more incidents of terrorism in the United States today than there were before September 11, 2001?" a group will want to clearly define what an "incident of terrorism" is before answering the question. Does it mean *any* act of violence? By reducing the ambiguity of a question, a group can save considerable time in agreeing on a final answer.

Your group's objective will determine whether or not you should investigate a question of fact. If the group needs to discover what is true and what is false, then formulate a question of fact and define the key words in the question to give it greater focus and clarity. If the group needs to make a less objective value judgment or to suggest solutions to a problem, choose one of the types of questions discussed below.

Questions of Prediction

Will a tuition increase result in the university's having a balanced budget? Will the levee withstand a force-3 hurricane? Will the new airport security measures make air travel safer? A **question of prediction** asks whether something is likely to occur or may occur under a certain set of circumstances. In the question "Will a tuition increase result in the university's having a balanced budget?" the set of circumstances is a tuition increase.

How does a group attempt to answer such a question? Groups look for examples of what happened in similar situations. For instance, the university might survey other universities to see how their budgets were affected when tuition was increased. Groups may also simply use logic and reasoning based on the available evidence to determine what will or will not happen in the future. Will you use questions of prediction when communicating with others in small groups? That's a question of prediction that you'll answer based on your past experiences.

Group researcher Dennis Gouran suggests that, when investigating questions of prediction, an appropriate agenda for groups to follow would include the following four steps:[26]

1. *Develop if-then statements:* Identify one or more if-then statements to focus and clarify the issues. Here's an example of an if-then statement: If tuition is increased, then the university will have a balanced budget. Here's another if-then statement: If tuition is increased, then the university can continue its expansion program.

2. *Analyze the problem:* Spend time analyzing the likelihood that what is suspected (a balanced budget) will actually occur. What are the causes, effects, and symptoms of the problem? What impact have previous tuition increases had on the budget in the past?

3. *Use evidence:* Present evidence that documents the likelihood that X will lead to Y. In this example, X = a tuition increase and Y = a balanced budget.

4. *Evaluate the quality of the evidence:* Determine whether the evidence that attempts to document the likelihood that X will lead to Y is high-quality evidence (e.g., Is the evidence recent? Is the evidence from a credible source?).

Using this four-step agenda, groups can efficiently focus on determining whether the suspected outcome will likely occur.

Questions of Value

A **question of value** generally produces a lively discussion because it concerns attitudes, beliefs, and values about what is good or bad or right or wrong. Answering a question of value is more complicated than simply determining whether an event did or did not occur. "Which political party in the United States produced the best presidents?" is an example of a question of value. Group members' responses to this question depend on their attitudes toward Democrats, Republicans, or other political parties.

An **attitude** is a learned predisposition to respond to a person, object, or idea in a favorable, neutral, or unfavorable way. In essence, the attitudes you hold about the world determine whether you like or dislike what you experience and observe. A favorable attitude toward Democrats will affect your response to the value question, "Which political party in the United States produced the best presidents?"

A **belief** is what you hold to be true and false. Put another way, it is the way you structure reality. If you believe in God, you have structured your reality to assume that God exists. If you do not believe in God, you have structured your perception of what is true and false so that God is not part of your reality.

A **value** is often defined as an enduring conception of good and bad. Your values affect your perceptions of right and wrong. A value, such as the importance of being honest, is more resistant to change than an attitude or a belief.

What are your values? Which of your values have the most influence on your behavior? Because values are so central to how you respond in the world, you may have trouble coming up with a tidy list of your most important values. You may be able to list things you like and do not like (attitudes) or things that you classify as true and not true (beliefs), but your values—the guiding forces affecting your behavior—are sometimes difficult to identify.

In looking at relationships between attitudes (likes and dislikes), beliefs (what is perceived as true or false), and values (what is perceived as good or bad), it is important to note that values change infrequently and attitudes are most susceptible to change. Figure 8.1 shows values in the center of the diagram because they are central to how you make sense out of what you experience; if you valued honesty yesterday you will probably still value

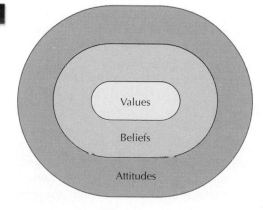

FIGURE 8.1

Interrelationship of Values, Beliefs, and Attitudes

Values

Beliefs

Attitudes

honesty today and in the future. Beliefs, the next ring, may change depending on your experiences and your perception of what is true and false. Attitudes are shown in the outer ring because they are likely to change more often; our attitudes may change daily. For example, one day you may like your small group communication class, and the next day you don't. Yet the underlying value of obtaining a good education probably will not vary.

Understanding the differences among attitudes, beliefs, and values helps you better understand what happens when a group discusses a value question. You base your response to a value question on your own attitudes, beliefs, and values, as do other group members. If you can identify the underlying attitudes, beliefs, and values that influence the responses to a value question, you can examine and discuss them.

Questions of Policy

Most problem-solving discussions revolve around **questions of policy**—questions that help groups determine what course of action or policy change would enable them to solve a problem or reach a decision. "What should be done to improve the quality of education in U.S. colleges and universities?" and "What can Congress do to reduce America's trade deficit?" are examples of policy questions. These questions can be identified easily because answers to them require changes of policy or procedure. Discussion questions including phrases such as "What should be done about…?" or "What could be done to improve…?" are policy questions. Most legislation in the U.S. Senate and House of Representatives is proposed in response to specific policy questions. A well-written policy question should adhere to three criteria: It should imply that a problem exists, it should be limited in scope, and it should be controversial enough to spark discussion.

1. *A policy question should imply that a specific problem exists and must be solved.* The question "What should be done about UFOs?" is not an appropriate policy question, because it does not provide enough direction to a specific problem. Do not confuse a discussion *topic* with a discussion *question*. If your group is going to discuss UFOs, it has a topic, but it is not trying to solve a problem. The group could rephrase the discussion question to make it more policy-oriented: "What could be done to improve the way the government handles and investigates UFO sightings in the United States?" The rephrased question more clearly implies that there is a problem in the way the government investigates sightings of UFOs. The latter question provides clearer direction for research and analysis.

2. *A policy question should be limited in scope.* Do not try to tackle a complex problem unless your group has the time and resources to solve it. For example, a group of students was assigned the task of formulating a policy question, discussing it, and then reporting the results of the discussion to the class. The students had three weeks to analyze and suggest possible solutions to the problem they had chosen to investigate, which was "What should be done to deal with Social Security?" Although the question clearly implies a specific problem, its lack of focus frustrated the group. A more limited discussion question, such as "What should be done to improve the tax base in our community?" would have been more manageable. You would do better to consider a simple, clearly worded question that can be analyzed in the time period allotted to your group than a question that would keep the U.S. Congress busy for several months or even years. On the other hand, a group should not phrase a policy-discussion question so that it requires only a yes or no answer or limits the group's options for solutions. Given

this criterion, "Should safety belts be required by law?" is a less-satisfactory policy discussion topic than "What can be done to ensure greater highway safety?"

3. *A policy question should be controversial.* A policy question should be about an important issue. An issue is a question about which individuals disagree. If group members disagree about how to solve a problem, they should not necessarily select another issue. Conflict, controversy, and disagreement should not always be viewed negatively. If group members agreed on how to solve a problem at the beginning of a discussion, they would have nothing to discuss. The purpose of a group discussion is to consider all alternatives and to agree on the best one. Therefore, do not reject a discussion question because other group members may hold contrasting points of view.

The four types of discussion questions (of fact, of prediction, of value, and of policy) may not appear to overlap, but as one researcher observed, groups must concern themselves

Case Study

Imagine that your instructor has just announced a semester-long group project for your small group communication course. You are assigned to work with a group of five people to develop a solution to a problem and, in so doing, answer a specific policy question. Your group has been assigned the following issue: What should be done to make college textbooks at our school bookstore more affordable for students at our school? You know that textbooks take quite a bite out of your budget, but you and other group members really don't understand how textbook prices are set or why used textbooks still have a high price tag. You also don't understand why popular books on best-seller lists at large bookstores cost under $30 while most of your textbooks cost over $60, with many over $100.

At the first group meeting, group members aren't quite sure how to begin addressing the question. You need to know more about how your local bookstore decides to set prices for both new and used books. Many students are buying their textbooks on the Internet and skipping the bookstore altogether. You've also heard that your school's bookstore generates a profit that is used to support other activities at your school, but you're not sure of the specific relationship between the bookstore and your school's budget.

Practice in Applying Principles

1. Although the policy question is clear, what are related questions of fact, prediction, and policy that your group may need to investigate before answering the larger policy question?

2. What should the group do to develop a plan for gathering information and analyzing the issues that contribute to the problem under discussion?

3. What information do you think is available through electronic sources to help your group analyze the issues being investigated? What information is probably not going to be available on the Internet and will call for other research strategies? How would you go about dividing up the work to gather the information you need?

4. Based on the information in this chapter and the information about developing an agenda for a meeting included in Appendix A, prepare an agenda for your group's next meeting.

5. Develop a reasonable timeline for accomplishing your group's goal.

6. Your instructor has asked your group to present analysis and recommendations to the class. Based on information included in Appendix B, what would be an appropriate format for your group's presentation?

with questions of fact, prediction, and value when considering questions of policy.[27] They must judge evidence as true or false (question of fact). They must ponder whether the proposed solution will be effective in the future (question of prediction). Their attitudes, beliefs, and values (questions of value) will influence the decisions they make on policy changes (questions of policy).

A discussion question serves a valuable function in providing direction to group deliberations. Once groups devise discussion questions, however, they can still modify them. Decide whether your group is considering a question of fact, of prediction, of value, or of policy. Identifying the type of question helps you understand the dynamics of the issue under discussion. If you realize that the question "Should we legalize casino gambling in our community?" involves value judgments, you will be less likely to condemn group members who disagree with you. Even in the face of disagreement, frustration and defensiveness can yield to understanding and compromise. Remember, too, that even though a discussion question may be clearly identified as one of fact, value, or policy, your discussion probably will include other types of questions. Once your group has a well-defined problem to discuss, members should begin researching and analyzing it.

*R*EVIEW

FOUR TYPES OF GROUP-DISCUSSION QUESTIONS

Question Type	Definition	Example
Question of fact	A question that asks whether something is true or false	Did university officials violate the freshman-admission policy last year?
Question of prediction	A question that asks whether something is likely to occur	Will the building renovations be completed by Christmas?
Question of value	A question that considers something's worth or desirability	What are the virtues of a democratic form of government?
Question of policy	A question that considers whether a change in procedure should be made	What should be done to curtail gang violence?

*U*SING LOGIC AND REASONING

In the search for truth, you will need to develop logical arguments and reach reasoned conclusions. **Reasoning** is the process of drawing a conclusion from evidence. Your evidence will consist of the facts, examples, statistics, and opinions you use to support the point you wish to make. For over two thousand years, students have studied the principles of critical analysis that we now present. Although you may have been introduced to a discussion of logic, reasoning, and evidence in another course (such as public speaking, argumentation, or philosophy), we think it's important to apply these important principles to group and team deliberations. First we will provide an overview of reasoning strategies and then we'll describe how to use evidence effectively. There are three major ways of structuring an argument to reach a logical conclusion: (1) inductive reasoning, (2) deductive reasoning, and (3) causal reasoning.

Inductive Reasoning

Inductive reasoning is a method of arriving at a general, or "bottom-line," conclusion through the use of specific examples, facts, statistics, and opinions. For example, suppose you recently bought a used personal computer that didn't work the way it was supposed to when you got it home. You learn that one of your classmates also bought a used computer that didn't work well. Your uncle also bought a used computer from someone who ran an ad in the paper; his computer didn't work properly either. Based on those three examples, you reach a conclusion that buying used computers will give you trouble. You've reached a general conclusion based on the specific examples you know about.

To help answer your group-discussion question, you need to make sure you reach a valid or logical conclusion. When you reason inductively (from specific examples to a general conclusion), keep the following questions in mind:

1. *Are there enough specific examples to support the conclusion?* Are three examples of problems with used computers enough to prove your point that all used computers don't work well? There are millions of used computers; three is not a very large sample. If you coupled your examples with additional statistical evidence that over 30 percent of people who purchased a used computer experienced computer problems, then your evidence would be more convincing.

2. *Are the specific instances typical?* Were the three examples you cited representative of all used computers? How do you know? Perhaps you, your classmate, and your uncle bought computers that were not typical of most used computers. For example, maybe you all bought them from the same guy, who sells them out of the trunk of his car, whereas most people buy them from a reputable retail outlet. If the examples you use to develop your point aren't representative of the entire population, you run the risk of reaching a flawed conclusion.

3. *Are the instances recent?* How long ago did you purchase your used computers? If you made your purchase three years ago, conditions may have changed. Perhaps used computers on the market today are more reliable.

Deductive Reasoning

Deductive reasoning is the process of going from a general statement or principle to a specific conclusion. This is the reverse of inductive reasoning. Deductive reasoning can be presented in the form of a **syllogism**—a way of organizing or structuring an argument in three parts: (1) a major premise, (2) a minor premise, and (3) a conclusion.

To reach a conclusion deductively, you start with a generalization that serves as the **major premise.** "All students who take a course in small group communication will have a successful career" is an example of a major premise. The **minor premise** is a more specific statement about an example that is linked to the major premise. "Mark Stevens has taken a course in group communication" is an example of a minor premise. The **conclusion** is based on the major premise and the more specific minor premise. In reasoning deductively, you should ensure that the major and minor premises are true and can be supported with evidence. The conclusion to our syllogism is "Mark Stevens will have a successful career."

To test the truth or validity of an argument organized deductively, consider the following questions.

1. *Is the major premise (general statement) true?* Will all students who take a course in small group communication necessarily have successful careers? What evidence exists to support that generalization? The most important part of making a deductive argument hinges on whether your major premise is true. It takes evidence to document the soundness of your major premise. Obviously, just asserting that a statement or generalization is true and labeling it a major premise is not enough. You need facts, examples, statistics, or expert opinion to support your generalization.

2. *Is the minor premise (the particular statement) also true?* If your minor premise is not true, your syllogism will fall apart. In our example, it is easy to confirm whether Mark Stevens has taken a course in small group communication. But not all minor premises can be verified as easily.

Causal Reasoning

The third way to reach a logical conclusion is through **causal reasoning**—the process of relating two or more events and concluding that one event caused the other. For example, you might reason that in 2000 the use of a confusing "butterfly ballot" in some counties in Florida resulted in voter error.

You can structure a causal argument in two ways. First, you can reason from cause to effect, moving from a known fact (cause) to predict a result (effect). You know that the number of drug arrests in your community has increased; you know this is a fact because you have researched the police records. You reason that crime will decrease in your community if the drug offenders are locked up. Weather forecasters use the same method of reasoning when they predict the weather. They base a conclusion about what will happen tomorrow on what they know about today's weather.

The second way to structure a causal argument is to reason backward, from a known effect to an unknown cause. You know, for example, that interest rates have decreased in the past six months. You hypothesize that the decrease has occurred because of a healthy economy. You can't be absolutely sure of your analysis, but you do know that interest rates have decreased (the effect). As with other forms of reasoning, you develop strong causal arguments by using evidence to link something known with something unknown. If you understand how to use evidence effectively, you can enhance your use of inductive, deductive, and causal reasoning.

$\mathcal{E}$VALUATING EVIDENCE IN GROUP DISCUSSION

After you formulate your discussion question, you need to define key terms and gather information on the issues implied by the question. Group members should also know something about the four kinds of evidence available: (1) facts, (2) examples, (3) opinions, and (4) statistics. Group members who use evidence effectively make better decisions. A research study found that the key element in swaying a jury is the quality and quantity of the evidence presented.[28]

Research also suggests that when reaching a final conclusion about the validity of an argument, most people find that an argument that is supported by multiple types of evidence is more persuasive than one backed up by only one source or one type of evidence.[29] Let's examine each of the four types of evidence in more detail.

Facts

A *fact* is any statement proven to be true. A fact cannot be a prediction about the future, because such a statement cannot be verified; it must be a report of something that has already happened or that is happening. "It will rain tomorrow" cannot be a fact, because the statement cannot be verified. "The weather forecaster predicts rain" may be a fact if the weather forecaster has made such a prediction; the accuracy of the forecast has nothing to do with whether the statement is a fact. Ask yourself these questions to determine whether a statement is a fact:

1. Is it true?
2. Is the source reliable?
3. Are there any contrary facts?

Examples

An *example* is an illustration of a particular case or incident and is most valuable when used to emphasize a fact. An example may be real or hypothetical. A real example can also be called a fact; it actually exists or has happened. A hypothetical example is of little use in proving a point but can add color and interest to illustrate an otherwise dry or boring factual presentation. Apply the following tests to examples:

1. Is it typical?
2. Is it significant?
3. Are there any contrary examples?

Opinions

An *opinion* is a quoted comment. The fact-based opinions of unbiased authorities are most valuable as evidence. Like examples, opinions can dramatize a point and make it more interesting. Opinions are most effective when used in conjunction with facts or statistics. The following questions can help you determine the usefulness of opinions:

1. Is the source reliable?
2. Is the source an expert in the field?
3. Is the source free from bias?
4. Is the opinion consistent with other statements made by the same source?
5. Is the opinion characteristic of opinions held by other experts in the field?

Statistics

Because they cannot present dozens of facts or examples in a given time limit, people often rely on statistics. A *statistic* is simply a number: 10,000 people, 132 reported cases of child abuse, 57 Western nations. Statistics provide firm support for important points. Pay special attention, though, to the tests of statistics listed next, because statistics are probably the most frequently misgathered and misinterpreted type of evidence.

1. Is the source reliable?
2. Is the source unbiased?
3. Are the figures recent? Do they apply to the time period in question?
4. How were the statistics drawn? If from a sample, is the sample representative of the total population? Is the sample big enough to be reliable?
5. Does the statistic actually measure what it is supposed to measure?
6. Are there contrary statistics?

Once you have located and collected your evidence, keep in mind a couple of guidelines for applying it effectively. First, never take evidence out of context. Even if you find a statement that seems to be exactly the evidence you need, do not use it if the next sentence following it says something like, "However, this idea has recently been proved false." Second, try to gather and use as many types of evidence from as many sources as possible to support a point.

Gathering and Evaluating Evidence: A Special Emphasis on Web Resources

Although traditional library sources are still excellent for gathering evidence used in group discussion, more and more research is conducted via the Internet. Newspapers, research journals, and a multitude of other resources are now available online; it's likely that you and your group members will find a significant amount of information on the Web.

There is no single index to all the information available in that portion of the Internet known as the World Wide Web. One of the most frequently used Web browsers (computer programs that allow you to access the Web) is Internet Explorer. Once you access the Web, you can find the information you need by using a search engine, which is really nothing more than a large index, organized by subject, of literally millions of Web sites. Two of today's more popular search engines are Yahoo! (www.yahoo.com) and Google (www.google.com); there are scores of others. Google has emerged as the most popular and comprehensive search engine. Lexis-Nexis is another powerful electronic research tool available through many university libraries; it can provide complete texts of periodicals and newspapers, as well as legal and government documents. Although a single search engine may not find everything you need, diligence and persistence should enable you to find what you are looking for.

Other useful resources include your professors, your school's own Web page, and the staff in the library and information technology department. Never underestimate the value of asking others about their experience doing Web research; people you already know may point you to great Web sites.

As technology continues to progress, it will likely become easier to locate resources. You will be able to locate more complete texts of books and articles on the Web rather than just finding references sites. Search engines will continue to improve in accuracy. But the Web is only a means of *finding* information; you will need to use your skill in identifying the most useful information.

The challenge in electronic research is deciding which data are relevant to your question. Although you can access hundreds of libraries and end up with a ream of documents, the volume of information is not nearly as important as your ability to use the information you gather. In the medical profession, *triage* is the process of making decisions about which patients need the most attention or medical care, in an emergency room, for example. **Information triage** is the process of sorting through information you have gathered from your search to determine what is most useful or needs the most critical attention. You will also need to cite the sources that you find on the Internet. Most new style manuals will tell you how to prepare a bibliographical entry to document an Internet citation.

As with any type of evidence, just because you find it on the Web does not mean the evidence or information is accurate or reliable. Anyone with a computer and software can construct a Web site. Information on the Web may not have gone through an editorial process to be checked for accuracy. For example, information that you glean from the Web site of the *New York Times* is more credible than that from someone's personal Web site or the Web site of an organization with a particular political or profit-based agenda. When evaluating information you retrieve from the Web, consider the following criteria:

1. *Accountability.* Who is responsible for the Web site? What can you find out about the sponsor? To whom do the sponsors of the Web site owe allegiance? Knowing who is placing the information on the site can help you evaluate whether the information is biased or unbiased.
2. *Objectivity.* Related to accountability for the Web site is the objectivity of the information presented. Consider the interests and philosophical or political biases of the organization or individual responsible for the site.
3. *Accuracy.* Is the information accurate? Is the information verifiable by other sources? Web resources should also be relatively free of common grammar, spelling, and punctuation errors.
4. *Recency.* How current and up to date is the information on the Web site? Look for clues that the site was recently posted or is kept current. Many sites indicate when they were posted and when they were last updated. As a general rule, the more recent the information (especially facts, statistics, and other data) the better.
5. *Usability.* Is there information that you can actually use? Does it relate to the group or team's goal? Also, consider the overall layout and design of the site, which should facilitate its use.

USING CRITICAL-ANALYSIS SKILLS: AVOIDING REASONING FALLACIES

It's not enough just to have evidence or to be able to label the kind of reasoning that you're using to reach conclusions. If you want to critically analyze information and ideas, you must evaluate both the logic and the evidence used to reach a conclusion. Critical thinkers who are members of groups and teams need to develop key technical skills:

Discovery: The ability to seek and find relevant information

Organization: The ability to categorize and structure information

Analysis: The ability to break information down into pieces and interpret each piece

Synthesis: The ability to combine information, to see new patterns and put information together in new and meaningful ways

Clarification: The ability to focus the group on the important information and to differentiate between key and secondary information.[30]

In addition to identifying and analyzing information, groups need to avoid committing **fallacies**—false reasoning that occurs when someone attempts to arrive at a conclusion without adequate evidence or with arguments that are irrelevant or inappropriate. Avoiding reasoning fallacies in your own arguments will enhance your critical-thinking skills. Being able to spot reasoning fallacies that others are using will make you a more discriminating and effective listener. Here are some of the most common fallacies.

Causal Fallacy

The causal fallacy is the inappropriate assumption that one event is the cause of another when there is little evidence to connect the two events. The Latin phrase used to summarize this fallacy is *post hoc, ergo propter hoc,* which translates as "after this, therefore because of this." Superstitions are prime examples of causal fallacies. Your assumption that your "lucky" rabbit's foot helps you perform better on math tests probably can't be demonstrated with facts and evidence. It's your ability to study and learn math that determines your test results, not whether you have a rabbit's foot in your pocket. Be on the lookout for group members who inappropriately try to connect one event to another without adequate cause and effective evidence.

Either/Or Fallacy

The either/or fallacy occurs when someone argues that there are only two approaches or solutions to a problem; it oversimplifies the options by suggesting we must do either X or Y. "It's either vote for new school taxes or we will have to send our kids to the next county to be educated," claims a parent at a school-board meeting. Usually there are a range of options to consider in any discussion. In fact, one hallmark of successful groups is the ability to identify several options to solving a problem.

Bandwagon Fallacy

"Everybody is in favor of expanding the city park, so you should favor it too," is an example of the bandwagon fallacy. Someone using this fallacy tries to convince you that an idea is good simply because "everybody" else thinks it's a good idea; hence, you should jump on the bandwagon and support the idea. Judge an idea on its merits, not just because of a popular opinion poll. As we noted in Chapter 1, one disadvantage of group discussion is that the group may give in to pressure from others.

Hasty Generalization

A person reaching a conclusion on the basis of too little evidence or evidence that doesn't exist is making a hasty generalization. As we noted when we discussed tests of evidence or tests of inductive reasoning, one or two examples do not prove your point. For example, because a friend of yours got ripped off by a service station when vacationing in Texas doesn't mean that you should avoid all service stations in Texas. Here's another example: "We don't need to spend more money on music education in our schools; my son listens to classical music at home, and so can other students."

Attacking the Person

This fallacy—also known as *ad hominem,* Latin for "to the man"—involves attacking irrelevant personal characteristics about someone rather than examining the idea or proposal he

It is a fallacy to attack someone's personal characteristics rather than examining the idea the person proposes. How can you improve your group discussion skills?

or she advances. "We all know that Sue's idea won't work because she's been in local politics for years and we just can't trust her" does not really deal with the soundness of the idea, which may be a great one.

Red Herring

The red herring fallacy, which occurs when someone undermines an idea by using irrelevant facts or arguments as distractions, gets its name from the old trick of dragging a red herring across the trail to divert the sniffing dogs who may be following. Someone uses a red herring fallacy to divert attention or distract listeners from the real issues. For example, someone who claims "The real problem is not sexual harassment in the military, but the fact that we need to pay our military personnel more money." Is trying to divert attention from the issue of sexual harassment and change the subject to the salary of military personnel. A group member who listens critically will recognize this distraction and return the discussion back to the issue at hand.

If in the course of your discussion you detect that someone reaches a conclusion using a reasoning fallacy, how do you bring it to his or her attention? We don't suggest that you use an accusatory voice and pounce on someone for the lousy logic. As we pointed out in Chapter 5, making someone defensive doesn't do much for maintaining a quality group climate. Your first effort to draw attention to a reasoning fallacy should be to calmly and tactfully describe how the evidence offered does not support the point. Consider using an "I" statement: "I'm not sure I follow that argument. ..." Describing how you don't see the logic of their point is a better way to challenge fellow group members than immediately labeling their logic as a "fallacious argument" and trying to belittle them. "You" statements ("You're wrong! Your evidence is terrible!") tend to raise the hackles of your listener and create a defensive, disconfirming climate.

Collaborating Ethically: What Would You Do?

When preparing for a group discussion or a team meeting, consider the following ethical obligations.

- *Use sound evidence and reasoning.* As we have discussed in this chapter, using appropriate evidence and reasoning will help ensure that your group reaches a quality decision. It is unethical to claim you have found "the truth" without adequately researching the issues you discuss. Furthermore, a discussion peppered with reasoning fallacies can lead to inaccurate conclusions and an insensitivity to the ideas and positions of others. Asserting your conclusions without evidence and overrelying on emotional appeals at the expense of rational, logical reasoning are also unethical.

- *Give credit to your sources.* Avoid **plagiarism**—presenting the words and ideas of others as your own without giving proper credit to the source. Don't use quotes or paraphrase the ideas of others without acknowledging them. Give proper credit to ideas and information that are not your own, both when speaking and writing. In group discussions you can provide an oral footnote: Simply tell your listeners where you got the idea or information you are using. In your written work, use footnotes or references to document the original source of the ideas.

- *Follow through on commitments.* Working in a group means that others depend on you to fulfill your assignments and workload. When you don't follow through on work you have promised to perform, you are not being an ethical group communicator. Don't promise to do more than you can accomplish, but accomplish all that you promise to do.

What would you do in the following situation? While watching television you see an interesting program that includes a wealth of statistics documenting the problem of climate change. Not long afterward, you are assigned to work on a group project that focuses on this policy question: Should the government take more aggressive steps to manage the worldwide problem of climate change? You remember several of the statistics that were presented in the TV program, but you don't remember the precise program that included those statistics. Is it acceptable to share your information with your group and "make up" a source for the statistics? You're fairly certain that your information is accurate and reliable; you just don't remember the exact source. No one will ever know that your figures aren't from the source you cite. Do you share the statistics with your group even though you can't remember the correct source of the information? *What would you do?*

Putting Principles into Practice

If you understand how to go about the process of preparing for group discussion, your group interactions will be not only more informed but also more productive. The following suggestions should help you apply the concepts presented in this chapter.

Develop a Discussion Plan

- Group members should try to get to know each other; exchange phone numbers and e-mail addresses.
- Develop a strategy for gathering information and researching your topic.
- Determine whether you have expert group members who can help address the issues confronting your group.
- Divide and conquer: Ask for volunteers or assign group members to gather appropriate information.
- Give your group interim deadlines; don't wait until the last minute to share your information; pool your information and ideas early in the process.
- Put your discussion plan in writing rather than relying on memory as to who will do what by a specific date.

Formulate Discussion Questions

- To focus and direct the deliberations of your group, formulate a discussion question. If your group is trying to decide whether something is true or false or whether something did or did not occur, formulate a question of fact. If your group is attempting to determine whether something will happen in the future, formulate a question of prediction. If your group is trying to decide whether one idea or approach to an issue is better than another, formulate a question of value. If your group is trying to develop a solution to a problem, formulate a question of policy.

Test Your Use of Logic and Reasoning

- When using inductive reasoning, make sure you have enough examples that are typical or representative of other examples and that are recent.

- When using deductive reasoning, make sure that the general premise is true and that you have evidence to support it.
- When using causal reasoning, make sure that there is actually a cause-and-effect relationship between the events you link together; simply because two things happen at the same time (because they are correlated) does not mean one event causes the second event.

Test the Quality of the Evidence You Use

- When relying on facts to prove a point, ask yourself three questions: Are the facts true? Is the source of the facts reliable? Are there any contrary facts?
- When relying on examples, determine if the examples are typical and significant and whether there are any contrary examples.
- When quoting opinions of others, determine if the source of the opinion is reliable, if the person is an expert, if the source is free from bias, and if the opinion is consistent with other statements made by the source and other experts in the field.
- When using statistics, determine if the source is reliable and unbiased, the information is up-to-date, the sampling method used to gather the statistics was sound, and whether there are any contrary statistics.
- Develop the skill of information triage; sort out useful from less important ideas and data that you retrieve from your Internet searches or library research; evaluate Web information for accountability, objectivity, accuracy, recency, and usability.

Use Critical-Thinking and Analysis Skills to Evaluate Reasoning

- Don't assume a cause-and-effect relationship without adequate evidence (causal fallacy).
- Don't suggest that options boil down to either one solution or another (either/or fallacy).
- Don't accept an idea or solution just because numerous people are in favor of it (bandwagon fallacy).

- Don't reach a conclusion without adequate evidence (hasty generalization).
- Don't criticize a person in order to attack an idea; focus on evaluating the quality of the idea, not the person (attacking-the-person fallacy).

- Don't let the group get away with diverting attention from the key issue under discussion (red herring fallacy).

𝒫RACTICE

Identifying Questions of Fact, Prediction, Value, and Policy

Read the following narrative, then formulate the main discussion question and indicate whether it is a question of fact, of prediction, of value, or of policy. Identify at least one question of fact and at least one question of value suggested by the narrative.

A new liberal divorce law has come up for discussion in the state senate. Senator Smith, who introduced the bill, has lobbied hard for it because she has found evidence to suggest that rather than deterring divorce, complications in the current law only result in lengthy delays and higher fees for divorce lawyers. Senator Williams also supports the new law; he was recently divorced and experienced much frustration and irritation in the process. Senator Schwartz, in contrast, is happily married and quite conservative; he leads opposition to the new law.

Critical Thinking and Analysis: Identifying Reasoning Fallacies

Read the following statements. Working with your group members, determine whether there is a flaw in the analysis or logic. If there is fallacious reasoning, identify which reasoning fallacy is illustrated.

1. Everyone in our city drinks fluoridated water. Therefore it's safe to drink fluoridated water.

2. Your idea can't be a good one. You grew up in a small town in the rural area of Missouri where it would be impossible to get a good education.

3. We either increase tuition or tell 10 percent of the faculty that they're fired; those are the only ways to balance the budget.

4. Each year the El Niño weather pattern is active, the economy improves; clearly, El Niño has an impact on stock prices.

5. Of course eating a good breakfast makes you smarter. My nephew Mike eats a good breakfast, and he has an IQ of over 130.

6. A recent survey found that 52 percent of respondents approved of modifying a résumé to make credentials appear better than they actually are; therefore it would be appropriate for you to modify your résumé credentials.

7. The school board should either add a new class period at the end of the school day or leave the schedule the way it is now.

8. Everyone knows a talk-show host is primarily an entertainer and therefore couldn't make a meaningful comment about the proposal to salvage Social Security.

9. The university should plan for more parking spaces, because when I arrive on campus I often can't find a place to park.

10. Even though we are discussing whether to raise admissions standards at our university, I think you will all agree that the real reason we don't have high-quality students is that many of them lack good oral communication skills.

CHAPTER NINE

Making Decisions and Solving Problems

"There's nothing in the middle of the road but yellow stripes and dead armadillos."

—Jim Hightower

OBJECTIVES

After studying this chapter, you will be able to:

- Differentiate between group decision making and group problem solving.
- Describe the elements of group decision making.
- List and describe characteristics of effective group decision makers.
- Compare and contrast descriptive, functional, and prescriptive approaches to problem solving in small groups.
- Identify the four phases of the group process.
- Discuss the three types of group activity tracks.

AS THE CHAPTER-OPENING QUOTE *from Jim Hightower suggests, if you stay in the middle of the road you are likely to get run over. As another saying goes, "Not to decide is to decide." Many North Americans value decisiveness and action rather than indecisiveness and muddled thought. More research has been conducted about group problem-solving and decision-making communication than about any other group objective. Groups discuss issues to search for truth; groups make decisions; and groups solve problems. In this chapter and the next, we turn our attention to principles and strategies that provide structure and guide interaction to help groups do the work of choosing among several options or circumventing vexing obstacles to solve problems.*

This chapter builds on the information presented in the last chapter, which discussed how to focus on a discussion question, conduct research, think critically, and test and evaluate evidence and reasoning. Here we focus on the communication strategies that help groups make quality decisions. First we describe the process of group decision making by identifying elements, methods, and obstacles to quality decision making. Then we describe the nature of group problem solving, including three approaches to examining how groups solve problems: descriptive, functional, and prescriptive. We end the chapter by identifying cultural assumptions about group problem solving and decision making. In Chapter 10 we continue our discussion of group problem solving with a look at strategies and techniques that can help groups do their work effectively and efficiently.

GROUP DECISION MAKING: CHOOSING AMONG ALTERNATIVES

One critical task of groups is **decision making**—the process of choosing from among several alternatives. For example, in deciding which college or university to attend, you probably considered several choices. Perhaps you started by gathering information about as many as fifteen or twenty schools and then narrowed the alternatives as you considered the advantages and disadvantages of each institution. Eventually you narrowed your choice to two and made a final decision. Groups make decisions in essentially the same way. In this section we consider the elements, methods, and characteristics of group decision making and also examine some of the obstacles that keep groups from making high-quality decisions. Later we contrast the decision-making (choice-making) process with the process of solving problems, a more comprehensive process that involves making choices to overcome an obstacle or barrier to achieve a goal.

Elements of Group Decision Making

According to Randy Hirokawa, Dennis Gouran, and several other group communication scholars, group decision making usually follows a predictable pattern.[1] Groups tend to make better decisions if the pattern is explicitly identified so that the group can structure its discussion.[2] Group decision making includes the following steps.[3]

1. *The group assesses the present situation.* A group analyzes a situation based on available information and realizes that it needs to make a decision. For example, an airline's board of directors must decide whether to lower fares. Thus, they look at competitors' fares and the number of passengers those competitors transport each day.

2. *The group identifies its goals.* After assessing the current situation, the group should identify its objectives. A group uncertain about its task will have difficulty making a quality decision. If its goal is clear, a group begins to identify alternatives or choices.

3. *The group identifies several alternatives.* The greater the number of alternatives a group generates, the greater the likelihood it will make a good decision. Poor decisions usually occur when a group fails to generate enough good possible choices.

4. *The group evaluates the positive and negative consequences of alternatives.* A group must do more than identify alternatives; it should also assess the positive and negative implications of each alternative before making a decision.

5. *The group selects the alternative (makes a decision).* The alternative selected should potentially have a maximum positive outcome with minimal negative consequences. A group is more likely to select the best alternative if it has carefully assessed the situation, considered group goals, identified several choices, and noted the positive and negative implications of each.

Methods of Group Decision Making

After the alternatives have been narrowed and weighed, what methods can groups use to make a decision? Knowing these methods can give you and your group options to consider when a decision needs to be made.[4]

Decision by Expert in Group   One person in a group may seem to be the best informed about the issue, and members can turn to this person to make the choice. This expert may or may not be a group's designated leader. Deferring to an expert from within a group may be an efficient way to make a decision, but if there is not adequate discussion, the group may not be satisfied with the outcome.

Decision by Expert Outside Group   A group may decide that none of its members has the credibility, knowledge, or wisdom to make a particular decision, and it may feel unable or unwilling to do so. Members can turn to someone outside the group who has authority to make a decision. Although an outside expert may make a fine decision, a group that gives up its decision-making power to one person loses the advantages of the greater input and variety of approaches that come from being a group in the first place.

Averaging Individual Rankings or Ratings   Group members can be asked to rank or rate possible alternatives. After the group averages the rankings or ratings, it selects the alternative with the highest average. This method of making decisions can be a useful way to start discussions and to see where the group stands on an issue. However, it is not the best way to make a final decision, because it does not take full advantage of the give-and-take of group discussion.

Random Choice   Sometimes groups become so frustrated that they make no decisions. They resort to coin tosses or other random approaches. These methods are not recommended for groups that take their decision making seriously.

Majority Rule   This is the method of group decision making most often used. Majority rule can be swift and efficient but can also leave an unsatisfied minority. Unless it allots time for discussing an issue, a group that makes a decision on the basis of majority rule may sacrifice decision quality and group cohesiveness for efficiency.

Decision by Minority   Sometimes a minority of group members makes a decision. The minority may yell the loudest or threaten to create problems for the group unless it gets its way. Members may ask, "Does anyone have any objections?" and, if no one answers immediately, consider the decision made. Minority members whose decision is adopted may temporarily rejoice, but over time the group will have difficulty implementing a decision that is not widely accepted. On the other hand, research suggests that when a majority of members support an idea and then the majority evaporates because several group members change their minds, the group is in a vulnerable position; a view that was previously held by a minority can swiftly become the majority view. So, in cases when you side with the minority, keep in mind that things change. Don't side with the majority simply because it's the majority. Groups work best when there is honest dialogue in the search for truth.[5]

Decision by Consensus   Consensus occurs when all group members can support a course of action. This decision-making method is time-consuming and difficult, but members are usually satisfied with the decision. If group members must also implement the solution, this method works well. To reach a decision by consensus, group members must listen and respond to individual viewpoints and manage conflicts that arise. Consensus is facilitated when group members are able to remain focused on the goal, emphasize areas of agreement, and combine or eliminate alternatives identified by the group. Although desirable, consensus sometimes is not possible. A fallback approach is to seek a **supermajority decision.** A supermajority is two-thirds of the group or team.

Obstacles to Quality Group Decision Making

We've more than once referred to the saying that a camel is a horse designed by a committee. Groups sometimes make foolish decisions. Knowing some of the typical pitfalls groups encounter when choosing among alternatives can help your group avoid them. Consider the following obstacles.[6]

■ *The group fails to analyze the present situation accurately.*   If a group improperly analyzes its current situation, it's likely to make a bad decision. To analyze something is to break it down into smaller parts. Research suggests that how a group analyzes the information can dramatically affect the group's decision.[7] Having too little evidence—or none—is one of the reasons groups sometimes fail to analyze the present situation accurately. Even if group members do have ample evidence, it may be defective if they have not applied the proper tests of evidence discussed in Chapter 8.

*R*EVIEW

METHODS OF GROUP DECISION MAKING

Method of Making a Group Decision	Advantages	Disadvantages
Decision by Expert: Group defers to the member who has the most expertise or experience or to someone outside the group with authority to make decisions	■ Decision is made quickly ■ Uses the expertise of a knowledgeable source of information	■ Group members may not be satisfied with the decision ■ The expert could be wrong
Averaging Individual Rankings or Ratings: Group members rank or rate possible outcomes, and the alternative with the highest ranking or best rating is selected	■ Uses a democratic process that taps all group members' thinking ■ Useful when the group needs to assess where it stands on an issue	■ The average ranking or rating may be an alternative that no group member supports ■ Group loses the opportunity for give-and-take discussion
Random Choice: Group members flip a coin or use a similar technique so they can move forward	■ Easy ■ Fast	■ More likely to result in an ineffective outcome because group members have not discussed the issues thoroughly ■ Suggests that the group does not care about making a high-quality decision
Majority Rule: Decision is made by the majority of group members	■ Often perceived as a fair way of making decisions ■ Can be an efficient way of making a decision	■ Those who do not support the majority opinion may feel left out of the process ■ Group may lose cohesiveness
Decision by Minority: Group decides to support a position advocated by a vocal minority of group members	■ Decision is made by those who feel most passionate about the outcome ■ Helps to avoid groupthink by acknowledging opposing points of view	■ The majority of group members may feel disenfranchised from the decision ■ Group decision may be difficult to implement because the majority of group members do not support the outcome
Decision by Consensus: Through discussion, group members reach a decision that all members can support	■ Group members are more likely to be satisfied with the outcome ■ Group members are more likely to participate in implementing a decision that all members support	■ Takes time ■ Takes skill

- *The group fails to establish a clear and appropriate goal.* A group that has not clearly spelled out what it hopes to accomplish by making a decision has no way to assess the effectiveness of the decision. It will be more difficult for you to select the right college or university if you do not know what your major will be or what your future plans are.
- *The group fails to identify the positive and negative consequences of the alternatives.* A group that is so eager to make a decision that it does not take time to consider the pros and cons of its actions is setting itself up to make a bad decision. A critical error by ineffective groups is failing to consider the consequences of their decision before they make it.[8]
- *The group has bad information.* As we pointed out in the last chapter, if a group has flawed or outdated evidence, the decision will also be flawed.[9] Whether the information they have is good or bad, group members will tend to use the information if all members receive it, group members discuss it, and at least one group member champions the information.[10]
- *The group does not think critically about the data it has.* Just having information does not mean the group will use it well. Reasoning is the process of drawing conclusions from information. Flawed reasoning, like flawed data, can contribute to a bad decision. Chapter 8 reviews several reasoning fallacies. Research suggests that groups perform better if they not only critically evaluate the information they have but also consider the impact of their final decision on solving the problem.[11]
- *Too few people are involved in the discussion.* One primary advantage of working in groups and teams is the opportunity to tap the knowledge base of many people rather than just of a few individuals. Research by John Oetzel documents what makes intuitive sense: Groups make better decisions when there is more equal participation in the discussion.[12] If several members dominate the conversation, decision quality suffers. Group members who believe they did not have an opportunity to voice their opinions and share information with others will not perceive the decision to have been reached fairly.[13]

Research suggests that our conclusions about group decision making apply to groups that interact online and in virtual group settings, as well as those that meet face to face. Yet there is some evidence that online groups may reach less effective decisions than groups that

REVIEW

COMPARING EFFECTIVE AND INEFFECTIVE GROUP DECISION MAKING

Effective Decision Making Results When the Group . . .	Ineffective Decision Making Results When the Group . . .
Accurately assesses the present situation	Improperly analyzes the present situation
Establishes clear and appropriate group goals	Does not establish clear and appropriate group goals
Accurately identifies positive and negative consequences of decision alternatives	Fails to identify enough positive and negative consequences of decision alternatives
Has accurate information	Works from too little information or faulty information
Draws reasonable conclusions from available information	Fails to think critically or logically about the available information
Encourages participation by many people	Allows (or settles for) participation by too few people

"Whew! That was close!
We almost decided something!"

© Ted Goff

meet in person.[14] Additionally, virtual group members report less satisfaction with their computer-mediated group experience. Virtual group members say that it typically takes more time, rather than less time, to work with people online compared with face-to-face interaction.

What can group members do to make effective and efficient decisions? Research by Michael Roberto suggests that groups that make the most efficient decisions (that use their time wisely) and reach high-quality decisions, do the following three things:[15]

1. They use clear criteria; they know what "good" looks like, and they make a decision based on clear standards for a good decision. They start the decision-making process with a vision of what the final outcome will look like.
2. They focus on finding high-quality, useful information directly related to the issue at hand, rather than gathering a large amount of information just for the sake of gathering it.
3. They break up big issues into smaller, more manageable issues to discuss.

Uncertainty in Group Decision Making

If a group is confused or uncertain how to proceed, are there any underlying principles that can help the group make a wise decision? Amos Tversky and Daniel Kahneman, a team of Nobel Prize–winning economists, have identified a framework to help reduce the uncertainty that a group or individual may face when making a decision.[16] Although their theory is complicated and abstract, we've reduced their suggestions to two underlying questions to consider when making any decision.

- Is the decision a routine decision or an unusual decision? The more representative or typical the decision and the facts and information gathered to help make the decision, the less uncertainty you should experience.
- Have you or others made decisions in the past similar to the one you now face? If you or others made similar decisions, what were the outcomes of those decisions?

Underlying each of these questions is a quest to manage the uncertainty that confronts an individual or a group when a decision should be made. If the decision is similar to other decisions that have been made previously and similar information is available to the group or individual, that information can make the choice confronting the group seem less mysterious and more manageable.

GROUP PROBLEM SOLVING: OVERCOMING OBSTACLES TO ACHIEVE A GOAL

The board of directors of a multinational corporation, a band-booster fund-raising committee, and a group of students doing a project for a group communication class all have something in common—they have problems to solve. Have you ever been involved in group problem solving and thought to yourself, "If I weren't working in this silly group, I could be more productive"? Despite such frustrations, a small group of people has the potential of arriving at a better solution than do individuals working alone. As we noted in Chapter 1, groups have more information and more creative approaches to surmounting obstacles than individuals do, and these advantages contribute to a higher-quality decision.

Problem Solving Defined

Problem solving is the process of overcoming obstacles to achieve a goal. Whereas decision making involves making a choice from among alternatives, problem solving usually requires a group to make *many* decisions or choices as it identifies a problem and determines how to solve it.

A problem consists of three elements: (1) an undesirable existing situation, (2) a goal a group wishes to achieve, and (3) obstacles that keep a group from achieving its goal.[17] Problem solving allows a group to eliminate or manage the obstacles that keep it from achieving its objective.

Like decision making, problem solving begins with assessing the present situation. What's wrong with what is happening now? *Almost every problem can be phrased in terms of something you want more of or less of.*[18] Problems often can be boiled down to such things as lack of time, money, information, or agreement. For example, a school board that decides a district needs a new high school yet realizes it lacks the money for a new school has a problem: The district has too many students for existing facilities. The board needs fewer students or more space. The goal the board wants to achieve is quality education for all students. The board cannot achieve this goal with the existing undesirable situation. The obstacles that keep the board from reaching its goal include lack of classroom space and lack of money to build more space. Every problem can be identified by noting its three elements just mentioned: the undesirable present, the group goal, and the obstacles to achieving it.

$\mathcal{R}$EVIEW

THREE ELEMENTS OF A PROBLEM

Undesirable existing situation: Something is wrong with the way things are

Goal: What the group wants to achieve

Obstacle: Something that keeps a group from achieving its goal

Barriers to Group and Team Problem Solving

What keeps groups and teams from working at their full capacity? Knowing what these barriers are can help you spot and eliminate them from your group or team. Thus, before we spend the bulk of this chapter and the next one suggesting principles and strategies to help groups work better, we lay out problems you and your group may face. Benjamin Broome and Luann Fulbright spent over six years asking people who participated in group discussions what barriers kept their group from operating at full capacity. What is significant about the following list is that these are problems that group members reported; they are not just problems that an observer noted. Here's their list of the top ten barriers.[19]

1. *Lack of structure:* Group members wanted specific methods to help their group function more efficiently.

All decision making involves assessing a situation, identifying alternative solutions, and selecting the best alternatives. What group decision methods have worked well in your group?

2. *Lack of cultural sensitivity:* Some group members were put off by biases, prejudice, sexist comments, and the failure of some to take cultural differences into account when interacting with others.

3. *Lack of planning:* Group members often weren't prepared or were unsure what the focus of the group was supposed to be.

4. *Lack of resources:* Sometimes groups had to meet in an inadequate physical space or just didn't have all the information and technical support to get the job done.

5. *Wrong people present:* The key people with the authority or information weren't involved in the discussion.

6. *Time pressure:* Groups felt pressured to achieve immediate results and to tell those in authority what they wanted to hear.

7. *Poor communication:* Misunderstandings, inattentiveness, and dominance by one group member or a faction of members within the group were cited as reasons for ineffective communication.

8. *Unsupportive social climate:* Group members sometimes did not feel they were cohesively working together, and they could not support or trust one another.

9. *Negative attitudes:* Some group members weren't flexible, were unwilling to compromise about procedures, or had unrealistic expectations about the group.

10. *Lack of problem-solving skill:* Group members tended to focus on the solution before defining the problem, or there was a lack of balanced participation.

THREE APPROACHES TO GROUP PROBLEM SOLVING

Thus far we have defined group decision making and problem solving, noted the obstacles to and the characteristics of effective group decisions, and noted barriers that keep groups from working well. We now examine three different approaches to understanding group problem solving:

1. *The* **descriptive approach** *to problem solving:* This approach identifies the typical patterns of communication that occur when people interact to solve problems.
2. *The* **functional approach** *to problem solving:* This approach identifies key task requirements and stresses the importance of effective communication as major factors that contribute to effective problem solving.
3. *The* **prescriptive approach** *to problem solving*: This approach identifies specific agendas and techniques to improve group problem-solving performance.

In this chapter we discuss the descriptive and functional approaches to group problem solving; we introduce the prescriptive approach here but reserve a detailed discussion of it for Chapter 10.

Descriptive Approach

When you describe something, you use words to categorize, classify, and clarify your subject. A descriptive approach to group problem solving identifies how groups *do* solve problems, not how they *should* solve problems.[20]

A descriptive approach does not offer specific guidelines and techniques for solving problems in groups; rather, it outlines how most groups go about solving problems. B. Aubrey Fisher makes two assumptions about the descriptive approach: (1) There is a "natural," or normal, process of group problem solving, and (2) a group will follow a normal problem-solving approach unless some external authority interferes with its freedom to solve its problem (for example, a supervisor gives the group an agenda or a strong-willed

Collaborating Ethically: What Would You Do?

Imagine that you are a member of a community advisory group whose task is to advise the city council on whether a large, well-known retail store should be permitted to build a new supercenter in the community. You think the supercenter would be a good addition to the community. One highly influential member of the group, the owner of a small clothing store on the town square, opposes the retail store. This group member is also the primary contributor to the popular "Sights and Sounds of the Holidays" celebration that's held every year in the square. She says the new supercenter will drive her and others out of business. Furthermore, she says that if the group recommends that the supercenter be approved she will withdraw her support of the community holiday celebration, which will disappoint many members of the community, including hundreds of school children who look forward to the annual performances at the celebration. Do you give in to the group member so that the community can continue to enjoy a popular celebration? Or, do you vote for what you want, knowing that while the community may gain a new larger retail store, it will lose some of the aspects that make the community a good place to live (small shops on the square, a popular holiday celebration)?
      What would you do?

group leader dictates how the group should approach its task).[21] One of the most fruitful areas of research from a descriptive perspective seeks to identify the normal phases, or cycles, that groups experience when solving problems.

Describing Group Phases   "Don't worry, Mom, I'm just going through a phase." Does this sound like something you may have said at one time? Maybe you were trying to alleviate your mother's concern by assuring her that your behavior was not at all uncommon and that it surely would pass in time. Implicit here is an assumption that individuals pass through several identifiable developmental stages, each of which leads to the next. Problem-solving groups, like individuals, go through several stages. If you understand these stages, you can learn to communicate in ways that expedite a group's passage from one stage to the next.

Does every group neatly cycle through the same phases of group discussion? The answer is no. As we will discuss later in the chapter, not all groups take the same path to solve a problem. Group discussion is often messy. Many groups do, however, go through phases. Knowing what these phases are can help you spot them if they occur in your group; it's like having a map that lets you know where you are in your group deliberations.

Several researchers have attempted to identify the phases of a problem-solving group. They have observed and recorded who speaks to whom and have categorized the comments group members exchange. Over the past fifty years researchers have used various labels to describe these phases, and despite differing terminology, they have reached similar conclusions. Although some researchers describe five phases, most scholars identify four.

Of the research on developmental phases of groups, Fisher's is the most significant for small group communication. He focused primarily on what was said throughout the development of his test groups. We use his terminology in the following sections.

Phase 1: Orientation   In the first phase of small group interaction, "group members break the ice and begin to establish a common basis for functioning."[22] Communication during this phase tends to be oriented toward getting to know one another, sharing backgrounds, and tentatively approaching the group's task. You are not likely to say anything that might prompt the rest of the group to reject you. Fisher noted that "more ambiguous comments . . . are contained in Phase 1 than in any other phase except the third, which is also characterized by ambiguity."[23]

Research on the **orientation phase** suggests that group members' communication is directed at orienting themselves toward others as well as to the group's task, which can also be said about the other phases. What sets this phase apart from the others is the degree to which the social dimension is emphasized and the tentative, careful way in which the task dimension is approached.

Yet another characteristic of the orientation phase is primary tension. **Primary tension** occurs when group members are uncertain how to behave and feel somewhat awkward about what to do or say. Clear group role expectations have not emerged; clear social norms are not yet developed. Some group members may be quiet, others may be exceptionally polite, yet others may laugh nervously and smile—all of which are manifestations of the primary tension that occurs when groups first congregate.

Even the most efficient, task-motivated group will spend some time socializing and getting acquainted. Do not underestimate the importance of this type of interaction. Interpersonal trust—an essential ingredient for an effective working environment—does not happen all at once. You begin slowly, with small talk, to determine whether it is safe to move on to deeper levels of interaction. The orientation phase, then, develops trust and group cohesiveness, which are important for the group's survival in the second phase—conflict.

Phase 2: Conflict   During the orientation phase, group members begin to form opinions about their own positions in the group and about the group's task. By the second phase they start asserting these opinions. They have tested the water in the first phase and now are ready to jump in. On the process, or social, level, this is a period in which individuals compete for status in the group. Two or more potential leaders may emerge, with the support for each dividing the group into camps. This jockeying for leadership, power, and position in a group has been called **secondary tension.**[24] This secondary tension occurs after the initial, or primary, tension has diminished and the group settles down to focus on both the task at hand and who will be influential in helping the group reach a conclusion. Secondary tension can occur abruptly. The group may be making progress, but conflict suddenly erupts over an issue and the group gets off its agenda.

Communication during the **conflict phase** is characterized by persuasive attempts at changing others' opinions and reinforcing one's own position. Some participants relish the idea of a good argument, whereas others see conflict as something to avoid at all cost. Avoiding conflict, however, means avoiding issues relevant and even crucial to the group's success. Just as individuals need to assert their own points of view, so do groups need to investigate all relevant alternatives in order to select the best solutions.

The conflict phase is necessary to both the task and the process dimensions of small group communication. Through conflict, you begin to identify the task issues that confront the group and clarify your own and others' roles. This clarification leads toward greater predictability, less uncertainty, and the establishment of group norms. There is evidence that groups that spend a considerable amount of time together may have a less prolonged period of conflict, but they nonetheless do experience conflict.[25]

Phase 3: Emergence   In Phase 3, new patterns of communication indicate a group's emergence from the conflict phase. If a group is going to function as a cohesive unit, it must resolve the conflict of Phase 2. Although conflict remains in Phase 3, what sets the **emergence phase** apart from the preceding conflict phase is the way in which members deal with conflict. This shift is most apparent in the reappearance of ambiguity in task-related statements.

Task and process dimensions are interwoven at this stage. Although the group is divided, there is also clarity. Leadership patterns and roles have been established, the issues and problems confronting the group have been identified, and the need to settle differences and reach consensus has become apparent. Ambiguity appears to be the means by which individual group members can comfortably shift their positions toward group consensus. The group settles on norms and moves toward consensus via ambiguous statements that gradually modify dissenting positions. Such ambiguous statements might take the form of qualifiers or reservations to the previous position: "I still would like to see our company merge with the Elector Electronics Corporation, but maybe we could consider a merger later in the year. A merger may be more appropriate next fall." Such a statement allows a person to save face and still allows the group to reach consensus.

Phase 4: Reinforcement   A spirit of unity characterizes the final phase of group interaction. In the preceding three phases, group members struggle through getting acquainted, building cohesiveness, expressing individuality, competing for status, and arguing over issues. The group eventually emerges from those struggles with a sense of direction, consensus, and a feeling of group identity. Not surprisingly, then, the fourth phase is characterized by positive feelings toward the group and its decisions. Finally, members feel a genuine sense of accomplishment.

Reinforcement predominates in communication:

Jim: I may have been against it at first, but I've finally seen the light. We're going in the right direction now.

Marilyn: Yes, but don't shortchange your contribution, Jim. If you hadn't opposed it so vehemently, we never would have developed the idea so fully.

Fisher noted that ambiguous and unfavorable comments all but disappear in the fourth phase, being replaced by uniformly favorable comments and reinforcement. At this time, all the hassle of group decision making and problem solving seems worthwhile. The group is at its most cohesive, individual satisfaction and sense of achievement are high, and uncertainty is at a low level.

Other Descriptive Models of Group Problem Solving

Although it may appear from our discussion that a group goes through four distinct phases of development in a predictable, easy-to-identify way, group deliberations are seldom that orderly. Communication does not typically operate in such a linear, step-by-step manner.[26]

Dialectical Theory   One theory that helps to explain the messiness of group interaction is dialectical theory. **Dialectical theory** suggests that during communication there are often competing tensions pulling the conversation into multiple directions.[27] For example, groups like a sense of stability; they want to predict what will happen because many group members like familiar patterns.[28] Yet, because communication is dynamic, there is also an interest in developing new ideas and procedures—groups expect change. Another dialectical tension is being separate from others while also being connected. The team versus the individual and structure versus interaction are other dialectical tensions that occur when groups communicate.

Because of these tensions and because communication is not usually (or even often) orderly and neat, the descriptive phases that we've described have been observed in some but not all groups. Group communication researchers have identified several other models that describe the patterns of communication within groups: the spiraling model, the punctuated equilibrium model, and the multisequence model.

Spiraling Model   Group-communication scholars Tom Scheidel and Laura Crowell's research suggests that groups may not march through four phases but rather cycle, or spiral, through them throughout the group or team's development.[29] For example, the first issue confronting the group may be "What's the purpose of this group?" A group will probably spend some time getting oriented to this task, conflict may follow as members learn each person's objectives, and after discussion, a consensus may emerge about the group's purpose. Finally, members may assure one another that their purpose has been developed clearly. Perhaps the next issue to come before the group is "How will we organize our work—should we have a subcommittee?" Again, the members may go through orientation, conflict, emergence, and reinforcement about a specific issue. Because group discussions

Virtual Communication

Research continues to describe the impact of technology on group problem solving.[30] The following strategies and observations may offer some guidance if your group seeks to solve problems and make decisions using e-mail and other electronic meeting tools.

- Electronically mediated communication seems to work best for more structured, linear tasks.
- In computer-mediated meetings, ideas can be captured and recorded quickly and accurately.
- The increased speed of information transfer allows less time for reflection. Thus, technology may sometimes help us make mistakes faster.
- Some group members do a less thorough job of evaluating the pros and cons of alternatives when using computer-mediated technology than when interacting in face-to-face settings.
- The use of computer technology does not inherently result in better solutions and decisions. Problems are solved and decisions are made by people. Technology may allow greater access to accurate information, help structure the process, and keep a group focused on facts—but decisions will continue to be made by people skilled in the art and science of decision making and problem solving.

tend to hop from topic to topic, a group may get bogged down in conflict, abandon the issue, and move to another issue. Thus, groups may spiral through phases for each issue, or group members may get sidetracked and abandon discussions about a particular topic.

Research by Charles Pavitt and Kelly Johnson found that groups do seem to exhibit spiraling tendencies, but not all groups behave in quite the same way, thus confirming the challenge of formulating tidy descriptions of how groups do their work.[31] Pavitt and Johnson's research also suggests that the order in which groups discuss topics and issues may not be as important as whether the topics are discussed or not. Therefore, the content of what you say may be more important than the precise sequence in which the content is discussed.

J. E. McGrath is another prominent small group researcher who suspects that groups and teams cycle through their work rather than following specific phases.[32] His theory includes the dimensions of time, interaction, and performance, which he calls TIP theory. McGrath hypothesizes that groups do what they need to do at a given moment based on their needs at that moment and on what function the group needs to perform. A group will become oriented or focused on a task when there is uncertainty, not just when it is first formed.

Punctuated Equilibrium Model   Connie Gersick describes what she calls a pattern of "punctuated equilibrium."[33] During the first half of a group's existence, group members may experience uncertainty and indecision about what to do or how to proceed, resulting in inertia; nothing seems to be happening. And then, about midway through the group's deliberation, a revolutionary transition, or **breakpoint,** punctuates the seeming equilibrium, and "nothing happening" changes to "something happening." The equilibrium of inertia is punctuated by a burst of activity. Then there will be a second inertia phase—a phase when the group seems to stop and again ponder which direction to go next before moving on to accomplishing the task. Gersick thinks this punctuated equilibrium model may only occur in groups that are working within a specific time limit; it may be less likely to occur in a group with an unstructured or open-ended time frame.

Additional research suggests that punctuated equilibrium can occur within the phases of group discussion that we described earlier.[34] During the conflict phase, for example, there will be bursts of progress in resolving the conflict, as well as periods of time when it appears nothing much is happening.

Multisequence Model   Yet another descriptive, nonphase model of how groups and teams typically function is proposed by M. Scott Poole.[35] As the term *multisequence* implies, groups and teams may be doing several things at once rather than cycling though predictable phases. Poole builds on Fisher's phase research by suggesting that groups engage in three types of **activity tracks** that do not necessarily follow logical step-by-step patterns. Poole believes that three types of activities best describe group interaction:[36]

1. **Task-process activities** help the group accomplish its work, such as analyzing a problem, becoming oriented to the components of a problem, establishing criteria, and evaluating proposed solutions. Answering such questions as "What's the problem here?" "How can we better understand the problem?" and "How effective will our solution be?" are examples of task-process activities. Furthermore, Poole indicates that there are three types of task-process activities: (1) activities that focus on the problem, (2) activities that serve executive functions (such as keeping the discussion oriented and on task), and (3) solution activities.[37]

2. **Relational activities** manage relationships and help maintain the group climate. For example, verbal or nonverbal communication that indicates who likes and dislikes whom can be categorized as relational activity. As noted in Chapter 4, communication has both a task dimension and a relationship dimension. Relational activities are also communication behaviors that sustain or damage interpersonal relationships among group members. Criticism, conflict, praise, and encouragement help group members understand their relationships with one another. Relational activities also affect a group's working climate. The specific relational activities that Poole identifies include (a) discussion about work-focused relationships, (b) discussion that manages conflict, (c) integration talk (connecting one person's ideas to those of others), and (d) discussion about ambiguous relationships (expressing uncertainty about relationships).[38]

3. **Topical focus activities** deal with the "general themes, major issues, or arguments of concern to the group at a given point in the discussion."[39] Ernest Bormann and other researchers have noted that groups often focus their conversations on themes or topics that serve as the groups' actual agendas.[40] This third type of activity, then, deals with major topics that do not relate to a group's specific task or to member relationships.

Poole's three activity tracks do not all develop at the same rate or according to the same pattern. Some groups spend a considerable portion of their time developing relationships before discussing their tasks in great detail. In contrast, task-oriented groups often devote considerable energy to completing their tasks, letting relationships play minor roles in group deliberations. Groups switch activity tracks at various breakpoints, which occur as

A COMPARISON OF DESCRIPTIVE MODELS OF GROUP PROCESS

Phase Models

Groups go through predictable phases (such as orientation, conflict, emergence, reinforcement) when working on a task or solving a problem.

Spiral Models

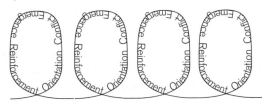

Groups may go through several phases and then repeat the cycle again and again throughout the history of the group.

Punctuated Equilibrium Models

Groups go through a period of uncertainty and indecision punctuated by a breakthrough, followed by more uncertainty, until a pattern emerges.

Multisequence Models

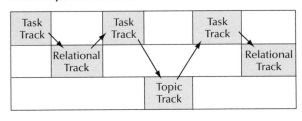

Groups switch from one activity track to another as they engage in task-process activities, relational activities, or topical focus activities.

---

groups switch topics, adjourn, or schedule planning periods. Another type of breakpoint, called a delay, occurs because of group conflict or inability to reach consensus. Whereas groups may expect and schedule some breakpoints, they usually do not schedule delays. Poole notes, "depending on the nature of the delay and the mood of the group, [a] break-point can signal the start of a difficulty or a highly creative period."[41] A disruption, the third type of breakpoint, results from a major conflict or a realization that a group may not be able to complete its task. To manage disruption, a group must be flexible.

Poole's analysis of group phases and group activity emphasizes the process nature of group communication and problem solving, rather than assuming that groups proceed through a linear, step-by-step approach. Although several researchers have documented chronological phases in a group's efforts, a group's communication can also be described by the three activity tracks Poole identifies. A descriptive approach to group communication can help you better understand and explain why certain types of statements are made in groups and how a group develops over time. With an *understanding* of the process, you should be in a better position to evaluate and improve your participation in group meetings.

Functional Approach

The descriptive approach to group problem solving does exactly what it implies: It describes what happens when groups communicate, whether the interaction involves going through phases, spirals, or sequences. The functional approach emphasizes that members of effective groups perform certain task requirements when they communicate with one another.[42] The functional approach has elements of description, because the researchers who propose this approach have observed groups and described the task requirements of effective groups. There's also a hint of prescription in this approach, in that the task requirements are presumed to be useful strategies that will help groups make better-quality decisions and arrive at good solutions. Thus, the functional approach includes elements of the conceptual frameworks of both descriptive and prescriptive approaches.

The functional approach assumes that groups are goal-oriented and that to accomplish the group goal, certain activities or communication functions need to be performed. Groups and teams become effective, argue the functional theorists, not just by applying communication techniques (the prescriptive approach) but also by communicating in ways that affect the fundamental processes of how the group achieves its goal.[43] It is through communication that group members perform key functions that enhance group problem solving and decision making.

The primary way researchers have identified the functions of effective problem solving is by examining the behaviors of both effective and ineffective groups. Certain types of communication and critical thinking distinguish effective groups from ineffective ones.[44]

What are the key functions of effective problem solving? According to Randy Hirokawa, groups must perform five key functions in order to develop a high-quality solution:[45]

1. *Develop an accurate understanding of the problem.* Specify precisely what the problem is. Identify the causes, symptoms, and history of the problem. Use data and information to help the group understand the problem.
2. *Develop requirements for an acceptable choice.* Establish criteria—explicit standards for an acceptable solution. Identify what a good solution will look like so members will know one when they see it.
3. *Develop many alternatives to solve the problem.* The more high-quality alternatives generated, the greater the chance that the group will find a high-quality solution. Just one or two ideas suggested early in the discussion will usually result in a less-effective solution.
4. *Assess the positive features of the alternatives or options for solving the problem.* Systematically identify the merits or benefits that will occur if the suggested solution or solutions are implemented.
5. *Assess the negative features of the alternatives or options for solving the problem.* Balance the positive benefits that have been identified with negative features or disadvantages of the suggested solution or solutions.

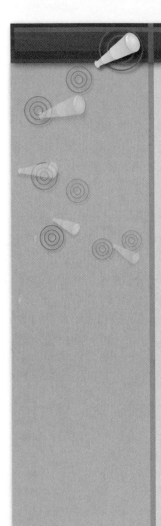

Cutting Edge Theory

THE BONA FIDE PERSPECTIVE ON GROUPS

It is increasingly likely that if you work in an organization you will be participating in many groups at the same time. Most people do not belong to just one team and focus all of their energy and talent on one primary task. The **bona fide perspective on groups** suggests that the context for and boundaries of the groups in which we participate move and change.[46] The phrase *bona fide* simply means authentic or genuine. Thus, a bona fide perspective on groups is concerned with how actual groups function in organizations. A bona fide perspective encourages us to look not at how groups are described in a textbook, but at how they operate in the real world with the tensions, pressures, and reality of being part of many groups simultaneously. Groups and teams are connected to and genuinely influenced by what else is happening in an organization. If, for example, the organization is losing money and on a tight budget, then the lack of money affects how a group operates within the organization. A group does not do its work in isolation. Another aspect of a bona fide perspective involves the other people who work in the group. You may be assigned to work with others who are not in the same physical location as you; they may work in another city, state, or country.

According to Linda Putnam, who has done extensive research and writing about bona fide groups, we need to be more sensitive to how groups really operate in natural settings. Most groups and teams do not exist in isolation from other groups and from the larger organization of which they are a part. Therefore, Putnam suggests focusing on two elements when considering bona fide groups:

1. how the group is connected to other groups and the larger organization and
2. how the group operates in relationship to its external context.

Group communicators who incorporate these functions into their interactions with others are what Hirokawa and other researchers call **vigilant thinkers.** Vigilant thinkers are critical thinkers. They pay attention to the process of problem solving. There is evidence that groups that believe they will be effective in using vigilant thinking skills will, in fact, do a better job of thinking critically and effectively.[47]

Of these five functions, is one more important than the others? Recent research points to the importance of all the functions, but the best predictors of quality group performance are functions 1, 2, and 5. So, for best results, (1) analyze the problem; be sure to use data and information rather than just sharing opinions when analyzing the current situation; (2) establish criteria—know what a good solution looks like; and (3) evaluate the potential negative consequences of possible solutions. Discuss certain standards or expectations before hunting for a solution.[48]

Communication researcher Elizabeth Graham and her colleagues found that effective

Real-Life Applications

What real-world applications does a bona fide perspective on groups have for the groups and teams to which we belong?

- If you're a leader or manager in an organization, a bona fide perspective suggests that you need to be aware that the people who work under your supervision have multiple roles and multiple jobs. Just as your instructor needs to be aware that you're likely taking more than one class, so should a manager realize that her or his employees are working on multiple projects at the same time.

- Remember that the groups and teams you work with today may not be the same groups and teams you work with tomorrow. Group membership changes. The changing composition of the group may result in the group's having to go through numerous periods of reorientation as group members come and go.

- Group members may participate in the group via e-mail or phone and not face to face. Special effort must be made to integrate the long-distance group members into the fabric of the group.

- Remember that when people work on a group or team task, they are constrained by the environment of the larger organization in which they work. Groups do not work in isolation—group members are connected to others even though all they may be aware of is the interaction in the group or team in which they work.

Naturally occurring groups are complex and have changeable boundaries and group members. The bona fide approach to groups calls on us to be realistic when we apply principles and practices of group theory to groups and teams.

groups established and used clear criteria and made positive comments about the alternative solutions that group members suggested; in essence, such groups had clear goals and said nice things about solutions.[49] The researchers suspected that the positive comments helped to establish a supportive group climate. In contrast, Kevin Barge suggests that the following functions are essential for an effective problem-solving group. Group members should (1) network with others within and outside the group to gather effective information; (2) acquire the skill of data splitting—that is, analyzing information effectively; (3) generate and evaluate solutions; and (4) manage their relationships effectively by means of listening, feedback, and negotiation skill.[50]

The vigilant-thinking functions suggested by Hirokawa and his colleagues, as well as the functions identified by Barge, are similar to those suggested by Irving Janis: Gather accurate information, analyze the information, draw reasonable conclusions from the data, generate solutions, evaluate the costs and risks of the solutions, and select the best one.[51]

Communication Functions of Effective Group Problem Solvers   The functional perspective assumes that a group will make a higher-quality decision if group members analyze information appropriately, generate an ample number of ideas, evaluate information and solutions, and remain sensitive to others. Based on the work of several group communication researchers, the following specific communication functions are considered essential to effective problem solving.[52]

1. *Analysis function:* Group members who effectively analyze information and ideas do several things:
   - *They establish clear criteria.*   Groups and teams have their goal clearly in mind as they analyze the issues.
   - *They see the problem from a variety of viewpoints.*   Individuals often look at a problem as it affects themselves. A skilled problem solver considers how the problem affects others, too, and is able to think about an issue from other people's vantage points.[53]
   - *They gather data and research issues.*   Good problem solvers do not rely on their own opinions. They spend time in the library or develop surveys to gather information and others' opinions about an issue.
   - *They use evidence effectively to reach a valid conclusion.*   Beyond just collecting evidence, a good problem solver needs to know how to use evidence to reach a conclusion.
   - *They ask appropriate questions.*   One big problem groups have is keeping the discussion focused on the issues. Members often bounce from one idea or topic to the next. Good problem solvers know this and use questions to help keep the group moving toward its goal. Questions such as "Where are we now?" or "What's the next step in solving our problem?" or "Aren't we getting off the track here?" can help the group get back to the task.

2. *Idea-generation function:* An essential aspect of a well-functioning problem-solving group is group members who are creative and inventive, who find ways to keep ideas flowing.
   - *They search for many alternatives or solutions to a problem.*   Effective groups are not content to have just one or two approaches to a problem. They identify many solutions that may help overcome the obstacles keeping the group from reaching its goal.
   - *They make high-quality statements to the group.*   According to several researchers, high-quality statements are precise rather than rambling and abstract. They are also consistent with previous evidence and relevant to the topic under discussion, and they positively reinforce the comments of other group members.[54]
   - *They take a vacation from a problem to revitalize the group.*   If the group gets bogged down and cannot reach agreement, postpone further discussion if possible. Sometimes you get a burst of creativity when you are not even thinking about a problem.[55] Have you ever had an idea come to you while you were jogging, driving somewhere, or taking a shower? Give your mind a chance to work on the problem by giving yourself a break from agonizing over a solution.

3. *Evaluation function:* Being able to separate good ideas from bad ideas is a critical function of group members who are good problem solvers.
   - *They examine the pros and cons of potential solutions.*   Give special attention to considering what might go wrong before implementing a solution.

According to the functional perspective, effective group members take breaks when they are having trouble solving a problem, instead of agonizing over a solution. What activities help you generate ideas?

■ *They evaluate the opinions and assumptions of others.* Do not just accept another person's conclusion or opinion at face value. One study found that groups that reach better solutions include members who take the time to test the assumptions of others.[56] Although you should not attack another person's credibility, all opinions and assumptions need to be supported by evidence. A group that tactfully examines the basis for an opinion can determine whether the opinion is valid.

■ *They test solutions to see if they meet preestablished criteria.* Criteria are standards for acceptable solutions. Such criteria as "It should be within the budget" and "It should be implemented within six months" are important to problem solving. If a group has generated criteria for a solution, a good problem solver reminds the group what the criteria are and evaluates possible solutions according to these previously identified standards.

4. *Personal-sensitivity function:* As we have emphasized throughout the book, groups have both a task and a relationship dimension. Members of successfully functioning teams or groups are other-oriented, empathic, sensitive to the needs of others, and thoughtful listeners.[57]

■ *They are concerned for both the group task and the feelings of others.* Being too task-oriented is not good for the overall group climate. As discussed in Chapter 5, sensitivity to the feelings of others can enhance the group climate and foster a supportive, rather than a defensive, approach to achieving a group goal. One study found that group members who engage in storytelling, especially stories relevant to the task at hand, help the group balance the deliberative task talk with a more relationally focused story; the use of stories helps the group achieve a more effective outcome.[58]

■ *They listen to minority arguments and opinions.* It is always tempting to disregard the voice of a lone dissenter. That individual may, however, have a brilliant idea or a legitimate complaint about the majority point of view. Assume that all ideas have merit; do not discount ideas because they come from members who are not supporting the majority at the moment.

A SUMMARY OF GROUP COMMUNICATION FUNCTIONS

Functions	Characteristics of an Effective Group Problem Solver
Analysis function	Sees the problem from a variety of viewpoints
	Gathers data and researches the issues
	Uses evidence effectively
	Asks appropriate questions
Idea-generation function	Searches for many solutions to a problem
	Makes high-quality statements
	Takes a vacation from the problem to revitalize the group
Evaluation function	Evaluates the pros and cons
	Evaluates the opinions and assumptions of others
	Tests proposed solutions to see if they meet preestablished criteria
Personal sensitivity function	Shows concern for both the group task and the feelings of others
	Listens to minority arguments

Prescriptive Approach

When the doctor gives you a prescription, he or she is telling you to do something very specific: Take a measured dose of a particular medicine to treat your medical problem. A prescriptive approach to group problem solving is based on the assumption that groups need more than a general understanding of how groups solve problems or what the key functions of group communication are. The prescriptive approach offers specific do's and don'ts for structuring a group's problem-solving agenda. Prescriptive approaches invite group members to perform certain behaviors in a specific order to achieve a group goal. Fisher describes the prescriptive approach as providing "guidelines, a road map, to assist the group in achieving consensus. A prescriptive approach is based on an assumed 'ideal' process."[59] According to Fisher, two assumptions underlie the prescriptive approach to problem solving: (1) Group members are consistently rational, and (2) the prescribed agenda or set of techniques will result in a better solution.

The descriptive approach to group problem solving and decision making helps a group understand *how* groups usually solve problems. The functional approach identifies tasks that should be performed to enhance the group's effectiveness. The prescriptive approach offers specific recommendations for sequencing certain types of communication in a group. Which approach is best? Some scholars advocate the descriptive approach, pointing out that it does not constrain a group from its normal or natural process. These scholars reject the prescriptive approach as being too rigid. Others suggest that groups should consciously perform key functions to maximize effectiveness. Yet others contend that the prescriptive approach gives a group needed structure for solving problems, because working in groups often results in uncertainty and ambiguity.[60]

Arthur VanGundy categorizes problems as either structured or unstructured.[61] An unstructured problem is one about which we have little information and thus high uncertainty. The more unstructured the problem, the greater the need for a prescriptive technique of gathering and analyzing information to solve the problem. One study suggests that leaders who give a group a structure by setting goals, monitoring time, and providing sugges-

Case Study

The school board was at an impasse. Board members had been debating whether to present a bond proposal for a new high school to the voters. The group had spent several sessions hashing through mounds of reports, population projections, data, and survey results from parents. Some board members thought the evidence did not support the need for a new high school. Yes, they knew the current high school was overcrowded and that more people were moving into the district, but despite these facts, survey results clearly suggested that most people thought taxes were already too high and that they would therefore not support additional bonds for the new school. Other board members felt it was their duty, regardless of what survey results suggested, to propose that the district build a new school.

The board decided to hire a trained group facilitator to help them overcome their impasse. The facilitator had looked at the minutes of previous board meetings and could see that the group was stuck in conflict and not yet oriented to the issues. Board members struggled with analyzing the mounds of information they had received. They also had difficulty generating options other than building or not building a high school.

Practice in Applying Principles

1. Think back on the discussion of methods of group decision making presented on pages 209–210. What method or methods would you recommend if you were the facilitator for the school board?
2. Based on the information in the case, what possible obstacles to quality group decision making (pages 211–212) may be hindering the school board from making a decision?
3. How could the facilitator help the group by using a descriptive approach to group problem solving and decision making, as described on pages 216–219?
4. What critical communication functions should the facilitator ensure the school board use (see pages 226–227) to help them move forward?

tions about procedure enhance the group's perceived effectiveness.[62] VanGundy has identified over 70 techniques that help provide structure to the problem-solving process.

Clearly each approach has its unique advantages. Draw on all three approaches as you work at becoming an effective problem-solving group participant. If the task is very simple, a group may not need a cumbersome, predetermined set of prescriptions. Research suggests, however, that if the task is complex (as many group tasks are) specific guidelines and procedures will help the group work more effectively.[63]

In this chapter we have emphasized descriptive and functional perspectives. In Chapter 10 we describe in more detail prescriptive approaches, formats, and techniques to give you some options in structuring group problem solving.

CULTURAL ASSUMPTIONS ABOUT GROUP PROBLEM SOLVING AND DECISION MAKING

As we conclude this chapter, we remind you that assumptions about the descriptions, functions, and prescriptions of group and team problem solving and decision making will be filtered through the cultural perspective group members hold. As we noted in Chapter 1, some cultures (notably those of the United States, Britain, and northern Europe) assume an individualistic approach to accomplishing work, whereas other cultures (such as Asian cultures) assume a collaborative or collectivistic mind-set.[64]

In addition to culture, gender also contributes to group differences that researchers suggest influence how group members interact. For example, Katherine Hawkins and Christopher Power found that females tend to ask more probing questions during group deliberations than do males.[65]

You need not travel abroad to experience different cultural perspectives. In the United States you are likely to encounter individuals with a wide range of cultural and ethnic traditions. Even within one region of the United States, group members may differ in their approaches to and assumptions about problem solving, collaboration, and teamwork.

What strategies can bridge these cultural differences? Consider these suggestions.[66]

■ *Develop mindfulness.*   To be mindful is to be consciously aware of cultural differences and to note that there are differences between your assumptions and the assumptions of others.[67] Consciously say to yourself, "These group members may have a different assumption about how to accomplish this task. Before I impose my strategies on them, I'll listen and make sure I understand what they are saying."

■ *Be flexible.*   Realize that you may have to adapt and change according to the perceptions and assumptions others hold.

■ *Tolerate uncertainty and ambiguity.*   Working with others from a culture or cultures different from your own is bound to create a certain amount of uncertainty and confusion. Being patient and tolerant will help you manage cultural differences when collaborating with others.[68]

■ *Resist stereotyping and making negative judgments about others.*   Ethnocentrism is the assumption that your cultural heritage is superior. Assuming superiority when evaluating others typically produces defensiveness.

■ *Ask questions.*   An essential element of any effective team is common ground rules; these can best be established simply by asking others how they work and solve problems and about their preferences for establishing norms and ground rules.

■ *Be other-oriented.*   Empathy and sensitivity to others are keys to bridging cultural differences. Although simply considering an issue from someone else's point of view will not eliminate the difference, it will help enhance understanding.[69] One of the seven habits of highly effective people identified by Stephen Covey nicely summarizes this principle: Seek to understand before being understood.[70]

 ## Putting Principles into Practice

If you understand how groups go about the task of solving problems, you will be better able to manage the problem-solving process in small groups. The following suggestions should help you apply the concepts presented in this chapter.

Group Decision Making

■ Start the decision-making process by accurately assessing the present situation.

■ Establish clear and appropriate group goals to frame the decision-making objective.

■ Identify positive and negative consequences of the alternatives identified.

■ Ensure that group members have accurate information.

■ Determine whether group members are drawing reasonable conclusions for the information that is available.

Group Problem Solving

- With other group members, answer the question "What do we want more or less of?" Analyze the problem by identifying (1) the undesirable present, (2) the group's goal, and (3) obstacles that may keep you from achieving the goal.
- Give all group members the opportunity to help formulate appropriate group goals.
- Even when the first proposed solution seems reasonable or workable, examine other alternatives.
- Effective problem solvers:

  Are vigilant thinkers; they appropriately analyze information and data.

  Identify criteria; they define standards so they'll recognize a good solution when they see it.

  Generate creative ideas; they search for many high-quality solutions.

  Evaluate ideas and solutions; they examine the costs and benefits of solutions.

  Are sensitive to others; they are concerned both about the task and about the feelings of other group members.

- Interpret and evaluate the information you collect. Do not just accept the information at face value.
- Do not let yourself be satisfied after you generate a few potential solutions. Keep searching, unless the group needs a break.

Approaches to Group Problem Solving

- Use a descriptive approach as a road map to help you determine where you are in the group problem-solving process.
- Adopt a functional approach to group problem solving by performing the functions of effective problem solvers.

- Adopt a prescriptive approach to problem solving if your group needs the structure that a problem-solving agenda provides.
- Do not be concerned if your group takes time to orient itself to the problem-solving process. Orientation is a normal part of group work.
- Expect some conflict and differences of opinion after a group clarifies its task and passes through the orientation phase of problem solving.
- Even though conflict may appear to impede a group's efforts to solve a problem, expect a decision to emerge after a thorough discussion and analysis of the issues.
- Do not overlook the importance of the reinforcement phase of group problem solving. Group members need to feel a sense of accomplishment after making a decision. Take time to celebrate.

Bridging Cultural Differences

- Develop mindfulness: Become consciously aware of cultural differences.
- Be flexible: Be ready to adapt to the cultural expectations and traditions of others.
- Tolerate uncertainty and ambiguity: Be patient when working with those who have a cultural background different from your own.
- Avoid stereotyping and making negative judgments: Avoid an ethnocentric mind-set that assumes your cultural traditions are superior to those of others.
- Ask questions: Reduce your uncertainty by asking questions to help you and your team members develop common ground rules and norms.
- Be other-oriented: Cultivate the skill of empathy and seek to understand others before forcing your ideas and opinions on others.

*P*RACTICE

Description of Group Process

Attend a meeting of your school board or city council or another public meeting in which problems are discussed and solutions are recommended. Prepare a written analysis of the meeting in which you attempt to identify phases in the group's discussions. Also, try to identify examples of the three activity tracks discussed in this chapter (task process, relational, and topical focus). In addition, provide examples of breakpoints in the discussion of the group.

Hurricane Preparedness Case

Imagine that you are a resident of a coastal city during hurricane season. Although you have idly watched local meteorologists track Hurricane Bruce's destructive course through the Caribbean for several days, you have not given any serious thought to the possibility that the storm might directly affect you. However, at about seven o'clock this morning, the storm suddenly veered northward, and it is now on course for a direct hit. The National Hurricane Center in Miami has posted a hurricane warning for your community. Forecasters predict landfall in approximately nine to twelve hours. Having taken no advance precautions, you are stunned by the amount of work you now have to do to secure your three-bedroom suburban home, which is about half a mile from the beach. You have enough food in the house for two days. You also have one candle and a transistor radio with one weak battery; you have no other hurricane supplies. Your task is to rank the following items in terms of their importance for ensuring your survival and the safety of your property, with number 1 being the first thing you should do, 2 the second, and so on. Work individually.

_____ Fill the gas tank of your car

_____ Trim your bushes and trees

_____ Fill the bathtub with water

_____ Construct hurricane shutters for the windows

_____ Buy enough food for a week

_____ Buy batteries and candles

_____ Bring in patio furniture from outside

_____ Buy dry ice

_____ Invite friends over for a hurricane party

_____ Drain the swimming pool

_____ Listen to TV and radio for further bulletins before doing anything

_____ Make sure you have an evacuation plan

_____ Stock up on charcoal and charcoal lighter for the barbecue grill

After you have made your individual rankings, work in a small group again and rank these items according to their importance. Your group's task is to reach consensus.

Stranded in the Desert Situation[71]

You are a member of a geology club that is on a field trip to study unusual formations in the New Mexico desert. It is the last week in July. You have been driving over old trails, far from any road, in order to see out-of-the-way formations. At about 10:30 A.M. your club's specially equipped minibus overturns, rolls into a 20-foot ravine, and burns. The driver and the club's professional adviser are killed; the rest of you are uninjured.

You know that the nearest ranch is approximately 45 miles east of where you are. There is no closer habitation. When your club does not report to its motel that evening, you will be missed. Several people know generally where you are but will not be able to pinpoint your whereabouts.

The area around you is rugged and dry. There is a shallow waterhole nearby, but the water is contaminated by worms, animal feces and urine, and several dead mice. Before you left you heard a weather report that the temperature would reach 108°F, making the surface temperature 128°F. All of you are dressed in lightweight summer clothing and all have hats and sunglasses.

In escaping from the minibus, each group member salvaged a couple of items; there are twelve items in all. Assume that your small group are the members of the geology club and that you all have agreed to stick together. Your group's task is to rank the salvaged items according to their importance to your survival, starting with 1 for the most important through 12 for the least important.

_____ Magnetic compass

_____ A piece of heavy-duty, light blue canvas, 20 square feet in area

_____ A book: *Plants of the Desert*

_____ Rearview mirror

_____ Large knife

_____ Flashlight

_____ One jacket per person

_____ One transparent plastic ground cloth (6 feet by 4 feet) per person

_____ A .38 caliber loaded pistol

_____ One 2-quart plastic canteen of water per person
_____ An accurate map of the area
_____ A large box of kitchen matches

Assessing Group Communication Skills

Communication researchers Katherine Hawkins and Bryant Fillion surveyed personnel managers to find out what the managers considered the most important skills necessary for success in groups and teams.[72] Their results are reflected in the following scale. Rate each member of a group you are in on the following skills, using a scale from 1 to 5 (1 = not at all effective; 2 = generally not effective; 3 = uncertain; 4 = effective; 5 = very effective).

Skill	Group Member	Group Member	Group Member	Group Member	Group Member
1. Listens effectively	_____	_____	_____	_____	_____
2. Understands roles and responsibilities	_____	_____	_____	_____	_____
3. Actively contributes to the group	_____	_____	_____	_____	_____
4. Asks clear questions	_____	_____	_____	_____	_____
5. Establishes and maintains rapport with others	_____	_____	_____	_____	_____
6. Is sensitive to people with different cultural backgrounds	_____	_____	_____	_____	_____
7. Uses clear, concise, accurate, and professional language	_____	_____	_____	_____	_____
8. Communicates well with people who have different professional backgrounds	_____	_____	_____	_____	_____
9. Gives clear and accurate instructions	_____	_____	_____	_____	_____
10. Presents a positive professional image nonverbally (through appropriate grooming and attire)	_____	_____	_____	_____	_____
11. Helps resolve conflicts	_____	_____	_____	_____	_____
12. Accurately summarizes information to the group	_____	_____	_____	_____	_____
13. Gives brief, clear, and well-organized, informative presentations to the group when appropriate	_____	_____	_____	_____	_____
Total	_____	_____	_____	_____	_____

Scoring: Total the score for each group member. A perfect score is 65; the lowest possible score is 13. Your instructor may invite you to share your ratings of other group members anonymously. Or, if you don't share your ratings, simply note how you evaluate your skill in comparison to your ratings of other group members.

CHAPTER TEN

Using Problem-Solving Techniques

"*The best way to escape from a problem is to solve it.*"

—*Anonymous*

CHAPTER OUTLINE

An Overview of Prescriptive Problem-Solving Strategies

Finding a Balance Between Group Structure and Interaction

Reflective Thinking: The Traditional Approach to Group Problem Solving

Question-Oriented Approaches to Problem Solving

Case Study

Beyond Technique

Putting Principles into Practice

Practice

OBJECTIVES

After studying this chapter, you will be able to:

- Use the steps and tools of reflective thinking to solve a problem in a small group discussion.
- Apply the ideal-solution problem-solving method to a group discussion.
- Apply the single-question problem-solving approach to a group discussion.
- Determine which problem-solving approach is most suitable for a given group discussion.

WHENEVER WE PRESENT *corporate communication training seminars for executives or business leaders on the topic of group or team problem solving, we begin our session by asking a simple question: What do you want to learn about group problem solving? Their responses are predictable. They want to know precisely what to do to make working in groups and teams more effective. They ask questions like "How do I develop an agenda when the group has a problem to solve?" "What are the best techniques to help a group arrive at the best solution?" "What should I do to ensure that my team operates at peak efficiency?" They want precise prescriptions for success.*

In the last chapter we introduced three approaches to understanding problem solving: descriptive, functional, and prescriptive. If you're leading a group or are a member of a group, you could adopt a descriptive approach to problem solving and clue group members in to some of the processes and phases that groups experience when trying to solve problems. You could, in essence, give them a road map to help them understand how groups operate. Or, you could hand out a list of the group functions—task requirements for groups—that we unveiled in Chapter 9: assess the problem, establish criteria, develop alternatives, and evaluate both the pros and cons of the options identified, giving special attention to reviewing negative consequences of options you may consider.

There's a third approach—the prescriptive approach to problem solving. To prescribe is to offer specific and sometimes detailed do's or don'ts to help a group perform well. However, as there is no single best way to solve problems in groups, *no list of prescriptive problem-solving techniques always works. Each group is unique, as is each group member. Yet evidence indicates that guiding a group through a structured agenda can enhance its effectiveness.[1] This chapter gives you several suggestions for solving problems in groups. We focus on the problem-solving task in this chapter and review prescriptions for enhancing creativity in the next chapter.*

AN OVERVIEW OF PRESCRIPTIVE PROBLEM-SOLVING STRATEGIES

There are a vast number of specific strategies and techniques that can help you facilitate group problem solving.[2] Most include references to five key elements: (1) identify and define the problem, (2) analyze the problem, (3) identify possible solutions, (4) select the best solution, and (5) implement the solution. These steps outline the primary way most scientists in any discipline go about finding answers to puzzling questions. We will examine the origin of these steps as well as why they continue to be used to structure group problem-solving discussion.

The Origin of Prescriptive Problem-Solving Strategies

In 1910, philosopher and educator John Dewey, in his book *How We Think,* identified the steps most people follow to solve problems. According to Dewey, a reflective thinker considers these key questions.[3]

1. What is the "felt difficulty" or concern?
2. Where is it located, and how is it defined?
3. What are possible solutions to the felt difficulty?
4. What are logical reasons that support the solution?
5. What additional testing and observation need to be done to confirm the validity of the solution?

These five steps should look familiar. They are very close to the five steps we just mentioned. Even though Dewey did not focus specifically on small groups, the steps he outlined, called **reflective thinking**—a series of logical, rational steps based on the scientific method of defining, analyzing, and solving a problem—have been used by many groups as a way to structure the problem-solving process. As new courses in group discussion were being designed in the 1920s and 1930s, teachers and authors adapted Dewey's framework as a standard agenda that could be used to tackle any problem-solving group discussion. One of the first texts to adapt these steps explicitly was Alfred Dwight Sheffield's brief book *Creative Discussion: A Statement of Method for Leaders and Members of Discussion Groups and Conferences,* first published in 1926.[4] Soon other scholars began making similar references to this sequence, and, as you will see in the discussion that follows, it has become a **standard agenda** for structuring group problem solving.[5]

*F*INDING A BALANCE BETWEEN GROUP STRUCTURE AND INTERACTION

Communicating with others in small groups to solve a problem is often a messy and disorganized process.[6] Even though some researchers have identified distinct phases in the course of a group's deliberation (orientation, conflict, emergence, reinforcement), others find that group discussion often bounces from person to person and can be an inefficient, time-consuming process.[7] And, as we discussed in Chapter 2, groups also develop fantasy themes that can trigger a chain of stories—some that are related to the group's task and some that are not. Although these stories and group fantasies are important to a group's identity, extended off-task "storytelling" can have a negative effect on the group's productivity.

To help group members manage the messiness of group discussion, a group needs a certain amount of structure to keep the discussion focused. Group **structure** consists of the agenda and other techniques and procedures to help a group stay focused on the task at hand.

A group also needs the energy that comes from interaction. **Interaction** is simply the give-and-take conversation that occurs when people collaborate. We suggest that a group needs a balance of structure and interaction to be both efficient and effective.

Groups Need Structure

To counteract the messiness of group interaction, researchers investigating groups have suggested that an agenda be used to structure the discussion. The purpose of a group agenda is to help keep the discussion on track, not to stifle group interaction or consciousness raising. Robert Bales found that most task-oriented groups spend a little over 60 percent of their time talking about the task and almost 40 percent of their time talking about social, relational, or maintenance matters.[8] An agenda ensures that the time spent talking about the task helps the group accomplish its goal.

Researchers have found that groups and teams that have no planned structure or agenda have many more procedural problems. Here's a summary of what researchers have found by observing "naturally occurring" or unhindered discussion, where there is little or no structure.

1. The group takes more time to deliberate; interaction is inefficient and often off task.
2. Group members prematurely focus on solutions rather than analyzing issues.
3. The group often jumps at the first solution mentioned.
4. Group members hop from one idea or proposal to the next without seeing the larger issues.
5. The group is more likely to be dominated by an outspoken group member.
6. Conflict is likely to go unmanaged.[9]

The conclusion to be drawn from this research: Groups and teams need help to keep them on track.

Of all the various ways to organize or structure discussion, which method seems to be the best? Many sequences of techniques have not been tested empirically. Among those sequences that have been compared in controlled studies, no single method seems to work best all of the time. One powerful conclusion, however, emerges from the research: *Any method of structuring group problem solving is better than no method at all.*[10]

Groups need structure because members have relatively short attention spans and because uncertainty results both from the relationships among group members and from the group's definition of the task. In separate studies, researchers found that groups shift topics about once a minute.[11] As noted in the last chapter, Poole argues that group members consider task process, relational concerns, and topical shifts with varying degrees of attention. Thus, groups benefit from an agenda that keeps the discussion focused on their task. And one research study found that some members need more structure than others. Group members who have a preference for using more rigid procedures arrived at higher-quality decisions than those using a less-structured approach to organizing their discussion.[12]

Think of the various steps and tools in this chapter as a way to impose a common structure on a group's deliberation. Without that structure, a group is more likely to wobble, waste time, and be less productive.

"Wait a minute! This budget meeting appears to have lost its focus!"

© Ted Goff

Groups Need Interaction

In addition to a structured agenda and procedures to help the group stay on task, groups need interaction—give-and-take conversation, talk, dialogue, and reaction to the

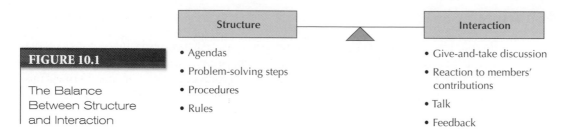

FIGURE 10.1

The Balance
Between Structure
and Interaction

messages of others. A group that has too much structure and not enough interaction is a group out of balance; participating in such a group would be like listening to someone give a speech rather than engaging in an interactive discussion.

In this chapter we identify techniques that not only help your group stay on track (structure) but also facilitate group conversation about the topic at hand (interaction). Ideally, a group should have balanced participation to which all members contribute.[13] A group member who talks too much can throw the group off balance. As Figure 10.1 suggests, the goal is to find the right balance between structure and interaction. Based on his effective decision-making theory, John Oetzel has found that groups that have more equal participation enjoy better-quality results; this research supports the assumption that groups need balanced interaction to achieve their goals.[14] Some research studies suggest that groups that used networked computers to share information (a highly structured situation) generated lots of ideas but had difficulty reaching a decision.[15] A less-structured, interactive, face-to-face situation was better for discussing alternatives and reaching a final decision. Many of the prescriptive agendas we discuss in this chapter incorporate the key communication functions of effective groups, discussed in the last chapter.

ℛEFLECTIVE THINKING: THE TRADITIONAL APPROACH TO GROUP PROBLEM SOLVING

Some researchers and numerous group communication textbooks recommend reflective thinking (or one of its many variations) as the standard agenda for organizing or structuring group problem solving. However, many group communication theorists today believe that reflective thinking is more useful as a description of the way some people solve problems than as an ideal pattern for all groups to solve problems. We describe the procedures and tools that can assist you and your groups in organizing the sometimes uncertain and fractious process of problem solving. The steps we present here are not intended to be a one-size-fits-all approach. They do, however, provide a logical, rational way of structuring group interaction.[16]

Step 1: Identify and Define the Problem

Perhaps you have heard the saying "A problem well stated is a problem half solved." A group first has to recognize that a problem exists. This may be the group's biggest obstacle. The problem should be limited so that members know its scope and size. After members identify and limit the problem, they should define key terms in light of the problem under consideration, so that they have a common understanding of the problem. For example, one student group recently decided to solve the problem of student apathy on campus. The students phrased their problem as a question: "What can be done to alleviate student apathy on campus?" They had identified a problem, but they soon discovered that they needed to decide what they meant by the word *apathy*. Does it mean poor attendance at football games? Does it mean a sparse showing at the recent fund-raising activity, "Hit Your Professor with a Pie"? After additional efforts to define the key word, they decided to limit their problem to low attendance at events sponsored by the student activities committee. With a clearer focus on their problem, they were ready to continue with the problem-solving process.

Researchers have consistently found that groups develop better solutions to their problems if they take the time to analyze the issues *before* jumping in and listing possible solutions; groups and teams have a tendency, however, to leap to a solution before looking at and analyzing the issues.[17]

Consider the following questions when attempting to identify and define a problem for group deliberations:

1. What is the specific problem the group is concerned about?
2. What obstacles are keeping the group from its goal?
3. Is the question the group is trying to answer clear?
4. What terms, concepts, or ideas need to be defined?
5. Who is harmed by the problem?
6. When do the harmful effects of the problem occur?

Tools for Defining the Problem

In addition to using the questions listed above to identify and define the problem, three techniques that provide even more structure—the *is/is not* analysis, the *journalist's six questions*, and *Pareto charts*—may be useful when your group needs "super" structure to clarify and define the problem.

Is/Is Not Analysis The **is/is not analysis** technique is a way to ensure that a group is, in fact, investigating a problem and not just a symptom of the problem.[18] Early in a group's deliberation, group members consider such questions as "What is the area or object with the problem?" "What is not the area or object with the problem?" "Where does the problem occur?" "Where does the problem not occur?" The chart below includes other questions that can help

	Is	Is Not
What	What is the area or object with the problem?	What is not the area or object with the problem?
Symptoms	What are the symptoms of the problem?	What are not the symptoms of the problem?
When	When is the problem observed?	When is the problem not observed?
Where	Where does the problem occur?	Where does the problem not occur?
Who	Who is affected by the problem?	Who is not affected by the problem?

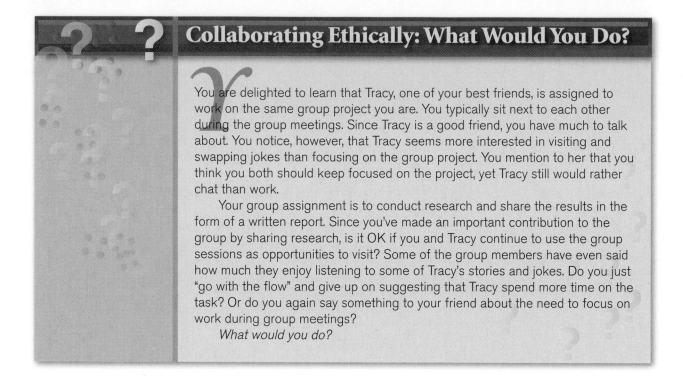

Collaborating Ethically: What Would You Do?

You are delighted to learn that Tracy, one of your best friends, is assigned to work on the same group project you are. You typically sit next to each other during the group meetings. Since Tracy is a good friend, you have much to talk about. You notice, however, that Tracy seems more interested in visiting and swapping jokes than focusing on the group project. You mention to her that you think you both should keep focused on the project, yet Tracy still would rather chat than work.

Your group assignment is to conduct research and share the results in the form of a written report. Since you've made an important contribution to the group by sharing research, is it OK if you and Tracy continue to use the group sessions as opportunities to visit? Some of the group members have even said how much they enjoy listening to some of Tracy's stories and jokes. Do you just "go with the flow" and give up on suggesting that Tracy spend more time on the task? Or do you again say something to your friend about the need to focus on work during group meetings?

What would you do?

give the group the structure it needs to clearly identify and define a problem. Group members can use the chart to focus on the specific problem under consideration. Members could first write down their answers and then share their responses one at a time. Having group members write before speaking is a way to help further structure their comments.

For example, one group was attempting to investigate the declining standardized test scores in one elementary school in their community. They thought the problem they were trying to solve was inadequate teaching that resulted in lowered scores. But when the group used the *is/is not* technique to identify when and where the problem was and was not observed, they discovered that the low test scores occurred in only three classrooms, which were in the same wing of the building and all cooled by the same air-conditioning system. On further investigation, they realized that the air-conditioning units were not functioning, which meant that classrooms in that wing were uncomfortably hot—which in turn affected student performance on the examinations. The problem changed from trying to eliminate bad teaching to repairing the air-conditioning system. The *is/is not* technique is a way to identify and define the problem rather than the symptoms of the problem.

Who?	
What?	
When?	
Where?	
Why?	
How?	

Journalist's Six Questions   Most news reporters are taught to quickly identify the key facts when writing a news story or broadcasting a news event. The key elements of almost any newsworthy story can be captured by addressing a **journalist's six questions:** Who? What? When? Where? Why? How? Using these questions can help a group quickly structure how a problem is defined. Group members could be given a worksheet such as the one shown here and asked to answer these six questions before the group's next meeting.[19] The group could then pool the results and

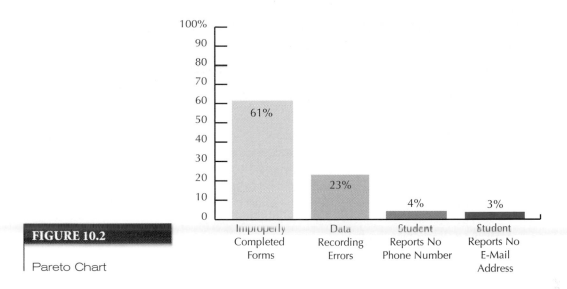

FIGURE 10.2

Pareto Chart

be well on the way to analyzing the problem. Or, the group could brainstorm answers to these questions while the group leader records the responses on a flip chart or chalkboard.

Pareto Charts A Pareto chart is a bar graph that shows data that describe the cause, source, or frequency of a problem. The chart is arranged with the tallest bars on the left and the shortest bars on the right. A Pareto chart makes it easy to look at data and identify the source of the problem. The chart gets its name from the **Pareto Principle.** Perhaps you've heard it: *The source of 80 percent of the problem comes from 20 percent of the incidents.*[20] Here are some examples: Eighty percent of the dirt on your carpet is on 20 percent of the carpet's surface; 80 percent of the food you order comes from 20 percent of the menu; 80 percent of the conflict in a group is created by 20 percent of the group members. Most groups find that the primary source of the problem comes from only a few examples. When a group or team is struggling to figure out exactly what the problem is, a Pareto chart can help the group spot the issue easily.

Consider an example: One group was interested in why there were so many errors on financial aid statements at their university; students weren't receiving their financial aid on time. They gathered data and found that 61 percent of the problem was caused by improperly completed financial-aid forms, 23 percent was related to errors in entering data into the computer, 4 percent of the mistakes were caused by the fact that students provided no phone number, and 3 percent arose because students did not provide their e-mail addresses. When the group displayed these data on a Pareto chart, as shown in Figure 10.2, they could easily see the main source of the problem—the forms weren't being completed properly.

Step 2: Analyze the Problem

Ray Kroc, founder of McDonald's, was fond of saying that nothing is particularly hard if you divide it into small jobs. To analyze a problem is to break a problem into causes, effects, symptoms, and subproblems. During the analysis phase of group problem solving, members need to research and investigate the problem. In analyzing the problem, a group may wish to consider the following questions:

1. What is the history of the problem? How long has it existed?
2. How serious is the problem?
3. What are the causes of the problem?
4. What are the effects of the problem?
5. What are the symptoms of the problem?
6. What methods does the group already have for dealing with the problem?
7. What are the limitations of those methods?
8. How much freedom does the group have in gathering information and attempting to solve the problem?
9. What obstacles keep the group from achieving the goal?
10. Can the problem be divided into subproblems for definition and analysis?

Tools for Analyzing a Problem

Groups may need help in breaking a problem down into its subcomponents. Two techniques can help a group sort out factors contributing to the problem: (1) force-field analysis and (2) cause-and-effect (fishbone) diagram. Each technique can help a group focus on data and facts rather than on vague impressions of what may be causing the problem.

Force-Field Analysis   This technique is based on the assumptions of Kurt Lewin, often called the father of group dynamics.[21] To use **force-field analysis,** a group needs to have a clear statement of its goal, which can be stated in terms of what the group wants more of or less of (for example, "We need more money, more time, or less interference from others"). The group analyzes the goal by noting what driving forces make it likely to be achieved and what restraining forces make it unlikely to be achieved.

Follow these steps to complete a force-field-analysis chart such as the one in Figure 10.3.[22]

Step 1.   Identify the goal, objective, or target the group is trying to achieve (such as more money, fewer errors).

Step 2.   On the right side of the chart, list all the restraining forces—those that currently keep the group from achieving its goal.

Step 3.   On the left side of the chart, list all the driving forces—those that currently help the group achieve its goal.

Step 4.   The group can now decide whether to do one of three things: (a) increase the driving forces; (b) decrease the restraining forces; (c) increase selected driving forces and decrease those restraining forces over which the group has control.

After the group has sorted through the facts and identified the driving and restraining forces, it will more likely be able to focus on the essential causes of a problem rather than on the problem's symptoms.

Say, for example, you are working in a group whose goal is to increase teamwork and collaboration among faculty and students. Driving forces—forces that favor teamwork—include such factors as faculty members who are motivated to work with students, students who also want to work with faculty, an existing training program that teaches teamwork and collaboration skills to both students and faculty. These and other driving forces could be

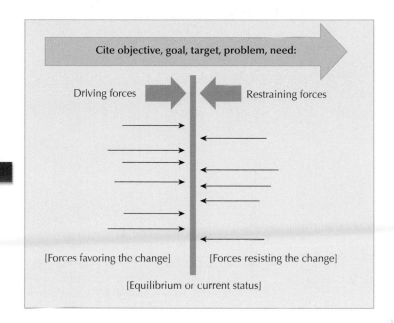

FIGURE 10.3

Force-Field Analysis Chart

included on the left-hand side of the force-field chart. Restraining forces—forces that work against increased collaboration—include current lack of knowledge of teamwork principles, the negative attitudes of a small but vocal group of faculty members who want to use more individual approaches to education, and the lack of a tradition of collaboration. These obstacles would be listed on the right side of the chart. Ideally, the group should work together on the force-field analysis diagram by using a flip chart or projecting the chart using an overhead projector. After generating additional driving and restraining forces, the group then turns its attention to the question "What can be done to increase the driving forces and decrease the restraining forces?" The group's force-field analysis of the problem can provide new insights for overcoming the obstacles and achieving the goal.

Cause-and-Effect (Fishbone) Diagram   Another problem analysis tool often used in groups and teams is the **cause-and-effect diagram,** also often called a **fishbone diagram** because the completed diagram looks like the skeleton of a fish. Developed by Kaoru Ishikawa, a Japanese specialist in quality management, this diagram helps groups and teams visually examine the relationship between causes and their probable effects.[23]

To develop a cause-and-effect diagram, first think of the possible effect you want to analyze. For example, imagine your group is trying to identify possible causes in the drop in students' standardized test scores in your community high school. The drop in test scores is the effect, but you aren't sure what's causing the drop. To prepare a cause-and-effect diagram, draw a long horizontal line on a piece of paper, chalkboard, or flipchart. Then, angling out from the long line, draw lines to represent possible causes of the drop in scores. Here you must use your analytical skills. For example, as illustrated in Figure 10.4, the major causes could be that the test-administration instructions are unclear; that parents are not involved; that teachers may not have time to prepare students for the test; or that students may have too many competing activities. Then, on each of the four angled lines, list possible contributing factors for each of the four main problem causes. For example, on the line suggesting that students have competing activities, you could draw lines to specify

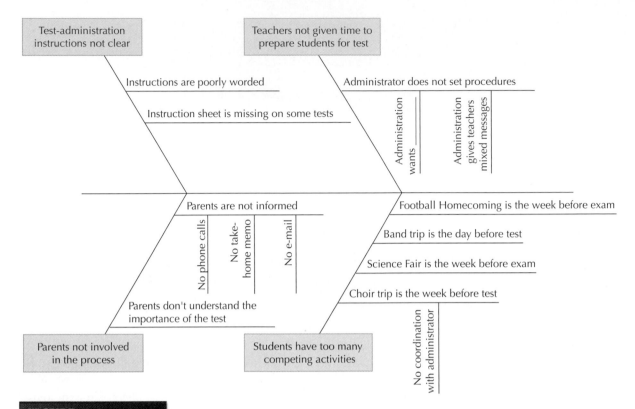

FIGURE 10.4

Cause-and-Effect
(Fishbone) Diagram

those competing activities. If you're stumped for a way to get started analyzing the problem, Ishikawa suggested that almost all problems boil down to issues related to the "four M's": Manpower (people), Machines, Materials, and Methods. You could begin your analysis by drawing a line angling off the horizontal line to represent each of these four categories.

The advantage of the cause-and-effect diagram is that all group members can work together to show relationships between causes and effects. For groups and teams to collaborate, they need a common format that helps them collaborate. A cause-and-effect diagram creates that shared space in which to work. You don't need to make your diagram complicated; you don't always need four lines angling off the center line. Often, simpler is better. The key is to write down the potential causes so all group or team members can see the relationships among possible causes and the known effect. As suggested by management consultant Peter Scholtes, "One of the biggest challenges in creating a cause-and-effect diagram is to have the bones show cause-and-effect relationships."[24] He cautions that cause-and-effect diagrams only depict *potential* causes. Once you have a list of potential causes, your group will need to verify the relationship between the cause and the effect with data and evidence.

How to Establish Criteria

Another task often part of the analysis step of the reflective-thinking process is to formulate **criteria**—standards or goals for an acceptable solution. Articulating criteria helps the group know when it has developed a good solution, because the criteria spell out what the final

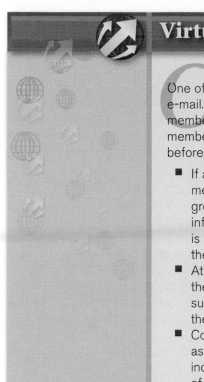

Virtual Communication

One of the ways a group can create structure is to do some of its work via e-mail. Rather than having people generate ideas face to face, assign group members some homework, to be submitted online. Or, consider inviting group members to share their ideas for defining and analyzing problems via e-mail before meeting face to face. Here are some examples:

- If a group is attempting to define a problem, take time during a face-to-face meeting to teach the group how to conduct is/is not analysis. Then each group member should complete an is/is not analysis and submit the information to one individual via e-mail. The person to whom the information is sent can then cull out duplicated information and prepare a summary of the information that the group can discuss at its next meeting.
- At a face-to-face meeting, the group could begin a general discussion about the nature of the problem it is attempting to solve. Then group members can submit e-mail responses to the journalist's six questions. One person can then collate and summarize the responses for the group to discuss.
- Conduct a force-field analysis via e-mail. After clarifying the group goal, assign some group members to identify the driving forces that would increase the likelihood of the goal being achieved. Others could submit a list of restraining forces. The information could be summarized and then discussed at the next meeting.
- Invite the group to do an analysis of the pros and cons of a particular suggestion via e-mail.

outcome should look like. Here are some questions that can help your group develop criteria.

1. What outcome are we trying to accomplish?
2. How will we know when we have completed our task?
3. Which criteria or standards are most important?
4. Which criteria are less important?

For example, criteria for a solution might include the following:

1. The solution should be inexpensive.
2. The solution should be implemented by a certain date and time.
3. The solution should address the causes of the problem, not just the symptoms.
4. All group members should agree to the solution.

Although we describe the setting of criteria as integral to analyzing the problem, the research literature is mixed as to when a group should explicitly identify criteria. One study found that the precise point during the problem-solving process when criteria were discussed did not seem to make a difference in the group's final outcome.[25] In fact, group members thought it made more sense to them to discuss criteria *after* they had identified several possible solutions. Consider this principle: *The more uncertain group members are about the goal of the discussion, the more important it is to explicitly talk about criteria.* If the goal is fairly obvious (for example, if a group is given the task of cutting 10 percent of a budget), then it's probably not necessary to ask, "OK, what are we looking for in a solution?" Everyone already knows what the standard for the solution is. But if the goal is less clear-cut, it may be helpful to make sure that the group knows what the outcome of its discussion should be. As you learned in Chapter 1, one of the most important behaviors of an effective team is to develop a clear, elevating goal.[26] Developing clear criteria is another way of ensuring that all group members know what the goal of the group is, so that group members know when they've identified a good solution.

Step 3: Generate Several Possible Solutions

After analyzing a problem and identifying criteria for a solution, the group should turn its attention to listing possible solutions in tentative, hypothetical terms. It's important that the group not be tempted to start listing solutions too early in the discussion; better solutions occur when groups take time to thoroughly define and analyze the issues.

Creativity is needed at each step of the problem-solving process, but it is especially important when the group attempts develop solutions. Creativity is such an important part of group deliberations that we devote the next chapter to discussing the principles and practices of group creativity.

Step 4: Evaluate Options and Select the Best Solution or Combination of Solutions

After a group has compiled a list of possible solutions to a problem, it should be ready to evaluate the various possible solutions and then select the best one. How do you narrow down a long list of proposed solutions? One way is to refer to the criteria proposed during the analysis stage of the discussion (or to take time now to develop crtiteria) and consider each tentative solution in light of these criteria. The group should decide which proposed solution or combination of solutions best meets its criteria. Narrowing a list of possible solutions down to one or two options is usually much harder for groups than generating options in the first place. Our discussion of how to facilitate consensus, presented in Chapter 7, offers several strategies for narrowing the number of options. The following questions may be helpful in analyzing the proposed solutions:

1. What are the advantages of each solution?
2. Are there any disadvantages to a solution? Do the disadvantages outweigh the advantages?
3. What would be the long-term and short-term effects of this solution if it were adopted?
4. Would the solution really solve the problem?
5. Does the solution conform to the criteria formulated by the group?
6. Should the group modify the criteria?

If group members agree, the criteria for a best solution may need to be changed or modified.[27]

Tools for Evaluating the Solutions

In addition to asking questions to guide discussion of the solutions or alternatives that the group has identified, the following are additional ways of focusing or structuring discussion.

Pros	Cons

Analyze the Pros and Cons   One of the most consistent findings of functional communication researchers is that when groups weigh the positive and negative outcomes of solutions, they make better decisions.[28] One method of facilitating such a discussion is to make a **T-chart** (named for its shape), like the one here, to evaluate solution pros and cons. If the group is large and you want to make sure everyone participates, you can have members first write their own lists of pros and cons (or risks and benefits) and then share their responses with the group. For example, if a group is trying to decide whether to purchase a new piece of property, one side of the center line might list positive aspects of the purchase (good investment, property values increasing, good location, and so on). On the other side would be negative implications of the purchase (reduced cash flow, increased property taxes, expensive lawyer fees, and so on). A thorough look at pros and cons can help a group consider alternatives before it makes a final decision.

Average Rankings and Ratings   It is usually easier for a group to identify possible solutions than it is to narrow the list of alternatives and select the best solution. If a group has many solutions to evaluate, one way to narrow the list is to ask group members to either rank or rate the solutions and then average the rankings or ratings to see which solutions emerge as the most and least popular. Ranking or rating should be done after a group has discussed the pros and cons of the solutions. Ranking solutions works best if you have no more than five to seven solutions; group members often have a difficult time ranking more than seven items. If you have a very long list of solutions—a dozen or more—you may ask the group members to rank their top five choices, assigning a rank of 1 to their top choice, 2 to their next choice, and so on. One researcher has found that asking the group to rank-order a list of possible alternatives is a better procedure than asking the group to pick the best solution. By ranking each option, group members are forced to critically evaluate each alternative.[29]

Besides ranking solutions, group members could also assign a rating score to each solution. Each solution could be rated on a five-point scale, with a rating of 1 being a very positive evaluation and 5 being a negative evaluation. Even a long list of 20 or more potential solutions could be rated. Group members' ratings for each solution could be averaged, and the most highly rated solutions could be discussed again by the entire group.

Step 5: Test and Implement the Solution

Group members should be confident that the proposed solution is valid—that it will solve the problem. After a group selects the best solution, it must determine how the solution can be put into effect. You may wish to consider the following questions:

1. How can the group get approval and support for its proposed solution?
2. What specific steps are necessary to implement the solution?
3. How can the group evaluate the success of its problem-solving efforts?

In many groups, those who choose a solution are not the same people who will implement it. If this is the case, members who select the solution should clearly explain why they selected it to members who will put the solution into practice. If they can demonstrate that the group went through an orderly process to solve the problem, they usually can convince others that their solution is valid.

Tools for Implementing a Solution

There are two key tools for implementing a solution: (1) an action chart and (2) a flowchart. An **action chart** is a grid that lists the tasks that need to be done and identifies who will be responsible for each task. Such a chart is based on more elaborate diagrams and procedures, such as a PERT diagram. PERT (the initials stand for Program Evaluation and Review Technique) was originally developed by the U.S. Navy in the late 1950s to assist with the *Polaris* missile program.[30] The action chart here was developed by using the following steps:

1. Identify the project goal.
2. Identify the activities needed to complete the project.
3. Identify the sequence of activities (what should be done first, second, third, and so on).
4. Estimate the amount of time it should take to complete each task.
5. Determine which group members should be responsible for each task.
6. Develop a chart that shows the relationships among the tasks, times, people, and sequence of events that are needed to accomplish the project.

Names								
Ken	●	●			●	●		●
Daryl		●			●			
Steve			●		●			
Janice			●		●		●	
Carl				●	●	●	●	
Assignment	Conduct needs assessment	Write behavioral objectives	Develop training content outline	Write training facilitator guide	Develop audio-visual resources	Conduct training pilot test	Conduct training for client	Analyze evaluation data
Week	Week 1		Week 2		Week 3		Week 4	
Day	Monday	Friday	Monday	Friday	Monday	Friday	Monday	Friday

One reason solutions do not get implemented is that people are uncertain about who should do what. An action chart provides needed structure to reduce this uncertainty. An action chart also helps ensure that everybody is aware of what needs to be done and reduces the risk that nobody will do anything.

A **flowchart** is a step-by-step diagram of a multistep process. Consider an example: One group was charged with choosing and carrying out a fund-raising activity. The chart in Figure 10.5 shows how the group described the essential steps involved holding a fundraiser. Flowcharts can help a group see whether the various procedures they have identified to solve a problem are practical and fit together. A flowchart can also help your group work through logistics and identify practical problems of moving from an idea's conception to its implementation. Like an action plan, a flowchart is a way to give structure to group thought. Flowcharts can be simple, like our example, or very complex, like those used by computer programmers when writing sophisticated programs.

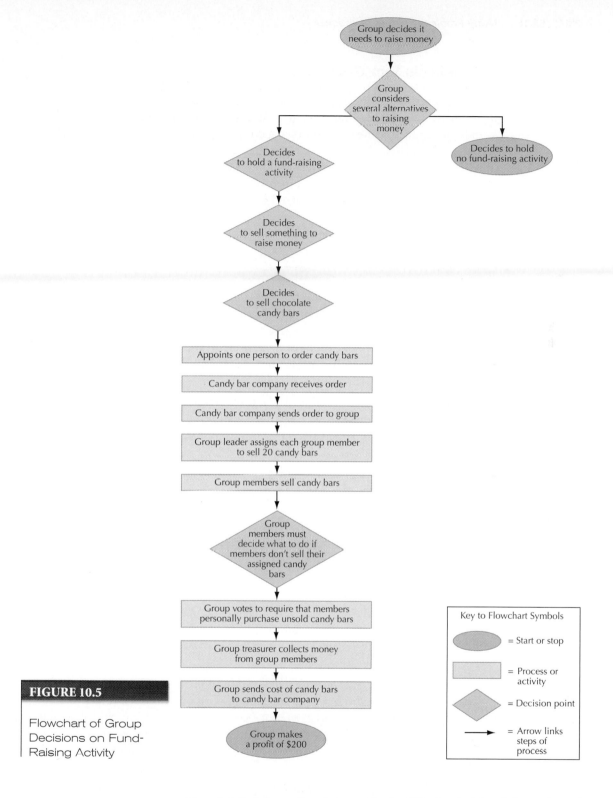

FIGURE 10.5

Flowchart of Group
Decisions on Fund-
Raising Activity

Flowchart content:

Group decides it needs to raise money

Group considers several alternatives to raising money

Decides to hold a fund-raising activity

Decides to hold no fund-raising activity

Decides to sell something to raise money

Decides to sell chocolate candy bars

Appoints one person to order candy bars

Candy bar company receives order

Candy bar company sends order to group

Group leader assigns each group member to sell 20 candy bars

Group members sell candy bars

Group members must decide what to do if members don't sell their assigned candy bars

Group votes to require that members personally purchase unsold candy bars

Group treasurer collects money from group members

Group sends cost of candy bars to candy bar company

Group makes a profit of $200

Key to Flowchart Symbols

= Start or stop

= Process or activity

= Decision point

= Arrow links steps of process

How detailed does a flowchart need to be? The level of detail depends on the needs of the group. We caution you, however, not to make the flowchart so detailed that your goal becomes developing a flowchart rather than describing and implementing a process. Use a flowchart as a tool to make sure all group members have a clear understanding of the critical parts of a more complex process.

How to Use Reflective Thinking in Your Group or Team

Reflective thinking assumes that groups work best when their discussions are organized rather than disorganized or random. Remember that you should use reflective thinking as a guide, not as an exact formula for solving every problem. As noted earlier, several group communication researchers have discovered that groups do not necessarily solve problems in a linear, step-by-step process.[31] The process by which groups solve problems goes through several phases of growth and development as members interact.[32] Reflective thinking is most useful in helping groups understand the phases of problem solving. As Ernest Bormann has noted, "Difficulties arise when [group] participants demand rationality from a group throughout its deliberations."[33]

In trying to apply reflective thinking to group problem solving, consider the following suggestions.

1. *Clearly identify the problem you are trying to solve.* Make sure that you are not just discussing a topic. For example, one group decides to discuss the quality of the U.S. judicial system. The group selects a topic area, but it does not identify a problem. It should focus clearly on a specific problem, such as "How can we improve the quality of the judicial system in the United States?" or "What should be done to improve the education and training of lawyers in the United States?"

2. *Phrase the problem as a question to help guide group discussion.* Stating your group's problem as a question adds focus and direction to your deliberations. When formulating a problem-solving discussion question, keep in mind the guidelines discussed in Chapter 8.

3. *Do not suggest solutions until you have analyzed the problem.* Many group communication researchers agree that until your group has researched the problem, you may not have enough information and specific facts to reach the best solution.[34]

4. *In the definition and analysis steps of reflective thinking, do not confuse the causes of the problem with its symptoms.* A fever and headache are symptoms, not necessarily causes, of a patient's ill health. The cause may be a cold or flu virus or a number of other things. A doctor tries to identify the cause of symptoms by running tests and analyzing a patient's medical history. In other words, a doctor needs to define, analyze, and solve a problem. You should try to clarify the differences between the causes and the symptoms (effects) of a problem. Perhaps your only goal is to alleviate the symptoms. However, you can better understand your group's goal if you can distinguish causes and symptoms.

5. *Constantly evaluate your group's problem-solving method.* For many years the only problem-solving method suggested to group-discussion classes was reflective thinking. Some communication theorists suggest, however, that for certain types of problems, alternative problem-solving methods work just as well, if not better, than reflective thinking. The final part of this chapter discusses some of these other problem-solving strategies.

6. *Appoint one or more group members to remind the group to use a structured method of solving problems.* One study found that groups in which one member is trained to help the group be mindful of the procedures it uses will make high-quality decisions.[35] Raters were trained to remind the group to use effective problem-solving and decision-making skills by asking the following questions at appropriate times:

Do we have enough evidence to support our choice of solution?

Have we looked at a sufficient number of alternatives?

Have we reexamined alternatives we rejected previously?

Have we avoided stereotypical thinking or premature judgments?

Because you're taking a course in small group communication, you now know the importance of helping a group stay on track and be vigilant thinkers, so you can periodically ask these questions. Even if you're not the appointed leader of a group, you can have a positive impact on the quality of the group's discussion by helping the group examine its process.

QUESTION-ORIENTED APPROACHES TO PROBLEM SOLVING

Another approach to problem solving requires groups to consider a series of questions to keep them oriented toward their goal. Two such approaches are discussed in the following sections: (1) the ideal-solution format and (2) the single-question format. Both formats help groups identify the critical issues they need to resolve and organize their thinking about the best possible solutions.

Ideal-Solution Format

Obviously, problem-solving groups want to identify the best solutions to problems. In the **ideal-solution format,** groups answer questions designed to help them identify ideal solutions. Alvin Goldberg and Carl Larson have devised the following agenda of questions:

1. Do all members agree on the nature of the problem?
2. What would be the ideal solution from the point of view of all parties involved in the problem?
3. What conditions within the problem could be changed so that the ideal solution might be achieved?
4. Of the solutions available, which one best approximates the ideal solution?[36]

These questions help groups recognize the barriers that the problems under consideration have created. The questions also encourage groups to analyze a problem's cause and to evaluate proposed solutions. The advantage of the ideal-solution format over other problem-solving approaches is its simplicity. Group members simply consider each of the above questions one at a time. One expert recommends the ideal-solution format for discussions among people with varied interests; this format works best when acceptance of a solution is important.[37] The format enables group members to see the problem from several viewpoints in their search for the best solution.

Although the ideal-solution format is similar to reflective thinking, its chief value is that it uses questions to help a group systematically identify and analyze a problem, pinpoint the best possible solution, and formulate specific methods for achieving a solution. Like the other problem-solving formats presented in this chapter, it helps a group—particularly one whose members have varying viewpoints and experiences—to focus on a problem and devise ways to solve it in a rational, structured way.

Single-Question Format

Like the ideal-solution format, the **single-question format** poses a series of questions designed to guide the group toward a best solution. Goldberg and Larson suggest that the answers to the following five questions can help a group achieve its goal:

1. What question does the group need to answer in order to accomplish its purpose?
2. What subquestions must be answered before the group can answer the single question it has formulated?
3. Does the group have sufficient information to answer the subquestions confidently?
4. What are the most reasonable answers to the subquestions?
5. Assuming that the answers to the subquestions are correct, what is the best solution to the problem?[38]

Unlike the ideal-solution format, the single-question format requires a group to formulate a question to help obtain the information needed to solve a problem. The single-question format also helps a group identify and resolve issues that must be confronted before it can reach a solution. As Goldberg and Larson note, "An assumption of the single-question form seems to be that issues must be resolved, however tentatively."[39] Thus, the single-question format probably works best for a group that is capable of reaching agreement on what the issues are and how they can be resolved. A group characterized by conflict and contention would probably not find the single-question approach productive.

The success of the single-question format depends on a group's agreeing on the subissues before trying to agree on the major issues. If you are working with a group that has difficulty reaching agreement, the single-question format may not be the best approach. The group may become bogged down arguing about trivial matters while the major issues remain unexamined. Decide whether your group will be able to reach agreement on the minor issues before you decide to use the single-question format. If your group cannot reach agreement, either the ideal-solution format or the reflective-thinking format may be a better method of organizing your group's deliberations.

How to Use Question-Oriented Approaches in Your Group or Team

You may have noticed some similarities among the single-question, the ideal-solution, and the reflective-thinking formats. By guiding groups toward their goals with questions, the ideal-solution and single-question formats help groups agree on minor issues before they try to agree on solutions to problems. Carl Larson tried to find out whether an ideal-solution, single-question, or reflective-thinking format, or no format at all, would produce better solutions.[40] His study indicates that ideal-solution and single-question formats generated better solutions than did the reflective-thinking approach. All three approaches fared better than no approach at all.

Of course, a single study does not prove that the single-question and ideal-solution formats are superior to the reflective-thinking format, but it does suggest that under certain conditions, goal-oriented approaches may have certain advantages. In Larson's study, when groups were given alternatives and told to choose the best solution to a problem, their discussions lasted only about twenty minutes. That is, by considering specific questions, members were able to solve problems efficiently. Norman Maier also concluded that a

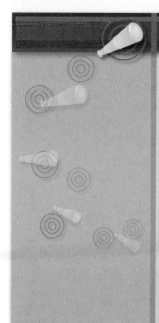

Cutting Edge Theory

TOTAL QUALITY MANAGEMENT

Total quality management (TQM) is a management approach that began to be used in the 1990s and continues to be used in organizations today. At its essence, total quality is an approach to accomplishing work that emphasizes minimizing errors and building quality into any task or process.

One of the principal leaders of the quality movement was the late W. Edwards Deming.[41] He was a professor of statistics who realized that applying data in a meaningful way and empowering team collaboration would enhance work quality. Deming is often credited with helping Japanese organizations to increase their work quality dramatically. He identified 14 points that he believed would, if implemented, transform an organization into an effective community producing quality goods and services. Many of his ideas emphasize the importance of collaboration and coordinated group effort when solving problems and improving quality.

Real-Life Applications

How can groups and teams in which you participate adopt a TQM approach to accomplishing your task? Although it does not list all of Deming's 14 suggestions, the list below is based on his core ideas. Consider the following practices.

- Develop a written group or team goal that places an emphasis on producing high-quality work. Rather than just trying to get the job done, stress the value of producing a final product or service that is the best it can be. Frequently talk about the importance of doing quality work.
- Keep a written record of errors and mistakes that the group makes—not so you can place blame on anyone or emphasize what the group does wrong, but so you can avoid making the same mistake in the future.
- Don't place emphasis on work quotas. Set high expectations and encourage group members to continue working—rather than suggesting that once they have gathered, say, ten sources of information (or done whatever the group is trying to accomplish), they can stop. Work quotas set limits on work quality.
- Examine the process the group or team uses to do its work. If the process is well designed, then the outcome will be of high quality. Focus on, for example, how the group solves problems or the effectiveness of agendas used to organize group discussion. Also, monitor whether everyone is participating in the group process.
- Make efforts to help each group or team member do a better job. Each group member can be a leader to improve quality; leadership is not just the job of a single individual.
- Emphasize encouragement and positive reinforcement for both individual and team accomplishments. Catch people doing something right and praise them.
- Encourage group and team members to continue to learn new ways of doing their jobs. Invest in education. Encourage innovation by learning new ways of doing things better.

Recording group members' ideas on a flip chart can help provide necessary structure when the group is trying to solve problems. What other equipment might help solve group problems?

problem-solving approach that has a group consider minor issues before major issues can improve group decisions.[42]

If you are going to lead a group discussion, the following suggestions may help you apply the ideal-solution and single-question approaches to problem solving:

1. *When using the ideal-solution or single-question approach, provide group members with copies of the questions that will guide their discussion.* You can reduce some of the uncertainty that occurs normally in groups by making sure that each person knows the procedure. Tell the group to use the questions as a guide.

2. *Explain why you are using the format you have selected.* Most groups are willing to go along with a particular discussion agenda, especially if you give them reasons for having selected it. Tell the group that considering specific questions in a developmental format can keep the discussion on track. If your group has a specified time period in which to meet, you can explain that using questions to guide the discussion can help make the discussion more efficient.

3. *Keep the discussion focused on the specific question under consideration.* Whether the group is using the ideal-solution or single-question format, some group members may be tempted to skip a question or may want to discuss an unrelated issue. You may have to help the group focus on one question at a time. Several studies suggest that groups with members who try to keep participants aware of the pertinent issues by summarizing the discussion and requesting clarification have a good chance of agreeing on a solution and of being satisfied with their discussion.[43]

4. *Agree to use a collaborative approach to solving the problem.* Frank LaFasto and Carl Larson suggest that the single-question format can be enhanced if group members explicitly consider the question "What principles should we agree on in order to maintain a reasonable and collaborative approach through the [problem-solving] process?"[44] Consider this question early in the problem-solving process. Making collaboration a problem-solving value can enhance teamwork and cooperation.

Case Study[45]

You are one of the managers of a department store in your community. You have just been informed by your supervisor that one of your employees will have to be laid off because of company cutbacks. You meet with your managerial colleagues to decide which employee will be chosen. All employees are full-time, and all work the same number of hours. There is one formal rule you have to follow: The reason for laying a person off must be job-related. Which of the following employees would you and your colleagues choose? Make the best decision you can with the limited information you are given. Be prepared to discuss the reasoning behind your group's decision.

Masha: Aged 33, married, with two children, Masha has worked for the company for five years. She loves her job and requires little or no supervision. You have considered giving her a promotion when the opportunity arises. Other people go to Masha when they have questions, because she is good at training others. She has been going to school part time to get a management degree and will graduate in another year.

Bob: Aged 49, divorced, with one child, Bob has worked with the company for 22 years. He keeps to himself but always gets work done. You never have to give Bob instructions, because he knows his job so well. Others in the department call him "Pop" because he seems like a father figure to everyone and is well liked. He really adds a great deal of stability to your department. He does not want to change his job at all because he is happy. You put Bob in charge in your absence.

Trent: Aged 19, single, a Native American, Trent just began working for your company 11 months ago. He went to an accelerated school as a child and started college when he was 15 years old. He has since graduated with a business degree and shows promise of going far in your company. He is already the best salesperson in your department. Most people get along with him well. Because he is new, Trent needs a lot of training, but his sales are worth your extra time.

Madeline: Madeline is 25, married, and three months pregnant. She transferred to your store only last month but has over three years total experience in the company. You have not been very satisfied with her attendance because she is calling in sick a lot. However, she is the only person that you feel you can give your most difficult tasks to, because she is very thorough. She also has had more customer compliments than any other person in your department.

Catrina: Catrina is 40, single, has three children, and is a recovering alcoholic. She fulfills a very necessary function in your department by doing maintenance work, which no one else really has time for. Catrina is efficient and is never late; however, she does not really associate with the others. She has worked with the company for over 10 years but she cannot read or write; it is likely that this is one of the few places she could find work.

Antonio: Aged 27, single, with no children, Antonio has worked for two years in your department, and in that time he has won three awards for creating outstanding merchandise displays (the heart and soul of retail). He is your most conscientious worker and keeps your department looking great. You have wondered, though, whether he comes to work under the influence of drugs. Several customers have complained about poor grooming habits and language he uses. In the last month, however, he has made significant improvements.

Practice in Applying Principles

1. What is the problem facing your group?
2. What criteria did your group use to help develop a solution?
3. How would you assess the balance between structure and interaction in your group?
4. Before making a decision, how did your group assess the advantages and disadvantages of each option?
5. Did your group use any specific problem-solving or decision-making technique to help structure the discussion? If not, which structured technique could you have used to create a balance between structure and interaction and produce a good solution?

BEYOND TECHNIQUE

Throughout this book we've offered skills, strategies, tips, and techniques for improving group process. We conclude this chapter with a caution: Participating in groups and teams is more than simply applying "how to's." As we've repeatedly noted, communicating in groups and teams is often a zipping, buzzing, humming, halting, and cacophonous process. Systems theory, discussed in Chapter 2, teaches that group communication is an interrelated, fragile process in which each person or element affects the entire group. Group and team research has not advanced to a state where we can certify that using the various techniques we've discussed will *always* result in high-quality solutions and decisions. Working in a group is more complicated than that.[46]

How do you know when to adopt a specific technique to help improve a group's process? The key, we believe, is to listen to your group, watch, observe, and identify what the group needs at a given time. In a word: adapt. Adapt to the needs of the group rather than assuming that a predetermined strategy or technique will somehow miraculously help the group or team achieve a breakthrough. If the group seems confused, disoriented, or stuck when defining or analyzing the task in front of it, then a more structured technique such as the cause-and-effect diagram or force-field analysis may be what the group needs. But if the group is making progress, we don't recommend that you haul out a group technique such as is/is not analysis, a fishbone diagram, a T-chart, or some other structured technique. The power of a group does not reside in technique. In fact, group researchers have had some difficulty documenting precisely what makes a group successful—and we don't believe groups will always be successful. There is no *one* approach or technique that always works.

Use your knowledge of group problem-solving techniques in combination with your understanding of group process to assess whether your group needs the structure of a specific technique or tool. Effective groups and group members use techniques and strategies thoughtfully to help them make progress toward their goal depending on what is (or is not) happening in the group. Use techniques wisely.

Putting Principles into Practice

In this chapter we discussed several prescriptive approaches that a group or team can use to solve a problem. Groups often need some plan or structure to help their members define, analyze, and solve a problem. We described three kinds of problem-solving formats: (1) reflective thinking, (2) ideal-solution format, and (3) single-question format. Review the following suggestions for applying these problem-solving approaches to the groups in which you participate.

Reflective Thinking: Traditional Problem Solving

- To help your group or team define and limit a problem, phrase it as a question.
- Do not start suggesting solutions until your group has thoroughly analyzed a problem.
- Consider using tools such as is/is not analysis, force-field analysis, journalist's six questions, Pareto charts, and cause-and-effect (fishbone) diagrams to help your group analyze the problem.

- Formulate criteria for a good solution before you begin suggesting solutions.
- If the other group members agree, you may need to change the criteria you have selected during the analysis phase of reflective thinking.
- Make sure that reflective thinking is the best method for your group; another problem-solving approach may work better.
- To help make sure that everyone knows and follows through on his or her assignment, consider using an action chart or a flowchart.

Ideal-Solution and Single-Question Formats

- If you are the leader of a group, tell the group why you have selected either the ideal-solution format or the single-question approach to problem solving.
- Use the ideal-solution format to help the group come to agreement on the nature of the problem.
- Use the single-question format if you are sure that your group is capable of agreeing on the issues and on how they can be resolved.
- Provide members with copies of the questions used in the ideal-solution format or the single-question format; this will help to keep your discussion on track.
- Remind group members to address only those questions and issues that are relevant to the discussion.

$\mathcal{P}$RACTICE

Earthquake

According to the *Worst-Case Scenario Survival Handbook,* there are certain things you should do if you experience an earthquake.[47] Individually rank-order the following suggestions from most important to least important. Then work with a small group to compare and revise your answers based on the collective wisdom of the group. Your instructor will give you the experts' rankings.

_____ If you are driving, stop, but carefully.

_____ Check food and water supplies.

_____ Check for gas leaks and damaged electrical wires.

_____ Put on a pair of thick-soled shoes.

_____ Be prepared for aftershocks.

_____ If you are indoors, stay indoors.

_____ Check for injuries and administer first aid.

_____ Get out in the open if you are inside.

_____ If you are in a mountainous area, watch out for landslides.

Using Interaction Process Analysis

Sociologist Robert Bales significantly advanced the study of communication in small groups by developing a method of describing and analyzing the interaction that occurs in groups. Bales identified four major categories of interaction and further specified twelve subcategories of comments group members typically make during group discussion. Two of Bales's major categories focus on social/emotional aspects of group conversation; the other two categories describe talk that focuses on completing the task. His categories are listed below.[48]

Positive Reactions

1. Shows solidarity, raises others' status, gives help, rewards
2. Shows tension release, jokes, laughs, shows satisfaction
3. Shows agreement, shows passive acceptance, understands, concurs, complies

Attempted Answers

1. Gives suggestion, direction, implying autonomy for others

2. Gives opinion, evaluation, analysis, expresses feeling, wish

3. Gives information, orientation, repeats, clarifies, confirms

Questions

1. Asks for information, orientation, repetition, confirmation

2. Asks for opinion, evaluation, analysis, expression of feeling

3. Asks for suggestions, direction, possible ways of action

Negative Reactions

1. Disagrees, shows passive rejection, formality, withholds help

2. Shows tension, asks for help, withdraws out of field

3. Shows antagonism, deflates others' status, defends or asserts self

Although it takes extensive training to gain maximum benefit from Bales's Interaction Process Analysis, communication researchers and educators Alvin Goldberg and Carl Larson suggest that you can develop a simple version of Bales's categories to describe group interaction.[49] On the left side of a sheet of paper, list the 12 subcategories of comments. Next, draw vertical lines to create a column for each group member. As you listen to a group discussion, simply make a mark to code each piece of conversation made by each group member. If, for example, Bill makes a comment that indicates friendly support for a person or idea, you would make a mark in Bill's column on line 1 for "shows solidarity." If Carmelita disagrees with Bill's idea, you would make a mark in her column on line 10 ("disagrees"). You continue to code the group members' comments until the end of the conversation. The key to using this method of analyzing group talk is to make sure you understand each of the 12 subcategories of interaction and can code them accurately. Each comment can be coded only once in only one category, so you have to make quick decisions as to how to code a group member's comments.

When you're finished, you can total the number of marks you've made for each person. With total numbers in hand, you can calculate the percentage of the time each individual made comments. You can also total the number of *types* of comments the group members made by adding the number of marks made on each row. Calculate the percentage of time group members made comments from each subcategory. The resulting percentage for each of the 12 lines will let you see whether the group was more concerned with the task or more concerned with social/emotional issues. You can also see which of the 12 interaction categories was used most and least during the discussion. You can more accurately assess people's comments if you videotape a group discussion and then watch the video while completing your analysis of the group; if necessary you can watch the video more than once. Group communication scholar Joann Keyton points out that the Bales Interaction Process Analysis system is an efficient way to analyze a group's behavior because it offers a descriptive, quantitative measure based on what group members say.[50]

CHAPTER ELEVEN

Enhancing Creativity in Groups and Teams

"Imagination is more important than knowledge."

—*Albert Einstein*

CHAPTER OUTLINE

What Is Creativity?

Why Study Creativity?

Myths about Creativity

Barriers to Group and Team Creativity

Principles of Group and Team Creativity

Techniques for Enhancing Group and Team Creativity

Case Study

Putting Principles into Practice

Practice

OBJECTIVES

After studying this chapter, you will be able to:

■ Define creativity.

■ Identify reasons for studying creativity.

■ List and describe three myths about group and team creativity.

■ Identify barriers to group and team creativity.

■ Identify principles that enhance group and team creativity.

■ Describe and use brainstorming, the nominal-group technique, the Delphi technique, electronic brainstorming, and the affinity technique.

■ Apply creativity principles and strategies when working in groups and teams.

IT'S OFTEN SAID *that the best predictor of longevity in individuals or groups is the well-known principle of "survival of the fittest." However, rather than fitness or brute strength, it may be that the "survival of the most creative" is what predicts long-term success.[1] For it is the creative person or group that is often able to surmount the most vexing problems. Being able to develop new ideas, figure out how to navigate through problems, and make decisions are some of the most valued skills you can master. In the previous chapters, we've emphasized the importance of using logical, structured approaches to solving problems and making decisions in groups and teams. And it's true that logic, careful analysis of the evidence, and systematic evaluation of the pros and the cons of proposals are essential elements in predicting group success. But being imaginative and creative can be equally vital to group achievement.[2]*

One of the key prescriptive steps in solving problems that we introduced in the last chapter is the ability to generate options and discover new approaches to problem solving. In this chapter, we turn our attention to the principles and practices of enhancing creativity in groups and teams. Specifically, we define creativity and discuss why it's so important for group and team members. We review commonly held myths about creativity and note barriers that inhibit creativity in groups, as well as identify characteristics that nurture the creative sprit. In the last part of the chapter, we offer specific methods and prescriptive strategies for structuring creative interaction in groups and teams.

WHAT IS CREATIVITY?

Many people have defined creativity—one research duo counted over 100 different definitions of creativity. The definition we like best has been distilled from several approaches to creativity. **Creativity** is the generation, application, combination, and extension of new ideas.[3] Essentially, to be creative is to invent something new that wasn't in existence before you invented it. In the context of groups and teams, we're not necessarily talking about inventing a tangible object (although a group could very well create something real), but inventing or creating a new idea, strategy, principle, or approach to solving a problem. Some researchers make a distinction between creativity (thinking of new ideas) and **innovation** (putting new ideas into action). Communication scholar Phil Clampitt describes innovation as including four steps: (1) idea generation, (2) feasibility analysis, (3) reality testing, and (4) implementation.[4] Innovation extends the notion of creativity by transforming a creative idea into something that is put into practice. Usually group members want not only to develop creative ideas but also to implement them. Creativity researcher Jill Nemiro suggests that creativity and innovation are really intertwined. Both involve the generation of something, whether an idea or product, that didn't exist before.[5] So, whether you call that being creative or being innovative, it's the same basic process.

Just as problem solving has phases, researchers have identified predictable phases in group creativity. Interestingly, Nemiro found parallel phases in face-to-face and virtual teams that are involved with developing creative ideas.[6] Phase one is the idea-generation phase, in which group members actively identify a range of new ideas, possibilities, and approaches to the issue at hand. Phase two is called development. In this phase, ideas are extended and more information is gathered to support the initial nuggets of ideas. In the third phase, called finalization and closure, the group agrees on the best ideas. In the forth and final phase, called evaluation, the team assesses the value and worth of the idea selected.

Because this book is about small group communication, we're more interested in creative messages than in the mental and psychological processes of creativity. Although some books provide detailed commentary about how the brain functions in creative contexts, communication researchers are more interested in such questions as "What should people say or do to enhance creativity?" or "How does a group or team organize the agenda of a meeting to produce a creative solution or outcome?" Of course, the psychological or mental aspects of creativity are clearly linked to how we talk and what we do. But interaction and dialogue are what communication researchers focus on most, and those are our focus in this chapter.

WHY STUDY CREATIVITY?

Long ago the ancient Romans identified *invention* as one of the classical canons, or key elements, of the communication process. **Invention** is the process of developing new ideas as we communicate with others and attempt to persuade them to adopt our ideas and suggestions. Being inventive or creative is just as important today. Especially in groups and teams, it's vital to be able to generate and articulate ideas and suggestions.

But you may be wondering whether systematically studying creativity is useful. Can people be trained to be more creative? The answer to the "Why study creativity?" question is unequivocal: Yes, people who are trained to be more creative are, in fact, more creative.[7] As we've suggested many times throughout this book, there are no sure-fire techniques that always enhance a person's skill. But several research studies suggest a clear link between being trained in creative skills and the resulting "creative competence" of the individuals taught. Whether it focuses on elementary school children or adults, research clearly suggests that creativity can be learned.[8]

Roger Firestien was particularly interested in the effects of creative problem solving training on communication behaviors in small groups.[9] Group members in the trained group were taught a six-stage model of creative problem solving:

Step 1. Mess finding: Isolating a concern or problem on which to work.

Step 2. Data finding: Generating and selecting the most important data regarding the mess.

Step 3. Problem finding: Generating and selecting a statement that captures the "essence" of the situation.

Step 4. Idea finding: Generating and selecting the best available alternative(s) for solving the problem.

Step 5. Solution finding: Using criteria to screen, select, and support ideas selected in idea finding.

Step 6. Acceptance finding: Generating ways to implement the solution and developing a plan for action.[10]

Firestien's research found clear evidence that trained group members used humor to enhance the creative process and were more supportive and less critical of the ideas suggested by others (a very important element of being creative). Ultimately, groups that received training in creative problem-solving techniques produced many more ideas than did groups that had not.

So, why learn about creativity? Because being creative is an essential skill, and there is ample evidence that people who learn creativity do's and don'ts are more creative.

*M*YTHS ABOUT CREATIVITY

Although you may be convinced of the value of learning creativity skills, you may still find the process clouded in mystery. Many people harbor misconceptions about who can be creative and how creativity works. Let's consider three common misunderstandings or myths about the creative process.[11] Discrediting these myths can give you insight into how you can enhance your own creative powers.

Creativity Myth 1: Creativity Is a Mysterious Process That Can't Be Learned

We've already addressed the myth that creativity can't be learned. Research clearly documents that people *can* learn to be more creative.[12] And as for its being a mysterious process—yes, we're still learning more about how the brain works, both from a biological and from a psychological perspective, but as you will learn in this chapter, there are some well-documented principles and strategies that have been demonstrated to enhance creativity. It's a mistake to think that you can't enhance your creative skill. Labeling yourself as "uncreative" can become a self-fulfilling prophecy: If you think you can't learn to be creative, you won't. So, don't buy in to the myth that you can't improve your creative skills. There is clear evidence that you can.

Creativity Myth 2: Only a Few Gifted People Are Creative

Most of us have been around someone who has a special creative talent. Maybe someone in your family is gifted in art, music, or drama and you think that only certain people can be creative. While it's true that some people have special talents in the creative arts, or just seem to have a knack for coming up with new, creative ideas, most people can be taught to enhance their creative skill. And if you're one of the talented people who have creative ability, there is evidence that you can further enhance your creative skills with both knowledge and practice.

Creativity Myth 3: Creativity Just Happens

Creativity is not a muse that periodically appears and disappears. Creativity can be cultivated and made to blossom. In the next section we'll identify certain barriers that keep cre-

Steve Jobs, CEO of Apple, is credited with being part of an innovative team that created such products as the iPod and the iPhone. Research suggests that creativity is not a mysterious process only a few can master. In fact, most people can learn principles and strategies to enhance their creativity.

ativity from growing, as well as key attributes that nurture it. Being creative is not a random, happenstance process; it can be nurtured.

BARRIERS TO GROUP AND TEAM CREATIVITY

Having had your misconceptions about creativity dispelled, you might expect your own creativity to start flowing unchecked. But research has identified several conditions and behaviors that inhibit creativity.[13] We'll identify them so you can spot them and eliminate them from your group and team collaborations.

Premature Evaluation of Ideas

Creativity is often inhibited by inappropriate evaluation of ideas as they are shared with the group. If group members feel that their ideas will be negatively evaluated, they will be less likely to share them with the group. Several of the techniques that we discuss later in the chapter specify that ideas not be evaluated in any way when they are first offered to the group. Eventually, ideas and suggestions need to be sorted through, and the best ideas should be chosen from those offered. But when members first offer ideas, avoid pouncing on them—you not only eliminate the idea you criticize but also potentially eliminate other ideas that might have been forthcoming from your group or team members.

Poor Physical Surroundings

Our creative abilities are affected by our physical space. It's hard to be creative if your group meets in a dingy, poorly lit, drafty, or too warm location. If too many people are crowded around a cramped table or in a room that wasn't designed for that size of group, creative juices will be less likely to flow. Distractions such as outside noise can also inhibit creativity.

Too Many People

In a large group—say, more than 12 to 15 people—it's difficult to have equal participation when the group shares ideas orally. Research clearly documents that communication apprehension is very real.[14] Many people are fearful, not just of giving a speech but also of speaking up in a group. Yet people who are anxious about speaking up may have just the creative idea your group needs. Asking people to be creative in a large group or conference setting may achieve some results, but many people will not generate as many creative ideas as they might in a smaller group.

Poor Timing

It sometimes takes time for groups to be creative. Not giving group members enough time to let ideas bubble up can reduce the group's creativity. On the other hand, some groups may be galvanized into action if given a tight deadline.[15] One study found that when a group was given a tight deadline it went into high gear and was highly productive—but that productivity wasn't very creative. Yet later on, when the same group was given another tight deadline, creativity increased.[16] They may have learned to deal with tight deadlines and thus improved their creativity. Another study found that when given longer periods in which to do their work, groups were more creative.[17] The key to interpreting these studies may lie in looking at what the group does with the time it has. A group is either on task or off task. If a short time period can spur a group to focus on its task, then a short time period may be best. Depending on the nature of the creative task, group members may need more time to accomplish high-quality results. Group leaders and participants should monitor how time affects the level of creativity of the group.

Stinking Thinking

Motivational speaker Zig Ziglar often challenges his audience to get rid of what he calls "stinking thinking." **Stinking thinking** consists of thoughts that limit the possibilities of an individual, group, or organization. Creativity is reduced when group or team members utter "sound bites" that discourage rather than encourage the group to think of new possibilities. Here are some examples:

- "We simply can't do this."
- "We've never done it this way before."
- "We tried that a few years ago and it didn't work."
- "They won't let us do this."
- "You can't be serious."

You can probably identify other comments that bring creative conversation to an abrupt halt. We don't recommend that you instantly silence the person who offers such a comment. Rather, gently and tactfully invite the group to continue considering possibilities. As we discussed in Chapter 4, use an "I" message ("I think there are options that we have yet to consider") rather than a "you" message ("You always offer negative comments!") when attempting to change the tenor of thought in your group.

PRINCIPLES OF GROUP AND TEAM CREATIVITY

Understanding how creativity works and knowing underlying principles that enhance the creative process can help you and your group and team members become more innovative. Creativity researcher Simon Taggar suggests that groups will be more creative if they are motivated; if they use creativity-fostering processes such as having everyone participate in the discussion; and if they communicate effectively by involving everyone, providing useful feedback, and addressing conflict when it arises.[18] Broadly speaking, group creativity research suggests that groups are more likely to be creative if they appropriately analyze and define the problem, intentionally foster a climate of freedom to be creative, listen to minority points of view, encourage members to assume new perspectives or roles, and find ways to structure the process.

Appropriately Analyze and Define the Problem

It's difficult to come up with a creative solution to a problem if the problem has not been clearly defined and analyzed. As we pointed out in previous chapters, groups that jump to solutions before thoroughly analyzing what is known and not known are less likely to have high-quality solutions. Before attempting to come up with creative solutions to a problem, make sure the group knows what the problem is and has some information, data, or evidence to serve as a springboard for possible solutions.

Arthur VanGundy suggests that the group may need to reframe the problem or reanalyze the issues to come up with a creative slant on what confronts the group.[19] For example, a group trying to develop a Web site where it could post answers to frequently asked questions decided that it already had a wealth of information; the group did not need to develop additional answers to questions, but rather to identify and highlight what information already existed. By reframing the problem, the group made a subtle yet useful distinction that saved the group much time and energy.

Create a Climate of Freedom

For maximum creativity, group members need to have the freedom to express ideas, even partial ideas, without fear of being ridiculed. Consultants at one firm claim they can unlock creativity by encouraging group members to be playful and even somewhat silly. As part of the creativity training, group members are given toys such as modeling clay, rubber-band powered airplanes, Nerf balls, and wooden blocks and are invited to play. Being playful encourages freedom of expression—a key ingredient of creativity. If, for example, your group is stymied by a problem, take time off to "play"; taking a walk, going for a snack, or doing something else the group members consider fun may be just what the group needs to boost its creativity.[20]

One study found that groups in which members retain their individualism rather than going along with a collectivistic group identity generate more creative ideas. This finding suggests that it's a good thing that group members bring their individual points of view to a group.[21] Just make sure that each group member feels free to share his or her ideas with others.

Listen to Minority Points of View

Creativity research suggests that groups with a diversity of opinions and ideas are more creative. Specifically, some researchers have concluded that groups that have more ethnic and racial diversity develop more creative solutions to problems.[22] Minority points of view challenge traditional thinking and ideas; and, if listened to, they can help group members see things in a new light. Groups in which one or two people dominate the discussion, either because of extreme status differences or because of their lack of sensitivity to the need for balanced discussion, are less likely to develop creative ideas. Just as groupthink (the false consensus that occurs when groups quickly agree with an idea so as to minimize conflict) can quash ideas and limit logical decision making, so too can it smother creative minority points of view. Encourage quiet group members to contribute to the group. And when they do, thoughtfully listen to what they have to say.

Encourage People to See Things and Themselves Differently

It's become a cliché to say, "let's think outside the box." Yet often, phrases become clichés because they express ideas succinctly. "Thinking outside the box" expresses the power of seeing facts, issues, and problems from a new vantage point. Instead of analyzing a problem from your own point of view, consider taking on a new role to gain a different point of view. For example, rather than thinking about a problem from the point of view of a student trying to identify solutions to the dramatically rising cost of tuition or attempting to solve the vexing parking problem on your campus, imagine that you're the president of your university. How would she or he view the problem? Try to consider an alternative entry point into the problem.

Another specific way to help group members see familiar problems and issues in a fresh light is to bring new members into the group. Changing the membership in a group can spur group creativity because new people bring in new ideas.[23]

Selectively Increase Group and Team Structure

Creative ideas come not only during periods of high stimulation but also during quiet periods, when the ideas silently creep into our consciousness. Invite group and team members to write and think individually before sharing ideas orally. Increasing group structure by alternating periods of personal reflection and writing with oral sharing of ideas may help prime the group's creative pump. Group and team members sometimes need the necessary space for ideas to emerge—not only physical space (although, as discussed above, groups need a good environment in which to work) but also psychological space, so that ideas can percolate.

Research suggests that people who can live with some uncertainty and who don't need immediate closure are more likely to generate creative ideas than are people who need to find the right answer in a short period of time.[24] So, people who are patient and don't try to force an immediate answer to a question or a speedy solution to a problem are likely to be more creative.

Problem-solving procedures such as reflective thinking or techniques such as journalist's six questions, force-field analysis, and fishbone analysis, discussed in the last chapter, are techniques designed to give the problem-solving process additional structure. Structure helps channel a group's attention and energies to stay focused on the task at hand. Several prescriptive techniques are designed to facilitate the generation of creative ideas. In the next section of this chapter we describe several methods.

REVIEW

HOW TO ENHANCE CREATIVITY IN YOUR GROUP

WHAT TO DO	HOW TO DO IT
Appropriately analyze and define the problem to be solved.	■ Write the specific problem some place where all can see it.
	■ Have each group member write a statement of precisely what the group wants to achieve.
	■ Separate the symptoms of the problem from the causes of the problem by using is/is not analysis.
Create a climate of individual freedom.	■ Use structured methods of capturing ideas—for example, have group members first write ideas on paper or share ideas via e-mail or a Web site.
	■ Encourage other group members by expressing positive reinforcement for ideas shared.
	■ Encourage the group to play together; do something fun.
	■ Take a break; take a walk; take time away from the problem.
Listen to minority points of view.	■ When someone disagrees with the majority point of view, make sure that the minority point of view is not quickly dismissed.
	■ Encourage quiet members to talk, and reinforce their ideas when they do contribute.
Encourage people to see things and themselves differently.	■ Try "rolestorming": Ask group members to assume a role (e.g., president of the company, a customer) different from their actual role.
	■ Try reverse brainstorming: Ask the group to generate ideas that would make the problem worse. Then see if any of these ideas can be flipped to help solve the problem or generate fresh insights.
	■ Bring new members into the group.
Selectively increase group and team structure.	■ Use techniques that help the group dissect the problem, such as force-field analysis (p. 242), the fishbone diagram (p. 243), or analyzing the pros and cons (p. 247).
	■ Use the affinity technique (p. 275) to get people moving and on their feet.

TECHNIQUES FOR ENHANCING GROUP AND TEAM CREATIVITY

Group and team members often want to know "What techniques will enhance our creativity?" Beyond understanding general principles of creativity and promoting conditions to enhance creativity, what are specific methods, approaches, or techniques that can boost creativity? As noted above, sometimes groups and teams need the structure of a technique to have a creative breakthrough. Such techniques include brainstorming, the nominal-group technique, the Delphi technique, electronic brainstorming, and the affinity technique—each a prescriptive technique for structuring the process of generating creative ideas. Research suggests that having standard procedures and some structure can enhance group member creativity.[25] We conclude the chapter by suggesting specific tips for incorporating these techniques into your group and team deliberations.

Brainstorming

Imagine that your employer assigns you to a task force whose goal is to increase the productivity of your small manufacturing company. Phrased as a policy question, the problem is "What can be done to increase efficiency and productivity for our company?" Your group is supposed to come up with ideas to help solve the problem. Assume that your boss has clearly identified the problem for the group and has provided you with several documents analyzing the problem in some detail. Your group may decide that reflective thinking, which focuses on identifying and analyzing problems, is not the best process to follow. Your group needs innovative ideas and creative, original solutions. Perhaps your group could benefit from brainstorming.[26]

Brainstorming is a creative technique designed to help a group generate several solutions to a problem. It was first developed by Alex Osborn, an advertising executive who felt the need for a creative technique that did not emphasize evaluating and criticizing ideas but instead would focus on developing imaginative and innovative solutions.[27] Brainstorming has been used by businesses, committees, and government agencies to improve the quality of group decision making. Although it can be used in several phases of many group discussions, it may be most useful if a group needs original ideas or has trouble coming up with any ideas at all. Research suggests that a trained facilitator can improve the execution of group brainstorming.[28]

The general assumption underlying brainstorming is that the more ideas generated, the more likely it is that a creative solution will be found. Research largely supports the brainstorming procedure; yet some studies suggest that generating quality ideas may be more useful to groups than merely identifying lots of bad ideas.[29] Groups who use brainstorming earlier in their deliberations perceive brainstorming to be more valuable in helping them generate quality ideas.[30] And brainstorming is helpful when the group must use evidence to help them find a specific, correct solution to a problem. Research also suggests that the most effective brainstorming groups keep at it—the more persistent group members are in generating ideas, even when idea generation slows, the better the result.[31] And there is evidence

A group may be more creative while brainstorming if they are comfortable and in a relaxed environment. What environmental factors might contribute to a creative brainstorming session for this group?

that women are more persistent than men in continuing to generate ideas during brainstorming.[32]

Traditional brainstorming steps   Traditional brainstorming is a process that follows certain specific guidelines.

1. *Select a specific problem that needs solving.* Be sure that all group members can identify and clearly define the problem.
2. *Set a clear time limit.*
3. *Ask group members to temporarily put aside all judgments and evaluations.* The key to brainstorming is ruling out all criticism and evaluation. Osborn makes these suggestions:
   - Acquire a "try anything" attitude.
   - Avoid criticism, which can stifle creativity.
   - Remember that all ideas are thought-starters.
   - Today's criticism may kill tomorrow's ideas.
4. *Ask group or team members to think of as many possible solutions to the problem as they can and to share the ideas with the group.* Consider the following suggestions:
   - The wilder the ideas, the better.
   - It is easier to tame ideas down than to think ideas up.
   - Think out loud and mention unusual ideas.
   - Someone's wild idea may trigger a good solution from another person in the group.
5. *Make sure the group understands that "piggybacking" off someone else's idea is useful.* Combine ideas; add to previous ideas. Adopt the philosophy that once an idea is presented to the group, no one owns it. It belongs to the group and anyone can modify it.
6. *Have someone record all the ideas mentioned.* Ideas could be recorded on a flipchart, chalkboard, whiteboard, or an overhead projector so that each group member can see them. You could also tape-record your discussions.
7. *Evaluate ideas when the time allotted for brainstorming has elapsed.* Consider these suggestions:
   - Approach each idea positively, and give it a fair trial.
   - Try to make ideas workable.
   - Encourage feedback about the success of a session. If only a few of the ideas generated by a group are useful, the session has been successful.

The Nominal-Group Technique

The **nominal-group technique** is a procedure that uses some of the principles and methods of brainstorming but has members write their ideas individually before sharing them with the group.[33] The nominal-group technique gets its name from the principle that the group is nominal (it is a group in name only), in the sense that members work on problems individually rather than during sustained group interaction. This technique uses **silent brainstorming** to overcome some of the disadvantages researchers have discovered in exclusively oral brainstorming.

Why does silent brainstorming often produce better results than oral brainstorming? During traditional brainstorming, group and team members blurt out their ideas. But if

Case Study

Business was terrible. The Paper Clip Company, the primary supplier of paper clips to big box discount stores, was having a sales slump. Because more people were using e-documents and e-files, fewer people were buying paper clips to fasten paper together. For the past three years sales had dropped by 15 percent each year. The company had already been forced to reduce the size of its manufacturing plant and lay off several employees.

The vice president of marketing decided to increase sales by identifying new, creative uses for paper clips other than holding sheets of paper together. She had assembled her brightest, most creative managers to develop possible new ways paper clips could be used. The vice president decided to use the brainstorming method. She announced the rules of brainstorming as described on page 269 and set a 15-minute time frame. She turned on a digital audio recorder to capture the verbal comments and the ideas suggested; her administrative assistant would type the list later and share them with the group.

It didn't go well. Several team members couldn't resist critiquing the ideas of others. The senior managers did more talking than the junior managers. One of the junior managers tried to share some ideas but received a glowering frown from a senior manager, and all the junior managers realized that they would risk being criticized if they shared their ideas. After about eight minutes of brainstorming, the senior managers had offered a few ideas, the junior managers had not spoken, and the vice president was becoming increasingly frustrated. She finally blurted out, "Oh, this isn't working!"

Practice in Applying Principles

1. What are the key problems with the brainstorming done by The Paper Clip Company's managers? Why did those problems occur? What should the vice president have done differently to set up the brainstorming session? What were the managers doing wrong?

2. Other than oral brainstorming, what are some alternative techniques that could be used to generate ideas?

3. Based on the principles of group and team creativity presented on pages 265–267, what could be done, regardless of the specific technique used, to develop a creative group climate?

4. In a group of five to seven people, select one of the creative idea-generation techniques discussed in this chapter. Take on the roles of managers at The Paper Clip Company, and see how many ideas you can generate. Alternative suggestion: Each group uses a different idea-generation technique (e.g., nominal-group technique, Delphi method, affinity technique); all groups have the same amount of time. At the end of the idea-generation process, see which groups have developed the most ideas. Discuss how the specific idea-generation technique you were required to use influenced your group's creativity.

someone laughs at an idea or says, "That's cool" or "That won't work," then the idea has been evaluated. *The key to making brainstorming work is that the generation of ideas is separated from the evaluation of ideas.* In oral brainstorming it's hard not to evaluate ideas. During traditional brainstorming, despite their best intentions, group members often evaluate ideas as soon as they are verbalized, so group members may be less likely to share ideas. As we discussed earlier in the chapter, criticism and evaluation diminish creativity.[34] Even if group members do not verbalize their evaluation, their nonverbal expressions often convey positive or negative evaluation of ideas. Some people are apprehensive or nervous about speaking up in a group, and traditional oral brainstorming makes it less likely that the communication-apprehensive members will participate. Silent brainstorming overcomes that problem by encouraging even apprehensive group and team members to participate by first writing their ideas. Once they have a written "script," they are more comfortable sharing their ideas. Researchers also found that people work more diligently if they have an individual assignment than if they have a group assignment.[35] In addition, researchers have found that sometimes with traditional brainstorming, the creative talents of some members seem to be restricted just by the very presence of others.[36] Group and team members may generate more ideas if members first work alone and then regroup. After they reconvene, group members can modify, elaborate on, and evaluate ideas. The generation of ideas (writing them down) has been separated from the evaluation of ideas. Silent brainstorming can be done even before a group meets for the first time; you could describe a problem and ask group members to brainstorm individually before assembling. E-mail makes this easier; communication researcher Henri Barki found that electronic brainstorming worked just as well as face-to-face brainstorming.[37] In the pages ahead, we talk about electronic brainstorming as a separate technique for developing creative ideas.

The nominal-group technique adds structure to the brainstorming process. The following steps summarize how to use the nominal-group technique.

1. All group members should be able to define and analyze the problem under consideration.
2. Working individually, group members write down possible solutions to the problem.
3. Group members report the solutions they have identified to the entire group one at a time. Each idea should be noted on a chart, chalkboard, whiteboard, or overhead projector for all group members to see.
4. Group members discuss the ideas gathered, not to advocate for one idea over another but rather to make sure that all the ideas are clear.
5. After discussing all proposed solutions, each group member ranks the solutions. If the list of solutions is long, the group members can rank the five solutions they like best. The results are tabulated.
6. The entire group discusses the results of the rankings. If the first round of ranking is inconclusive or if the group is not comfortable with the results, the options can be

DILBERT © Scott Adams/Dist. by United Feature Syndicate, Inc.

ranked again after additional discussion. Research suggests that using this organized method of gathering and evaluating information results in better solutions than if the group attacks a problem in a disorganized fashion.[38] One researcher has found that the nominal-group technique works better than other prescriptive approaches such as reflective thinking.[39]

This individual method of idea generation and evaluation has the advantage of involving all group members in deliberations. It can be useful if some group members are uncomfortable making contributions because of status differences in the group. Also, alternating group discussion with individual deliberation can be useful in groups plagued by conflict and tension.

Both traditional brainstorming and the nominal-group technique can be used at any phase of the problem-solving process. For example, you could combine the nominal-group technique with force-field analysis by asking group members to silently brainstorm about the forces driving and restraining attainment of a group goal. Or, you could ask members to brainstorm possible causes or symptoms of the problem during problem analysis. Or, you could use brainstorming or the nominal-group technique to generate possible strategies for implementing a solution the group has settled on.

The Delphi Technique

Whereas the nominal-group technique invites participants to contribute ideas by first writing them down and then sharing them with the group, the **Delphi technique** takes this idea one step further. This method, named after the ancient oracle at Delphi, has been called "absentee brainstorming," because individuals share ideas in writing or via e-mail, without meeting face-to-face. One person coordinates the information and shares it with the rest of the group. This approach is especially useful when conflict within the group inhibits effective group interaction, or when time and distance constraints make it diffi-

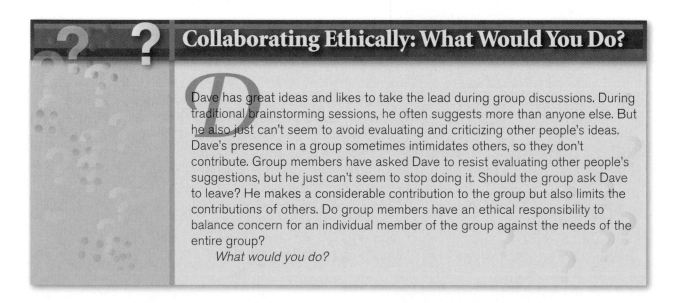

Collaborating Ethically: What Would You Do?

Dave has great ideas and likes to take the lead during group discussions. During traditional brainstorming sessions, he often suggests more than anyone else. But he also just can't seem to avoid evaluating and criticizing other people's ideas. Dave's presence in a group sometimes intimidates others, so they don't contribute. Group members have asked Dave to resist evaluating other people's suggestions, but he just can't seem to stop doing it. Should the group ask Dave to leave? He makes a considerable contribution to the group but also limits the contributions of others. Do group members have an ethical responsibility to balance concern for an individual member of the group against the needs of the entire group?

What would you do?

cult for group members to meet. Here is a step-by-step description of the Delphi technique.[10]

1. The group leader selects a problem, issue, policy, or decision that needs to be reviewed.
2. The leader corresponds with group members in writing, informing them of the task and inviting their suggestions and input. A specific questionnaire may be developed, or the group members may be asked to individually brainstorm suggestions or reactions to the issue confronting the group.
3. The respondents complete the questionnaire or generate a list of their brainstormed responses and send it to the leader.
4. The leader then summarizes all the responses from the group and shares the summary with all group members, asking for additional ideas, suggestions, and reactions. Team members are asked to rate or rank the ideas and return their comments to the leader.
5. The leader continues the process of summarizing the group feedback and asking for more input until general consensus emerges and decisions are made. It may take several rounds of soliciting ideas and evaluating ideas before consensus is achieved.

This method often produces many good ideas. All participants are treated equally, because no one is aware of who submitted which idea. It is, however, a time-consuming process. And because there is no face-to-face interaction, some ideas that are worthy of elaboration and exploration may get lost in the shuffle. Using the Delphi technique in combination with face-to-face meetings can help eliminate some disadvantages of the procedure.

Electronic Brainstorming

Electronic brainstorming is a technique that makes it possible for a group to generate solutions or strategies by typing ideas at a computer keyboard and having them displayed to the entire group. This high-tech method resembles the nominal-group technique in that group members write ideas before sharing them with the group. Because they can see ideas in written form, group members can piggyback off the ideas of others. Electronic brainstorming can be performed with all group members in the same room or computer lab or with members at their own home or office computers.

Research suggests that groups using electronic brainstorming generate more ideas than traditional face-to-face brainstorming groups.[41] One research team found that when some members of a group meet face to face and are supported with ideas from group members not physically present but using electronic means to share information, more ideas are generated and these are of higher quality than if all members meet face to face.[42] Some researchers theorize that this happens because the ideas are generated anonymously.[43] Members feel less fear or anxiety about being criticized for unconventional ideas, because no one knows who suggested them. Thus, when group members move to the phase of evaluating ideas, they are not sure whether they are evaluating an idea coming from a boss or a group leader or a new intern. All ideas are considered on their merit and quality. Another reason more ideas may be generated is because of the "piggyback effect." Group members may be stimulated to build on the ideas of other group members.

One obvious disadvantage of electronic brainstorming is the need to have access to a computer network and appropriate software. But recent evidence strongly supports the value of this variation of the brainstorming method, in which computers add structure to the process.

Cutting Edge Theory

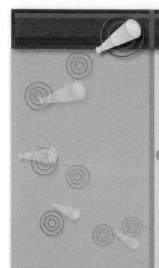

COGNITIVE STIMULATION AND CREATIVITY

Much research seems to suggest that oral brainstorming typically results in the generation of fewer ideas than such silent brainstorming techniques as the nominal-group technique, the Delphi technique, or the affinity technique, for several reasons:[44]

- Group members may not share their ideas orally because they fear that their suggestions will be criticized by others.
- Group members may just loaf when they hear others suggesting ideas.
- Some group members may not be able to create ideas while listening to others—they can't do two things at once.
- Group members may compare their ideas with the ideas they hear from others and think their own ideas are inferior and thus not share them.

However, an interesting theory called the **cognitive stimulation theory of creativity,** which describes how new and innovative ideas are stimulated in our brains, predicts that there may be some situations in which collaborative brainstorming may be best. This theory suggests that hearing words and phrases from others stimulates your own ideas because it jogs your memory of experiences and ideas that may result in a creative idea. One study explicitly tested this theory.[45] Group members who had been asked to brainstorm were first trained in techniques to increase their memory and retention of ideas that they heard. Then, while brainstorming, people listened to a prerecorded tape of someone suggesting ideas. The participants who had received memory training and who heard other ideas being suggested produced more ideas than a group that did not have the benefit of training and did not hear someone making suggestions. The researchers concluded that hearing ideas from others coupled with knowing some tips for remembering what one hears results in better brainstorming, especially if all ideas are not written out for all to see.

Real-Life Applications

The research seems to suggest that oral brainstorming can be improved if group members use the ideas of others to stimulate their own creativity.[46] What are the practical implications of this research? You will probably participate in groups that use oral brainstorming. If you do, these suggestions can help you become more creative.

- First and foremost, listen to and try to remember what others say during the brainstorming period.
- Build on the ideas of others. Turn someone else's idea inside out or upside down and come up with something completely different.
- Consciously avoid some of the documented pitfalls of oral brainstorming: Don't assume others will do all the work; don't hold back your ideas; freely share your ideas, even whacky, off-beat ones.
- Express your ideas, any ideas, boldly, even if you think they may not be well received; don't censor yourself.
- Work hard not to evaluate the ideas of others while listening to them.

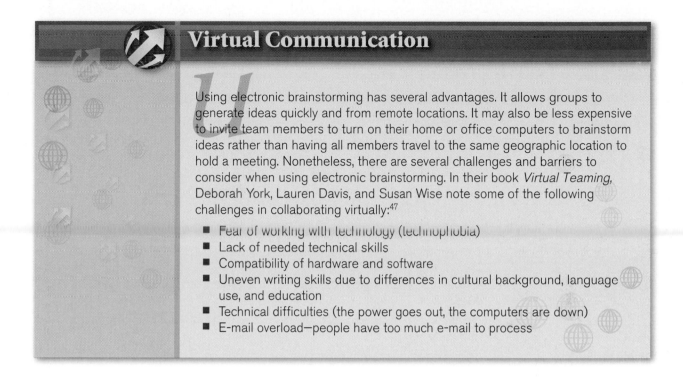

Virtual Communication

Using electronic brainstorming has several advantages. It allows groups to generate ideas quickly and from remote locations. It may also be less expensive to invite team members to turn on their home or office computers to brainstorm ideas rather than having all members travel to the same geographic location to hold a meeting. Nonetheless, there are several challenges and barriers to consider when using electronic brainstorming. In their book *Virtual Teaming*, Deborah York, Lauren Davis, and Susan Wise note some of the following challenges in collaborating virtually:[47]

- Fear of working with technology (technophobia)
- Lack of needed technical skills
- Compatibility of hardware and software
- Uneven writing skills due to differences in cultural background, language use, and education
- Technical difficulties (the power goes out, the computers are down)
- E-mail overload—people have too much e-mail to process

The Affinity Technique

Have you ever sat down at a desk cluttered with papers from a variety of projects and realized that you needed to sort the papers into piles to help you organize your desk? The **affinity technique** is a method for sorting through and organizing ideas that a group may generate.[48] The affinity technique is similar to the nominal-group technique, but instead of listing ideas on paper, group members write ideas on Post-it® notes. Like the other variations of brainstorming that we've discussed, the group is assigned an issue or problem about which to generate ideas. The entire group (or a smaller subcommittee) then organizes the ideas that have an "affinity," or are similar to each other, into categories.

The affinity technique is a way to make brainstorming sessions more fun and let people move around during a meeting. You can ask group members to post their notes on a wall or other smooth surface such as a chalkboard or white board and then to move around the room, review the ideas, and group them into categories. If your group sticks the notes on a chalkboard or white board, you could draw a circle around the notes and label the category using a word or terms that capture the theme of the suggestions. This technique will allow your group to quickly identify how many people have generated the same idea. The group will be able to see that one affinity category may have six or seven ideas, whereas another category may have only one or two. After creating the categories, the group may decide to combine them. Someone should be assigned to record the ideas that have been developed. The affinity technique may take a bit longer than the nominal-group technique, but for certain groups it may be the best way to develop a sense of collaboration in generating ideas.

ℛEVIEW

COMPARING CREATIVE TECHNIQUES

	ADVANTAGES	DISADVANTAGES
Brainstorming	Easy to use	High potential for group members to evaluate ideas as they are being generated
	No special materials needed	Takes more time than highly structured methods
	Group members can piggyback off of each other's ideas	Quiet members less likely to participate
Nominal-group technique	Can build on ideas of others	Requires good leader to organize the process
	Provides a written record of ideas suggested	Less time for free flow of ideas
	Controls more talkative, dominating group members	Difficult to implement with a large group
Delphi technique	Group does not have to meet face to face	No synergy created by hearing the ideas of others
	Provides a written record of ideas suggested	Minimizes opportunities for elaborating on ideas
	Helps group members prepare for upcoming meeting	Group members may be suspicious that someone has manipulated the results
Electronic brainstorming	Very efficient	Need special equipment
	Anonymity increases number of ideas generated	Need training in using computer software
		It takes time to describe procedures of electronic brainstorming
Affinity technique	Builds acceptance	Need Post-it notes
	Provides for interaction and acceptance of ideas	Takes more time than other techniques
	Preserves a written record of ideas presented	A skilled facilitator must orchestrate the technique

Source: Adapted from E. K. Aranda, L. Aranda, and K. Conlon, *Teams: Structure, Process, Culture, and Politics* (Upper Saddle River, NJ: Prentice Hall, 1998) 89.

How to Use Brainstorming in Your Group or Team

Although you should now understand how brainstorming, in its various forms, works, you may still have some questions about how you can apply this method of creative problem solving to your group discussions. Consider the following suggestions:[49]

- *Set aside a definite amount of time for brainstorming.*   Decide as a group how much time you want to devote to brainstorming. You may want to set a goal for a certain number of ideas that should be recorded: "We'll stop brainstorming when we get sixty ideas."

- *Do not make the time limit for brainstorming too short.*   Research suggests that groups given only a short time (four minutes) to brainstorm can be very productive, but not as creative as groups that have a longer time.[50] If you brainstorm orally, do not worry about a little silence while people think. If you use silent brainstorming (the nominal-group technique), it is okay if people don't write furiously during the entire brainstorming period. Don't cut off the brainstorming period early simply because people are silent or not writing.

- *Be certain that each group or team member understands the specific problem to be solved.*   A problem must be clearly defined and understood and must also be limited in size and scope. A broad, vaguely worded problem must be clarified before a group attempts to identify possible solutions.

- *Make sure that each group member follows the brainstorming rules.*   Brainstorming will be most effective if group members stop criticizing and evaluating ideas. Don't forget that group members can criticize nonverbally through tone of voice, facial expression, or posture. Everyone in the group must feel completely free to communicate ideas that may solve the problem. What should you do if a few members just cannot stop evaluating the ideas that are suggested? You may have to remind them courteously to follow the rules, ask them to be quiet, ask them to record the ideas of others, or ask them to leave the group. You may also consider using another technique (the nominal-group or the affinity technique or electronic brainstorming) as an alternative to oral brainstorming.

- *If you serve as the group's leader, try to draw less-talkative group members into the discussion.*   Call people by name: "Curt, you look like you've got some good ideas. What do you suggest?" You can also compliment the entire group when members do a good job of generating ideas: "Good job, group! We've got thirty ideas so far. Let's see if we can come up with thirty more."

- *Consider reverse brainstorming.[51]*   With this method, group members brainstorm ideas or solutions that would make the problem *worse*. After generating such a list, the group can consider the implications of doing the opposite of what was identified.

- *Consider rolestorming.[52]*   Rolestorming is one way of "thinking outside the box." With this method, group members assume the roles of someone else to help unlock ideas and increase group creativity. If you focus on a problem in your community, ask group members to assume the role of the mayor, the school superintendent, or the city manager. If it is a government problem, have them imagine that they are the governor, a member of the legislature, or even the president of the United States.

- *Tell the group what will happen with the ideas and suggestions generated.[53]*   Do not finish the brainstorming session with a long list of ideas that may be shelved. Perhaps a subcommittee can be formed to combine ideas and eliminate obvious overlapping suggestions. The subgroup might also be asked to evaluate the ideas or determine which ideas need further exploration or more information.

- *Try the random-word technique.*   One strategy to enhance the power of brainstorming that seems to work for some groups is the **random-word technique.** As described by Edward de Bono, while a group is brainstorming or pondering a problem, one person is assigned the task of saying a random word so others can hear it. The word is selected from a list of random words.[54] The spoken word is supposed to act as a trigger for new or creative ideas. This technique is another way to stimuate "thinking outside the box."

REVIEW

AN OVERVIEW OF PROBLEM-SOLVING STEPS AND TECHNIQUES

STEPS	TECHNIQUES
Identify and define the problem	*Is/is not* analysis Journalist's six questions Gather data Pareto charts
Analyze the problem	*Is/is not* analysis Cause-and-effect (fishbone) diagram Journalist's six questions Force-field analysis Develop criteria Identify history, causes, effects, symptoms, goals, obstacles
Generate solutions	Brainstorm Rolestorm Reverse brainstorm Nominal-group technique Delphi technique Affinity technique Electronic brainstorming
Evaluate solutions and select the best solution or combination of solutions	Compare pros and cons Apply solutions to criteria Appoint a subgroup Combine alternatives Average rankings and ratings
Test and implement the solution	Identify implementation steps Develop a group action plan Develop a flowchart

 ## Putting Principles into Practice

Overcome Barriers to Creativity

■ Don't seek creative solutions to problems prematurely; wait until the problems have been clearly defined and analyzed.

■ Find a suitable place to meet and work; groups and teams are more creative in a comfortable physical space.

■ Make sure the group is not too large; creative thinking is less likely in groups much larger than 12 or 15 people.
■ Give groups enough time to be creative.
■ Be positive; don't cut off creative efforts with negative and discouraging comments.

Use Principles of Group and Team Creativity to Your Advantage

■ Create a climate that encourages free thinking and spontaneity.
■ Listen to minority points of view.
■ Encourage people to see things from a new perspective or role.
■ Structure the conversation so as to balance participation and time to think.

Use Creativity Techniques Appropriately

■ Follow the rules of brainstorming and encourage others to follow the rules, especially the rule about not evaluating ideas until the proper time.
■ Consider using a silent or more structured brainstorming technique, such as the nominal-group technique, the Delphi technique, or the affinity technique, to encourage all group and team members to contribute.
■ Use electronic brainstorming to eliminate status differences and to permit anonymous contributions by group members that may otherwise feel too inhibited to contribute creative ideas.
■ Try to draw less-talkative group members into the discussion; compliment members when they come up with good ideas during the period of evaluating ideas.

𝒫RACTICE

Creativity Exercise

Solving this problem requires creativity. The class should divide into groups of three. Each group's assignment is to connect all nine dots with only four straight and connected lines without lifting your pen or pencil from the page.

Assessing Competencies of Problem-Solving Groups[55]

Competencies are specific behaviors that group and team members perform (review Chapter 1,

pages 26–28). The assessment form on the following pages lists nine competencies organized into four general categories. Use the evaluation form to assess small group communication competencies in a group or team discussion. Here's how to use the form:

1. Observe a group or team that is attempting to solve a problem. Write the names of the group members at the top of the form. (If the group includes more than six group members, photocopy the form so that each group member can be evaluated.)
2. When using the form, first decide whether each group member has performed each competency. Circle NO if the group member was not observed performing the competency. Circle YES if you did observe the group member performing the competency (e.g., defining the problem, analyzing the problem, identifying criteria, and so on.)

The Competent Group Communicator Assessment Form

Problem-Solving Competencies	Group Member	
Problem-Oriented Competencies		
1. Defined the problem by identifying the obstacle(s) that prevent the group from achieving its goal; identified what the group wants more of or less of to achieve the goal.	NO YES 0 1 2 3	
2. Analyzed the problem the group attempted to solve: Used relevant information, data, or evidence; discussed the causes, history, symptoms, or significance of the problem.	NO YES 0 1 2 3	
Solution-Oriented Competencies		
3. Identified criteria for an appropriate solution to the problem; developed standards for an acceptable solution; identified ideal outcomes of the solution.	NO YES 0 1 2 3	
4. Generated solutions or strategies that would solve the problem the group identified.	NO YES 0 1 2 3	
5. Evaluated solution(s): Identified positive and/or negative consequences of the proposed solutions; considered the pros and cons of suggested solutions.	NO YES 0 1 2 3	
Discussion-Management Competencies		
6. Maintained task focus: Helped the group stay on or return to the task, issue, or topic the group was discussing.	NO YES 0 1 2 3	
7. Managed group interaction: Appropriately initiated and terminated discussion, contributed to the discussion, or invited others to contribute to the discussion.	NO YES 0 1 2 3	
Relational Competencies		
8. Managed conflict: Appropriately and constructively helped the group stay focused on issues rather than on personalities when conflict occurred.	NO YES 0 1 2 3	
9. Maintained climate: Offered positive comments or non-verbal expressions that helped maintain a positive group climate.	NO YES 0 1 2 3	

Scoring: NO = Not observed   YES   0 = Inappropriate or inadequate performance of competency overall   1 = Adequate performance of competency overall

Problem-Oriented Competencies (0–6)		
Solution-Oriented Competencies (0–9)		
Discussion-Management Competencies (0–6)		
Relational Competencies (0–6)		

	Group Member _____	Group Member _____	Group Member _____	Group Member _____	Group Member _____	Group Assessment
	NO YES	NO YES	NO YES	NO YES	NO YES	NO YES
	0 1 2 3	0 1 2 3	0 1 2 3	0 1 2 3	0 1 2 3	0 1 2 3
	NO YES	NO YES	NO YES	NO YES	NO YES	NO YES
	0 1 2 3	0 1 2 3	0 1 2 3	0 1 2 3	0 1 2 3	0 1 2 3
	NO YES	NO YES	NO YES	NO YES	NO YES	NO YES
	0 1 2 3	0 1 2 3	0 1 2 3	0 1 2 3	0 1 2 3	0 1 2 3
	NO YES	NO YES	NO YES	NO YES	NO YES	NO YES
	0 1 2 3	0 1 2 3	0 1 2 3	0 1 2 3	0 1 2 3	0 1 2 3
	NO YES	NO YES	NO YES	NO YES	NO YES	NO YES
	0 1 2 3	0 1 2 3	0 1 2 3	0 1 2 3	0 1 2 3	0 1 2 3
	NO YES	NO YES	NO YES	NO YES	NO YES	NO YES
	0 1 2 3	0 1 2 3	0 1 2 3	0 1 2 3	0 1 2 3	0 1 2 3
	NO YES	NO YES	NO YES	NO YES	NO YES	NO YES
	0 1 2 3	0 1 2 3	0 1 2 3	0 1 2 3	0 1 2 3	0 1 2 3
	NO YES	NO YES	NO YES	NO YES	NO YES	NO YES
	0 1 2 3	0 1 2 3	0 1 2 3	0 1 2 3	0 1 2 3	0 1 2 3

2 = Good performance of competency overall   3 = Excellent performance of competency overall

3. For each competency for which you circled YES, determine how effectively the competency was performed. Use the scale, which ranges from 0 to 3.

   0 = This competency was performed, but it was performed inappropriately or inadequately. For example, the person observed tried to define a problem but did so poorly.
   1 = Overall, performance of this competency was adequate.
   2 = Overall, performance of this competency was good.
   3 = Overall, performance of this competency was excellent.

4. Total the score for each group member in each of the four categories. If the competency was performed, the total number of points will range from 0 to 6 or 0 to 9. The higher the number of points, the better the individual performed on this competency.

   Problem-Oriented Competencies consists of items 1 and 2. These behaviors help the group or team member define and analyze the problem.
   Solution-Oriented Competencies include items 3, 4, and 5, with a point range from 0 to 9. These competencies focus on how well the team member helped develop and evaluate a solution to the problem.
   Discussion-Management Competencies, items 6 and 7, help the group or team remain focused or manage interaction. The points for this category range from 0 to 6.
   Relational Competencies are behaviors that focus on dealing with conflict and developing a positive, supportive group climate. Items 8 and 9 reflect this competency; points range from 0 to 6.

5. You can also assess the group's or team's ability to perform these competencies. The column marked "Group Assessment" can be used to record your overall impression of how effectively the group or team behaved. Circle NO if no one in the group performed a particular competency. Circle YES if at least one person in the group or team performed a competency. Then evaluate how well the entire group performed each competency, using the 0 to 3 scale.

Sometimes it is difficult to make judgments about group competencies by just viewing a group discussion once. Many people find that it's easier to videotape a group discussion so that you can observe the group discussion more than once.

CHAPTER TWELVE

Leadership

"The first responsibility of a leader is to define reality. The last is to say thank you. In between, the leader is a servant."

—Max De Pree

OBJECTIVES

After studying this chapter, you will be able to:

- Discuss three approaches to the study of leadership.
- Describe three styles of leadership.
- Explain the relationship between situational variables and the effectiveness of different leadership styles.
- Analyze a small group meeting and determine which leadership behaviors will move the group toward its goal.
- Describe your own leadership style.
- Determine those situations in which you are most likely to be an effective leader.
- Be a more effective group leader and participant.
- Identify three transformational leadership skills.
- Explain the purpose of simulation in leadership training.

BEFORE BEGINNING THIS CHAPTER, *consider the following statements about leadership:*

Leaders are born, not made.

An effective leader is always in control of the group process.

A leader is a person who gets others to do the work.

Leadership is a set of functions distributed throughout the group.

The leader should know more than other group members about the topic of discussion.

An authoritarian leader is better than one who allows the group to function without control.

It is best for a group to have only one leader.

A person who has been appointed leader is the leader.

What do you think about these statements? Which ones do you agree with? Disagree with? If it has not happened already, be assured that one day you will find yourself in a leadership position—on a committee, in an organization, or perhaps in the military. In fact, whenever you participate in a decision-making group, your attitudes about leadership will affect your behavior, the behavior of others, and the effectiveness of the group.

This chapter provides information about the nature of leadership in groups, which should help you become a more effective group participant, and offers some specific suggestions to help you become an effective leader.

WHAT IS LEADERSHIP?

When you think about "leadership," what comes to mind? A fearless commanding officer leading troops into battle? The president of the United States addressing the country on national television? The student-body president coordinating and representing student efforts? Perhaps you think of the chairperson of a committee you are on. For our purposes, we define **leadership** as behavior or communication that influences, guides, directs, or controls a group. Communication scholar Dennis Gouran argues that leadership can be seen as a *counteractive influence* when groups get off track. He says leadership constitutes the behavior required when groups experience difficulty establishing the conditions necessary for making the best possible choices.[1]

Traditionally, the study of leadership has centered on people who are successful in leadership positions. Researchers argued that by looking at successful leaders, they could identify attributes or individual traits that best predict good leadership ability. Identifying such traits would be tremendously valuable to those in business, government, or the military who are responsible for promoting others to positions of leadership.

TRAIT PERSPECTIVE: CHARACTERISTICS OF EFFECTIVE LEADERS

Over the last several decades, researchers have conducted scores of trait studies indicating that leaders often have attributes such as intelligence, enthusiasm, dominance, self-confidence, social participation, and egalitarianism.[2] Other researchers found physical traits to be related to leadership ability. Leaders seemed to be larger, more active and energetic, and better looking than other group members.[3] Still other researchers found that leaders possess tact, cheerfulness, a sense of justice, discipline, versatility, and self-control.

The **trait perspective**—a view of leadership as the personal attributes or qualities that leaders possess—seemed like a reasonable one when it was first proposed, but it actually yielded very little useful information. Traits useful in one situation, such as leading troops into battle, are not necessarily the traits required for other leadership positions, such as conducting a business meeting.

A further problem with the trait approach is that it does not identify which traits are important to *becoming* a leader and which are important to *maintaining* the position. These studies also fail to adequately distinguish between leaders and followers who possess the same traits, and they are not useful to group participants wishing to improve their leadership skills. Therefore, although the trait approach is of interest from a historical perspective, we will move on to consider other, more useful, approaches.

FUNCTIONAL PERSPECTIVE: GROUP NEEDS AND ROLES

Rather than focusing on the characteristics of individual leaders, the **functional perspective** examines leadership as behaviors that may be performed by any group member to maximize group effectiveness. Dean Barnlund and Franklyn Haiman identify leadership behaviors as those that guide, influence, direct, or control others in a group.[4] This is a much more fruitful approach for those interested in improving their leadership abilities. Although the trait approach might help identify the sort of person who should be appointed to a leadership position, the functional approach describes the specific communicative behaviors a leader needs in order to help a group to function effectively. By understanding these behaviors, people can participate more effectively in group discussions.

According to advocates of the functional approach, the major leadership behaviors fall into two categories: (1) **task leadership** and (2) **process leadership** (also called *group building* or *maintenance*). Task-oriented behaviors aim specifically at accomplishing a group goal. Process-oriented behaviors help maintain a satisfactory interpersonal climate within a group. Both types of leadership are essential.

Task Leadership

When groups convene to solve problems, make decisions, plan activities, or determine policy, they are frequently hampered by group members' random behavior. Even when they get

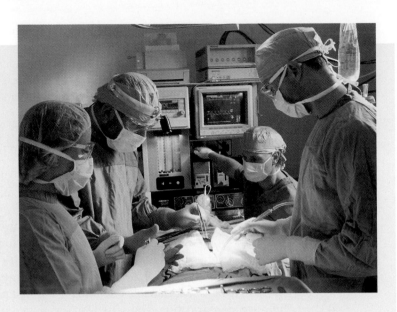

In an operating room, the role of each member of the surgical team is defined by the tasks required. What type of leader is best suited to lead such a team?

down to business, group process strays. Discussion becomes tangential, and groups lose track of where they are going. Sometimes one person monopolizes the conversation while others remain silent. Sometimes groups just cannot seem to get started. At such times, members may blame their designated leaders for their failure.

A group leader has a responsibility to keep a group moving, but research in group process has shown that anyone can perform the behaviors that keep a group on track. Just because a person has the title "leader" does not necessarily mean that he or she is best equipped to do the job. If leadership is a set of functions that are often distributed, a group is still quite capable of getting its job done regardless of who is designated leader. If you are a member of a disorganized group, you can provide the leadership the group needs even though you are not the "leader."

Chapter 4 describes the diversity of roles in small groups. The following list summarizes a few task-leadership behaviors and the ways in which they help a group move toward its goal:

■ *Initiating:* Task-oriented group discussions need to generate ideas. Sometimes ideas are related to procedural matters; at other times a group needs to generate ideas to solve problems. If, for example, you just read Chapter 9 on problem solving and can see that your group has not adequately defined its problem before suggesting solutions, you might say, "Listen. I think we're all proposing solutions before we've really agreed on the nature of the problem. Let's take a few minutes and talk some more about the problem so that we know we're all discussing the same thing."

By proposing a change in the group's deliberations, you initiate a procedural change—in this case, one that will probably benefit the group. To "initiate" means to "begin." If you say "Let's get this meeting under way," you have begun a change (assuming the group follows your suggestion). If, later in the meeting, you say, "Let's consider an alternative plan" or "Let's generate some more ideas before evaluating what we have here," you will again probably alter the course of the group's action. Without someone who initiates discussion, a group has no direction. The ability to initiate is an important group behavior, one that anyone can contribute.

- *Coordinating:* Different people bring different expectations, beliefs, attitudes, values, and experiences to a group. The contributions of each member are unique, yet all should be directed toward a common group goal. Given the diversity in small groups, coordinating is often an important leadership function. Communicative behavior that helps a group explore the contributions of all members is valuable. If, for example, you see a connection between the ideas that two members bring to the group, you should point it out to help focus the group. Coordinating members' efforts can help them see the "groupness" of their activities and reduce their uncertainty about the group, its problem, and its solutions.
- *Summarizing:* Groups can get long-winded. Often, people who are in the middle of a discussion cannot tell just where the discussion began and where it is going. It does not take many tangential remarks to get the group off track. Even when the group is on track, it is sometimes useful to stop and assess its progress. Summarizing reduces group uncertainty by showing how far the discussion has progressed and what it still needs to accomplish. By understanding when a group needs a summary—and then providing it—you can help move the group toward its goal. Even if the group does not accept your summary, you will still reveal discrepancies among group members' perceptions, thus opening the door to more clarification and less uncertainty.
- *Elaborating:* Sometimes good ideas are ignored until they are elaborated on enough to be visualized. Suppose you attend a meeting of your fraternity or sorority, which is trying to determine ways of increasing next year's pledge class. Someone in the group suggests that redecorating the recreation room might help. Several things might happen in the discussion: (1) Members might begin to evaluate the idea, some being in favor and some not; (2) another idea might be suggested and recorded; or (3), you (or someone else) might elaborate on the idea by describing how the room might look with new carpeting, a pool table, soft lighting, and a new sofa. Whereas redecoration might have fallen flat by itself, your elaboration gives it a fighting chance.

Initiating, coordinating, summarizing, and elaborating are types of communicative behaviors. Although these are some of the more important types of contributions you can make, the list is by no means complete. Task leadership is any behavior that influences group process and helps accomplish the group's task. Making suggestions, offering new ideas, giving information or opinions, asking for more information, and making procedural observations or recommendations are all task-oriented leadership behaviors that can contribute to a group's effort. The functional approach reveals that leadership skill is associated with the ability to analyze a group's process and to choose appropriate behaviors to further that process.

Process Leadership

For a group to function effectively, it needs to *concern itself with itself.* Groups are composed of people, and people have needs. (In fact, the family is a small group specifically adapted to meeting individual needs.) People do not leave their needs at home when they come to a meeting; they bring them along. Effective group communication must be addressed to both the external task of the group and the needs of its members. Failing to maintain a satisfying group climate can lead to a breakdown in a group's performance. In this respect, small groups resemble automobiles. Cars are great for getting you where you want to go, but they require regular tuning and maintenance in order to run reliably and efficiently. In fact, if an owner does not maintain a car, eventually it will break down. So it is with groups: They, too, need tuning and maintenance.

Leadership research consistently indicates that groups have both task and process needs. The process dimension is often called "group building and maintenance." Process leadership behaviors maintain interpersonal relations in a group and facilitate a climate satisfying to members and conducive to accomplishing the group's task. Group process leaders are really communication facilitators.

Chapter 5 discusses group climate from the perspective of individual and interpersonal needs. The following list presents some specific process-leadership behaviors that enhance climate:

- *Releasing tension:*   Think of times you have studied for exams. You cram more and more information into your head until you reach a point where it all seems futile. Everything runs together; ideas blur. You know it's time for a break. After a cup of coffee and some relaxing conversation, you return to your books with renewed energy.

    Sometimes the most effective leadership you can provide for a group is suggesting a coffee break. When a group is tired, when its task is difficult, when the hour is late, when tension and stress are high, a group needs relief. A joke, a bit of humor, a break, or even a motion to adjourn can often provide just what a group needs—tension release. An occasional break or a good laugh can renew a group's energy and improve member satisfaction.

- *Gatekeeping:*   As we note in Chapter 1, an advantage of working in small groups is that several heads are better than one. The very diversity that makes group communication so complex also gives it strength. A group possesses more experience and intelligence than does any individual, but experience and individual insight are only useful to a group if they are shared.

    Some people like to talk more than others, and in some groups, two or three people monopolize the conversation while others remain relatively silent. This fairly common occurrence poses a problem for a group in two ways: First, quiet members are just as likely as more vocal group members to possess useful information and ideas, and their ideas may never surface unless they say something. Second, people who talk more tend to be more satisfied with a group. Thus, members who do not talk much can have a negative effect on a group in both the task and process dimensions.

    Gatekeeping is aimed at coordinating discussion so that members can air their views. It may take the form of eliciting input ("Harvey, you must have given this a lot of thought. What are your views of the problem?") or even of limiting the contributions of more verbal group members ("Can we perhaps limit our comments to two or three minutes so that we can get everyone's ideas before we have to adjourn?"). Gatekeeping is an important leadership function because it ensures more input along the task dimension and higher member satisfaction along the process dimension.

- *Encouraging:*   People like praise. They feel good when someone recognizes them for their contributions. Offering encouragement is a leadership behavior aimed at increasing the self-esteem of group members and raising their hopes, confidence, and aspirations. Improving the morale of a group can increase cohesiveness, member satisfaction, and productivity.

- *Mediating:*   Conflict is a normal, healthy part of group interaction. However, mismanaged conflict can lead to hurt feelings, physical or mental withdrawal from a group, reduced cohesiveness, and general disruption. Mediating is aimed at resolving conflict between group members and releasing any tension associated with the conflict. When-

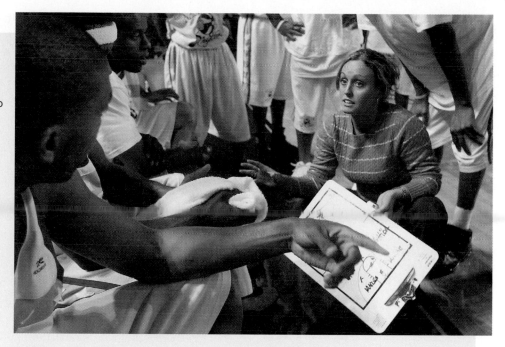

Coaching is an activity that requires both task and process leadership skills. What might happen if this coach had poor leadership skills?

ever conflict becomes person-oriented rather than issue-oriented, it is a particularly appropriate time for mediation.

Wanda: I think that the plan I'm proposing has considerable merit and meets our needs.

Harold: That's ridiculous. It'll never work.

Wanda: Get off my case! I don't see you proposing any better solutions.

This potentially volatile situation could easily disrupt the group. You often have to work in groups with people you do not especially like. Obviously, Harold and Wanda do not get along well, but groups can function effectively in spite of personality clashes. They need to focus discussion on issues rather than on personalities. At times, interpersonal difficulties become so severe that they cannot be resolved by simply focusing on a group's task. Such difficulties can be a serious encumbrance to a group and need to be dealt with either within or outside the group; ignoring problems will not make them go away.

The preceding list of behaviors that contribute to a group's process or maintenance needs is not complete. More complete lists appear in Chapter 4. The behaviors just described are some of those that are more essential to task and process leadership. They are included here to emphasize their importance and to help you identify your own leadership behavior in groups.

Both task and process leadership are essential to the success of a small group. If a group does not make progress on its task, members probably will feel frustrated and unsatisfied. In addition, if a group does not maintain a comfortable environment, members will tend to focus their attention and energy on their own dissatisfaction with the group rather than on their assigned task.

SITUATIONAL PERSPECTIVE: ADAPTING STYLE TO CONTEXT

Thus far we have discussed the trait and functional approaches to leadership study and explored some task and process leadership roles. The **situational perspective** to group leadership accommodates all these factors—leadership behaviors, task needs, and process needs—but also takes into account leadership style and situation.

Leadership Style

Your beliefs and attitudes about leadership will affect your behavior in small groups. **Leadership style** is a relatively consistent pattern of behavior reflecting a leader's beliefs and attitudes. Although no two people act as leaders in precisely the same way, people do lead with three basic styles: (1) authoritarian (or autocratic), (2) democratic, and (3) laissez-faire.

Authoritarian leaders assume positions of intellectual and behavioral superiority in groups. They make the decisions, give the orders, and generally control all activities. Democratic leaders have more faith in the group than authoritarian leaders do and consequently try to involve members in making decisions. Laissez-faire leaders see themselves as no better or no worse than other group members. They assume the group will direct itself. Laissez-faire leaders avoid dominating groups. In one of the earliest studies of the effects of leadership style, researchers compared groups of school children led by graduate students who had been specifically trained in one of the three leadership styles. The researchers defined the styles as shown in Table 12.1.[5] Here is a brief summary of the results of the study:

1. Groups with democratic leaders generally were better satisfied and functioned in a more orderly and positive way.
2. Groups with authoritarian leaders were more aggressive or more apathetic (depending on the group).
3. Members of democratic groups were better satisfied than members of laissez-faire groups; a majority of group members preferred democratic to authoritarian leadership, although some members were better satisfied in authoritarian groups.
4. Authoritarian groups spent more time engaged in productive work, but only when the leader was present.

It is tempting to conclude that humanistic, participatory, democratic leadership will invariably lead to greater satisfaction and higher productivity. Unfortunately, the evidence does not warrant such a generalization. Several studies have shown that no single leadership style is effective in all situations. What works at General Motors may not work in a family business. An effective student

"Any other objections?"

TABLE 12.1   **Leader Behavior in Three "Social Climates"**

Authoritarian	Democratic	Laissez-Faire
Leader makes all determination of policy.	Leader encourages and directs, but all policies are a matter of group discussion and decision.	Leader participates at a minimum level; complete freedom for group or individual decisions.
Leader dictates techniques and activity steps one at a time, so group members are always largely uncertain of future steps.	Leader discusses activity steps with group before group begins work; general steps to group goal are sketched, and when technical advice is needed, leader suggests alternative procedures.	Leader supplies various materials, making it clear he or she will supply information when asked, but taking no other part in discussion.
Leader usually dictates work task and work companion for each member.	Leader leaves division of tasks to group; members are free to work with anyone.	Leader does not participate in task or work companion assignments.
Leader tends to be personal in praise and criticism of each member's work; remains aloof from active group participation except when demonstrating.	Leader tends to be objective or "fact-minded" in praise and criticism and tries to be regular group member in spirit without doing too much of the work.	Leader makes only infrequent, spontaneous comments on member activities unless questioned; makes no attempt to appraise or regulate course of events.

body president may be a poor camp counselor. The expectations of one group differ from those of other groups.[6]

Recent research on the effectiveness of different leadership styles has suggested that effective leadership is contingent on a variety of interrelated factors, such as culture, time constraints, group compatibility, and the nature of a group's task. Although the functional approach reveals the importance of fulfilling various leadership roles in a group, it does not explain which roles are most appropriate in which situation. It is clear that you need to consider the setting in which leadership behavior occurs.

The situational approach views leadership as an interaction between style and various situational factors. David Korten proposes that under certain conditions groups are pressured to have centralized, authoritarian leadership but that as these conditions change, groups often develop a more democratic, participative form of leadership.

Korten says that groups with highly structured goals and high stress move toward authoritarian leadership. Think of times when you were in a group with clear goals but with members uncertain of how to achieve them. Remember when a group felt stress because of an impending deadline or a group grade. At such times, group members will gladly follow any leader who can give direction and show them the means to their goal. When the situation changes—that is, when the group feels less uncertain, has less stress, and has less structured goals—it has less of a need for authoritarian leadership and instead needs more participative, democratic leadership. Figure 12.1 represents Korten's situational leadership

FIGURE 12.1

Relation of Stress,
Goal, Structuring,
and Leadership
Patterns

Source: D. C. Korten,
"Situational Determinants of
Leadership Structure,"
Journal of Conflict Resolu-
tion 6 (1962) 222–35.

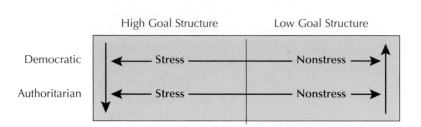

model. Note the flow of the model showing that as stress and goal structure increase, the tendency of a group to accept authoritarian leadership increases. As stress and goal structure decrease, groups need more democratic—or even laissez-faire—leadership. When the room is on fire, we want someone who will take charge and lead us to safety. But when the task is to discuss the book of the month, such take-charge leadership seems inappropriate.

Korten's model is applicable even on an international scale. Consider the differences between leadership and goal structure in the developing world and in the United States. Citizens of developing countries seek new ways of life that they as yet have not attained; their goals are structured, concrete, and operational. By contrast, Americans focus more on maintaining processes than on changing them. The relationship of these goals to leadership styles in the two regions is obvious.

Hersey and Blanchard's Situational Model

Like other situational leadership theories, Paul Hersey and Kenneth Blanchard's model uses various combinations of task- and relationship-oriented leadership behavior to describe leadership style as it relates to different situations.[7] In this case, the maturity of the group is the situational variable.

Take a few minutes to examine Hersey and Blanchard's model in Figure 12.2. Note that the two axes of the model represent the now-familiar task and relationship (process) dimensions of leadership behavior, reflecting different leaders' orientations. Quadrant S1 represents a leader who strongly emphasizes performance of the group task and pays little attention to relationship issues—that is, his or her orientation is high task and low relationship; quadrant S2, high task and high relationship, and so on. To these various combinations, Hersey and Blanchard gave the terms *telling, selling, participating,* and *delegating.* A telling style is extremely directive. A selling style is also directive, but a leader is concerned that the group accept and internalize orders given. A participating style is driven primarily by concern for relationships and a need for all group members to share in decision making. A leader with a delegating style takes a hands-off attitude and allows the group to direct itself.

According to Hersey and Blanchard, these four leadership styles are more or less appropriate depending on a group's maturity. Note across the bottom of the Hersey and Blanchard model a scale that goes from M4 (high maturity) to M1 (low maturity). Here, "maturity" refers not to chronological age or emotional maturity, but to the degree of experience group members have with one another in that group. When you view maturity in

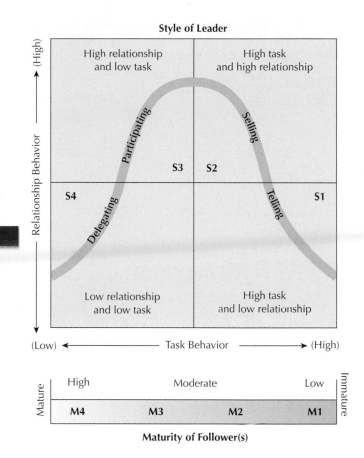

Style of Leader

FIGURE 12.2

Hersey and Blanchard's Situational-Leadership Model

SOURCE: Paul Hersey and Ken Blanchard, *Management of Organizational Behavior: Utilizing Human Resources,* 6th ed. (Englewood Cliffs, NJ: Prentice Hall, 1992) 248. Reprinted by permission.

combination with the rest of the model, you can see that a "telling" style is most appropriate with groups that are just starting out, perhaps in their orientation stage of development. As groups mature, effective leadership allows for more autonomy. "Just as parents should relinquish control as a function of the increasing maturity of their children, so too should leaders share more decision-making power as their subordinates acquire greater experience with and commitment to their tasks."[8]

Communication scholar Sarah Trenholm offers the following example of how Hersey and Blanchard's model might apply to a classroom:

> Consider teaching style as a form of leadership. Hersey and Blanchard would suggest that at the beginning of a course of study, with inexperienced students, a highly directive telling style is best. The teacher who tells a freshman class, "You decide what and how you want to learn. It's entirely up to you," is using a delegating style, which will fail, because at this point, students are not yet ready to take full responsibility for their own learning. As the course progresses, however, and as the students feel more comfortable with the course and each other, the teacher might use selling and participating styles, and perhaps end up with a delegating approach. More mature students may be ready for autonomy and may even resent being told what to do.[9]

The Hersey and Blanchard model is widely used in training managers and executives, probably because it shows how managers can change styles according to their subordinates'

Virtual Communication

Virtual teams will not survive or thrive without good leadership.[10] But leading a virtual team is not easy—in fact, it can be more difficult and demanding than leading a traditional team. In general, the role of a virtual team leader is to facilitate, coach, and consult rather than to direct (that is, telling others what to do and how to do it). However, it does take more than one person to make a virtual team successful. Shared leadership is important and necessary because virtual team members have varied skills and need to feel comfortable stepping in when necessary, based on the task at hand. Following are some important tasks for virtual team leaders:

- Establish clear channels of communication with your team, such as when to use voice mail, e-mail, phone calls, faxes, pagers, groupware, and face-to-face meetings.
- Maintain focus on the team mission, goals, and objectives. Remind people of the mission, goals, and objectives often; be willing and able to define goals and objectives and manage priorities in a fast-paced environment.
- Help members connect with one another. Be a role model for sharing ideas, resources, and information.
- Actively support team communication, collaboration, and coordination. Remember, if you do not participate, other group members will not; be hands-on and active in the work.
- Establish a process for storing and retrieving critical team knowledge, such as in shared folders, databases, or shared work spaces.
- Work continuously to improve relationships among team members. Provide occasions for team members to meet face to face and get to know one another.
- Help team members stay connected with the larger organization. Communicate the company vision, share new projects, and build links with other key stakeholders.
- Keep the larger organization informed about what the team is working on. Share team success stories and alert others about challenges.
- Be aware of differences in perspectives and work practices. Help by bridging gaps in understanding, reducing confusion, and adding clarification.

maturity level. A delegating style can be used with one employee or group and a telling style with another.[11]

Some Observations on the Situational Approach to Leadership

At first glance, the situational approach seems to cover all bases. It looks at the style of leadership, the group's task needs and process needs, and situational variables that influence groups. Unfortunately, most research using this approach has focused on the behavior of leaders rather than on leadership as a process of realizing group goals.[12] Thus, while the sit-

Case Study

Having been offered some very attractive extra retirement benefits by top management, Arthur agreed to take early retirement at age 62. Once an ambitious young junior executive for the company, Arthur had, in recent years, taken a rather relaxed, anything-goes attitude as director of his division. As a result, his team showed the lowest productivity record in the company, and the employees under his supervision did not receive attractive salary increments and other rewards from top management. Morale was very low, and the employees were discontented.

Hoping to rejuvenate the group, management replaced Arthur with an extremely bright, dynamic, and aggressive young manager named Marilyn. Marilyn's instructions were these: "Get your team's productivity up by 20 percent over the next twelve months, or we'll fire the whole group and start from scratch, with a new manager and new employees."

Marilyn began by studying the records of employees in her group to determine the strengths and weaknesses of each. She then created goals and objectives for each employee and made assignments accordingly. She set a rigid timetable for each employee and made all employees directly accountable to her.

Employee response was overwhelmingly positive. Out of chaos came order. Each person knew what was expected and had tangible goals to achieve. Employees felt united behind their new leader as they all strove to achieve their objective of a one-year, 20 percent increase in productivity.

At the end of the year, productivity was up not 20 percent but 35 percent! Management was thrilled and awarded Marilyn a large raise and the company's certificate of achievement. All of her team members received a handsome bonus.

Feeling that she had a viable formula for success, Marilyn moved into the second year as she had into the first—setting goals for each employee, holding them accountable, and so forth. However, things went less smoothly the second year. Employees who had been quick to respond the first year were less responsive. Although the work Marilyn assigned was usually completed on time, its quality declined. Employees had a morale problem: Those who had once looked up to Marilyn as "Boss" were now sarcastically calling her "Queen Bee" and reminiscing about "the good old days" when Arthur was their manager.

Marilyn's behavior as a manager had not changed, yet her leadership was no longer effective. Something needed to be done, but what?

Practice in Applying Principles

1. Analyze this situation. What are the important elements to consider when diagnosing Marilyn's leadership problem? How would you describe her leadership style?
2. What situational variables changed from the first to the second year of Marilyn's leadership?
3. Why was Marilyn's leadership successful in the first year but not in the second?
4. How did team goals change from the first to the second year? How about stress levels? Were they the same, or did they change?
5. What would you recommend to Marilyn to help her be more successful? First, use David Korten's model and language to make your recommendations. Then, make recommendations based on the Hersey and Blanchard model.

uational approach is useful, it is, perhaps, not as helpful to the student of small group communication as is the functional approach. Achieving a group goal involves everyone in the group, not just the leader. Consequently, students and scholars continue to be interested in the influence of group members' verbal and nonverbal statements on group goals—that is, in group members' communication.

PERSPECTIVES ON LEADERSHIP

Trait approach: Attempts to identify characteristics common to successful leaders

Functional approach: Views leadership as a set of behaviors that may be enacted by any group member

Situational approach: Relates effective leadership to interaction between leadership style and the group situation

TRANSFORMATIONAL LEADERSHIP

A relatively new theory of leadership, which describes leadership in organizations, is **transformational leadership.** As described in management and public administration literature, transformational leadership has four defining characteristics, called the Four I's: (1) Idealized leadership, (2) Inspirational motivation, (3) Intellectual stimulation, and (4) Individual consideration.

Contrasted with transactional leaders, who manage within the existing norms of their organizations, the transformational leader changes the organization by realigning its culture with a new vision and restructuring its shared assumptions and norms. Transformational leaders have a sense of vision and purpose. Author Peter Senge proposes three critical skills of transformational leadership: (1) building shared vision, (2) surfacing and challenging mental models, and (3) engaging in systems thinking.[13] *Building shared vision* is similar to establishing mutuality of concern (see Chapter 3). It involves encouraging individuals to express their visions of group or organizational goals while encouraging the development of a common, positive view. *Surfacing and challenging mental models* is a process of identifying and challenging assumptions without creating defensiveness—a daunting task requiring supportive communication skills (see Chapter 5). *Systems thinking* is a process we have argued for throughout this book. Understanding groups and organizations and the great complexity that characterizes them requires that leaders look beyond day-to-day operations to find underlying themes, forces of change, and interrelationships.[14]

In the film *The Empire Strikes Back,* Luke Skywalker watches as Yoda levitates his spaceship out of the swamp.

> *Luke:*   "I don't believe it!"
>
> *Yoda:*   "That is why you fail."

Often, the secret to *reaching* a goal (or vision) lies in the *belief* that it *can* be reached. Belief in the vision becomes more powerful than the followers' sense of lack, limitation, and doubt. This *belief-system shift* empowers followers to a higher level of commitment and achievement. Its effect may even be so powerful as to convert followers into leaders and leaders into moral agents.[15]

Transformational leadership is not so much a set of behaviors that one can observe or emulate as it is a philosophy of leadership and change.[16] Small groups and teams everywhere operate within the cultures of larger organizations and thus are affected by and a part of those cultures. In innovative transformational organizational cultures, we are likely to see assumptions that people can be trusted, that everyone has a contribution to make, and that complex problems should be handled at the lowest possible level. In a transformational culture, norms are flexible enough to adapt to changing external environments. Superiors serve as mentors, coaches, role models, and leaders.[17] Transformational leadership has the greatest capacity to motivate group members to debate ideas constructively.[18]

EMERGENT LEADERSHIP IN SMALL GROUPS

The Minnesota Studies

A fascinating series of leadership studies begun at the University of Minnesota (called the Minnesota Studies) sought the answer to the question "Who is most likely to emerge as the perceived leader of a leaderless discussion group?" Led by Professor Ernest Bormann, the Minnesota Studies formed and observed "test-tube groups" that engaged in leaderless group discussions.

Collaborating Ethically: What Would You Do?

Some research indicates that the behavior of leaders or superiors in an organization is among the strongest influences on ethical behavior, playing a larger role than the actions of peers or, in some cases, people's individual ethical frameworks.[19] When you're a leader, you're a role model. As such, your power may go far beyond your direct, immediate influence on your group's work.

Often, group and team leaders are privy to information that other group members do not have. Organizations often communicate with groups only through their designated leaders. Thus, the leader is a gatekeeper for the group, a channel through whom information passes from superiors to the group and from the group back to those above.

Suppose that you are the leader of a team working on a project nearing completion. You are relieved, because the holidays are approaching rapidly, your group has been working night and day, and the project must be completed so that the exhausted group members can take some time off with their families. You schedule the final meeting for tomorrow, when the team will put the finishing touches on the project and you will tell them they can have some time off.

Your boss has just brought you a report from another team, which he believes may have bearing on your project. You review the report, and while you understand your boss's view, you don't believe the other team's data are really relevant to your project. If you forward the report to your group, they will have to take time to process it, which will cut into their much-needed vacation time.

What would you do?

Most people think of a leader as someone who takes charge and organizes a discussion. Predictably, group members often perceive those who actively participate in the group and who direct communication toward procedural matters as leaders. Although studies show a clear correlation between perceived leadership and talkativeness, especially task-oriented talkativeness,[20] those who talk most are not the only ones who become leaders in leaderless groups. In fact, most groups do not select leaders at all. The Minnesota Studies show that leaders emerge through a "method of residues," whereby group members are rejected for the role of leader, until only one remains. The first members to be eliminated from consideration are the quiet ones who do not actively participate in the early stages of a group's discussion. The next to go are the talkative but overaggressive or dogmatic group members who are perceived to be too inflexible for leadership positions.

After this initial phase of elimination, a group enters a second phase, in which roughly half the group members remain in contention for the leadership role. This phase moves much more slowly than the first phase, and it is a good deal more painful and frustrating. One by one, the group rejects contenders for the leadership role, until only one or two remain. Often, members reject would-be leaders because their style is perceived as disturbing. In the Minnesota Studies' classroom discussion groups, members often rejected an authoritarian style on the grounds that the person was "too bossy" or "dictatorial." (Of course, as the situational perspective would suggest, the authoritarian style might be inappropriate in a classroom discussion group but highly appropriate in other situations, especially those that involve extreme stress.) In another study, Deborah Baker found that specific communication behaviors increase the likelihood of rejection as leader.[21] Group members who seem unable to contribute to either the group's tasks or organization because they are quiet, vague, tentative, self-effacing, or always asking others for direction are usually rejected. In this second phase of role emergence, the Minnesota Studies also found that, to some extent, groups with two or more men rejected female contenders for the leadership role. Groups containing only one man often selected a female leader and isolated the man— a pattern that may be changing.

Task-motivated group members often rejected a contender who was perceived as too process-oriented—that is, too concerned about everyone's feelings and moods to be decisive. Likewise, process-oriented members tended to reject those they saw as too concerned with the task. According to Bormann,

> In the final analysis, groups accepted the contender who provided the optimum blend of task efficiency and personal consideration. The leader who emerged was the one that others thought would be of most value to the entire group and whose orders and directions they trusted and could follow.[22]

The Minnesota Studies give fascinating insight into the process through which group leaders emerge. Although this information does not tell you how to behave in order to rise to leadership positions, it does alert you to the process through which leadership emerges. These studies also highlight the complexity of small groups and explain, to an extent, why a person who assumes a leadership role in one group may not do so in another and why a person who is perceived to be a leader in two groups may not assume the same role in each.

Research is adding to our knowledge of emergent leadership in groups. Emergent leaders typically display more effective listening skills and may be more extroverted.[23] Individual task ability contributes to emergent leadership, as does commitment to the group's assigned

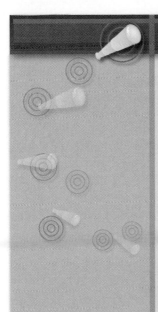

Cutting Edge Theory

LEADERSHIP AND GENDER

Communication scholars Susan Shimanoff and Mercilee Jenkins have conducted extensive reviews of the research literature on gender and group leadership, and they have drawn several conclusions.

- In problem-solving groups, both male and female leaders concentrate on task behaviors, but female leaders are slightly more responsive to the group's social-emotional needs.
- Males tend to talk more, which can increase their power, but women are equally effective in using evidence and making procedural suggestions, which are two critical leadership behaviors.
- Generally, men and women lead equally well. However, there is some evidence that because of sex role biases, female leaders may need to perform better than their male counterparts to be considered as good as the men.

Men and women appear to be equally suited to positions of leadership, yet men are still more likely to rise to positions of power. The authors note that it is disturbing to think that gender alone can change how people and behaviors are perceived.

Real-Life Applications

Groups are most productive and satisfied when they have effective leadership. Men and women are equally qualified to provide that leadership, yet barriers still remain that slow women's rise to leadership positions. Shimanoff and Jenkins have offered the following suggestions for group members who wish to lower these barriers and maximize effective leadership.

- Acknowledge and challenge sex-role biases; affirm egalitarian attitudes, and remind group members of their importance.
- Celebrate the "traditional" strengths of women, but don't assume women alone have these strengths.
- Increase the visibility and support of female role models.
- Designate leaders only after interacting, if at all.
- Listen attentively; support members and treat them with respect.
- Ask others for their opinions; invite others to participate.
- Draw on the strengths of all group members; recognize the contributions of each as a valuable resource.
- Make procedural suggestions and offer relevant information.
- Provide evidence for claims.
- Be an active participant, but monitor how much time you spend talking.
- Discourage interruptions, especially those that change the subject.
- Learn from diverse groups and individuals.[24]

goals.[25] Group goals are often strongly influenced by the emergent leader's personal goals for the group.[26] Verbal aggressiveness is *not* associated with leadership emergence.[27]

Leadership and Gender

A review of research literature on the subject of gender and leadership reveals that the times, indeed, are changing.[28] Research in the 1960s and 1970s found that women were reluctant to assume leadership roles.[29] Group members perceived males as more independent, rational, confident, and influential than females and viewed males as leaders more often than females.[30] In 1979, however, one team of researchers noted that females were more receptive to ideas and to fostering interpersonal relations, showing concern, and being attentive to others than males. Males in the same study in actual organizational settings were more dominant than females and quicker to challenge others and to control the course of conversation. The researchers noted that female leadership styles were more compatible with human-resource theories of how managers should behave.[31]

In 1981, research reported that the influence of gender on the emergence of leadership was most evident early in the process and dissipated over time.[32] By the late 1980s, some studies were reporting no difference in the way males and females are perceived in leadership roles.[33] Also in the 1980s, there was a substantial body of research distinguishing *psychological gender* (introduced in Chapter 4) from *biological gender.* This research supported the argument that the most effective leader was that androgynous individual who could draw from a repertoire of both traditionally male and traditionally female behaviors.[34] Research in the 1990s continued to support this view.[35]

Researcher Katherine Hawkins identified task-relevant communication as the sole significant predictor in her study of emergent leadership, regardless of the gender of the candidate for leadership. Her study also noted no significant gender differences in the production of task-relevant communication.[36] Such communication, it seems, is the key to emergent leadership in task-oriented group interaction, for either gender. Other research has found that female managers are considered to be better at putting people at ease but that gender makes no difference in perceptions of leadership ability once a manager has gained organizational experience.[37] Gender composition, too, may have an effect on team outcomes. Some research has suggested that having more females as informal leaders within a team enhances the team's performance.[38] More recent studies have found no preference for men over women in ratings of competence.[39]

LEADERSHIP AND SELF-DECEPTION IN ORGANIZATIONS

Leaders in organizations often have a tendency to ignore upward communication from nonmanagerial staff members, especially when such communication is critical of management and even when staff members have specifically been asked to communicate. This tendency can lead to flawed decision making and poorer performance.[40]

As we have noted throughout the book, higher-status members of a group or organization do not necessarily have the best ideas or the clearest vision. Managers deceive themselves if they think this. At best, their understanding is incomplete if they have not considered all points of view. Developing awareness of their own tendencies toward self-deception is the first step leaders can take toward more intentionally soliciting and attending to upward communication from lower-status members.

LEADERSHIP TRAINING

Research consistently indicates that the productivity of a group improves if its members are trained. In one study, team-building intervention among a group of department leaders resulted in a measurable increase in the ability to raise issues and manage conflict; an increase in mutual praise, support, and cooperation; clarification of roles and responsibilities; and long-term commitment to teamwork and innovation. The author concluded that a communication-focused team-building intervention can have positive, lasting results.[41] **Training** involves instruction to develop skills. Most of the instruction you receive in university classrooms involves what and how you *think;* training emphasizes what you can *do.*

The simplest form of leadership training provides members with feedback on their performance.[42] Evidence suggests that when members receive such feedback, they tend to work harder, particularly when they are being evaluated by an expert.[43] This technique of observation and feedback is the mainstay of most leadership training programs. Whether other group members provide feedback, or an observer or a video monitor does, people need a more objective eye than their own to see what they are doing and how they can do it better. Beyond the basics, leadership training ranges from the simple and inexpensive to the elaborate and expensive. Given the various definitions of leadership outlined in this chapter, training may justifiably encompass any or all of the principles and skills outlined in this book. Often, training includes simulation exercises.

A **simulation** is a structured exercise that creates conditions that participants might confront outside the training environment. It provides a context in which participants can experiment with new behaviors without any risks. The war games that are a part of military training are one example of simulation; the conditions of war are recreated so that trainees can try out new behaviors in a situation that is not life threatening. Likewise, many leadership and management training programs recreate conditions of the work environment in which trainees can experiment with hypothetical written reports, financial documents, and background information. Thus, simulations are important to leadership training because they add a context that approximates the actual circumstances for which participants are being trained.

Although most training focuses more on behavior than it does on cognition, good training is multidimensional; that is, it incorporates more than one level of learning. Training effectiveness depends on many factors, including team and individual competencies, task requirements, and features of the work environment.[44]

Good training should provide you with an expanded repertoire of behaviors and the understanding and awareness to make judgments about why, how, and when to use those behaviors. To learn effectively, you need to be aware of both principles and practice.

We conclude this chapter as it began, with a quotation, this time from Lao Tsu, who wrote these words 2,500 years ago. They remain as true today as ever:

> The wicked leader is he whom the people despise,
> The good leader is he whom the people revere.
> The great leader is he of whom the people say,
> "We did it ourselves."

Putting Principles into Practice

The most effective leadership behavior is behavior that best meets the needs of the group. Groups have both task and process needs; these and other situational variables determine the most appropriate type of leadership behavior for groups. Here are some suggestions on how to apply what you have learned, if and when you are the designated leader or chairperson of a group:

- The rest of the group will have certain expectations of you as leader. For example, they may expect you to be particularly influential on matters of procedure. You should meet such expectations.
- Prepare a realistic agenda well in advance and distribute it to all group members. At meetings, help the group stick to its agenda.
- Analyze the group's situation—its time constraints, goal structure, stress, leader–member relations, and so on.
- Remember that groups have task and process needs. Members need to get the job done, but they also need encouragement, praise, and thanks.
- Consider your own orientation toward group work. Are you motivated primarily by task concerns or by people concerns? Some situations call for decisive, authoritarian action. Is this what you are good at? If not, you may want to delegate authority to someone who is more task-oriented, at least in crisis situations. Does your concern for task outweigh your concern for group–member relations? At times you may want to follow a laissez-faire leadership style and let person-oriented group members take over for a while. Adapt your style to the situation, and use the resources of the group to everyone's advantage.
- In an ad hoc group that meets only once or twice, the leadership style you choose is not nearly as important as in a committee that meets regularly over a long period of time. In most long-term situations, a democratic style of leadership is preferable. Provide procedural structure for the group, but encourage as much participation as possible. Increased member participation can breed a better solution.

If you are not the designated leader or chairperson of the group:

- Although you have less control in this situation because of the different expectations the group has of you, you are still influential. You can still demonstrate leadership behavior.
- Use your knowledge about small group communication to analyze what is going on in the group. Consider your own strengths as a group member. What roles do you fulfill best in the group? Use your strengths to provide what the group needs and to support those who have other needed skills.
- Occasionally a group suffers a leadership void. This often occurs when leaders are appointed by an outside source or when leaders are elected at a group's first meeting before group members have had a chance to evaluate one another as potential leaders. In these cases, rely on the functional approach, because any member of the group (including you) can provide leadership. But watch out for delicate egos. When leaders do not live up to expectations, group members will disapprove of them. In a small group, this can result in an attempt to overthrow a leader or in a resentful and ineffectual group climate. Members set aside the group's task while they hassle over who is in charge. Almost invariably, such groups produce unsatisfactory results and bruised egos. For a more effective strategy, work around an ineffectual leader. Any group member can provide leadership while leaving a leader's self-esteem intact.
- Sometimes a small group contains a wealth of leadership talent. The process of establishing group leadership is not (or should not be) a contest for status and power. Individual goals must be placed behind group goals. Good leaders need good followers and supporters.

Usually, the most effective leaders are those who put the group ahead of their own ego needs. In every group the effectiveness of leadership depends on the situation, sensitivity to the group's needs, and the ability to adapt your communicative behavior to meet those needs. Effective leaders bring out the leadership in others.

PRACTICE

1. Chapter 4 introduced you to functional leadership roles that help groups move toward their goals by addressing task as well as process concerns (group building and group maintenance). Begin this exercise by writing these roles on index cards, one role per card. Distribute the cards randomly, and anonymously, throughout your group. Take a few minutes to review the sections in Chapter 4 that describe these roles.

   Spend 15 to 20 minutes discussing an ongoing project or a topic assigned by your instructor, during which you assume the role written on your index card. After 20 minutes, reshuffle and redistribute the role cards. Assume your new role and continue the discussion for another 15 to 20 minutes.

   Now discuss the following questions in your groups:

   - Can you identify who was enacting each role?
   - Whose roles were most consistent with their natural behavior?
   - Whose roles were the most "out of character"?
   - With people assuming these assigned roles, did the group seem to function better or worse than usual? Why?
   - Were some roles difficult or impossible to enact in this situation? Why?
   - Who in your group is naturally most task oriented? Most process oriented?

2. Consider the stages in problem solving that are described in Chapter 10. Identify which leadership functions might be the most appropriate at each stage of development.

3. Consider the dialogue between Harold and Wanda presented early in this chapter. List five responses that would help the group, and especially Harold and Wanda, resolve the conflict.

Observing Group Leadership

The ability to lead a small group is, to a large extent, the ability to communicate effectively: to send and receive messages clearly and without disruption; to channel, focus, and interpret the communication of others so that the meanings of messages are shared by all; and to help the group avoid "anything that needlessly inflates the time and energy required to exchange meanings."[45] When we observe and evaluate leadership, then, we are analyzing the *quality* of communication in the small group. In this section we present an example of a rating scale. Rating scales are particularly valuable for measuring leadership, in that they go beyond the descriptive properties of category systems by including an evaluative component, which is essential if we are to measure the quality of communication.

Barnlund-Haiman Leadership Rating Scale

Instructions: This rating scale may be used to evaluate leadership in groups with or without official leaders. In the latter case (the leaderless group), use part A of each item only. When evaluating the actions of an official leader, use parts A and B of each item on the scale.

Influence on Procedure

Initiating Discussion

A.	3	2	1	0	1	2	3

Group needed more help
in getting started

Group got right
amount of help

Group needed less help
in getting started

B. **The quality of the introductory remarks was**

Excellent	Good	Adequate	Fair	Poor

Organizing Group Thinking

A.	3	2	1	0	1	2	3

Group needed more
direction in thinking

Group got right
amount of help

Group needed less
direction in thinking

B. **If and when attempts were made to organize group thinking, they were**

Excellent	Good	Adequate	Fair	Poor

Clarifying Communication

A.	3	2	1	0	1	2	3

Group needed more help in
clarifying communication

Group got right
amount of help

Group needed less help in
clarifying communication

B. **If and when attempts were made to clarify communication, they were**

Excellent	Good	Adequate	Fair	Poor

Summarizing and Verbalizing Agreements

A.	3	2	1	0	1	2	3

Group needed more help in
summarizing and verbalizing
agreements

Group got right
amount of help

Group needed less help in
summarizing and verbalizing
agreements

B. **If and when attempts were made to summarize and verbalize agreements, they were**

Excellent	Good	Adequate	Fair	Poor

Resolving Conflict

A.	3	2	1	0	1	2	3

Group needed more help
in resolving conflict

Group got right
amount of help

Group needed less help
in resolving conflict

B. **If and when attempts were made to resolve conflict, they were**

Excellent	Good	Adequate	Fair	Poor

Influence on Creative and Critical Thinking

Stimulating Critical Thinking

A.	3	2	1	0	1	2	3
	Group needed more stimulation of creative thinking			Group got right amount of help			Group needed less stimulation of creative thinking

B. **If and when attempts were made to stimulate ideas, they were**

Excellent	Good	Adequate	Fair	Poor

Encouraging Criticism

A.	3	2	1	0	1	2	3
	Group needed more encouragement to be critical			Group got right amount of help			Group needed less encouragement to be critical

B. **If and when attempts were made to encourage criticism, they were**

Excellent	Good	Adequate	Fair	Poor

Balancing Abstract and Concrete Thought

A.	3	2	1	0	1	2	3
	Group needed to be more concrete			Group achieved proper balance			Group needed to be more abstract

B. **If and when attempts were made to balance abstract and concrete thought, they were**

Excellent	Good	Adequate	Fair	Poor

Influence on Interpersonal Relations

Climate-Making

A.	3	2	1	0	1	2	3
	Group needed more help in securing a permissive (supportive) atmosphere			Group got right amount of help			Group needed less help in securing a permissive (supportive) atmosphere

B. **If and when attempts were made to establish a permissive atmosphere, they were**

Excellent	Good	Adequate	Fair	Poor

Regulating Participation

A.	3	2	1	0	1	2	3
	Group needed more regulation of participation			Group got right amount of help			Group needed less regulation of participation

B. **If and when attempts were made to regulate participation, they were**

Excellent	Good	Adequate	Fair	Poor

Overall Leadership

A.	3	2	1	0	1	2	3
	Group needed more control			Group got right amount of control			Group needed less control

B. **If and when attempts were made to control the group, they were**

Excellent	Good	Adequate	Fair	Poor

Source: D. C. Barnlund and F. S. Haiman, *The Dynamics of Discussion* (Boston: Houghton Mifflin Company, 1960), pp. 401–4.

Principles and Practices for Effective Meetings

A COMMITTEE MEETING IS A COLLECTION *of the unfit chosen from the unwilling by the incompetent to do the unnecessary.*

"At Electronic Data Systems," said Ross Perot, "when we saw a snake, we'd kill it. At General Motors, when they saw a snake, they'd form a committee."

If you want to get a job done, give it to an individual; if you want to have it studied, give it to a committee.

Sign on conference wall: "A meeting is no substitute for progress."

Business meetings are important. They demonstrate how many people the company can do without.

President John F. Kennedy said, "Most committee meetings consist of twelve people to do the work of one." Humorist Dave Barry compared business meetings with funerals, in the sense that "you have a gathering of people who are wearing uncomfortable clothing and would rather be somewhere else. The major difference is that most funerals have a definite purpose. Also, nothing is ever really buried in a meeting."[1]

Frankly, most people do not like meetings. Although this generalization has exceptions, it is safe to say that few individuals relish the thought of a weekly appointment calendar peppered with frequent meetings. MCI Worldcom Conferencing research found that most professionals spend nearly three hours a day in business meetings, and more than one-third of those surveyed reported that the meetings are a waste of time. Many of today's techno-savvy meeting-goers have learned the art of paging themselves to have an excuse to duck out of a meeting.[2] Why are meetings held in such low esteem? Probably because many meetings are not well managed, either by the meeting leader or the participants. What bothers meeting attendees the most? Listed below are the results of studies that ranked meeting "sins."[3]

1. *Getting off the subject*
2. *No goals or agenda*
3. *Too lengthy*
4. *Poor or inadequate preparation*
5. *Inconclusive*
6. *Disorganized*
7. *Ineffective leadership/lack of control*
8. *Irrelevance of information discussed*
9. *Time wasted during meetings*
10. *Starting late*
11. *Not effective for making decisions*
12. *Interruptions*
13. *Individuals who dominate discussion*
14. *Rambling, redundant, or digressive discussion*
15. *No published results or follow-up actions*
16. *No premeeting orientation*
17. *Canceled or postponed meetings*

To be effective, a meeting needs to balance two things: structure and interaction. Throughout this book, we talk about the importance of helping a group stay on task by structuring the interaction; following the steps of reflective thinking when solving a problem (as discussed in Chapter 10) is one way of helping a group stay on task. As you examine the preceding list, note how many of the problems associated with meetings stem from a lack of clear structure or agenda. But while structure is important, group members need to have the freedom to express ideas and react to the comments of others. If there is too much structure, the meeting is not really a meeting; it is a lecture—one person talks and others listen. In contrast, with too much unstructured interaction, a group meeting bounces along with no clear focus. In unstructured meetings, minimal attention is given to the time it takes to get the job done.[4] In the sections ahead, we offer suggestions for providing both structure and interaction in group meetings. An agenda is the prime tool for structuring a group meeting. Facilitation skills and an understanding of how to plan interaction can ensure that meeting participants will be free to interact and that their contributions will be relevant and on target.

GIVING MEETINGS STRUCTURE

Getting off the subject and having no goals or agenda are the two most often mentioned complaints about meetings. The principal tool that ensures that meetings are appropriately structured and that the deliberation achieves the intended goal is a meeting *agenda*—a list of key issues, ideas, and information that will be presented, in the order in which they will be discussed. Uncertainty and lack of an agenda can serve as major barriers to accomplishing a task as a group. Consider the following steps in drafting your meeting agenda.

Determine the Meeting Goal(s)

One cardinal rule of meetings is this: Meet only when there is a specific purpose and when it is advantageous or desirable to discuss issues, solve problems, or make decisions as a group. Before beginning to draft an agenda, you need to know the meeting goal. Most meeting have one or more of the following three goals: (1) information needs to be shared, (2) issues need to be discussed, or (3) action needs to be taken.

As you prepare for a meeting, identify what you would like to have happen as a result of the meeting.[5] A typical goal might be "At the end of this meeting we will have selected the firm that will produce our new advertising campaign," or, "At the end of this meeting we will have reviewed the applicants for the management position and identified our top three choices." Without a specific goal that leader and participants are all aware of, little is accomplished.

Identify Items That Need to Be Discussed to Achieve the Goal

With the goal in mind, you next need to determine how to structure the meeting to achieve the goal. Consider generating a list of topics that are essential to accomplishing the goal: What information needs to be shared, what issues need to be discussed, what action needs to be taken? In the brainstorming phase, do not worry about the order of the items; you can rearrange the items later.

Organize the Agenda Items to Achieve the Goal

After you have a list of items to be addressed, organize them in some logical way. A key constraint in organizing items and determining what to include on a meeting agenda is the amount of time budgeted for the meeting. Many meeting planners underestimate the amount of time discussion will take.

When you have identified potential agenda items, review your meeting goal and eliminate any items that do not help you achieve your goal. Armed with your meeting goal and your list of agenda items, begin drafting your meeting agenda.[6] Consider organizing it around the three meeting goals: information items, discussion items, and action items.

Most meeting experts suggest that your first agenda item should be to ask the group to approve or modify the agenda you have prepared. If meeting participants make no modifications, you then know that your agenda was on target. Before making final decisions about which items you should cover and the order in which you should cover them, estimate how long you think it might take to deal with each item. You may want to address several small issues first before tackling major ones. Or, you may decide to arrange your agenda items in terms of priority: Discuss the most important items first and less important ones later.

HOW TO PREPARE A GOAL-CENTERED MEETING AGENDA

1. Determine your meeting goals.
2. Identify what needs to be discussed to achieve the goals.
3. Organize the agenda items to achieve the goals.

John Tropman and Gershom Morningstar recommend using the "bell-curve agenda."[7] As indicated in Figure A.1, the middle of the meeting is reserved for the most challenging or controversial issues. The opening and closing of the meeting include more routine or less vital issues.

In contrast to Tropman and Morningstar's recommendations, others suggest that you avoid putting routine announcements and reports at the beginning of a meeting. The rationale is that meeting members are less sensitive to the time constraints of a meeting at its beginning and thus may spend too much time and energy on routine matters. To take advantage of the early energy in a group, you may want to start with a discussion or action item that will involve all meeting participants.

Often issues are discussed during meetings but nothing happens afterward. As the following sample meeting agenda shows, one of your last agenda items should be to summarize the actions that are to be taken following the meeting.

Sample Agenda

Meeting goal: To review updates from committees and make a decision about donating to the school-volunteer program.

  I. Finalize meeting agenda
 II. Discussion items
     A. What are the problems with our new work report system?

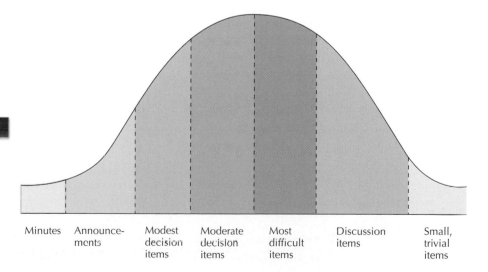

FIGURE A.1

Bell-Curve Agenda
Source: J. E. Tropman and G. C. Morningstar, *Meetings: How to Make Them Work for You* (New York: Van Nostrand Reinhold, 1985) 56. Reprinted by permission.

Minutes | Announcements | Modest decision items | Moderate decision items | Most difficult items | Discussion items | Small, trivial items

B. What are the advantages and disadvantages of the new product team proposal (distributed by e-mail)?

III. Action items

A. Approve new personnel policy (distributed by e-mail).

B. Make a decision about the following issue: Should we donate $5,000 to school-volunteer program?

IV. Information items

A. New employee orientation report

B. Planning committee report

C. Finance committee report

D. Announcements

V. Summarize action that needs to be taken after today's meeting.

Distribute your agenda to the meeting participants well in advance of the meeting. Meeting participants should come prepared to discuss the issues on the agenda. Obviously, if they do not have an agenda before the meeting, they cannot come prepared for a meaningful discussion.

*R*EVIEW

MEETING AGENDA PITFALLS AND STRATEGIES

Potential Pitfall	Suggested Strategy
Participants tend to spend too much time on early agenda items.	Make the first agenda item something worthy of discussion rather than beginning with a trivial report or announcement.
Participants will find a way to talk even if you don't want them to talk.	Invite input and discussion early in the meeting rather than having participants trying to interrupt.
Participants aren't prepared to have a meeting; they have not read what they were supposed to read.	Take a few minutes to have participants read information or have them prepare by writing ideas or suggestions using the silent-brainstorming technique.
Participants won't stick to the agenda.	Remind the group what the meeting goals are, or, with input from the group, change the agenda item.
A meeting is scheduled late in the day or participants are tired.	Schedule an early agenda item that involves all meeting participants rather than having participants sitting silently.
The agenda includes a controversial item that will create conflict and disagreement.	Put one or more items on the agenda ahead of the conflict-producing item. Addressing easier agenda items first will establish a feeling of accomplishment and agreement before the group tackles the more conflict-producing item.

*B*ECOMING A MEETING FACILITATOR: MANAGING GROUP AND TEAM INTERACTION

The essential task of a meeting facilitator is to manage the interaction in order to achieve the goals of the group. Without interaction—the give-and-take dialogue and contributions that participants make during meetings—meetings become monologues. But with too much interaction, meetings can become disorganized, with rambling, redundant, or digressive discussions that waste time and are inconclusive. Meeting leaders and participants can help ensure a balance of structure and interaction by using the facilitation skills of gatekeeping, reminding the group of meeting goals, helping the group be sensitive to the time that elapses during discussion, and using strategies that structure group interaction.

Be a Gatekeeper

As you learned earlier in the book, a gatekeeper encourages less-talkative members to participate and tries to limit lengthy contributions by other group members. Meetings should not consist of a monologue from the meeting leader or be dominated by just a few participants. As a meeting leader, it is your job to make sure that you involve all meeting participants in the discussion.

Focus on the Goal

As we have also stressed throughout this book, members need to understand a group's goals. Once they do, the group's agenda for each meeting should provide a road map for moving toward those goals. A leader often has to keep the group on course, and one of the most effective tools for doing so is summarizing. Periodically, use the metadiscussion skill (discussion about discussion) that we talked about in Chapter 7 and review your understanding of the group's progress with brief comments such as "Okay. Dennis agrees with John that we need to determine how much our project will cost. Are we ready for the next issue?" Such summaries help a group take stock of what it has done and what it has yet to accomplish. Communication researchers Fred Niederman and Roger Volkema, in studying the effects of meeting facilitators on group productivity, found that the most experienced facilitators helped orient the group toward the goal, helped them adapt to what was happening in the group, and involved the group in developing the agenda for the meeting.[8]

Monitor Time

Another job of a meeting leader is to keep track of how much time has been spent on the planned agenda items and how much time remains. Think of your agenda as a map, helping you plan where you want to go. Think of the clock as your gas gauge, telling you the amount of fuel you have to get where you want to go. In a meeting, just as on any car trip, you need to know where you are going and how much fuel you need to get you to your destination. If you are running out of fuel (time), you will either need to fill up the tank (budget more time) or recognize that you will not get where you want to go. Begin each meeting by asking how long members can meet. If you face two or three crucial agenda items, and one-third of your group has to leave in an hour, you will want to make certain to schedule important items early in the meeting.

Structure Interaction

To ensure that all members participate in the discussion, you may need to use some of the prescriptive decision-making and problem-solving tools and techniques mentioned in Chapters 10 and 11. For example, if your meeting goal is to identify new ideas to solve a particular problem, consider using brainstorming or the nominal-group technique as a way to generate ideas. The is/is not technique, journalist's six questions, and the Pareto chart are other tools you can use to invite people to contribute ideas yet structure the interaction so that meeting members do not lose sight of their goals. A key task of the meeting facilitator is to orchestrate meaningful interaction during the meeting so that all participants have the opportunity to give input. Structured methods of inviting involvement are effective in garnering contributions from all group members.

Another strategy that can help encourage interaction is to phrase each discussion item on the printed agenda as a question. Questions give the discussion focus. As we discussed in Chapter 8, discussion questions are a useful tool to help encourage focused and productive discussion.

HOW TO FACILITATE MEETING INTERACTION

Facilitation Skill	Description	Examples
Use gatekeeping skills.	Listen to the discussion to encourage less-talkative members to participate and limit the contributions of ververbalizers.	"Dale, we've not heard from you. Do you have some thoughts on this idea?" or, "Heather, I know you have some strong opinions about this project, but I'd like to hear from others who have not spoken on the issue."
Focus the group's attention on the agenda or goal of the discussion.	Especially when discussion seems to be off target, remind the group of the purpose of the meeting or state the goal of the group.	"Although we seem to be interested in talking about some of the recent hassles we've had at the university, I'd like to bring us back to the purpose of today's meeting. Let's return to our second agenda item, to help us solve the problem we're addressing."
Monitor the group's use of time.	Remind the group how much time is left for discussion if the group gets unnecessarily bogged down on one issue; suggest a strategy to help the group move on to another issue.	"I note that we've been talking about this issue for over 20 minutes, and we only have 15 minutes left in our discussion. Would you like to continue talking about this issue or appoint a subcommittee to tackle this problem and get back to us with a recommendation?"
Provide appropriate structure to channel discussion, and keep it focused on the issues at hand.	Consider inviting all group members to write their ideas on paper before verbalizing; consider using silent brainstorming, the nominal-group technique, the affinity technique, the is/is not technique, a T-chart, or force-field analysis. Also, phrase issues for discussion as a question on the printed agenda rather than just listing a topic to talk about.	"We have a couple of options to consider. Why don't we first each write down advantages and disadvantages of each option and then share our ideas with the entire group."

HOW TO LEAD MEETINGS

As mentioned, a meeting leader needs to be especially sensitive to balancing meeting structure with interaction. An effective meeting leader should facilitate rather than dictate how the group will conduct the meeting. One study found that groups generated more and better ideas when team leaders simply listened and waited for team members to contribute ideas before stating their own ideas than they did when the leader spoke first.[9] Different groups accept (or tolerate) different levels of direction from their designated leaders. One simple rule of thumb is this: *A group will generally allow a leader who emerges naturally from the group or who leads a one-time-only ad hoc group to be more directive.*

Certain tasks are generally expected of leaders. One of the most important leader tasks is to keep the group focused on its agenda during the meeting. Of course, that means the leader needs to have an agenda. We strongly urge that agendas be distributed well in advance of a meeting. As we have stressed, give participants a chance to shape the agenda both before the meeting and as the meeting opens. In general, meeting leaders are expected to do the following:

- Call the group together, which may involve finding out when participants can meet.
- Call the meeting to order.
- If it is a formal meeting, determine if there is a **quorum**—the minimum number of people who must be present to conduct business.
- Keep the meeting moving; go on to the next agenda item when a point has been thoroughly covered. Use effective facilitation and gatekeeping skills.
- Use a flipchart, chalkboard, or dry-erase board to summarize meeting progress; the written notes of a meeting become the "group mind" and help keep the group on track.
- If the meeting is a formal one, decide when to take a vote. Make sure the issues are clear before a vote is taken.
- Prepare a committee report (or delegate someone to prepare a report) after one or many meetings. Groups need a record of their progress. Many groups designate someone to be a secretary and prepare the minutes or summary of what occurred at the meeting.

One of the time-tested strategies for leading a large group is **parliamentary procedure**—a comprehensive set of rules that prescribe how to take action on specific issues that come before the group; it provides an orderly way for large groups (of twenty or more people) to conduct business, although it is less useful for small groups (in which it leads to win/lose patterns of decision making rather than consensus).

All groups need structure. The larger the group, the greater the need for structure. In effect, parliamentary procedure provides the needed structure to help large groups stay focused on the business at hand. Research suggests that parliamentary procedure can be an effective method of adding structure and rules to coordinate quality discussion in a large group.[10] For a complete guide to parliamentary procedure, consult *Robert's Rules of Order* at http://robertsrules.com.

HOW TO PARTICIPATE IN MEETINGS

So far we have stressed the meeting leader's responsibility to give the meeting structure and ensure interaction, but meeting participants have similar obligations. In many respects, each meeting participant has leadership responsibilities. Leadership, as noted in Chapter 12, means "to influence." As a meeting participant, you will have many opportunities to influence the group process. Be sensitive to both the level of structure and the interaction in the meeting. Use such skills as metadiscussion (discussion about discussion) to help keep the group on track.

Your key obligation as a meeting participant is to come to the meeting prepared to work. If the leader has distributed an agenda before the meeting (as leaders should), then you have a clear sense of how to prepare and what information you should bring to the meeting. Even if no agenda has been provided, try to anticipate what will be discussed. If you have no clue as to what will be on the agenda, contact the meeting leader and ask him or her how to prepare.

Roger Mosvick and Paul Nelson, in their book *We've Got to Start Meeting Like This!*, identify six guidelines of competent meeting participants.[11]

1. *Organize your contributions.* Just as a well-organized speech makes a better presentation, well-organized contributions make better meetings. Rambling, disorganized, disjointed ideas increase the likelihood that the meeting will become sidetracked.

2. *Speak when your contribution is relevant.* Before you make a comment, listen to the person who is speaking. Is your comment useful and helpful? Groups are easily distracted by irrelevant contributions.

3. *Make one point at a time.* Even though you may be bursting with good ideas and suggestions, your colleagues will be more likely to listen to your ideas if you present them one at a time rather than as a string of unrelated points.

4. *Speak clearly and forcefully.* No, we are not advocating that you aggressively try to dominate the conversation. Unassertive mumbling, however, will probably get lost in the verbal shuffle of most meetings.

5. *Support your ideas with evidence.* One of the key determinants of good decisions and effective solutions that we discussed in Chapter 8 is the use of evidence to support your ideas and opinions. Opinions are ubiquitous: Everyone has them. Facts, statistics, and well-selected examples help keep the group focused on the task.

6. *Listen actively to all aspects of the discussion.* Group meetings provide one of the most challenging listening contexts. When several people are attempting to make points and counterarguments, you will have to gear up your powers of concentration and listening. Checking your understanding by summarizing or paraphrasing can dramatically improve communication and decrease misunderstanding.[12]

*R*EVIEW

How to Give a Meeting Structure

- Prepare an effective agenda by determining your meeting goals
- Identify what needs to be discussed to achieve the goals
- Organize the agenda to achieve the goals

How to Ensure Managed Interaction

- Use effective gatekeeping skills.
- Use metadiscussion to help the group focus on the goals
- Help the group be sensitive to time that has elapsed and that remains for deliberation
- Use strategies to structure interaction (e.g., write before speaking, nominal-group technique, or silent brainstorming)

Putting Principles into Practice

The appendix reviewed several principles and skills to help make group meetings efficient and effective.

- Meetings need a balance of structure and information.
- When you lead a group, always prepare an agenda by (1) determining your meeting goal, (2) identifying items to achieve the goal, and (3) organizing the agenda items.
- Find ways to involve all members in the meeting.

Draw out quiet members; avoid letting a verbose member dominate a meeting.

- When conducting a formal meeting, use parliamentary procedure to help give the meeting structure and order.
- When you participate in a meeting, make sure your comments are organized, relevant, clear, and supported with evidence. Also, make sure you listen to others and monitor your nonverbal messages.

Principles and Practices for Communicating to an Audience

*T*HROUGHOUT THIS BOOK *we have featured principles and skills that can help you communicate with others in groups, meetings, and teams. Most of your group communication will be private discussions among members of your group. Some group discussions, however, are intended to be heard by others.* **Public-communication formats** *help an audience understand all sides of an issue, particularly if individuals with diverse viewpoints are involved in the discussion. Three public communication formats will be considered in the following sections: (1) panel discussions, (2) symposium presentations, and (3) forum presentations. We will also offer some general guidelines for speaking to an audience.*

PANEL DISCUSSIONS

A **panel discussion**—the most frequently used public group discussion format—is a group discussion that takes place before an audience with the purpose of (1) informing the audience about issues of interest, (2) solving a problem, or (3) encouraging the audience to evaluate the pros and cons of a controversial issue.

A panel discussion is usually facilitated by an appointed moderator or chairperson. The moderator's job is to keep the discussion on track. The moderator opens the discussion by announcing the discussion question. Most panel discussions include at least three panelists; if there are more than eight or nine, the panelists have difficulty participating equally. Because the panel is presented for the benefit of an audience, organizers should take care that the audience can see and hear the discussion clearly. Panelists usually sit in a semicircle or behind a table. Although they should be informed about the subject they will discuss, they should not rehearse their discussion; the conversation should be extemporaneous. Panelists may use notes to help them remember facts and statistics, but they should not use a prepared text.

After announcing the discussion question or topic, the moderator briefly introduces the panel members, perhaps noting each one's qualifications for being on the panel. To begin the discussion, the moderator may then direct a specific question to one or more panelists. An effective moderator encourages all panelists to participate. If one panelist seems reluctant, the moderator may direct a specific question to that person. If one panelist tends to dominate the discussion, the moderator may suggest politely that other panel members be given an opportunity to participate. Rather than let the discussion continue until the group has nothing more to say on the issue, the moderator usually sets a specific time limit. Most panel discussions last about an hour, but the time limit can be tailored to the needs of the audience and the topic. At the conclusion of the discussion, the moderator may either summarize comments made by the group members or ask another group member to do so. Often the summary is followed by an invitation to the audience to ask questions of the panel.

SYMPOSIUM PRESENTATIONS

A **symposium presentation** is another public discussion format, consisting of a series of short speeches usually unified by a central theme or issue. Unlike participants in a panel discussion, participants in a symposium either come with prepared speeches or speak extemporaneously from an outline. The speakers are usually experts who represent contrasting points of view. For example, imagine that your physics instructor has invited four experts in the field of nuclear energy to speak to your class. Each expert has selected a specific aspect of nuclear energy to present. Your instructor probably will briefly introduce the speakers, announce the central topic of discussion, and ask the speakers to address themselves to a discussion question. Then each will speak for eight or ten minutes. The speakers probably will not talk informally between speeches; they most likely will know in advance what general areas the other speakers will discuss. After the speeches, your instructor may summarize the major ideas presented and allow the audience to participate in an open forum.

Technically, a symposium is not really a form of group discussion, because there is little or no interaction among the participants. But a symposium often concludes with a more informal panel discussion or forum. There usually is a time limit for the audience forum following a symposium. A major advantage of the symposium is that it is easy to organize: Just line up three or four speakers to discuss a designated topic. In addition, when speakers with contrasting viewpoints present their ideas, a lively discussion often follows. The moderator of a symposium must make sure that the speakers know their time limits and address their assigned topics. An able moderator can prevent a symposium from digressing into a discussion of irrelevant issues.

FORUM PRESENTATIONS

Group discussion encourages more interaction and participation than other forms of communication (such as public speaking). A **forum presentation** takes maximum advantage of the principle that when many people participate, improved decisions can result. The word *forum* originated with the Romans: The forum was the public marketplace where Roman citizens could assemble and voice their opinions about the issues of the day. A forum discussion generally follows a panel discussion or symposium, but a forum can also come after a single speaker's presentation. A forum permits an audience to get involved in the discussion. Rather than playing a passive role, as in a panel discussion, the audience directs questions and responses to a chairperson or to a group of individuals. For example, when holding a news conference, the president of the United States presents a prepared statement, followed by questions and responses from reporters—a forum. Some talk radio stations have forum discussions on issues of the day. Many communities conduct town meetings or public hearings in which citizens can voice their opinions about issues affecting the community. The audience in a forum has an opportunity to provide feedback. Comments from audience members sometimes can be used to determine how successful a speaker or panel has been in enlightening the audience. The questions and responses also give the featured speakers an opportunity to clarify and elaborate their viewpoints.

REVIEW

PUBLIC COMMUNICATION FORMATS

Format	Description
Panel	An unrehearsed discussion that takes place before an audience to inform, solve a problem, or make a decision
Symposium	A series of short speeches unified by a central theme or issue
Forum	A discussion that frequently follows a panel or symposium presentation and allows audience members to respond

PLANNING WHAT TO SAY TO AN AUDIENCE

Speaking to an audience involves skills in planning what you are going to say and presenting your information to your listeners. Your school probably offers a course in public speaking. The discussion that follows highlights some of the essential skills public presenters should master when speaking to an audience, whether in a panel, symposium, or forum-group presentation.[1] The more formal the presentation (a symposium presentation, for example), the more planning it requires. We will offer some general tips for both planning a presentation and presenting your ideas to others.

Every speaker needs a plan. Speakers who are part of a group effort to communicate with an audience need to coordinate their plans with those of other group members. Central to all these planning elements is a consideration of your audience. Your first and foremost priority when speaking to an audience is to make sure you consider their needs and backgrounds. A speaking plan also typically involves clarifying and coordinating your topic with other group members, deciding on your specific purpose or objective, identifying your central ideas, and supporting and organizing your ideas.

Analyze Your Audience

Analyzing your audience means finding out as much as you can about your listeners. Why will they be listening to you? What are their expectations? What are their attitudes toward you, your group, and your topic? Answers to these questions can help you make choices throughout the planning process. If you are speaking to a captive audience—people who have little choice about listening to you, such as your classmates in small group communication class—you need to be especially sensitive to their needs. If class members have to show up, your group needs to work extra hard to immediately make the information interesting and relevant to the listeners.

Have a Clear Objective

Keep your specific presentation objective clearly in mind as you prepare for your public presentation. Is your goal primarily to inform the audience about decisions your group has already made? Or is your goal to persuade your listeners to adopt a solution you are proposing? You might give a public presentation to let the audience eavesdrop on your conversation as you debate issues and share information. If an audience is present, though, you should be keenly aware of the audience's needs and not become lost in a conversation that ignores those who came to hear what you have to say. It is a good idea for all group members involved in the presentation to talk explicitly about the overall goal of sharing information and ideas with the audience.

Identify Your Major Ideas

What are the key points you will make? When you speak in public, do not just start sharing unrelated pieces of information; think about major ideas you want to share. If you were to boil your information down to one, two, or three ideas, what would they be? The major points you want to address flow from the information you have gathered and the discussion that may have taken place in your group.

Support Your Major Ideas

A presentation to an audience does not consist of just asserting points or drawing a conclusion and sharing the conclusion with your listeners. Support your major points with evidence or examples. We discussed the types and tests of evidence in Chapter 8. In addition to using facts, examples, opinions, and statistics, you could also support a point you are making with a hypothetical example or a personal story. Realize, however, that although hypothetical examples and personal experiences can add interest to your presentation, they are not sufficient to prove a point. Their value lies in illustrating ideas and issues. Again, we urge you to keep your audience in mind as you make choices about how you will support your major points. It is also a good idea to check with other group members to make sure that you are not duplicating information your colleagues plan to share.

Organize Your Ideas

The last step in developing a presentation plan is to arrange your major ideas and supporting material in a logical way. If you are relating a sequence of steps or discussing the history of an issue, you probably will use *chronological order,* which means arranging your ideas by telling your listeners what happened first, second, third, and so forth.

Another classic method of organizing ideas is the *topical* method. With this approach, you simply organize your presentation by topics or natural divisions in your presentation. If you were informing an audience about the functions of your local government, for example, you could arrange your presentation topically by saying, "Our government provides for our safety through the police and fire departments, our education through schools and libraries, and our transportation through funding public transportation and maintaining our roads."

Spatial arrangement, in which you organize information according to location or position, is another approach. In describing your campus to your listeners, you might first talk about the west campus, then the central campus, and finally the east campus, rather than hopping around a map depicting the layout of your school.

There are other ways to organize information:

Problem/solution: First talk about the problem and then the solution

Pro versus con: Compare advantages and disadvantages

Complexity: Move from simple ideas to more complex ones

Regardless of the specific method you select, make sure your overall organizational strategy makes sense both to you and to your listeners. Most public-speaking teachers strongly urge speakers to develop an outline of their presentation. The introduction to the presentation should, at a minimum, provide an overview of the key ideas and catch and hold the listeners' attention. The body of the presentation covers the key ideas and supporting material. The conclusion's prime function is to summarize and, if appropriate, call for listeners to take specific action.

PRESENTING INFORMATION TO AN AUDIENCE

With your objective in mind, key ideas thoughtfully prepared, and a logical organization of your points at hand, you are ready to consider how to deliver your information to your listeners. As we discussed in Chapter 6, your unspoken messages play a major role in communicating your ideas and feelings to your listeners.

Select Your Method of Delivery

There are four primary delivery methods from which to select: (1) manuscript (reading), (2) memorized, (3) impromptu, and (4) extemporaneous style. Most speech teachers have definite biases about which methods are most and least effective. We do not recommend that you read from a manuscript. Such an approach is stilted and does not permit you to adapt to your listeners. Giving a presentation totally from memory also has its pitfalls, especially if you have many statistics or other forms of evidence that you want to share. You run the risk of forgetting key points. Speaking impromptu means that you speak with minimal preparation or none at all—you just try to wing it. This has some obvious disadvantages as well. Impromptu speaking negates all the suggestions we made for planning your presentation. The style of delivery that seems to work best is extemporaneous delivery. You know the major ideas you want to present, you also may have an outline, but you do not memorize the exact wording of your presentation. This approach has the advantage of encouraging you to plan your message but gives you the flexibility to adapt to the specific audience to which you are speaking. Your delivery also sounds more natural and interesting when you speak extemporaneously than when you read or memorize your remarks.

Use Effective Delivery Skills

When speaking to an audience, there are several fundamental principles to keep in mind. First and foremost, have eye contact with your audience. Research suggests this is the single most important nonverbal delivery variable.[2]

When you are giving your portion of a group presentation, it is not unusual to deliver your message while remaining seated at a table. If your group remains seated, you can still use gestures to emphasize key points and add interest and animation to your talk. Effective gestures should be natural, not overly dramatic, and be coordinated with your verbal message. Usually speakers use fewer gestures when seated than when standing to give a speech. If you are participating in a symposium presentation, more than likely you will be expected to stand when you speak. When standing, ensure that your posture communicates your interest in your listeners.

Besides having eye contact and monitoring your physical delivery, you have a fundamental obligation to speak so others can hear you and to convey interest and enthusiasm in your voice. Speaking with adequate volume and varying your vocal pitch, rate, and quality are essential to effective speech delivery.

Consider Using Visual Aids

Many groups find that visual aids help communicate statistical information and survey results and can help dramatize the problem the group is attempting to solve. One group, wanting to illustrate the parking problem on campus, made a video to show exactly how overcrowded the parking lots were. Audio and video interviews can also add interest and credibility to a group's effort to document problems and solutions. However, we caution you against overusing visual aids. The purpose of most group presentations is to present information, not to entertain. Resist the temptation to spend so much time and energy on visuals, video, and audio material that your overall objective takes a back seat to your method of presentation.

In addition to video and audio tapes, visual aids can include objects, models, people, drawings, photographs, slides, maps, charts, and graphs. Bar, pie, and line graphs are especially effective in presenting statistical information to an audience. Most audiences today expect to see high-quality, computer-generated visual aids.

Another often-used type of visual aid is overhead transparencies. These are usually inexpensive and can be made ahead of time to clearly present information in an effective way. When using an overhead projector and transparency, consider the following suggestions:

- Turn the projector off when you are not showing your visual.
- Do not put too much information on one visual. Many experts recommend no more than seven lines of type, using at least an 18-point type font.

- Consider revealing a transparency one line at a time rather than showing the entire transparency; you are better able to control your listeners' attention.
- Consider using color to add interest.

When using any type of visual aid, consider the following guidelines:

- Make sure all audience members can see the visual aid easily.
- Give yourself plenty of time to prepare your visual aid before you speak.
- Rehearse with your visual aid.
- Have eye contact with your audience, not with your visual aid.
- Talk about your visual aid, do not just show it.
- Do not pass objects among your audience while you are speaking; it distracts from your oral presentation.
- Use handouts during the presentation only if your listeners need to have the information in front of them while you speak.
- Keep your visual aids simple.

The last suggestion we offer for using visual aids is to have a backup plan if your visual aid is crucial to your presentation. Taking an extra extension cord, making another copy of your homemade video, or making sure the overhead projector has a spare bulb are examples of backup plans to ensure that your presentation goes smoothly.

Ask other group members to help you manage the visual aids. Consider asking someone to help change the transparencies on the overhead projector or ask for help in displaying charts or graphs. Since you are part of a team, involve other group members to help you present information clearly and effectively.

Using Computer-Generated Graphics

It is becoming increasingly common for public presentations to include computer-generated graphics. A computer-generated visual aid can add credibility and interest to your presentation if the technology is used effectively. There are several widely used software programs that make it very easy to produce professional-looking visual aids. Such software permits you to use color, pictures, sound, photographs, and even video footage in visual aids. Many college and university computer labs can give you access to both hardware and software to prepare computer-generated graphics. To present your visuals, you will need a computer and a video projection system. If you are inexperienced at using computer-generated graphics, find someone to teach you the basics of designing visuals.

When using a computer to develop your visuals, keep the following suggestions in mind.

- Allow plenty of time to design the graphics. If you are familiar with the software, it may not take you long to draft quality visuals, but you should still not wait until the last minute to develop them.
- Don't get carried away with the technology. Your goal is to communicate ideas, not to dazzle your listeners with glitzy graphics. Computer graphics programs such as Power-Point let you select a background for your messages. Use a common background or template for your presentation to give your information a unified look. As with other types of visual aids, simple ideas are best.
- Consider the effects of room lighting on your presentation. Fluorescent light, especially, washes out the image projected by video projectors. Make sure you have the proper equipment to project a clear image to your audience.

Accommodation. Conflict management style that involves giving in to the demands of others.

Action chart. A grid that lists tasks that need to be done and identifies who will be responsible for each task.

Activity tracks. Phases of problem solving that do not follow linear, step-by-step patterns.

Adaptor. A nonverbal behavior that helps people respond to their immediate environment.

Ad hoc committee. A committee that disbands when it completes its task.

Affect display. A nonverbal behavior that communicates emotion.

Affection. Human warmth and closeness.

Affinity technique. A method of generating and organizing ideas by using Post-it notes; group members write each idea on a note and then sort the ideas into common categories.

Agenda. A list of topics or tasks to be discussed or completed in a meeting.

Allness statement. A simple but untrue generalization.

Asynchronous communication. Interaction in which e-mail messages are responded to after a time delay; the communication thus does not occur in real time.

Attitude. A learned predisposition to respond to a person, object, or idea in a favorable, neutral, or unfavorable way.

Avoidance. Conflict management style that involves ignoring disagreements in order to sidestep conflict.

Belief. What someone considers to be true or false.

Bona fide perspective on groups. The view that the context and boundaries of groups change.

Brainstorming. A problem-solving technique that helps a group generate creative options.

Breakpoint. A point in a group discussion when members shift to a different activity.

Bypassing. A barrier to communication that occurs when two people interpret the same word differently.

Causal reasoning. Relating two or more events in such a way as to conclude that one event caused the other.

Cause-and-effect diagram. An analysis tool (also called a fishbone diagram) that charts the causes and effects of a problem or outcome.

Charge. The purpose of a team, group, or committee.

Coercive power. Power derived from the ability to punish people for acting or not acting in a certain way.

Cognitive stimulation theory of creativity. Theory that suggests that hearing words and phrases from others stimulates creativity and enhances the brainstorming process.

Collaborate. To use positive communication strategies in conflict management in order to achieve a positive solution for all involved.

Committee. A small group given a specific task by an individual or a larger group.

Communication. The process of acting on information; the process that allows a group to move toward its goals.

Communication network. A pattern of interaction within a group; who talks to whom.

Competent group communicator. A person who is able to interact appropriately and effectively with others in small groups.

Competition. Conflict management style that stresses winning at the expense of others involved.

Complementarity. The tendency of individuals to be attracted to others who have knowledge, skills, or other attributes that they themselves do not have but that they admire.

Compromise. Conflict management style that attempts to find the middle ground in the conflict.

Conclusion. The logical outcome of an argument that stems from the major premise and the minor premise.

Confirming response. A communication response that causes a person to value himself or herself more.

Conflict. An expressed struggle between at least two interdependent people who perceive incompatible goals, scarce resources, and interference from others in an attempt to achieve a specific goal.

Conflict phase. Fisher's second phase of group interaction, in which disagreement and individual differences arise.

Consensus. Support for and commitment to a decision on the part of all group members.

Control. The use of status and power to achieve a goal.

Creativity. The generation, application, combination, and extension of new ideas.

Criteria. Standards for an acceptable solution to a problem.

Cross-functional team-role training. Training that prepares members of a team to perform several roles or duties of other team members.

Culture. A learned system of knowledge, behavior, attitudes, beliefs, values, and norms that is shared by a group of people.

Decision making. Making a choice from among several alternatives.

Decision-making group. A group whose purpose is to make a choice from among several alternatives.

Deductive reasoning. The process of reasoning from a general statement or principle to a specific conclusion.

Delphi technique. A technique whereby people share ideas in writing, without meeting face to face; also known as absentee brainstorming.

Descriptive approach. An approach to problem solving that helps people understand how a group solves a problem.

Dialectical theory. Descriptive model of group problem solving that suggests that during communication competing tensions can pull the conversation in multiple directions; group members may feel simultaneously separate from the group and connected to the group.

Disconfirming response. A response that causes another person to value himself or herself less.

Discussion-management competencies. The communication skills that help a group maintain a focus on the task and manage interaction.

Dyad. Two people.

Ego conflict. Conflict that occurs when individuals become defensive because they feel they are being attacked.

Electronic brainstorming. A method of generating creative ideas using computers; group members write out their own ideas, which are then displayed to all other members.

E-mail. Electronic mail.

Emblem. A nonverbal cue with a specific verbal counterpart, such as a word, letter, or number.

Emergence phase. Fisher's third phase of group interaction, in which a group begins to manage disagreement and conflict.

Entropy. The measure of the randomness and chaos in a system.

Equifinality. A systems-theory principle that a final state may be reached by multiple paths and from different initial states.

Ethics. Beliefs, values, and moral principles by which people determine what is right and wrong.

Expert power. The influence someone has over others because of greater knowledge and information.

Explanatory function. The power of a theory to explain things.

Fact-inference confusion. Mistaking a conclusion drawn from an observation for a fact instead of limited inferential information.

Fallacy. False reasoning that occurs when someone attempts to persuade without adequate evidence or with arguments that are irrelevant or inappropriate.

Fantasy. In symbolic convergence theory, a group's creative and imaginative shared interpretation of events that fulfills a group psychological or rhetorical need.

Fantasy chain. A string of connected stories that revolve around a common theme and that is created when a group is sharing a group fantasy.

Fantasy theme. The common or related content of the stories that a group is sharing during a group fantasy.

Fishbone diagram. An analysis tool (also called a cause-and-effect diagram) that charts the causes and effects of a problem or outcome; so named because a completed chart resembles the skeleton of a fish.

Flowchart. A step-by-step diagram of a multistep process.

Focus group. A small group selected to discuss a particular topic so that others can better understand the group's responses to that topic.

Force-field analysis. A method of structuring the analysis of a problem to assess the driving and restraining forces that may affect the attainment of a goal.

Forum presentation. A discussion that directly follows a panel discussion or symposium and allows audience members to respond to ideas.

Function. The effect or consequence of a given behavior within a group system.

Functional approach. An approach to problem solving that emphasizes the performance of certain activities and effective communication to accomplish a group goal.

Functional perspective. A view of leadership that assumes all group members can initiate leadership behaviors.

Ground rules. Explicit, agreed-on prescriptions for acceptable and appropriate behavior in a group or team.

Group climate. The emotional environment of a group that affects and is affected by interaction among members.

Group cohesiveness. The degree of attraction members feel toward one another and their group.

Grouphate. The dread and repulsion people sometimes feel about working in groups and teams or participating in meetings.

Groupthink. The illusion of agreement exhibited by group members who try to minimize conflict and reach consensus without critically testing, analyzing, and evaluating ideas.

Gunny-sack. A poor communication technique of dredging up old problems and issues from the past to use against your communication partner, like pulling them out of an old gunny-sack.

Hidden agenda. A private goal toward which an individual works while appearing to work toward the group's goal.

High-contact culture. A culture in which people tend to touch others and to require less personal space.

High-context culture. A culture that emphasizes nonverbal communication.

Human communication. The process of making sense out of the world and sharing that sense with others by creating meaning through the use of verbal and nonverbal messages.

Ideal-solution format. A problem-solving method that helps a group define a problem, speculate about an ideal solution, and identify the obstacles that keep it from achieving its goal.

Illustrator. A nonverbal behavior that accompanies and embellishes verbal communication.

Inclusion. The human need for affiliation with others.

Individual roles. Roles characterized by behavior that calls attention to individual contributions of group members.

Inductive reasoning. The method of arriving at a general conclusion through the use of specific instances or examples.

Information triage. The process of sorting through information to assess its importance, value, or relevance.

Innovation. A creative process of putting new ideas into action; innovation includes idea generation, feasibility analysis, reality testing, and implementation of the idea.

Interaction. The give-and-take conversation, talk, dialogue, and reaction to the messages of others that occur during a group discussion.

Interaction diagram. A means of identifying and recording the frequency and direction of communication networks in groups.

Interdependence. A relationship among components in a system such that a change in one component affects all other components.

Interpersonal need. A human need that can be fulfilled by others.

Intimate zone. Zone of personal space between 0 and $1\frac{1}{2}$ feet from an individual.

Invention. The process of developing new ideas.

Is/is not analysis. A method of separating the causes from the symptoms of a problem by considering such questions as What is or is not the problem? What are or are not symptoms of the problem? and When and where does the problem occur or not occur?

Journalist's six questions. The six questions news reporters use to analyze an event: Who? What? When? Where? Why? and How?

Knowledge. Cognitive understanding or accurate information about a subject—one of the elements essential to being a competent communicator.

Leadership. Behavior or communication that influences, guides, directs, or controls a group.

Leadership style. A relatively consistent behavior pattern that reflects a leader's beliefs and attitudes; classified as authoritarian, laissez-faire, or democratic.

Legitimate power. Power derived from being elected or appointed to control a group.

Listening. The active process of selecting, attending, understanding, and remembering.

Listening style. An individual's preferred way of making sense out of spoken messages.

Low-contact culture. A culture in which people are uncomfortable being touched and require more personal space.

Low-context culture. A culture that emphasizes verbal expression.

Maintenance roles. Roles that influence a group's social atmosphere.

Major premise. A general statement that is the first element of a syllogism.

Media richness theory. The theory that a communication medium is rich if it has (1) potential for instant feedback, (2) verbal and nonverbal cues that can be processed by senders and receivers, (3) natural language, and (4) a focus on individuals.

Mediated setting. A context for communication that is not face to face but instead occurs through a phone line, fiber-optic cable, TV signal, or other means.

Message. Written, spoken, and unspoken elements of communication to which people assign meaning.

Metadiscussion. A statement about the process of discussion itself rather than about the discussion's topic; discussion about discussion.

Method theories. Theories that offer prescriptions for behavior.

Minor premise. A specific statement about an example that is linked to the major premise; it is the second element of a syllogism.

Mission statement. A concise description of the goals or desired outcomes of a team.

Monochronic. A typically Western view of time as linear and segmented; also, a person who is more comfortable doing one thing at a time.

Motivation. An internal drive to achieve a goal.

Nominal-group technique. A problem-solving brainstorming method in which members work individually on ideas, rank suggested solutions, and then report their findings for group discussion.

Nonverbal communication. Communication behavior that does not rely on written or spoken words.

Norm. A standard that determines appropriate and inappropriate behavior.

Orientation phase. Fisher's first phase of small group interaction, in which members try to understand one another and the task before their group.

Panel discussion. A group discussion intended to inform an audience about a problem or encourage the audience to evaluate the pros and cons of an issue.

Paralanguage. Vocal cues such as pitch, volume, speaking rate, and voice quality that provide information about the meaning of a message.

Pareto principle. The principle that the source of 80 percent of a problem comes from 20 percent of the incidents.

Parliamentary procedure. A comprehensive set of rules that prescribe how to take action on specific issues that come before a group and how to organize all aspects of group governance. For a complete guide to parliamentary procedure, see *Robert's Rules of Order.*

Perception checking. The skill of asking someone whether your interpretation of his or her message is accurate; the skill requires observing behavior, thinking about what the behavior may mean, and asking whether your interpretation is accurate.

Personal zone. Zone of personal space between 1½ and 4 feet from an individual.

Plagiarism. Presenting someone else's words and ideas as one's own.

Polychronic. A view of time that places less emphasis on punctuality; also, a person who is able to do many things simultaneously.

Power. The ability to influence or exert control over others.

Predictive function. The ability of a theory to predict events.

Prescriptive approach. An approach to solving problems that identifies specific agendas and techniques to improve problem solving.

Primary group. A group (such as a family) that fulfills people's needs to associate with others.

Primary tension. Anxiety and tension that occur when a group first meets and members feel awkward and uncertain how to behave.

Problem-oriented competencies. The communication skills of defining and analyzing a problem.

Problem solving. A process that attempts to overcome or manage an obstacle in order to reach a goal.

Problem-solving group. A group that exists to resolve an issue or overcome an obstacle.

Process leadership. Communication directed toward maintaining interpersonal relations and a positive group climate; also called group building or maintenance.

Process theories. Theories that explain human behaviors in a variety of contexts, including group and team phenomena.

Proxemics. The study of how close to or far away from other people and objects we choose to be.

Pseudo-conflict. Conflict that occurs when individuals disagree because of poor communication.

Public communication format. A format for presenting an organized group discussion to an audience.

Public zone. Zone of personal space beyond 12 feet from an individual.

Quality circle. A group of from three to fifteen employees who meet regularly to improve work productivity, company morale, and work quality.

Question of fact. A question that asks whether something is true or false or did or did not occur.

Question of policy. A question that asks about a course of action or a change in a procedure or behavior.

Question of prediction. A question that asks whether something is likely to occur under certain circumstances.

Question of value. A question that asks whether something is good or bad or right or wrong.

Quorum. The minimum number of people who must be present to conduct business.

Random word technique. A method used to enhance creative brainstorming in which one person says a random word to stimulate the development of new ideas.

Reasoning. The process of drawing conclusions from information.

Referent power. The power of interpersonal attraction.

Reflective thinking. John Dewey's problem-solving method, which includes defining a problem, analyzing it, suggesting possible solutions for it, selecting the best solution for it, and testing and implementing that solution.

Regulator. A nonverbal behavior that helps a group control the flow of communication.

Reinforcement. A fourth and final phase of group development in which group members express positive regard for the group and its members and offer comments that build cohesiveness.

Relational activity. An activity that sustains relationships among group members and manages the group climate.

Relational competencies. Small group communication competencies that help a group manage conflict and maintain a positive group climate.

Reward power. Power based on the ability to reward desired behavior.

Rule. A prescription for acceptable behavior. Rules identify the appropriate or expected behavior of team or group members.

Secondary group. A group that exists to accomplish a task or achieve a goal.

Secondary tension. Conflict and stress that occur in a group as members vie for positions of leadership and influence or when group members begin to openly express disagreement about the task at hand.

Self-concept. The characteristics and attributes an individual believes himself or herself to have; one's theory about oneself.

Self-disclosure. The deliberate communication of information about oneself to others.

Silent brainstorming. A period of individual brainstorming that occurs before group members share their ideas with the group; integral to the nominal-group technique; also may be used as part of traditional brainstorming.

Similarity. The tendency of individuals with like experiences, beliefs, attitudes, and values to be attracted to one another.

Simple conflict. Conflict that occurs when two people's goals or ideas are mutually exclusive or incompatible.

Simulation. A structured exercise that creates conditions that participants might encounter in the real world.

Single-question format. A problem-solving agenda that helps a group identify key issues and subissues of a problem.

Situational perspective. A perspective that views leadership as the interaction among group needs and goals, leadership style, and the situation.

Skill. An effective behavior that can be repeated when appropriate.

Small group. At least three people interacting with one another.

Small group communication. Interaction among a small group of people who share a common purpose, who feel a sense of belonging to the group, and who exert influence on one another.

Small group ecology. The consistent way in which people in small groups arrange themselves physically.

Social exchange theory. A description of human relationships in terms of costs and rewards or profits and losses.

Social facilitation. The tendency for the presence of others to affect human behavior, specifically, to cause people to work harder.

Social information-processing theory. A theory that suggests that relationships do develop via mediated channels but that expressing and interpreting relational cues takes longer than during face-to-face interaction.

Social loafing. The tendency for people to hold back from contributing (to loaf) in a group because they assume someone else will do the work.

Social zone. Zone of personal space between 4 and 12 feet from an individual.

Solution-oriented competencies. The communication skills of identifying solution criteria and generating and evaluating solutions.

Source. Originator of a thought or emotion, who puts it into a code that can be understood by a receiver.

Standard agenda. A prescriptive agenda for solving a group or team problem that includes (1) identifying and defining the problem, (2) analyzing the problem, (3) identifying possible solutions, (4) selecting the best solution, and (5) implementing the solution.

Standing committee. A committee that remains active for an extended period of time.

Status. An individual's importance.

Stinking thinking. Thoughts that limit a person's, group's, or organization's possibilities.

Structure. Methods used to keep a group discussion focused and on task, which include using an agenda, rules, procedures, and problem-solving steps.

Structuration theory. A general framework that explains how people use rules and resources to interact in a social system.

Study group. A group whose primary purpose is to gather information and learn new ideas.

Supermajority decision. A decision based on agreement on a solution, action, or decision by at least two-thirds of a group.

Syllogism. A way of structuring an argument in three parts: (1) a major premise, (2) a minor premise, and (3) a conclusion.

Symbol. Word, sound, or visual image that represents something else, such as a thought, concept, or object.

Symbolic convergence theory. The theory that a group develops a shared consciousness and identity through the sharing of fantasies or stories, which are often chained together and have a common theme.

Symposium presentation. A series of short speeches unified by a central issue or theme.

Synchronous communication. E-mail interaction that takes place in real time.

Synergy. A condition in which the whole is greater than the sum of its parts.

System. An organic whole composed of interdependent elements.

Systems theory. A theory that describes group behavior in terms of input, processes, and output.

Task leadership. Communication directed toward accomplishing a group's task or goal.

Task-process activity. An activity that helps a group manage its task or accomplish its work.

Task role. A role a member assumes to help accomplish the group's mission.

T-chart. A diagram (in the shape of a large T) on which the pros and cons of a particular proposition are listed on either side of the middle line.

Team. A group of individuals organized to work together to achieve a common goal.

Territoriality. Use of space to claim or defend a given area.

Theory. A set of interrelated facts, observations, and ideas that explains or predicts something.

Therapy group. A group led by a trained professional whose purpose is to help individuals with personal problems.

Topical focus activity. An activity that deals with the issues under discussion by a group at a given time.

Training. Instruction emphasizing skill development to achieve a specific task.

Trait perspective. A view of leadership as the personal attributes or qualities that leaders possess.

Transactional. Involving both sending and receiving simultaneously.

Transformational leadership. Leadership that aims at changing an organization by realigning its culture around a new vision.

Value. A person's perception of what is right or wrong, good or bad.

Video conference. A conference between two or more individuals who are linked by Internet, closed-circuit, or satellite-linked TV.

Vigilant thinkers. People who use logic, reasoning, evidence, and data to analyze issues and problems; they also establish clear decision criteria and evaluate the positive and negative consequences of a decision.

Virtual small group communication. Communication among group members who are not together in the same physical location.

X-Y-Z formula. A way to describe feelings by saying, "When you do X, in situation Y, I feel Z."

NOTES

CHAPTER 1

1. R. K. Mosvick and R. B. Nelson, *We've Got to Start Meeting Like This!* (Glenview, IL: Scott, Foresman, 1987); R. Y. Hirokawa, "Communication and Group Decision-Making Efficacy," in R. Y. Hirokawa, R. S. Cathcart, L. A. Samovar, L. D. Henman, eds., *Small Group Communication Theory and Practice: An Anthology* (Los Angeles, CA: Roxbury Publishing Company, 2002) 125.

2. S. Sorenson, "Grouphate," paper presented at the annual meeting of the International Communication Association, Minneapolis, Minnesota, May 1981.

3. F. E. X. Dance and C. Larson, *Speech Communication: Concepts and Behavior* (New York: Holt, Rinehart & Winston, 1972).

4. Our definition of human communication is based on a discussion in S. A. Beebe, S. J. Beebe, and M. V. Redmond, *Interpersonal Communication: Relating to Others,* 5th ed. (Boston: Allyn and Bacon, 2008).

5. A. K. Offner, T. J. Kramer, and J. P. Winter, "The Effects of Facilitation, Recording, and Pauses on Group Brainstorming," *Small Group Research* 27 (1996): 283–98; V. Brown and P. B. Paulus, "A Simple Dynamic Model of Social Factors in Group Brainstorming," *Small Group Research* 27 (1996): 91–114; M. W. Kramer, C. L. Kuo, and J. C. Dailey, "The Impact of Brainstorming Techniques on Subsequent Group Processes," *Small Group Research* 28 (1997): 218–42; V. Brown, M. Tumeo, T. S. Larey, and P. B. Paulus, "Modeling Cognitive Interactions During Group Brainstorming," *Small Group Research* 29 (1997): 495–526.

6. See S. G. Straus, "Getting a Clue: The Effects of Communication Media and Information Distribution on Participation and Performance in Computer-Mediated and Face-to-Face Groups," *Small Group Research* 27 (February 1996): 115–42; S. G. Straus, "Technology, Group Process, and Group Outcomes: Testing the Connections in Computer-Mediated and Face-to-Face Groups," *Human-Computer Interaction* 12 (1997): 227–66; S. P. Weisband, "Group Discussion and First Advocacy Effects in Computer-Mediated and Face-to-Face Decision Making Groups," *Organizational Behavior and Human Decision Processes* 53 (1992): 352–80.

7. C. Pavitt, "Does Communication Matter in Social Influence During Small Group Discussion? Five Positions," *Communication Studies* 44 (Fall 1993): 216–27.

8. A. J. Salazar, "Ambiguity and Communication Effects on Small Group Decision-Making Performance," *Human Communication Research* 23 (1996): 155–92; R. Y. Hirokawa, D. DeGooyer, and K. Valde, "Using Narratives to Study Task Group Effectiveness," *Small Group Research* 31 (2000): 573–91; S. Jarboe, "Procedures for Enhancing Group Decision Making," in R. Y. Hirokawa and M. S. Poole, eds., *Communication and Group Decision Making* (Thousand Oaks, CA: Sage, 1996).

9. A. B. Henley and K. H. Price, "Want a Better Team? Foster a Climate of Fairness," *Academy of Management Executive* 16 (August 2002): 153–54.

10. D. Romig, *Side by Side Leadership: Achieving Outstanding Results Together* (Austin, TX: Bard Press, 2001).

11. J. W. Bishop, K. D. Scott, and S. M. Burroughs, "Support, Commitment, and Employee Outcomes in a Team Environment," *Journal of Management* 26 (2000): 1113–32.

12. M. L. Miller Henningsen, D. D. Henningsen, M. G. Cruz, and J. Morrill, "Social Influence in Groups: A Comparative Application of Relational Framing Theory and the Elaboration Likelihood Model of Persuasion," *Communication Monographs* 70, 3 (September 2003): 175–97. For an excellent review of teamwork principles and strategies, see D. A. Romig, *Breakthrough Teamwork: Outstanding Results Using Structured Teamwork* (New York: Irwin, 1996); V. Rousscau, C. Aubé, and A. Savoie, "Teamwork Behaviors: A Review and an Integration of Frameworks," *Small Group Research* 37 (2006): 540–70.

13. J. R. Katzenback and D. K. Smith, *The Wisdom of Teams: Creating the High-Performance Organization* (New York: HarperBusiness, 1993); M. Schrage, *No More Teams! Mastering the Dynamics of Creative Collaboration* (New York: Currency Doubleday, 1995); Romig, *Breakthrough Teamwork;* D. D. Chrislip and C. E. Larson, *Collaborative Leadership* (San Francisco: Jossey-Bass, 1994).

14. See P. R. Scholtes, B. L. Joiner, and B. J. Streibel, *The Team Handbook,* 2nd ed. (Madison, WI: Joiner Associates, 1996); Romig, *Breakthrough Teamwork;* Schrage, *No More Teams!*

15. N. Katz and G. Koenig, "Sports Teams as a Model for Workplace Teams: Lessons and Liabilities," *Academy of Management Executive* 15 (August 2001): 56–67.

16. D. J. Devine, L. D. Clayton, J. L. Philips, B. B. Dunford, and S. B. Melner, "Teams in Organizations: Prevalence, Characteristics, and Effectiveness," *Small Group Research* 30 (1999): 678–711.

17. R. Y. Hirokawa and J. Keyton, "Perceived Facilitators and Inhibitors of Effectiveness in Organizational Work Teams," *Management Communication Quarterly* 8 (1995): 424–46; E. Salas, D. E. Sims, and C. S. Burke, "Is There a 'Big Five' in Teamwork?" *Small Group Research* 36 (2005): 555–99.

18. D. J. Devine and J. L. Philips, "Do Smarter Teams Do Better? A Meta-Analysis of Cognitive Ability and Team Performance," *Small Group Research* 32 (2001): 507–35.

19. C. E. Larson and F. M. J. LaFasto, *Teamwork: What Must Go Right/What Can Go Wrong* (Beverly Hills, CA: Sage, 1989).

20. M. Hoegl and K. Parboteeah, "Goal Setting and Team Performance in Innovative Projects: On the Moderating Role of Teamwork Quality," *Small Group Research* 34 (2003): 3–19.

21. M. A. Marks, J. E. Mathieu, and S. J. Zaccaro, "A Temporally Based Framework and Taxonomy of Team Processes," *Academy of Management Review* 26 (2001): 356–76.

22. Devine et al., "Teams in Organizations"; M. H. Jordan, H. S. Field, and A. A. Armenakis, "The Relationship of Group Process Variables and Team Performance: A Team-Level Analysis in a Field Setting," *Small Group Research* 35 (2002): 121–50.

23. A. M. Hardin, M. A. Fuller, and J. S. Valacich, "Measuring Group Efficacy in Virtual Team: New Questions in an Old Debate," *Small Group Research* 37 (2006): 65–85.

24. J. R. Hackman and R. Wageman, "A Theory of Team Coaching," *Academy of Management Review* 30 (2005): 269–87.

25. M. S. Limon and F. J. Boster, "The Effects of Performance Feedback on Group Members' Perceptions of Prestige, Task Competencies, Group Belonging, and Loafing," *Communication Research Reports* 20 (Winter 2003): 13–23; J. N. Choi, "External Activities and Team Effectiveness: Review and Theoretical Development," *Small Group Research* 33 (2002): 181–208.

26. F. LaFasto and C. Larson, *When Teams Work Best* (Thousand Oaks, CA: Sage, 2001). Our discussion of the six characteristics of effective team members is based on information presented in Chapter 1, pages 4–25.

27. A. English, R. L. Griffith, and L. A. Steelman, "Team Performance: The Effect of Team Conscientiousness and Task Type," *Small Group Research* 35 (2004): 643–65.

28. C. M. Anderson and M. M. Martin, "Communication Motives (State vs. Trait?) and Task Group Outcomes," *Communication Research Reports* 19 (Summer 2002): 269–82.

29. A. T. Pescosolido, "Group Efficacy and Group Effectiveness: The Effects of Group Efficacy Over Time on Group Performance and Development," *Small Group Research* 34 (2003): 20–43.

30. B. Beersma, J. R. Hollenbeck, S. E. Humphrey, H. Moon, D. E. Conlon, and D. R. Ilgen, "Cooperation, Competition, and Team Performance: Toward a Contingency Approach, *Academy of Management Journal* 46 (2002): 572–90.

31. M. A. G. Peeters, C. G. Rutte, H. F. J. M. vanTuijl, and I. M. M. J. Reymen, "The Big Five Personality Traits and Individual Satisfaction with the Team," *Small Group Research* 37 (2006): 187–211.

32. Adapted from D. W. Johnson and F. P. Johnson, *Joining Together: Group Theory and Group Skills* (Englewood Cliffs, NJ: Prentice Hall, 1975), 304.

33. S. A. Furst, M. Reeves, B. Rosen, and R. S. Blackburn, "Managing the Life Cycle of Virtual Teams," *The Academy of Management Executive* 18 (2004): 6–20.

34. J. A. Bonito, "Shared Cognition and Participation in Small Groups: Similarity of Member Prototypes," *Communication Research* 31 (2004): 704–30.

35. E. Salas, D. Rozell, J. E. Dirskell, and B. Mullen, "The Effect of Team Building on Performance: An Integration," *Small Group Research* 39 (1999): 309–29.

36. Devine et al., "Teams in Organizations"; Salas et al., "The Effect of Team Building on Performance."

37. R. Forrester and A. B. Drexler, "A Model for Team-Based Organization Performance," *Academy of Management Executive* 13 (1999): 36–49.

38. The discussion of the advantages and disadvantages of working in small groups is based in part on N. R. F. Maier, "Assets and Liabilities in Group Problem Solving: The Need for an Integrative Function," *Psychological Review* 74 (1967): 239–49. See also Michael Argyle, *Cooperation: The Basis of Sociability* (London: Routledge, 1991).

39. See F. C. Broadbeck and T. Breitemeyer, "Effects of Individual versus Mixed Individual and Group Experience in Rule Induction on Group Member Learning and Group Performance," *Journal of Experimental Social Psychology* 36 (October 2002): 621–48; G. S. Van Der Vegt and J. S. Bunderson, "Learning and Performance in Multidisciplinary Teams: The Importance of Collective Team Identification," *Academy of Management Journal* 48 (2005): 532–47.

40. R. A. Cooke and J. A. Kernaghan, "Estimating the Difference Between Group Versus Individual Performance on Problem-Solving Tasks," *Group & Organizational Studies* 12, no. 3 (September 1987): 319–42; P. R. Laughlin, E. C. Hatch, J. Silver, and L. Boh, "Groups Perform Better Than the Best Individuals on Letters-to-Numbers Problems: Effects of Group Size," *Journal of Personality and Social Psychology* 90 (2006): 644–51.

41. Cooke and Kernaghan, "Estimating the Difference."

42. D. D. Stewart, "Stereotypes, Negativity Bias, and the Discussion of Unshared Information in Decision-Making Groups," *Small Group Research* 29 (1998): 643–68; J. R. Larson, "Modeling the Entry of Shared and Unshared Information into Group Discussion: A Review and BASIC Language Computer Program," *Small Group Research* 28 (1997): 454–79.

43. J. Platania and G. P. Moran, "Social Facilitation as a Function of the Mere Presence of Others," *The Journal of Social Psychology* 141 (Spring 2001): 190–97

44. R. Zajonc, "Social Facilitation," *Science* 149 (1965): 269–74; M. Gagne and M. Zuckerman, "Performance and Learning Goal Orientations as Moderators of Social Loafing and Social Facilitation," *Small Group Research* 30 (1999): 524–41; R. G. Geen, "Social Motivation," *Annual Review of Psychology* 42 (1991): 377–99.

45. I. L. Janis, "Groupthink," *Psychology Today* 5 (November 1971): 43–46, 74–76.

46. Gagne and Zuckerman, "Performance and Learning Goal Orientations."

47. A. BarNir, "Can Group- and Issue-Related Factors Predict Choice Shift? A Meta-Analysis of Group Decisions on Life Dilemmas," *Small Group Research* 29 (1998): 308–38.

48. D. R. Forsyth, *An Introduction to Group Dynamics* (Monterey, CA: Brooks/Cole, 1983) 424.

49. S. N. Fraidin, "When Is One Head Better Than Two? Interdependent Information in Group Decision Making," *Organizational Behavior and Human Decision Processes* 93 (2004): 102–13.

50. G. Hofstede, *Culture's Consequences: International Differences in Work-Related Values* (Beverly Hills, CA: Sage, 1980) 221; S. B. Alavi and J. McCormick, "Theoretical and Measurement Issues for Studies of Collective Orientation in Team Contexts," *Small Group Research* 35 (2004): 111–27.

51. Hofstede, *Culture's Consequences.*

52. In addition to the work of Hofstede, see J. A. Wagner III and M. K. Moch, "Individualism-Collectivism: Concept and Measure," *Group and Organizational Studies* 11 (September 1986): 280–304; H. C. Triandis, C. McCusker, and C. H. Hui, "Multimethod Probes of Individualism and Collectivism," *Journal of Personality and Social Psychology* 59 (1990): 1006–20; C. H. Hui, "Measurement of Individualism-Collectivism," *Journal of Research in Personality* 22 (1988): 17–36; C. R. Bantz, "Cultural Diversity and Group Cross-Cultural Team Research," *Journal of Applied Communication Research* (February 1993): 1–20; M. R. Hammer and J. N. Martin, "The Effects of Cross-Cultural Training on American Managers in a Japanese-American Joint Venture," *Journal of Applied Communication Research* (May 1992): 161–82; T. H. Cox, S. A. Lobel, and P. L. McLeod, "Effects of Ethnic Group Cultural Differences on Cooperative and Competitive Behavior on a Group Task," *Academy of Management Journal* 34, no. 4 (1991): 827–47; B. L. Kirkman and D. L. Shapiro, "Understanding Why Team Members Won't Share: An Examination of Factors Related to Employee Receptivity to Team-Based Rewards," *Small Group Research* 31 (2000): 175–209.

53. For an excellent discussion of small group communication in naturalistic settings, see L. R. Frey, "The Naturalistic Paradigm: Studying Small Groups in the Postmodern Era," *Small Group Research* 25 (1994): 551–77; L. R. Frey, "Applied Communication Research on Group Facilitation in Natural Settings," in L. R. Frey, ed., *Innovations in Group Facilitation: Applications in Natural Settings* (Cresskill, NJ: Hampton, 1995) 1–23.

54. For a comprehensive review of the history of group decision-making research, see L. R. Frey, "Remember and 'Remembering': A History of Theory and Research on Communication and Group Decision-Making," in R. Y. Hirokawa and M. S. Poole, eds., *Communication and Group Decision Making,* 2nd ed. (Thousand Oaks, CA: Sage, 1996) 19–51.

55. C. E. Timmerman and C. R. Scott, "Virtually Working: Communicative and Structural Predictors of Media Use and Key Outcomes in Virtual Work Teams," *Communication Monographs* 73 (2006): 108–36.

56. D. Jude-York, L. D. Davis, and S. L. Wise, *Virtual Teaming: Breaking the Boundaries of Time and Place* (Menlo Park, CA: Crisp Learning, 2000) 71.

57. U. Becker-Beck, M. Wintermantel, and A. Borg, "Principles of Regulating Interaction in Teams Practicing Face-to-Face Communication versus Teams Practicing Computer-Mediated Communication," *Small Group Research* 36 (2005): 499–536.

58. See the excellent review of the effect of technology on group decision making in M. S. Poole and G. DeSanctis, "Microlevel Structuration in Computer-Supported Group Decision Making," *Human Communication Research* 19 (1992): 5–49.

59. V. J. Dubrovsky, S. Kiesler, and B. N. Sethna, "The Equalization Phenomenon: Status Effects in Computer-Mediated and Face-to-Face Decision-Making Groups," *Human Computer Interaction* 6 (1991): 119–46.

60. A. I. Shirani, M. H. A. Tafti, and J. F. Affisco, "Task and Technology Fit: A Comparison of Two Technologies for Synchronous and Asynchronous Group Communication," *Information & Management* 36 (1999): 139–50.

61. M. Adkins and D. E. Brashers, "The Power of Language in Computer-Mediated Groups," *Management Communication Quarterly* 8 (1995): 289–322.

62. R. E. Rice and G. Love, "Electronic Emotion: Socioemotional Context in a Computer-Mediated Communication Network," *Communication Research* 14 (February 1987): 85–108.

63. See R. Johansen, J. Vallee, and K. Spangler, *Electronic Meetings: Technical Alternatives and Social Choices* (Reading, MA: Addison-Wesley, 1979); B. L. Kirkman, P. E. Tesluk, and C. B. Gibson, "The Impact of Team Empowerment on Virtual Team Performance: The Moderating Role of Face-to-Face Interaction," *Academy of Management Journal* 47 (2004): 175–92.

64. P. L. McLeod and J. K. Liker, "Electronic Meeting Systems: Evidence from a Low Structure Environment," *Information Systems Research* 3 (1992): 195–223.

65. Michael Finley, "Welcome to the Electronic Meeting," *Training* (July 1991): 29–32. See also Poole and DeSanctis, "Microlevel Structuration."

66. For an excellent discussion of the effects of computer-mediated communication and interpersonal communication, see J. B. Walther, "Interpersonal Effects in Computer-Mediated Interaction: A Relational Perspective," *Communication Research* 19 (1992): 52–90; J. B. Walther, "Relational Aspects of Computer-Mediated Communication: Experimental and Longitudinal Observations," *Organization Science* 6 (1995): 186–203; J. B. Walther, J. F. Anderson, and D. Park, "Interpersonal Effects in Computer-Mediated Interaction: A Meta-Analysis of Social and Anti-Social Communication," *Communication Research* 21 (1994): 460–87; N. Negroponte, *Being Digital* (New York: Knopf, 1995); J. B. Walther and L. Tidwell, "When Is Mediated Communication Not Interpersonal?" in K. Galvin and P. Cooper, *Making Connections* (Los Angeles, CA: Roxbury Press, 1996); P. Wallace, *The Psychology of the Internet* (Cambridge, England: Cambridge University Press, 1999).

67. J. B. Walther and J. K. Burgoon, "Relational Communication in Computer-Mediated Interaction," *Human Communication Research* 19 (1992): 50–88.

68. M. E. Mayer, "Behaviors Leading to More Effective Decisions in Small Groups Embedded in Organizations," *Communication Reports* 11 (1998): 123–32.

69. B. H. Spitzberg, "Communication Competence as Knowledge, Skill, and Impression," *Communication Education* 32 (1983): 323–29.

70. A. B. Hollingshead, "Group and Individual Training: The Impact of Practice on Performance," *Small Group Research* 29 (1998): 254–80.

71. S. A. Beebe and J. K. Barge, "Assessing Small Group Problem Solving Communication Competencies," in R. Cathcart and L. Samovar, eds., *A Reader in Small Group Communication* (New York: Roxbury, 2004); S. A. Beebe, J. K. Barge, P. Motlet, and C. Tustl, "The Competent Group Communicator," presented at the National Communication Association annual conference, San Antonio, Texas (November 2006).

72. K. W. Hawkins and B. P. Fillion, "Perceived Communication Skill Needs for Work Groups," *Communication Research Reports* 16 (1999): 167–74.

73. Developed by Alvin Goldberg, University of Denver.

74. D. W. Johnson, *Reaching Out: Interpersonal Effectiveness and Self-Actualization* (Boston: Allyn and Bacon, 2000).

CHAPTER 2

1. F. E. X. Dance and C. E. Larson, *The Functions of Human Communication: A Theoretical Approach* (New York: Holt, Rinehart & Winston, 1976) 4.

2. G. A. Kelly, *A Theory of Personality: The Psychology of Personal Constructs* (New York: Norton, 1963) 18.

3. R. Buehler, D. Messervey, and D. Griffin, "Collaborative Planning and Prediction: Does Group Discussion Affect Optimistic Biases in Time Estimation?" *Organizational Behavior and Human Decision Processes* 97 (2005): 47–63.

4. D. Barnlund, "Toward a Meaning-Centered Philosophy of Communication," in K. G. Johnson et al., eds., *Nothing Never Happens* (Beverly Hills, CA: Glencoe Press, 1974) 213.

5. J. A. Bonito, "The Analysis of Participation in Small Groups: Methodological and Conceptual Issues Related to Interdependence," *Small Group Research* 33 (2002): 412–38.

6. J. K. Brilhart, *Effective Group Discussion*, 8th ed. (Dubuque, IA: Brown, 1995) 26.

7. S. W. Littlejohn, *Theories of Human Communication*, 7th ed. (Belmont, CA: Wadsworth, 1996).

8. M. W. Kramer, "Communication and Social Exchange Processes in Community Theatre Groups," *Journal of Applied Communication Research* 33 (2005): 159–82.

9. E. Bormann, *Small Group Communication: Theory and Practice*, 3rd ed. (New York: HarperCollins, 1990).

10. E. Bormann, "Symbolic Convergence Theory," in R. Y. Hirokawa, R. S. Cathcart, L. A. Samovar, and L. D. Henman, eds., *Small Group Communication Theory and Practice* (Los Angeles: Roxbury, 2003) 41.

11. K. M. Propp and G. Kreps, "A Rose by Any Other Name: The Vitality of Group Communication Research," *Communication Studies* 45 (1994): 7–19.

12. See A. Giddens, *New Rules of Sociological Method*, 2nd ed. (Palo Alto, CA: Stanford University Press, 1993) and A. Giddens, *Studies in Social and Political Theory* (New York: Basic Books, 1979).

13. M. S. Poole, D. R. Seibold, and R. D. McPhee, "A Structurational Approach to Theory Building in Group Decision-Making Research," in R. Y. Hirokawa and M. S. Poole, eds., *Communication and Group Decision Making*, 2nd ed. (Thousand Oaks, CA: Sage, 1996).

14. M. S. Poole, "Group Communication and the Structuring Process," in R. Y. Hirokawa, R. S. Cathcart, L. A. Samovar, and L. D. Henman, eds., *Small Group Communication Theory and Practice* (Los Angeles: Roxbury, 2003) 49.

15. D. F. Witmer, "Communication and Recovery: Structuration as an Ontological Approach to Organizational Culture," *Communication Monographs* 64 (1997): 324–49.

16. S. Siebold and D. R. Seibold, "Jurors' Intuitive Rules for Deliberation: A Structurational Approach to Communication in Jury Decision Making," *Communication Monographs* 65 (1998): 282–307.

17. M. S. Poole, "Group Communication Theory," in L. R. Frey, ed., *The Handbook of Small Group Research* (Thousand Oaks, CA: Sage, 1996).

18. D. S. Gouran and R. Y. Hirokawa, "Effective Decision Making and Problem Solving in Groups: A Functional Perspective," in R. Y. Hirokawa, R. S. Cathcart, L. A. Samovar, and L. D. Henman, eds., *Small Group Communication Theory and Practice* (Los Angeles: Roxbury, 2003).

19. D. Gouran and R. Y. Hirokawa, "Functional Theory and Communication in Decision-Making Groups: An Expanded View," in R. Y. Hirokawa and M. S. Poole, eds., *Communication and Group Decision Making*, 2nd ed. (Thousand Oaks, CA: Sage, 1996).

20. S. Tangirala and B. J. Alge, "Reactions to Unfair Events in Computer-Mediated Groups: A Test of Uncertainty Management Theory," *Organizational Behavior and Human Decision Processes* 100 (2006): 1–20.

CHAPTER 3

1. For an illuminating discussion of this topic, see S. Pinker, *How the Mind Works* (New York: Norton, 1997).

2. A. Maslow, *Toward a Psychology of Being*, 2nd ed. (Princeton, NJ: Van Nostrand, 1982).

3. D. Stacks, M. Hickson, III, and S. R. Hill, Jr., *Introduction to Communication Theory* (Chicago: Holt, Rinehart & Winston, 1991).

4. W. Schutz, *The Interpersonal Underworld* (Palo Alto, CA: Science & Behavior Books, 1958).

5. F. E. X. Dance, "A Helical Model of Communication," in F. E. X. Dance, ed., *Human Communication Theory* (New York: Holt, Rinehart & Winston, 1967) 294–98.

6. C. M. Mason and M. A. Griffin, "Group Task Satisfaction: Applying the Construct of Job Satisfaction to Groups," *Small Group Research* 33 (2002): 271–312.

7. For a full discussion of mutuality of concern, see R. Patton and K. Giffin, *Decision-Making Group Interaction*, 3rd ed. (New York: HarperCollins, 1990) 118–19.

8. M. A. G. Peeters, C. G. Rutte, H. F. J. M. van Tuijl, and I. M. M. J. Reyman, "The Big Five Personality Traits and Individual Satisfaction with the Team," *Small Group Research* 37 (2006): 187–211.

9. L. Mann, "Cross Cultural Studies of Small Groups," in H. Triandis, ed., *Handbook of Cross-Cultural Psychology,* vol. 5 (Boston: Allyn and Bacon, 1980).

10. J. K. Barge and L. R. Frey, "Life in a Task Group," in L. R. Frey and J. K. Barge, eds., *Managing Group Life: Communicating in Decision-Making Groups* (Boston: Houghton Mifflin, 1997) 39.

11. Barge and Frey, "Life in a Task Group" 39.

12. C. S. Palazzo, "The Social Group: Definitions," in R. S. Cathcart and L. A. Samovar, eds., *Small Group Communication: A Reader,* 6th ed. (Dubuque, IA: Brown, 1991) 11–12.

13. F. G. Chen and D. T. Kenrick, "Repulsion or Attraction? Group Membership and Assumed Attitude Similarity," *Journal of Personality and Social Psychology* 83 (2002): 111–25.

14. S. B. Feichtner and E. A. Davis, "Why Some Groups Fail: A Survey of Students' Experiences with Learning Groups," in A. Goodsell, M. Maher, and V. Tinto, *Collaborative Learning: A Sourcebook for Higher Education* (University Park, PA: National Center on Postsecondary Teaching, Learning, and Assessment [NCTLA], 1997) 59–67.

15. J. Thibaut and H. Kelley, *The Social Psychology of Groups* (New Brunswick, NJ: Transaction Publishing, 1986).

16. R. Zajonc, "Attitudinal Effects of Mere Exposure," *Journal of Personality and Social Psychology* 9 (1968): 1–29.

17. M. W. Kramer, "Communication in a Community Theatre Group: Managing Multiple Group Roles," *Communication Studies* 53 (2002): 151–70.

18. M. Shaw, *Group Dynamics: The Psychology of Small Group Behavior* (New York: McGraw-Hill, 1981) 93.

19. D. M. Buss, "Sex Differences in Mate Preferences: Evolutionary Hypotheses Tested in 37 Different Cultures," *Behavioral and Brain Sciences* 12 (1989): 1–49.

20. Shaw, *Group Dynamics* 85.

21. A. L. Johnson, M. T. Crawford, S. J. Sherman, A. M. Rutchick, D. L. Hamilton, M. B. Ferreira, and J. V. Petrocelli, "A Functional Perspective on Group Memberships: Differential Need Fulfillment in a Group Typology," *Journal of Experimental and Social Psychology* 42 (2006): 707–19.

22. D. Trafimow and K. A. Finlay, "The Accessibility of Group Memberships," *The Journal of Social Psychology* 141 (2001): 509–22.

23. D. L. Duarte and N. Tennant Snyder, *Mastering Virtual Teams* (San Francisco, CA: Jossey-Bass, 2001) 60. Based on research by Geert Hofstede.

24. *2006 Household Data* (pp. 220–221). Bureau of Labor Statistics, Department of Labor. Washington, DC.

25. J. E. Farley, *Majority–Minority Relations* (Englewood Cliffs, NJ: Prentice Hall, 1995).

26. M. Bayazit and E. A. Mannix, "Should I Stay or Should I Go? Predicting Team Members' Intent to Remain in the Team," *Small Group Research* 34 (2003): 290–321.

27. K. Fritz, "The Diversity Dilemma: Dealing with Difference," paper presented at the Vocation of a Lutheran Institution Conference, Selinsgrove, Pennsylvania, 1999.

28. B. W. Tuckman, "Developmental Sequence in Small Groups," *Psychological Bulletin* 63 (1965): 384–99.

29. N. Anderson and H. D. C. Thomas, "Work Group Socialization," in M. S. West, ed., *Handbook of Work Group Psychology* (Chichester, England: Wiley, 1996).

30. G. Chen and R. J. Klimoski, "The Impact of Expectations on Newcomer Performance in Teams as Mediated by Work Characteristics, Social Exchanges, and Empowerment," *Academy of Management Journal* 46 (2003): 581–607.

CHAPTER 4

1. J. Keyton, "Relational Communication in Groups," in L. Frey, D. S. Gouran, and M. S. Poole, eds., *The Handbook of Group Communication and Research* (Thousand Oaks, CA: Sage, 1999) 192.

2. For a full discussion of gender and communication, see J. T. Wood, *Gendered Lives: Communication, Gender and Culture,* 3rd ed. (Belmont, CA: Wadsworth, 1999) and D. K. Ivy and P. Backlund, "Exploring Gender Speak: Personal Effectiveness," in J. C. Pearson, L. H. Turner, and W. Todd-Mancillas, eds., *Gender and Communication* (New York: McGraw-Hill, 1994).

3. L. Stafford, M. Dainton, and S. Haas, "Measuring Routine and Strategic Relational Maintenance: Scale Revision, Sex versus Gender Roles, and Prediction of Relational Characteristics," *Communication Monographs* 67 (2000): 306–23; E. A. Seeley, W. L. Gardner, G. Pennington, and S. Gabriel, "Circle of Friends or Members of a Group? Sex Differences in Relational and Collective Attachments to Groups," *Group Process and Intergroup Relations* (6) (2003): 251–63.

4. M. S. Woodward, L. B. Rosenfeld, and S. K. May, "Sex Differences in Social Support in Sororities and Fraternities," *Journal of Applied Communication Research* 24 (1996): 260.

5. J. C. McCroskey and V. P. Richmond, "Willingness to Communicate: Differing Cultural Perspectives," *The Southern Communication Journal* 56 (1990): 72–77.

6. M. L. Hecht, S. Ribeau, and J. K. Alberts, "An Afro-American Perspective on Interethnic Communication," *Communication Monographs* 56 (1989): 385–410.

7. For a good review of role development in groups, see A. P. Hare, "Types of Roles in Small Groups: A Bit of History and a Current Perspective," *Small Group Research* 25 (1994): 433–48 and A. J. Salazar, "An Analysis of the Development and Evolution of Roles in the Small Group," *Small Group Research* 27 (1996): 475–503.

8. S. R. Bray and J. R. Brawley, "Role Efficacy, Role Clarity, and Role Performance Effectiveness," *Small Group Research* 33 (2002): 233–53.

9. K. D. Benne and P. Sheats, "Functional Roles of Group Members," *Journal of Social Issues* 4 (Spring 1948): 41–49.

10. E. G. Bormann, *Discussion and Group Methods: Theory and Practice*, 3rd ed. (New York: Harper & Row, 1989) 209.

11. J. W. Strijbos, R. L. Martens, W. M. G. Jochems, and N. J. Broder, "The Effect of Functional Roles on Group Efficiency: Using Multilevel Modeling and Content Analysis to Investigate Computer-Supported Collaboration in Groups," *Small Group Research* 35 (2004): 195–229.

12. T. Postmes, R. Spears, and S. Cihangir, "Quality of Decision Making and Group Norms," *Journal of Personality and Social Psychology* 80 (2001): 918–30.

13. S. Schacter, "Deviation, Rejection, and Communication," *Journal of Abnormal and Social Psychology* 46 (1951): 190–207.

14. M. S. Poole, "Group Communication and the Structuring Process," in R. S. Cathcart and L. A. Samovar, eds., *Small Group Communication: A Reader*, 6th ed. (Dubuque, IA: Brown, 1992) 275–87.

15. H. T. Reitan and M. E. Shaw, "Group Membership, Sex-Composition of the Group, and Conformity Behavior," *Journal of Social Psychology* 64 (1964): 45–51.

16. M. Shaw, *Group Dynamics: The Psychology of Small Group Behavior* (New York: McGraw-Hill, 1981) 281.

17. S. Asch, "Studies of Independence and Submission to Group Pressures," *Psychological Monographs* 70 (whole issue) (1956).

18. C. R. Graham, "A Model of Norm Development for Computer-Mediated Teamwork," *Small Group Research* 34 (2003): 322–52.

19. M. G. Cruz, D. Henningsen, and M. L. M. Williams, "The Presence of Norms in the Absence of Groups? The Impact of Normative Influence Under Hidden-Profile Conditions," *Human Communication Research* 26 (2000): 104–24.

20. S. B. Shimanoff, "Group Interaction via Communication Rules," in R. S. Cathcart and L. A. Samovar, eds., *Small Group Communication: A Reader*, 6th ed. (Dubuque, IA: Brown, 1992).

21. P. R. Scholtes, B. L. Joiner, and B. J. Streibel, *The Team Handbook*, 2nd ed. (Madison, WI: Joiner, 1996); J. R. Katzenbach and D. K. Smith, *The Wisdom of Teams: Creating the High-Performance Organization* (New York: HarperCollins, 1993); D. A. Romig, *Breakthrough Teamwork: Outstanding Results Using Structured Teamwork®* (Chicago: Irwin, 1996).

22. S. R. Covey, *The Seven Habits of Highly Effective People* (New York: Simon & Schuster, 1989).

23. Scholtes, Joiner, and Streible, *The Team Handbook*.

24. Bormann, *Discussion and Group Methods* 215.

25. J. I. Hurwitz, A. F. Zander, and B. Hymovitch, "Some Effects of Power on the Relations among Group Members," in D. Cartwright and A. Zander, eds., *Group Dynamics: Research and Theory* (New York: Harper & Row, 1953), 483–92.

26. Hurwitz, Zander, and Hymovitch, "Some Effects of Power."

27. Hurwitz, Zander, and Hymovitch, "Some Effects of Power."

28. D. C. Barnlund and C. Harland, "Propinquity and Prestige as Determinants of Communication Networks," *Sociometry* 26 (1963): 467–79.

29. L. Karakowsky and K. McBey, "Do My Contributions Matter? The Influence of Imputed Expertise on Member Involvement and Self-Evaluations in the Work Group," *Group and Organization Management* 26 (2001): 70–92.

30. G. C. Homans, *The Human Group* (New York: Harcourt Brace & World, 1992).

31. J. K. Brilhart and G. J. Galanes, *Effective Group Discussion* (Dubuque, IA: Brown, 1997) 36.

32. H. H. Kelly, "Communication in Experimentally Created Hierarchies," *Human Relations* 4 (1951): 36–56.

33. Kelly, "Communication in Experimentally Created Hierarchies."

34. Kelly, "Communication in Experimentally Created Hierarchies."

35. Bormann, *Discussion and Group Methods* 215.

36. Bormann, *Discussion and Group Methods* 215.

37. R. Bierstedt, "An Analysis of Social Power," *American Sociological Review* 6 (1950): 7–30.

38. R. S. Franz, "Task Interdependence and Personal Power in Teams," *Small Group Research* 29 (1998): 226–53.

39. J. R. P. French and B. H. Raven, "The Bases of Social Power," in D. Cartwright and A. Zander, eds., *Group Dynamics* (Evanston, IL: Row, Peterson, 1962) 607–23.

40. C. R. Berger, "Power in the Family," in M. Roloff and G. Miller, eds., *Persuasion: New Direction in Theory and Research* (Beverly Hills, CA: Sage, 1980) 217.

41. M. R. Singer, *Intercultural Communication: A Perceptual Approach* (Englewood Cliffs, NJ: Prentice Hall, 1987) 118.

42. R. S. Franz, "Task Interdependence and Personal Power in Teams."

43. K. M. Propp, "An Experimental Examination of Biological Sex as a Status Cue in Decision-Making Groups and Its Influence on Information Use," *Small Group Research* 26 (1995): 451–74. L. M. Grob, R. Meyers, and R. Schuh, "Powerful/Powerless Language Use in Group Interactions: Sex Differences or Similarities?" *Communication Quarterly* 45 (1997): 282–303.

44. L. M. Sagrestano, "Power Strategies in Interpersonal Relationships: The Effects of Expertise and Gender," *Psychology of Women Quarterly* 16 (1992): 481–95.

45. W. L. Gardner III, J. V. Peluchette, and S. K. Clinebell, "Valuing Women in Management: An Impression Management Perspective of Gender Diversity," *Management Communication Quarterly* 8 (1994): 115–64.

46. S. S. Li, "Power and Its Relationship with Group Communication," Ph.D. dissertation, U of Iowa, 1993.

47. V. I. Armstrong, *I Have Spoken: American History through Voices of the Indians* (Chicago: The Swallow Press, 1971).

48. J. M. Wilson, S. G. Straus, and B. McEvily, "All in Due Time: The Development of Trust in Computer-Mediated and Face-to-Face Teams," *Organizational Behavior and Human Decision Processes* 99 (2006): 16–33.

49. R. Reichert, *Self-Awareness Through Group Dynamics* (Dayton, OH: Pflaum/Standard, 1970) 21.

50. J. Powell, *Why Am I Afraid To Tell You Who I Am?* (Niles, IL: Argus Communications, 1990) 12.

51. Powell, *Why Am I Afraid To Tell You Who I Am?*, 54–58.

52. J. Luft, *Of Human Interaction* (Palo Alto, CA: National Press, 1969) 132–33.

53. Bormann, *Discussion and Group Methods* 181–82.

54. Definition based on one by A. G. Smith, ed., *Communications and Culture* (New York; Holt, Rinehart & Winston, 1966).

55. B. J. McCauliffe, J. Jetten, M. J. Hornsey, and M. A. Hogg, "Individualist and Collectivist Norms: When It's OK to Go Your Own Way," *European Journal of Social Psychology* 33 (2003): 57–70.

56. H. S. Park and T. R. Levine, "The Theory of Reasoned Action and Self-Construal: Evidence from Three Cultures," *Comunication Monographs* 66 (1999): 199–218; M.-S. Kim, J. E. Hunter, A. Miyahara, A.-M. Horvath, M. Bresnahan, and H. Yoon, "Individual- vs. Culture-Level Dimensions of Individualism and Collectivism: Effects on Preferred Conversational Styles," *Communication Monographs* 63 (1996): 29–49.

57. E. T. Hall, *Beyond Culture* (Garden City, NY: Doubleday, 1976).

58. Hall, *Beyond Culture.*

59. Hall, *Beyond Culture.*

60. C. H. Dodd, *Dynamics of Intercultural Communication* (Dubuque, IA: Brown, 1997).

61. F. Yousef and N. Briggs, "The Multinational Business Organization: A Schema for the Training of Overseas Personnel in Communication," *International and Intercultural Communication Annual* 2 (1975): 74–85.

62. E. T. Hall, *The Silent Language* (New York: Anchor, 1973).

63. R. Shuter, "A Field Study of Nonverbal Communication in Germany, Italy, and the United States," *Communication Monographs* 44 (1977): 298–305.

64. Dodd, *Dynamics of Intercultural Communication.*

65. C. Mayo and N. Henley, *Gender and Nonverbal Behavior* (New York: Springer, 1981).

66. D. K. Ivy and P. Backlund, *Exploring Gender Speak: Personal Effectiveness in Gender Communications,* 2d ed. (New York: McGraw-Hill, 2000).

67. G. Leventhal and M. Matturro, "Differential Effects of Spatial Crowding and Sex on Behavior," *Perceptual Motor Skills* 50 (1980): 111–19.

68. R. Sommer, "Studies in Personal Space," *Sociometry* 22 (1959): 247–60.

69. P. C. Ellsworth and L. M. Ludwig, "Visual Behavior in Social Interaction," *Journal of Communication* 22 (1972): 375–403.

70. A. Mehrabian, *Nonverbal Communication* (Chicago: Aldine Atherton, 1972).

71. N. M. Henley, *Body Politics: Power, Sex and Nonverbal Communication* (Englewood Cliffs, NJ: Prentice-Hall, 1977).

72. Henley, *Body Politics.*

73. N. N. Markel, J. Long, and T. J. Saine, "Sex Effects in Conversational Interaction: Another Look at Male Dominance," *Human Communication Research* 2 (1976): 35–64.

74. T. Katriel, "Communicative Style in Cross-Cultural Perspective: Arabs and Jews in Israel." Paper presented at the annual meeting of the Western Speech Communication Association, Sacramento, California, 1990.

75. D. Barnlund, *Communicative Styles of Japanese and Americans: Images and Realities* (Belmont, CA: Wadsworth, 1989).

76. S. Ishii and T. Bruneau, "Silence and Silences in Cross-Cultural Perspective: Japan and the United States," in L. A. Samovar and R. E. Porter, eds., *Intercultural Communication: A Reader,* 6th ed. (Belmont, CA: Wadsworth, 1991).

77. J. Condon, "... So Near the United States: Notes on Communication between Mexicans and North Americans," in L. A. Samovar and R. E. Porter, eds., *Intercultural Communication: A Reader,* 6th ed. (Belmont, CA: Wadsworth, 1991).

78. T. K. Fitzgerald, *Metaphors of Identity: A Culture-Communication Dialogue* (Albany: SUNY P, 1993).

79. E. T. Hall and M. R. Hall, *Understanding Cultural Differences* (Yarmouth, ME: Intercultural Press, 1989).

80. D. I. Ballard and D. R. Seibold, "Time Orientation and Temporary Variation Across Work Groups: Implications for Group and Organizational Communication," *Western Journal of Communication* 64 (Spring 2000): 218–42.

81. Ballard and Seibold, "Time Orientation and Temporary Variations Across Work Groups."

82. Adapted from D. W. Klopf, *Intercultural Encounters: The Fundamentals of Intercultural Communication* (Englewood, CO: Morton, 1998) and Hall and Hall, *Understanding Cultural Differences.*

83. Adapted from C. R. Bontz, "Cultural Diversity and Group Cross-Cultural Team Research," *Journal of Applied Communication Research* 21 (1993): 12.

CHAPTER 5

1. J. R. Gibb, "Defensive Communication," *Journal of Communication* 11 (September 1961): 141.

2. C. H. Tandy, "Assessing the Functions of Supportive Messages," *Communication Research* 19 (1992): 175–92.

3. E. B. Ray, "The Relationship Among Communication Network Roles, Job Stress, and Burnout in Educational Organizations," *Communication Quarterly* 39 (1991): 91–100.

4. A. Goldberg and C. Larson, *Group Communication: Discussion Processes and Applications* (Englewood Cliffs, NJ: Prentice Hall, 1975) 105.

5. E. Sieburg and C. Larson, "Dimensions of Interpersonal Response," paper delivered at the annual conference of the International Communication Association, Phoenix, April 1971, 1.

6. Goldberg and Larson, *Group Communication* 103–104.

7. A. V. Carron and L. R. Brawley, "Cohesion: Conceptual and Measurement Issues," *Small Group Research* 31 (2000): 89–106.

8. K. A. Bollen and R. H. Hoyle, "Perceived Cohesion: A Conceptual and Empirical Examination," *Social Forces* 69 (1990): 479.

9. P. G. Bain, L. Mann, and A. Pirola-Merlo, "The Innovation Imperative: The Relationships Between Team Climate, Innovation, and Performance in Research and Development Teams," *Small Group Research* 32 (2001): 55–73; A. Chang and P. Bordia, "A Multidimensional Approach to the Group Cohesion–Group Performance Relationship," *Small Group Research* 32 (2001): 379–405.

10. S. B. Fiechtner and E. A. Davis, "Why Some Groups Fail: A Survey of Students' Experiences with Learning Groups," in A. Goodsell, M. Maher, and V. Tinto, eds., *Collaborative Learning: A Sourcebook for Higher Education* (University Park, PA: National Center on Postsecondary Teaching, Learning, and Assessment (NCTLA), 1992) 59–67.

11. J. D. Shaw, "The Salieri Syndrome: Consequences of Envy in Groups," *Small Group Research* 31 (2000): 3–23.

12. C. A. Bowers, J. A. Pharmer, and E. Salas, "When Member Homogeneity Is Needed in Work Teams," *Small Group Research* 31 (2000): 305–27.

13. C. M. Anderson, M. M. Martin, and B. L. Riddle, "Small Group Relational Satisfaction Scale: Development, Reliability and Validity," *Communication Studies* 52 (2001): 220–23.

14. C. M. Mason and M. A. Griffin, "Identifying Group Task Satisfaction at Work," *Small Group Research* 34 (2003): 413–42.

15. E. G. Bormann, *Discussion and Group Methods: Theory and Practice,* 2nd ed. (New York: Harper & Row, 1975) 162–63.

16. R. E. de Vries, B. van den Hoof, and J. A. de Ridder, "Explaining Knowledge Sharing: The Role of Communication Styles, Job Satisfaction, and Performance Beliefs," *Communication Research* 33 (2006): 115–35.

17. G. C. Homans, *The Human Group* (New York: Harcourt Brace, 1992).

18. P. Chansler, P. Swamidass, and C. Cammann, "Self-Managing Work Teams: An Empirical Study of Group Cohesiveness in 'Natural Work Teams' at a Harley-Davidson Motor Company Plant," *Small Group Research* 34 (2003): 101–20.

19. A. P. Hare, *Handbook of Small Group Research,* 2nd ed. (New York: Free Press, 1976) 345.

20. J. A. Bonito, "The Effect of Contributing Substantively on Perceptions of Participation," *Small Group Research* 31 (2000): 528–53.

21. B. Prasad and D. A. Harrison, "Ties, Leaders, and Time in Teams: Strong Inference About Network Structure's Effects on Team Viability and Performance," *Academy of Management Journal* 49 (2006): 49–68.

22. M. G. Cruz, F. W. Boster, and J. I. Rodriguez, "The Impact of Group Size and Proportion of Shared Information on the Exchange and Integration of Information in Groups," *Communication Research* 24 (1997): 291–313.

23. B. Mullen, T. Anthony, E. Salas, and J. E. Driskell, "Group Cohesiveness and Quality of Decision Making," *Small Group Research* 25 (1994): 189–204.

24. H. A. Thelen, "Group Dynamics in Instruction: Principle of Least Group Size," *School Review* 57 (1949): 139–48.

25. C. W. Langfred, "Is Group Cohesiveness a Double-Edged Sword? An Investigation of the Effects of Cohesiveness on Performance," *Small Group Research* 29 (1998): 124–43.

26. S. J. Adams, S. G. Roch, and R. Ayman, "Communication Medium and Member Familiarity: The Effects on Decision Time, Accuracy, and Satisfaction," *Small Group Research* 36 (2005): 321–53.

27. J. C. Pearson and P. E. Nelson, *An Introduction to Human Communication* (Madison, WI: Brown and Benchmark, 1997).

28. Bormann, *Discussion and Group Methods* 145.

29. Bormann, *Discussion and Group Methods* 144–45.

30. D. Cartwright and A. Zander, *Group Dynamics: Research and Theory,* 3rd ed. (New York: Harper & Row, 1968) 104.

31. Hare, *Handbook of Small Group Research* 340.

32. C. Burningham and M. A. West, "Individual, Climate, and Group Interaction Processes as Predictors of Work Team Innovation," *Small Group Research* 26 (1995): 106–17.

33. B. H. Spitzberg, "Intercultural Communication Competence," in L. A. Samovar and R. E. Porter, *Intercultural Communication* (Belmont, CA: Wadsworth, 1997) 354.

34. C. M. Anderson and M. M. Martin, "The Effects of Communication Motives, Interaction, Involvement, and Loneliness on Satisfaction: A Model of Small Groups," *Small Group Research* 26 (1995): 119.

CHAPTER 6

1. J. Coupland, "Small Talk: Social Function," *Research on Language and Social Interaction* 36 (2003): 1–6; M. M. Step and M. O. Finucane, "Interpersonal Communication Motives in Everyday Interactions," *Communication Quarterly* 50 (2002): 93–100.

2. D. Tannen, *You Just Don't Understand: Women and Men in Conversation* (New York: Ballantine, 1995) 24.

3. L. Rehling, "Improving Teamwork through Awareness of Conversational Styles," *Business Communication Quarterly* 67 (2004): 475–82.

4. Rehling, "Improving Teamwork."

5. S. D. Johnson and C. Bechler, "Examining the Relationship Between Listening Effectiveness and Leadership Emergence: Perceptions, Behavior, and Recall," *Small Group Research* 29 (1998): 452–71; R. W. Young and C. M. Cates, "Emotional and Directive Listening in Peer Mentoring," *International Journal of Listening* 18 (2004): 21–33; also see, D. A. Romig, *Side by Side Leadership* (Marietta, GA: Bard, 2001).

6. For support of the validity and reliability of the Listening Styles Profile, see D. L. Worthington, "Exploring the Relationship between Listening Style Preference and Personality," *International Journal of Listening* 17 (2003): 68–87; also see J. B. Weaver, K. W. Watson, and L. L. Barker, "Individual Differences in Listening Styles: Do You Hear What I Hear?" *Personality and Individual Differences* 20 (1996): 381–87; S.

Sargent, J. B. Weaver, and C. Kiewitz, "Correlates between Communication Apprehension and Listening Style Preferences," *Communication Research Reports* 14 (1997): 74–78; M. K. Johnston, J. B. Weaver, K. W. Watson, and L. B. Barker, "Listening Styles: Biological or Psychological Differences?" *International Journal of Listening* 14 (2000): 32–46.

7. L. L. Barker and K. W. Watson, *Listen Up* (New York: St. Martin's Press, 2000); also see M. Imhof, "Who Are We as We Listen? Individual Listening Profiles in Varying Contexts," *International Journal of Listening* 18 (2004): 36–45.

8. B. J. Allen, "Diversity and Organizational Communication," *Journal of Applied Communication Research* 23 (1995): 143–55.

9. R. Leonard and D. C. Locke, "Communication Stereotypes: Is Interracial Communication Possible?" *Journal of Black Studies* 23 (1993): 332–43.

10. M. Imhof, "How to Listen More Efficiently: Self-Monitoring Strategies in Listening," *International Journal of Listening* 17 (2003): 2–19.

11. K. K. Halone and L. L. Pecchioni, "Relational Listening: A Grounded Theoretical Model," *Communication Reports* 14 (2001): 59–71.

12. A. Mehrabian, *Nonverbal Communication* (Chicago: Aldine Atherton, 1972) 108.

13. V. Brown, M. Tumeo, T. S. Larey, and P. B. Paulus, "Modeling Cognitive Interactions During Group Brainstorming," *Small Group Research* 4 (1998) 495–536.

14. R. L. Birdwhistell, *Kinesics and Context* (Philadelphia: U. of Pennsylvania, 1970). For a comprehensive review of nonverbal communication in small groups, see S. M. Ketrow, "Missing Link: Nonverbal Messages in Group Communication Research," paper presented at the annual meeting of the Speech Communication Association, November 1994.

15. For an excellent literature review of nonverbal communication and groups, see S. M. Ketrow, "Nonverbal Aspects of Group Communication," in L. Frey, ed., *The Handbook of Group Communication Theory and Research* (Thousand Oaks, CA: Sage, 1999): 251–87.

16. P. Ekman and W. V. Friesen, "The Repertoire of Nonverbal Behavior: Categories, Origins, Usage, and Coding," *Semiotica* 1 (1969): 49–98.

17. W. S. Condon and W. D. Ogston, "Soundfilm Analysis of Normal and Pathological Behavior Patterns," *Journal of Nervous and Mental Disease* 143 (1966): 338–47.

18. P. Ekman and W. V. Friesen, "Hand Movements," *Journal of Communication* 22 (1972): 353–74. See also P. E. R. Bitti and I. Poggi, "Symbolic Nonverbal Behavior: Talking Through Gestures," in R. S. Feldman and B. Rime, eds., *Fundamentals of Nonverbal Behavior* (Cambridge, England: Cambridge, 1991).

19. M. Argyle and A. Kendon, "The Experimental Analysis of Social Performance," in L. Berkowitz, ed., *Advances in Experimental Social Psychology*, vol. 3 (New York: Academic Press, 1967) 55–98.

20. M. L. Knapp and J. A Hall, *Nonverbal Communication in Human Interaction* (Fort Worth, TX: Harcourt Brace, 1997) 297.

21. A. Kendon, "Some Functions of Gaze-Direction in Social Interaction," *Acta Psychologica* 26 (1967): 22–63.

22. A. Kalma, "Hierarchisation and Dominance Assessment at First Glance," *European Journal of Social Psychology* 21 (1991): 165–81.

23. A. Kalma, "Gazing in Triads: A Powerful Signal in Floor Apportionment," *British Journal of Social Psychology* 31 (1992): 21–39.

24. P. Ekman and W. V. Friesen, *Unmasking the Face* (Englewood Cliffs, NJ: Prentice Hall, 1975).

25. P. Ekman, W. V. Friesen, and S. S. Tompkins, "Facial Affect Scoring Technique: A First Validity Study," *Semiotica* 3 (1971): 35–38; Eckman and Friesen, *Unmasking the Face.*

26. G. Baker, "The Effects of Synchronous Collaborative Technologies on Decision Making: A Study of Virtual Teams," *Information Resources Management Journal* 15 (2002): 79–93.

27. K. K. Sereno and G. J. Hawkins, "The Effect of Variations in Speakers' Nonfluency upon Audience Ratings of Attitude toward the Speech Topic and Speakers' Credibility," *Speech Monographs* 34 (1967): 58–64; G. R. Miller and M. A. Hewgill, "The Effect of Variations in Nonfluency on Audience Ratings of Source Credibility," *Quarterly Journal of Speech* 50 (1964): 36–44.

28. J. R. Davitz, *The Communication of Emotional Meaning* (New York: McGraw-Hill, 1964). See also A. Kappas, U. Hess, and K. R. Scherer, "Voice and Emotion," in R. S. Feldman and B. Rime, eds., *Fundamentals of Nonverbal Behavior* (Cambridge, England: Cambridge, 1991).

29. Baker, "The Effects of Synchronous Collaborative Technologies."

30. J. K. Burgoon, "Spatial Relationships in Small Groups," in R. Y. Hirokawa, R. S. Cathcart, L. A. Samovar, and L. D. Henman, eds., *Small Group Communication: Theory and Practice* (Los Angeles: Roxbury, 2003) 85–96.

31. E. T. Hall, *The Hidden Dimension* (Garden City, NY: Doubleday, 1966); also see R. Sommer, "Studies in Personal Space," *Sociometry* 22 (1959): 247–60; N. M. Henley, *Body Politics: Power, Sex and Nonverbal Communication* (Englewood Cliffs, NJ: Prentice Hall, 1977).

32. A. Mehrabian, "Significance of Posture and Position in the Communication of Attitude and Status Relationships," *Psychological Bulletin* 71 (1960): 363.

33. B. Steinzor, "The Spatial Factors in Face-to-Face Discussion Groups," *Journal of Abnormal and Social Psychology* 45 (1950): 552–55.

34. R. L. Michelini, R. Passalacqua, and J. Cusimano, "Effects of Seating Arrangements on Group Participation," *Journal of Social Psychology* 99 (1976): 179–86.

35. C. H. Silverstein and D. J. Stang, "Seating Position and Interaction in Triads: A Field Study," *Sociometry* (1976): 166–70.

36. L. T. Howells and S. W. Becker, "Seating Arrangements and Leadership Emergence," *Journal of Abnormal and Social Psychology* 64 (1962): 148–50.

37. F. Strodtbeck and L. Hook, "The Social Dimensions of a Twelve Man Jury Table," *Sociometry* 36 (1973): 424–29; A. Hare and R. Bales, "Seating Position and Small-Group Interaction," *Sociometry* 26 (1963): 480–86.

38. M. Dosey and M. Meisels, "Personal Space and Self Protection," *Journal of Personality and Social Psychology* 11 (1969): 93–97.

39. R. Sommer, "Studies in Personal Space," *Sociometry* 22 (1959): 247–60.

40. M. Cook, "Experiments on Orientation and Proxemics," *Human Relations* 23 (1970): 61–70.

41. J. E. Singer, "The Use of Manipulative Strategies: Machiavellianism and Attractiveness," *Sociometry* 27 (1964): 128–51; J. Kelly, "Dress as Non-Verbal Communication," paper presented at the annual conference of the American Association for Public Opinion Research, May 1969; M. Lefkowitz, R. Blake, and J. Mouton, "Status Factors in Pedestrian Violation of Traffic Signals," *Journal of Abnormal and Social Psychology* 51 (1955): 704–06; J. Mills and E. Aronson, "Opinion Change as a Function of the Communicator's Attractiveness and Desire to Influence," *Journal of Social Psychology* 1 (1965): 73–77. See also D. Leathers, *Successful Nonverbal Communication* (Boston: Allyn and Bacon, 1997).

42. J. O'Connor, "The Relationship of Kinesics and Verbal Communication to Leadership Perception in Small Group Discussion" (Ph.D. diss., Indiana University, 1971).

43. J. Baird, "Some Nonverbal Elements of Leadership Emergence," *Southern Speech Communication Journal* 40 (1977): 352–61; see also L. M. Childs et al., "Nonverbal and Verbal Communication of Leadership," paper presented at the annual meeting of the American Psychological Association, Los Angeles, 1981.

44. L. M. Van Swol, "The Effects of Nonverbal Mirroring on Perceived Persuasiveness, Agreement with an Imitator, and Reciprocity in a Group Discussion," *Communication Research* 30 (2003): 461–80.

45. A. Mehrabian and M. Williams, "Nonverbal Concomitants of Perceived and Intended Persuasiveness," *Journal of Personality and Social Psychology* 13 (1969): 37–58.

46. M. Reece and R. Whitman, "Expressive Movements, Warmth, and Verbal Reinforcement," *Journal of Abnormal and Social Psychology* 64 (1962): 234–36.

47. M. L. Knapp, R. P. Hart, G. W. Friedrich, and G. Schulman, "The Rhetoric of Goodbye: Verbal and Nonverbal Correlates of Human Leave-Taking," *Speech Monographs* 40 (1975): 182–98.

48. J. K. Burgoon, L. A. Stern, and L. Dillman, *Interpersonal Adaptation: Dyadic Interaction Patterns* (Cambridge, England: Cambridge, 1995); see also J. K. Burgoon, D. Buller, and W. G. Woodall, *Nonverbal Communication: The Unspoken Dialogue* (New York: McGraw-Hill, 1996).

49. W. S. Condon and L. W. Sander, "Neonate Movement Is Synchronized with Adult Speech: Interactional Participation and Language Acquisition," *Science* I (January 1974): 99–101; Condon and Ogston, "Soundfilm Analysis of Normal and Pathological Behavior Patterns."

50. A. Kendon, "Some Relationships between Body Motion and Speech: An Analysis of an Example," in A. W. Siegman and B. Pope, eds., *Studies in Dyadic Communication* (Elmsford, NY: Pergamon, 1972); see also F. J. Bernieri and R. Rosenthal, "Interpersonal Coordination: Behavior Matching and Interactional Synchrony," in R. S. Feldman and B. Rimes, eds., *Fundamentals of Nonverbal Behavior* (Cambridge, England: Cambridge, 1991).

51. D. Navarre and C. A. Emihovich, "Movement Synchrony and Self-Analytic Group," paper presented at the Eastern Communication Association, Boston, 1978.

52. E. A. Mabry, "Developmental Aspects of Nonverbal Behavior in Small Group Settings," *Small Group Behavior* 20 (May 1989): 190–202.

53. P. Ekman and W. V. Friesen, "Nonverbal Leakage and Clues to Deception," *Psychiatry* 32 (1969): 88–106.

54. Knapp and Hall, *Nonverbal Communication* 313.

55. J. Siegel, V. Dubrovsky, S. Kiesler, and T. W. McGuire, "Group Processes in Computer-Mediated Communication," *Organizational Behavior and Human Decision Processes* 33 (1986): 157–87; P. Bordia, N. DiFonzo, and A. Chang, "Rumor as Group Problem Solving: Development Patterns in Informal Computer-Mediated Groups," *Small Group Research* 30 (1999): 8–28.

56. S. G. Straus, "Testing Typology of Tasks: An Empirical Validation of McGrath's (1984) Group Task Circumplex," *Small Group Research* 30 (1999): 166–87.

57. A. Mehrabian, *Silent Messages* (Belmont, CA: Wadsworth, 1981) 108.

CHAPTER 7

1. G. Kraus, "The Psychodynamics of Constructive Aggression in Small Groups," *Small Group Research* 28 (1997): 122–45.

2. S. M. Farmer and J. Roth, "Conflict-Handling Behavior in Work Groups: Effects of Group Structure, Decision Processes, and Time," *Small Group Research* 29 (1998): 669–713.

3. W. W. Wilmot and J. L. Hocker, *Interpersonal Conflict* (New York: McGraw-Hill, 2007) 8.

4. M. Burgoon, J. K. Heston, and J. McCroskey, *Small Group Communication: A Functional Approach* (New York: Holt, Rinehart & Winston, 1974) 76.

5. O. Dahlback, "A Conflict Theory of Group Risk Taking," *Small Group Research* 34 (2003): 251–89.

6. B. A. Fisher, "Decision Emergence: Phases in Group Decision-Making," *Speech Monographs* 37 (1970): 60.

7. K. A. Jehn and E. A. Mannix, "The Dynamic Nature of Conflict: A Longitudinal Study of Intragroup Conflict and Group Performance," *Academy of Management Journal* 44 (April 2001): 238–52.

8. J. Li and D. C. Hambrick, "Factional Groups: A New Vantage on Demographic Faultlines, Conflict, and Disintegration in Work Teams," *Academy of Management Journal* 48 (2005): 794–813.

9. V. D. Wall and L. L. Nolan, "Small Group Conflict: A Look at Equity, Satisfaction, and Styles of Conflict-Management," *Small Group Behavior* 18 (May 1987): 188–211.

10. M. Nussbaum, M. Singer, R. Rosas, M. Castillo, E. Flies, R. Lara, and R. Sommers, "Decision Support System for Conflict Diagnosis in Personnel Selection," *Information & Management* 36 (1999): 55–62.

11. Portions of the following discussion of misconceptions about conflict were adapted from R. J. Doolittle, *Orientations to Communication and Conflict* (Chicago: Science Research Associates, 1976) 7–9.

12. See F. E. Jandt, ed., *Conflict Resolution Through Communication* (New York: Harper & Row, 1973).

13. C. R. Franz and K. G. Jin, "The Structure of Group Conflict in a Collaborative Work Group During Information Systems Development," *Journal of Applied Communication Research* 23 (1995): 108–27.

14. Doolittle, *Orientations to Communication* 8.

15. G. R. Miller and M. Steinberg, *Between People: New Analysis of Interpersonal Communication* (Chicago: Science Research Associates, 1975) 264.

16. S. D. Johnson and C. Bechler, "Examining the Relationship Between Listening Effectiveness and Leadership Emergence: Perceptions, Behaviors, and Recall," *Small Group Research* 29 (1998): 452–71.

17. Miller and Steinberg, *Between People.*

18. J. Sell, M. J. Lovaglia, E. A. Mannix, C. D. Samuelson, and R. K. Wilson, "Investigating Conflict, Power, and Status Within and Among Groups," *Small Group Research* 35 (2004): 44–72.

19. D. J. Devine, "Effects of Cognitive Ability, Task Knowledge, Information Sharing, and Conflict on Group Decision-Making Effectiveness," *Small Group Research* 30 (1999): 608–34.

20. B. M. Gayle and R. W. Preiss, "Assessing Emotionality in Organizational Conflicts," *Management Communication Quarterly* 12 (1998): 280–302; A. Ostell, "Managing Dysfunctional Emotions in Organizations," *Journal of Management Studies* 33 (1996): 525–57.

21. K. Lovelace, "Maximizing Cross-Functional New Product Teams' Innovativeness and Constraint Adherence: A Conflict Communications Perspective," *Academy of Management Journal* 44 (April 2001): 179–94; M. A. Von Glinow, D. L. Shapiro, and J. M. Brett, "Can We Talk, and Should We? Managing Emotional Conflict in Multicultural Teams," *Academy of Management Review* 29 (2004): 578–92.

22. V. Schei and J. K. Rognes, "Small Group Negotiation: When Members Differ in Motivational Orientation," *Small Group Research* 36 (2005): 289–320.

23. S. Ting-Toomey, "Toward a Theory of Conflict and Culture," in W. Gudykunst, L. Stewart, and S. Ting-Toomey, eds., *Communication, Culture, and Organizational Processes* (Beverly Hills, CA: Sage, 1985).

24. S. Ting-Toomey, "A Face Negotiation Theory," in Y. Kim and W. Gudykunst, eds., *Theories in Intercultural Communication* (Newbury Park, CA: Sage, 1988).

25. Ting-Toomey, "Conflict and Culture."

26. See also an excellent review of conflict and culture research in W. B. Gudykunst, *Bridging Difference: Effective Intergroup Communication* (Newbury Park, CA: Sage, 1994).

27. Ting-Toomey, "A Face Negotiation Theory."

28. For an excellent review of conflict and gender, see M. Argyle, *The Psychology of Interpersonal Behavior* (London: Penguin Books, 1994).

29. R. Rodriguez, "Challenging Demographic Reductionism: A Pilot Study Investigating Diversity in Group Composition," *Small Group Research* 26 (1998): 744–59.

30. L. Karakowsky and J. P. Siegel, "The Effects of Proportional Representation on Intragroup Behavior in Mixed-Race Decision-Making Groups," *Small Group Research* 30 (1999): 259–79.

31. T. A. Timmerman, "Racial Diversity, Age Diversity, Interdependence, and Team Performance," *Small Group Research* 31 (2000): 592–606.

32. Lovelace, "New Product Teams' Innovativeness and Constraint Adherence."

33. R. Kilmann and K. Thomas, "Interpersonal Conflict-Handling Behavior as Reflections of Jungian Personality Dimensions," *Psychological Reports* 37 (1975): 971–80.

34. U. Becker-Beck, "Methods for Diagnosing Interaction Strategies: An Application to Group Interaction in Conflict Situations," *Small Group Research* 32 (2001): 259–82.

35. T. M. Brown and C. E. Miller, "Communication Networks in Task-Performing Groups: Effects of Task Complexity, Time Pressure, and Interpersonal Dominance," *Small Group Research* 31 (2000): 131–57.

36. D. Romig, *Side-by-Side Leadership: Achieving Outstanding Results Together*, (Austin, TX: Bard Press, 2001).

37. A. Sinclair, "The Effects of Justice and Cooperation on Team Effectiveness," *Small Group Research* 34 (2003): 74–100.

38. C. Kirchmeyer and A. Cohen, "Multicultural Groups," *Group & Organization Management* 17 (June 1992): 153–70; C. L. Wong, D. Tjosvold, and F. Lee, "Managing Conflict in a Diverse Work Force: A Chinese Perspective in North America," *Small Group Research* 23 (August 1992): 302–21.

39. D. Cramer, "Linking Conflict Management Behaviors and Relational Satisfaction: The Intervening Role of Conflict Outcome Satisfaction," *Journal of Social and Personal Relationships* 19 (2000): 425–32.

40. D. Weider-Hatfield and J. D. Hatfield, "Superiors' Conflict Management Strategies and Subordinate Outcomes," *Management Communication Quarterly* 10 (1996): 189–208; also see P. J. Carnevale and T. M. Probst, "Social Values and Social Conflict in Creative Problem Solving Categorization,"

Journal of Personality and Social Psychology 74 (1998): 1300–09.

41. R. Fisher and W. Ury, *Getting to Yes: Negotiating Agreement without Giving In* (Boston: Houghton Mifflin, 1991).

42. See J. L. Hocker and W. W. Wilmot, *Interpersonal Conflict-Management* (New York: McGraw-Hill, 2007); Fisher and Ury, *Getting to Yes;* R. Bolton, *People Skills: How to Assert Yourself, Listen to Others and Resolve Conflict* (New York: Simon & Schuster, 1979) 217; D. A. Romig and L. J. Romig. *Structured Teamwork Guide* (Austin, TX: Performance Resource, 1990); D. A. Romig, *Breakthrough Teamwork: Outstanding Results Using Structured Teamwork* (New York: Irwin, 1996).

43. J. Gottman, C. Notarius, J. Gonso, and H. Markman, *A Couple's Guide to Communication* (Champaign, IL: Research Press, 1976).

44. Hocker and Wilmot, *Interpersonal Conflict-Management.*

45. R. A. Meyers and D. E. Brashers, "Argument in Group Decision Making: Explicating a Process Model and Investigating the Argument-Outcome Link," *Communication Monographs* 65 (1998): 261–81.

46. Becker-Beck, "Methods for Diagnosing Interaction Strategies."

47. S. M. Miranda, "Avoidance of Groupthink: Meeting Management Using Group Support Systems," *Small Group Communication Research* 25 (February 1994): 105–36.

48. K. Thomas and W. Schmidt, "A Survey of Managerial Interests with Respect to Conflict," *Academy of Management Journal* 19 (1976): 315–18.

49. J. M. Juran, *Juran on Planning for Quality* (New York: Free Press, 1988).

50. Boulton, *People Skills,* 217.

51. Gayle and Preiss, "Assessing Emotionality in Organizational Conflicts."

52. A. Ostell, "Managing Dysfunctional Emotionality in Organizations," *Journal of Management Studies* 33 (1996): 523–57.

53. A. M. Bippus and S. L. Young, "Owning Your Emotions: Reactions to Expressions of Self- versus Other-Attributed Positive and Negative Emotions," *Journal of Applied Communication Research* 33 (2005): 26–45.

54. Becker-Beck, "Methods for Diagnosing Interaction Strategies."

55. R. J. W. Cline, "Detecting Groupthink: Methods for Observing the Illusion of Unanimity," *Communication Quarterly* 38 (Spring 1990): 112–26.

56. W. Safire, "On Language: Groupthink—A Collaborative Search for Coinage," *New York Times Magazine* (August 6, 2004), section 6, p. 16.

57. D. D. Henningsen, M. L. M. Henningsen, J. Eden, and M. G. Cruz, "Examining the Symptoms of Groupthink and Retrospective Sensemaking," *Small Group Research* 37 (2006): 36–64.

58. I. L. Janis, *Victims of Groupthink* (Boston: Houghton Mifflin, 1973).

59. R. K. M. Haurwitz, "Faculty Doubted Bonfire's Stability," *Austin-American Statesman* (December 10, 1999), p. A1.52.

60. R. Y. Hirokawa, D. S. Gouran, and A. Martz, "Understanding the Sources of Faulty Group Decision Making: A Lesson from the Challenger Disaster," *Small Group Behavior* 19 (November 1988): 411–33.

61. D. Jehl, "Panel Unanimous: 'Group Think' Backed Prewar Assumptions, Report Concludes," *New York Times* (July 10, 2004) p. 1; also see *The 9/11 Commission Report: Final Report of the National Commission on Terrorist Attacks Upon the United States* (Washington, DC: National Commission on Terrorist Attacks, 2004).

62. J. F. Veiga, "The Frequency of Self-Limiting Behavior in Groups: A Measure and an Explanation," *Human Relations* 44 (1991): 877–95.

63. M. D. Street. "Groupthink: An Examination of Theoretical Issues, Implications, and Future Research Suggestions," *Small Group Research* 28 (1997): 72–93; M. D. Street and W. P. Anthony, "A Conceptual Framework Establishing the Relationship Between Groupthink and Escalating Commitment Behavior," *Small Group Research* 28 (1997): 267–93; A. A. Mohaned and F. A. Wiebe, "Toward a Process Theory of Groupthink," *Small Group Research* 27 (1996): 416–30; K. Granstrom and D. Stiwne, "A Bipolar Model of Groupthink: An Expansion of Janis's Concept," *Small Group Research* 29 (1998): 32–56; W. Park. "A Comprehensive Empirical Investigation of the Relationships Among Variables in the Groupthink Model," *Journal of Organizational Behavior* 21 (2000): 873–87.

64. Adapted from I. L. Janis, "Groupthink," *Psychology Today* 5 (November 1971): 43–46, 74–76.

65. W. Park, "A Review of Research on Groupthink," *Journal of Behavioral Decision Making* 3 (1990): 229–45; Street, "Groupthink"; Street and Anthony, "A Conceptual Framework."

66. See R. Hotz and N. Miller, "Intergroup Competition, Attitudinal Projection, and Opinion Certainty: Capitalizing on Conflict," *Group Processes and Intergroup Relations* 41 (2001): 61–73.

67. Cline, "Detecting Groupthink."

68. See K. Andersen and T. Clevenger, Jr., "A Summary of Experimental Research in Ethos," *Speech Monographs* 30 (1963): 59–78.

69. C. B. Gibson and T. Saxton, "Thinking Outside the Black Box: Outcomes of Team Decisions with Third-Party Intervention," *Small Group Research* 36 (2005): 208–36.

70. M. A. Dorado, F. J. Medina, L. Munduate, I. F. J. Cisneros, and M. Euwema, "Computer-Mediated Negotiation of an Escalated Conflict," *Small Group Research* 33 (2002): 509–24.

71. A. Zornoza, P. Ripoll, and J. M. Peiro, "Conflict Management in Groups that Work in Two Different Communication Contexts: Face-to-Face and Computer-Mediated Communication," *Small Group Research* 33 (2002): 481–508.

72. M. Montoya-Weiss, A. P. Massey, and M. Song, "Getting It Together: Temporal Coordination and Conflict Management in Global Virtual Teams," *Academy of Management Journal* 44 (December 2001): 1251–62.

73. Miranda, "Avoidance of Groupthink."

74. Miranda, "Avoidance of Groupthink."

75. J. T. Polzer, C. B. Crisp, S. L. Jarvenpaa, and J. W. Kim, "Extending the Faultline Model to Geographically Dispersed Teams: How Colocated Subgroups Can Impair Group Functioning," *Academy of Management Journal* 49 (2006): 659–92.

76. For an excellent discussion of the definition of *consensus*, see M. A. Renz, "The Meaning of Consensus and Blocking for Cohousing Groups," *Small Group Research* 37 (2006): 351–76.

77. R. Y. Hirokawa, "Consensus Group Decision-Making, Quality of Decision and Group Satisfaction: An Attempt to Sort 'Fact' from 'Fiction,'" *Central States Speech Journal* 33 (Summer 1982): 407–15.

78. R. S. DeStephen and R. Y. Hirokawa, "Small Group Consensus: Stability of Group Support of the Decision, Task Process, and Group Relationships," *Small Group Behavior* 19 (May 1988): 227–39.

79. Portions of the following section on consensus were adapted from J. A. Kline, "Ten Techniques for Reaching Consensus in Small Groups," *Air Force Reserve Officer Training Corps Education Journal* 19 (Spring 1977): 19–21.

80. See D. S. Gouran, "Variables Related to Consensus in Group Discussions of Questions of Policy," *Speech Monographs* 36 (August 1969): 385–91; T. J. Knutson, "An Experimental Study of the Effects of Orientation Behavior on Small Group Consensus," *Speech Monographs* 39 (August 1972): 159–65; J. A. Kline, "Orientation and Group Consensus," *Central States Speech Journal* 23 (Spring 1972): 44–47.

81. Gouran, "Variables," 385–91; Knutson, "Experimental Study"; Kline, "Orientation."

82. See Hirokawa, "Consensus Group Decision-Making"; R. Y. Hirokawa, "Discussion Procedures and Decision-Making Performance: A Test of the Functional Perspective," *Human Communication Research* 12 (Winter 1985): 203–24; R. Y. Hirokawa and D. R. Scheerhorn, "Communication in Faulty Group Decision-Making," in R. Y. Hirokawa and M. S. Poole, eds., *Communication and Group Decision-Making* (Beverly Hills, CA: Sage, 1986).

83. Hirokawa, "Consensus Group Decision-Making."

84. See J. A. Kline and J. L. Hullinger, "Redundancy, Self-Orientation, and Group Consensus," *Speech Monographs* 40 (March 1973): 72–74.

85. C. A. VanLear and E. A. Mabry, "Testing Contrasting Interaction Models for Discriminating Between Consensual and Dissentient Decision-Making Groups," *Small Group Research* 30 (1999): 29–58.

86. A. Van Hiel and V. Franssen, "Information Acquisition Bias During the Preparing of Group Discussion: A Comparison of Prospective Minority and Majority Members," *Small Group Research* 34 (2003): 557–74.

87. See H. W. Riecken, "The Effect of Talkativeness on Ability to Influence Group Solutions of Problems," *Sociometry* 21 (1958): 309–21.

88. R. C. Pace, "Communication Patterns in High and Low Consensus Discussion: A Descriptive Analysis," *Southern Speech Communication Journal* 53 (Winter 1988): 184–202.

89. VanLear and Mabry, "Testing Contrasting Interaction Models."

90. A. Zornoza, P. Ripoll, and J. M. Peiro, "Conflict Management in Groups that Work in Two Different Communication Contexts: Face-to-Face and Computer-Mediated Communication," *Small Group Research* 33 (2002): 481–508.

91. S. Mohammed and E. Ringseis, "Cognitive Diversity and Consensus in Group Decision Making: The Role of Inputs, Processes, and Outcomes," *Organizational Behavior and Human Decision Processes* 85 (July 2001): 310–35.

92. J. W. Pfeiffer and J. E. Jones, eds., *A Handbook of Structured Experiences for Human Relations Training*, vol. 2 (La Jolla, CA: University Associates, 1974) 62–67.

CHAPTER 8

1. M. Schittekatte and A. Van Hiel, "Effects of Partially Shared Information and Awareness of Unshared Information on Information Sampling," *Small Group Research* 27 (1996): 431–49.

2. D. A. Romig, *Breakthrough Teamwork: Outstanding Results Using Structured Teamwork* (Chicago: Irwin, 1996); P. R. Scholtes, B. L. Joiner, and B. J. Streibel, *The Team Handbook,* 2nd ed. (Madison, WI: Joiner Associates, 1996).

3. S. Burkhalter, J. Gastil, and T. Kelshaw, "A Conceptual Definition and Theoretical Model of Public Deliberation in Small Face-to-Face Groups," *Communication Theory* (November 2002): 398–422; C. Pavitt, "Does Communication Matter in Social Influence During Small Group Discussion? Five Positions," *Communication Studies* 44 (1993): 216–27.

4. D. D. Stewart and G. Stasser, "Expert Role Assignment and Information Sampling During Collective Recall and Decision Making," *Journal of Personality and Social Psychology* 69 (1995): 619–28; also see D. D. Stewart, "Stereotypes, Negativity Bias, and the Discussion of Unshared Information in Decision-Making Groups," *Small Group Research* 29 (1998): 643–68; J. R. Larson, Jr., "Modeling the Entry of Shared and Unshared Information into Group Discussion: A Review and BASIC Language Computer Program," *Small Group Research* 28 (1997): 454–79; G. Stasser, "Pooling of Unshared Information During Group Discussion," in S. Worchel, W. Wood, and J. A. Simpson (eds.), *Group Process and Productivity* (Newbury Park, CA: Sage, 1992) 48–67; D. D. Henningsen and M. L. M. Henningsen, "The Effect of Individual Difference Variables on Information Sharing in Decision-Making Groups," *Human Communication Research* 30 (2004): 540–55.

5. G. M. Wittenbaum, A. B. Hollingshead, and I. C. Botero, "From Cooperative to Motivated Information Sharing in Groups: Moving Beyond the Hidden Profile Paradigm," *Communication Monographs* 71 (2004): 286–310; A. D. Galinsky and L. J. Kray, "From Thinking About What Might Have Been to Sharing What We Know: The Effects of Counterfactual Mind-Sets on Information Sharing in Groups," *Journal of Experimental Social Psychology* 40 (2004): 606–18.

6. Henningsen and Henningsen, "The Effect of Individual Difference Variables." For an excellent review of the literature on information sharing in small groups see J. A. Bonito, "A Local Model of Information Sharing in Small Groups," *Communication Theory* 17 (2007): 252–80.

7. T. M. Franz and J. R. Larson, "The Impact of Experts on Information Sharing During Group Discussion," *Small Group Research* 33, 4 (2002): 383–411.

8. J. R. Spoor and J. R. Kelly, "The Evolutionary Significance of Effect in Groups: Communication and Group Bonding," *Group Processes & Intergroup Relations* 7 (2004): 398–412.

9. K. B. Dahlin, L. R. Weingart, and P. J. Hinds, "Team Diversity and Information Use," *Academy of Management Journal* 48 (2005): 1107–23.

10. Burkhalter, Gastil, and Kelshaw, "A Conceptual Definition and Theoretical Model."

11. D. D. Chrislip and C. E. Larson, *Collaborative Leadership* (San Francisco: Jossey-Bass, 1994); J. R. Katzenback and D. K. Smith, *The Wisdom of Teams: Creating the High-Performance Organization* (New York: HarperBusiness, 1993); Romig, *Breakthrough Teamwork*.

12. L. A. Perlow, G. A. Okhuysen, and N. P. Repenning, "The Speed Trap: Exploring the Relationship Between Decision Making and Temporal Context," *Academy of Management Journal* 45 (October 2002): 931–35.

13. S. Covey, *The Seven Habits of Highly Effective People* (New York: Simon and Schuster, 1989).

14. J. Kruger and M. Evans, "If You Don't Want to be Late, Enumerate: Unpacking Reduces the Planning Fallacy," *Journal of Experimental Social Psychology* 40 (2004): 586–98.

15. R. Buehler, D. Messervey, and D. Griffin, "Collaborative Planning and Prediction: Does Group Discussion Affect Optimistic Biases in Time Estimation?" *Organizational Behavior and Human Decision Processes* 97 (2005): 47–63.

16. S. N. Fraidin, "When Is One Head Better Than Two? Interdependent Information in Group Decision Making," *Organizational Behavior and Human Decision Processes* 9 (2004): 102–13.

17. J. Campbell and G. Stasser, "The Influence of Time and Task Demonstrability on Decision-Making in Computer-Mediated and Face-to-Face Groups," *Small Group Research* 37 (2006): 271–94.

18. Fraidin, "When Is One Head Better than Two?"

19. C. Pavitt, M. Philipp, and K. K. Johnson, "Who Owns a Group's Proposals: The Initiator or the Group as a Whole?" *Communication Research Reports* 21 (2004): 221–30.

20. R. F. Bales, *Personality and Interpersonal Behavior* (New York: Holt, Rinehart and Winston, 1970).

21. G. E. Schrah, R. S. Dalal, and J. A. Sniezek, "No Decision-Maker Is an Island: Integrating Expert Advice with Information Acquisition," *Journal of Behavioral Decision Making* 19 (2006): 43–60.

22. R. E. de Vries, B. van den Hooff, J. A. de Ridder, "Explaining Knowledge Sharing: The Role of Team Communication Styles, Job Satisfaction, and Performance Beliefs, *Communication Research* 33 (2006): 115–35.

23. C. Saunders and S. Miranda, "Information Acquisition in Group Decision Making," *Information and Management* 34 (1998): 55–74.

24. E. G. Bormann, *Discussion and Group Methods: Theory and Practice* (New York: Harper & Row, 1969). For an excellent discussion about each of the four types of discussion questions, see D. S. Gouran, "Reflections on the Type of Question as a Determinant of the Form of Interaction in Decision-Making and Problem-Solving Discussions," *Communication Quarterly* 51 (2003): 111–25.

25. Gouran, "Reflections on the Type of Question."

26. Gouran, "Reflections on the Type of Question."

27. D. S. Gouran, *Discussion: The Process of Group Decision-Making* (New York: Harper & Row, 1974) 72.

28. A. B. Pettus, "The Verdict Is In: A Study of Jury Decision-Making Factors, Moment of Personal Decision, and Jury Deliberations—From the Jurors' Point of View," *Communication Quarterly* 38 (Winter 1990): 83–97.

29. N. Karelaia, "Thirst for Confirmation in Multi-Attribute Choice: Does Search for Consistency Impair Decision Performance?" *Organizational Behavior and Human Decision Processes* 100 (2006): 128–43.

30. E. K. Aranda, L. Aranda, and K. Conlon, *Teams: Structure, Process, Culture, and Politics* (Englewood Cliffs, NJ: Prentice-Hall, 1998).

CHAPTER 9

1. D. S. Gouran and R. Y. Hirokawa, "Functional Theory and Communication in Decision-Making and Problem-Solving Groups: An Expanded View," in R. Y. Hirokawa and M. S. Poole, eds., *Communication and Group Decision Making* (Thousand Oaks, CA: Sage, 1996) 55–80; D. S. Gouran, R. Y. Hirokawa, K. M. Julian, and G. B. Leatham, "The Evolution and Current Status of the Functional Perspective on Communication in Decision-Making and Problem-Solving Groups," in S. A. Deetz, ed., *Communication Yearbook* 16 (Newbury Park, CA: Sage, 1993) 573–600; E. E. Graham, M. J. Papa, and M. B. McPherson, "An Applied Test of the Functional Communication Perspective of Small Group Decision Making," *The Southern Communication Journal* 62 (1997): 169–279.

2. B. R. Newell, T. Rakow, N. J. Weston, and D. R. Shanks, "Search Strategies in Decision Making: The Success of 'Success,'" *Journal of Behavioral Decision Making* 17 (2004): 117–37.

3. Gouran and Hirokawa, "Functional Theory," 69.

4. See J. K. Brilhart and G. Galanes, *Communicating in Groups* (Madison, WI: Brown & Benchmark, 1997) 256; D. W. Johnson and F. P. Johnson, *Joining Together: Group Theory and Group Skills* (Englewood Cliffs, NJ: Prentice Hall, 1987) 99–104.

5. R. Prislin, W. M. Limbert, and E. Bauer, "From Majority to Minority and Vice Versa: The Asymmetrical Effects of Losing and Gaining Majority Position within a Group," *Journal of Personality and Social Psychology* 79, 3 (2000): 385–97.

6. R. Y. Hirokawa and D. R. Scheerhorn, "Communication in Faulty Group Decision-Making," in R. Y. Hirokawa and M. S. Poole, *Communication and Group Decision Making* (Beverly Hills, CA: Sage, 1986) 67.

7. D. A. Rettinger and R. Hastie, "Content Effects on Decision Making," *Organizational Behavior and Human Decision Processes* 85 (July 2001): 336–59.

8. Hirokawa and Scheerhorn, "Communication in Faulty Group Decision-Making."

9. A. R. Dennis, "Information Exchange and Use in Small Group Decision Making," *Small Group Research* 27 (1996): 532–50; see also G. M. Wittenbaum, "Information Sampling in Decision-Making Groups: The Impact of Members' Task-Relevant Status," *Small Group Research* 29 (1998): 57–84; K. M. Propp, "Information Utilization in Small Group Decision Making: A Study of the Evaluation Interaction Model," *Small Group Research* 28 (1997): 424–53.

10. O. S. Chernyshenko, A. G. Miner, M. R. Baumann, and J. A. Sniezek, "The Impact of Information Distribution, Ownership, and Discussion on Group Member Judgment: The Differential Cue Weighting Model," *Organizational Behavior and Human Decision Processes* 91 (2003): 12–25.

11. C. Gonzalez, "Decision Support for Real-Time, Dynamic Decision-Making Tasks," *Organizational Behavior and Human Decision Processes* 96 (2005): 142–54.

12. J. G. Oetzel, "Explaining Individual Communication Processes in Homogeneous and Heterogeneous Groups Through Individual-Collectivism and Self-Construal," *Human Communication Research* 25 (1998): 202–24.

13. K. H. Price, J. J. Lavelle, A. B. Henley, F. K. Cocchiara, and F. R. Buchanan, "Judging the Fairness of Voice-Based Participation Across Multiple and Interrelated Stages of Decision Making," *Organizational Behavior and Human Decision Processes* 99 (2006): 212–26.

14. B. B. Baltes, M. W. Dickson, M. P. Sherman, C. C. Bauer, and J. S. LaGanke, "Computer-Mediated Communication and Group Decision Making: A Meta-Analysis," *Organizational Behavior and Human Decision Processes* 87 (2002): 156–79.

15. M. A. Roberto, "Strategic Decision-Making Processes: Beyond the Efficiency-Consensus Trade-Off," *Group & Organization Management* 29 (2004): 626–58.

16. For a review of the work of Amos Tversky and Daniel Kahneman, see A. Tversky and D. Kahneman, "Judgment Under Uncertainty: Heuristics and Biases," *Science* 27 (September 1974): 1124–31; also see A. Tversky and D. Kahneman, "Rational Choice and the Framing of Decisions," *Journal of Business* 59 (1986): 251–78.

17. C. H. Kepner and B. B. Treogoe, *The Rational Manager* (New York: McGraw-Hill, 1965); see also J. K. Brilhart and G. Galanes, *Effective Group Discussion* (Dubuque, IA: Brown, 1992) 232.

18. We thank Dennis Romig for this observation. For additional information about structuring problem solving in teams, see

D. A. Romig, *Breakthrough Teamwork: Outstanding Results Using Structured Teamwork* (New York: Irwin, 1996).

19. B. J. Broome and L. Fulbright, "A Multistage Influence Model of Barriers to Group Problem Solving: A Participant-Generated Agenda for Small Group Research," *Small Group Research* 26 (February 1995): 24–55.

20. B. Aubrey Fisher, *Small Group Decision Making: Communication and the Group Process,* 2nd ed. (New York: McGraw-Hill, 1980) 132.

21. Fisher, *Small Group Decision Making,* 130.

22. B. Aubrey Fisher, "Decision Emergence: Phases in Group Decision Making," *Speech Monographs* 37 (1970): 60.

23. Fisher, "Decision Emergence," 130–31.

24. E. G. Bormann, *Discussion and Group Methods: Theory and Practice* (New York: Harper & Row, 1969).

25. S. Wheelan, B. Davidson, and T. Felice, "Group Development Across Time: Reality or Illusion?" *Small Group Research* 34, 2 (2003): 223–45.

26. J. A. Bonito, "The Analysis of Participation in Small Groups: Methodological and Conceptual Issues Related to Interdependence," *Small Group Research* 33, 4 (2002): 412–38.

27. For an excellent discussion of dialectical theory, see L. A. Baxter and B. M. Montgomery, *Relating: Dialogues and Dialectics* (New York: Guilford, 1996).

28. L. A. Erbert, G. M. Mearns, and S. Dena, "Perceptions of Turning Points and Dialectical Interpretations in Organizational Team Development," *Small Group Research* 36 (2005): 21–58.

29. T. M. Scheidel and L. Crowell, "Idea Development in Small Discussion Groups," *Quarterly Journal of Speech* 50 (1994): 140–45.

30. For an excellent review of communication technology and group communication, see C. R. Scott, "Communication Technology and Group Communication," in L. Frey, ed., *The Handbook of Group Communication Theory and Research* (Thousand Oaks, CA: Sage, 1999) 432–72; also see N. N. Kamel and R. M. Davison, "Applying CSCW Technology to Overcome Traditional Barriers in Group Interactions," *Information & Management* 34 (1998): 209–19; R. C. W. Kwok and M. Khalifa, "Effects of GSS on Knowledge Acquisition," *Information & Management* 34 (1998): 307–15; B. P. Robichaux and R. B. Cooper, "GSS Participation: A Cultural Examination," *Information & Management* 33 (1998): 287–300; A. Shirani, M. Aiken, and J. G. P. Paolillo, "Group Decision Support Systems and Incentive Structures," *Information & Management* 33 (1998): 231–40; B. A. Jain and J. S. Solomon, "The Effect of Task Complexity and Conflict Handling Styles on Computer-Supported Negotiations," *Information & Management* 37 (2000): 161–68; D. P. Brandon and A. B. Hollingshead, "Collaborative Learning and Computer-Supported Groups," *Communication Education* 48 (1999): 109–26; C. R. Scott, L. Quinn, C. E. Timmerman, and D. M. Garrett, "Ironic Uses of Group Communication Technology: Evidence from Meeting Transcripts and Interviews with Group Decision Support Systems Users," *Communication Quarterly* 46 (1998):

53–74; and K. J. Chun and H. K. Park, "Examining the Conflicting Results of GDSS Research," *Information & Management* 33 (1998): 313–25.

31. C. Pavitt and K. K. Johnson, "The Association Between Group Procedural MOPs and Group Discussion Procedure," *Small Group Research* 32, 5 (2001): 595–624; C. Pavitt and K. K. Johnson, "Scheidel and Crowell Revisited: A Descriptive Study of Group Proposal Sequencing," *Communication Monographs* 69 (March 2002): 19–32.

32. J. E. McGrath, "Time, Interaction, and Performance (TIP): A Theory of Groups," *Small Group Research* 22 (1991): 147–74.

33. C. J. Gersick, "Time and Transition in Work Teams: Toward a New Model of Group Development," *Academy of Management Journal* 32 (1989): 274–309; C. J. Gersick and J. R. Hackman, "Habitual Routines in Task-Performing Groups," *Organizational Behavior and Human Decision Processes* 47 (1990): 65–97.

34. A. Chang, P. Bordia, and J. Duck, "Punctuated Equilibrium and Linear Progression: Toward a New Understanding of Group Development," *Academy of Management Journal* 46 (2003): 106–17.

35. M. S. Poole, "Decision Development in Small Groups, III: A Multiple Sequence Model of Group Decision Development," *Communication Monographs* 50 (December 1983): 321–41.

36. Poole, "Decision Development in Small Groups, III."

37. M. S. Poole, "A Multisequence Model of Group Decision Development," in R. Y. Hirokawa, R. S. Cathcart, L. A. Samovar, and L. D. Henman, eds., *Small Group Communication Theory and Practice: An Anthology* (Los Angeles, CA: Roxbury Publishing Company, 2003).

38. Poole, "A Multisequence Model."

39. Poole, "Decision Development in Small Groups, III."

40. See E. G. Bormann, *Discussion and Group Methods* (New York: Harper & Row, 1975).

41. Poole, "Decision Development in Small Groups, III," 330.

42. G. M. Wittenbaum, A. B. Hollingshead, P. B. Paulus, R. Y. Hirokawa, D. G. Ancona, R. S. Peterson, K. A. Jehn, and K. Yoon, "The Functional Perspective as a Lens for Understanding Groups," *Small Group Research* 35 (2004): 17–43.

43. D. S. Gouran and R. Y. Hirokawa, "Effective Decision Making and Problem Solving in Groups: A Functional Perspective," in R. Y. Hirokawa, R. S. Cathcart, L. A. Samovar, and L. D. Henman, eds., *Small Group Communication Theory and Practice: An Anthology* (Los Angeles, CA: Roxbury Publishing Company, 2003).

44. For a discussion and critique of functional group communication theory, see L. VanderVoort, "Functional and Causal Explanations in Group Communication Research," *Communication Theory* (November 2002): 469–86.

45. R. Y. Hirokawa, "Discussion Procedures and Decision-Making Performance: A Test of a Functional Perspective," *Human Communication Research* 12, 2 (Winter 1985): 203–24; R. Y. Hirokawa and K. Rost, "Effective Group Decision-Making in Organizations: Field Test of the Vigilant Interaction Theory,"

Management Communication Quarterly 5 (1992): 267–88; R. Y. Hirokawa, "Why Informed Groups Make Faulty Decisions: An Investigation of Possible Interaction-Based Explanations," *Small Group Behavior* 18 (1987): 3–29; R. Y. Hirokawa, "Group Communication and Decision-Making Performance: A Continued Test of the Functional Perspective," *Human Communication Research* 14 (Summer 1988): 487–515; M. O. Orlitzky and R. Y. Hirokawa, "To Err Is Human, to Correct for It Divine: A Meta-Analysis of Research Testing the Functional Theory of Group Decision-Making Effectiveness." *Small Group Behavior* 32, 3 (2001): 313–41; R. Y. Hirokawa and A. J. Salazar, "Task-Group Communication and Decision-Making Performance," in L. Frey, ed., *The Handbook of Group Communication Theory and Research* (Thousand Oaks, CA: Sage, 1999) 167–91; D. Gouran and R. Y. Hirokawa, "Functional Theory and Communication in Decision-Making and Problem-Solving Groups: An Expanded View," in R. Y. Hirokawa and M. S. Poole, eds., *Communication and Group Decision Making* (Thousand Oaks, CA: Sage, 1996) 55–80.

46. For a comprehensive discussion of bona fide groups, see L. L. Putnam, "Rethinking the Nature of Groups: A Bona Fide Group Perspective," in R. Y. Hirokawa, R. S. Cathcart, L. A. Samovar, and L. D. Henman, eds., *Small Group Communication Theory and Practice: An Anthology* (Los Angeles, CA: Roxbury Publishing Company, 2003).

47. K. Tas and G. Whyte, "Collective Efficacy and Vigilant Problem Solving in Group Decision Making: A Non-Linear Model," *Organizational Behavior and Human Decision Processes* 96 (2005): 119–29.

48. Orlitzky and Hirokawa, "To Err Is Human, To Correct for It Divine."

49. Graham, Papa, and McPherson, "An Applied Test."

50. K. Barge, *Leadership: Communication Skills for Organizations and Groups* (New York: St. Martin's, 1994).

51. I. L. Janis, *Victims of Groupthink* (Boston: Houghton Mifflin, 1973); I. L. Janis, *Critical Decision: Leadership in Policymaking and Crisis Management* (New York: Free Press, 1989).

52. See R. Y. Hirokawa and R. Pace, "A Descriptive Investigation of the Possible Communication-Based Reasons for Effective and Ineffective Group Decision Making," *Communication Monographs* 50 (December 1983): 363–79. The authors also wish to acknowledge D. A. Romig, Performance Resources, Inc., Austin, Texas, for his contribution to the discussion.

53. K. A. Liljenquist, A. D. Galinsky, and L. J. Kray, "Exploring the Rabbit Hole of Possibilities by Myself or with My Group: The Benefits and Liabilities of Activating Counterfactual Mind-Sets for Information Sharing and Group Coordination," *Journal of Behavioral Decision Making* 17 (2004): 263–79.

54. D. G. Leathers, "Quality of Group Communication as a Determinant of Group Product," *Speech Monographs* 39 (1972): 166–73; R. Y. Hirokawa and D. S. Gouran, "Facilitation of Group Communication: A Critique of Prior Research and an Agenda for Future Research," *Management Communication Quarterly* 3 (August 1989): 71–92.

55. See F. J. Sabatine, "Rediscovering Creativity: Unlearning Old Habits," *Mid-American Journal of Business* 4 (1989): 11–13.

56. Graham, Papa, and McPherson, "An Applied Test."

57. J. R. Spoor and J. R. Kelly, "The Evolutionary Significance of Affect in Groups: Communication and Group Bonding," *Group Processes & Intergroup Relations* 7 (2004): 398–412.

58. D. Ryfe, "Narrative and Deliberation in Small Groups," *Journal of Applied Communication Research* 34 (2006): 72–93; also see Sunwolf, "Decisional Regret Theory: Reducing the Anxiety about Uncertain Outcomes During Group Decision Making through Shared Counterfactual Storytelling," *Communication Studies* 57 (2006): 107–34.

59. Fisher, *Small Group Decision Making*, 130.

60. S. A. Beebe and J. T. Masterson, "Toward a Model of Small Group Communication: Applications for Teaching and Research," *Florida Speech Communication Journal* 8, 2 (1980): 9–15.

61. See A. B. VanGundy, *Techniques of Structured Problem Solving* (New York: Van Nostrand Reinhold, 1981); see also Romig, *Breakthrough Teamwork*.

62. W. E. Jurma, "Effects of Leader Structuring Style and Task Orientation Characteristics of Group Members," *Communication Monographs* 46 (1979): 282–95.

63. S. Jarboe, "A Comparison of Input–Output, Process–Output and Input–Process–Output Models of Small Group Problem-Solving Effectiveness," *Communication Monographs* 55 (June 1988): 121–42; Hirokawa, "Group Communication and Decision-Making Performance."

64. See K. Y. Ng and L. Van Dyne, "Individualism-Collectivism as a Boundary Condition for Effectiveness of Minority Influence in Decision Making," *Organizational Behavior and Human Decision Processes* 84, 2 (March 2001): 198–225.

65. K. Hawkins and C. B. Power, "Gender Differences in Questions Asked During Small Decision-Making Group Discussions," *Small Group Research* 30 (1990): 235–56.

66. This discussion of bridging cultural differences is based on a discussion in S. A. Beebe, S. J. Beebe, and M. V. Redmond, *Interpersonal Communication: Relating to Others* (Boston: Allyn and Bacon, 2002).

67. See W. B. Gudykunst, *Bridging Differences: Effective Intergroup Communication* (Newbury Park, CA: Sage, 1998).

68. Oetzel, "Explaining Individual Communication Processes."

69. T. Reimer, "Attributions for Poor Group Performance as a Predictor of Perspective-Taking and Subsequent Group Achievement: A Process Model," *Group Processes and Intergroup Relations* 4, 1 (2001): 31–47.

70. S. R. Covey, *The 7 Habits of Highly Effective People* (New York: Simon & Schuster, 1989).

71. Johnson and Johnson, *Joining Together*.

72. K. W. Hawkins and B. P. Fillion, "Perceived Communication Skill Needs for Work Groups," *Communication Research Reports* 16 (1999): 167–74.

CHAPTER 10

1. J. K. Brilhart and L. M. Jochem, "Effects of Different Patterns on Outcomes of Problem-Solving Discussion," *Journal of Applied Psychology* 48 (1964): 174–79; W. E. Jurma, "Effects of Leader Structuring Style and Task Orientation Characteristics of Group Members," *Communication Monographs* 49 (1979): 282–95; S. Jarboe, "A Comparison of Input-Output, Process-Output, and Input-Process-Output Models of Small Group Problem-Solving Effectiveness," *Communication Monographs* 55 (June 1988): 121–42; A. B. VanGundy, *Techniques of Structured Problem Solving* (New York: Van Nostrand Reinhold, 1981).

2. J. K. Brilhart and G. J. Galanes, *Effective Group Discussion* (Dubuque, IA: Brown, 1992), J. F. Cragan and D. W. Wright, *Communication in Small Group Discussions* (St. Paul, MN: West, 1986); Brilhart and Jochem, "Effects of Different Patterns on Outcomes of Problem-Solving Discussion"; J. Dewey, *How We Think* (Boston: Heath, 1910); R. C. Huseman, "The Role of the Nominal Group in Small Group Communication," in R. C. Huseman, C. M. Logue, and D. L. Freshley, eds., *Readings in Interpersonal and Organizational Communication*, 3rd ed. (Boston: Holbrook, 1977) 493–507; C. E. Larson, "Forms of Analysis and Small Group Problem Solving," *Speech Monographs* 36 (1969): 452–55; N. R. F. Maier, *Problem Solving and Creativity in Individuals and Groups* (Belmont, CA: Brooks/Cole, 1970); J. H. McBuirney and K. G. Hance, *The Principles and Methods of Discussion* (New York: Harper, 1939); R. S. Ross, *Speech Communication: Fundamentals and Practice* (New York: McGraw-Hill, 1974); D. W. Wright, *Small Group Communication: An Introduction* (Dubuque, IA: Kendall/Hunt, 1975); C. H. Kepner and B. B. Tregoe, *The Rational Manager* (New York: McGraw-Hill, 1965); P. B. Crosby, *The Quality Is Free: The Art of Making Quality Certain* (New York: New American Library, 1979); S. Ingle, *Quality Circles Master Guide: Increasing Productivity with People Power* (Englewood Cliffs, NJ: Prentice-Hall, 1982); K. J. Albert, *How to Solve Business Problems* (New York: McGraw-Hill, 1978); D. L. Dewar, *Quality Circle Leader Manual and Instructional Guide* (Red Bluff, CA: Quality Circle Institute, 1980); D. S. Gouran, *Discussion: The Process of Group Decision-Making* (New York: Harper & Row, 1974); VanGundy, *Techniques of Structured Problem Solving*; F. LaFasto and C. Larson, *When Teams Work Best* (Thousand Oaks, CA: Sage, 2001).

3. Dewey, *How We Think*; see also R. V. Harnack, "John Dewey and Discussion," *Western Speech* 32 (Spring 1969): 137–49.

4. For a complete discussion of the history of teaching group discussion, see H. Cohen, *The History of Speech Communication: The Emergence of a Discipline, 1914–1945* (Annandale, VA: Speech Communication Association, 1994) 274–322.

5. For an excellent discussion of the history of teaching group discussion, see D. S. Gouran, "Communication in Groups: The Emergence and Evolution of a Field of Study," in L. R. Frey, ed., *The Handbook of Group Communication Theory and Research* (Thousand Oaks, CA: Sage, 1999) 3–36.

6. K. Atuahene-Gima, "The Effects of Centrifugal and Centripetal Forces on Product Development Speed and Quality: How Does Problem Solving Matter?" *Academy of Management Journal* 46 (2003): 359–73.

7. J. A. Bonito, "The Analysis of Participation in Small Groups: Methodological and Conceptual Issues Related to Interdependence," *Small Group Research* 33, 4 (2002): 412–38.

8. R. F. Bales, *Interaction Process Analysis* (Chicago, IL: University of Chicago Press, 1976).

9. For an excellent summary of the literature documenting these problems, see Sunwolf and D. R. Seibold, "The Impact of Formal Procedures on Group Processes, Members, and Task Outcomes," in L. Frey, ed., *The Handbook of Group Communication Theory and Research* (Thousand Oaks, CA: Sage, 1999) 395–431.

10. D. S. Gouran, C. Brown, and D. R. Henry, "Behavioral Correlates of Perceptions of Quality in Decision-Making Discussion," *Communication Monographs* 45 (1978): 60–65; L. L. Putnam, "Preference for Procedural Order in Task-Oriented Small Groups," *Communication Monographs* 46 (1979): 193–218; see also VanGundy, *Techniques of Structured Problem Solving*; B. J. Broome and L. Fulbright, "A Multistage Influence Model of Barriers to Group Problem Solving: Participant-Generated Agenda for Small Group Research," *Small Group Research* 26 (1995): 25–55; J. P. Klubuilt and P. F. Green, *The Team-Based Problem Solver* (Burr Ridge, IL: Irwin, 1994).

11. D. M. Berg, "A Descriptive Analysis of the Distribution and Duration of Themes Discussed by Task-Oriented Small Groups," *Speech Monographs* 34 (1967): 172–75; see also E. G. Bormann and N. C. Bormann, *Effective Small Group Communication,* 2nd ed. (Minneapolis: Burgess, 1976) 132; M. S. Poole, "Decision Development in Small Groups III: A Multiple Sequence Model of Group Decision Development," *Communication Monographs* 50 (1983): 321–41.

12. R. Y. Hirokawa, R. Ice, and J. Cook, "Preference for Procedural Order, Discussion Structure and Group Decision Performance," *Communication Quarterly* 36 (Summer 1988): 217–26.

13. C. Pavitt, M. Philipp, and K. K. Johnson, "Who Owns a Group's Proposals: The Initiator or the Group as a Whole?" *Communication Research Reports* 21 (2004): 221–30.

14. J. G. Oetzel, "Explaining Individual Communication Processes in Homogeneous and Heterogeneous Groups Through Individualism, Collectivism, and Self-Construal," *Human Communication Research* 25 (1998): 202–24.

15. S. R. Hiltz, K. Johnson, and M. Turoff, "Experiments in Group Decision Making: Communication Process and Outcome in Face-to-Face Versus Computerized Conferences," *Human Communication Research* 13 (Winter 1986): 225–52.

16. C. A. Van Lear and E. A. Mabry, "Testing Contrasting Interaction Models for Discriminating Between Consensual and Dissent Decision-Making Groups," *Small Group Research* 30 (1999): 29–58; R. Y. Hirokawa, "Group Communication and Decision-Making Performance: A Continued Test of the Functional Perspective," *Human Communication Research* 14 (1985): 487–515.

17. For an excellent review of the literature about various rational and nonrational problem-solving methods, see S. Jarboe, "Procedures for Enhancing Group Decision Making," in R. Y. Hirokawa and M. S. Poole, eds., *Communication and Group Decision Making* (Thousand Oaks, CA: Sage, 1996).

18. See Kepner and Tregoe, *The Rational Manager;* our application of is/is not analysis is based on D. A. Romig and L. J. Romig, *Structured Teamwork® Guide* (Austin, TX: Performance Resources, 1990); see also D. A. Romig, *Breakthrough Teamwork: Outstanding Results Using Structured Teamwork®* (Chicago: Irwin, 1996).

19. This discussion of the journalist's six questions is based on a discussion by J. E. Eitington, *The Winning Trainer* (Houston, TX: Gulf Publishing, 1989) 157.

20. P. R. Scholtes, B. L. Joiner, and B. J. Streibel, *The Team Handbook* (Madison, WI: Joiner and Associates, 1996) 2–20.

21. K. Lewin, "Frontiers in Group Dynamics," *Human Relations* 1 (1947): 5–42.

22. Eitington, *The Winning Trainer,* 158.

23. K. Ishikawa, *Guide to Quality Control* (Tokyo: Asian Productivity Organization, 1982).

24. Scholtes, Joiner, and Streibel, *The Team Handbook.*

25. Brilhart and Jochem, "Effects of Different Patterns."

26. C. E. Larson and F. M. J. LaFasto, *Teamwork: What Must Go Right/What Can Go Wrong* (Beverly Hills, CA: Sage, 1989).

27. For evidence to support this modification of the reflective-thinking pattern, see J. K. Brilhart, "An Experimental Comparison of Three Techniques for Communicating a Problem-Solving Pattern to Members of a Discussion Group," *Speech Monographs* 33 (1966): 168–77.

28. R. Y. Hirokawa, "Why Informed Groups Make Faulty Decisions: An Investigation of Possible Interaction-Based Explanations," *Small Group Behavior* 18 (1987): 3–29; R. Y. Hirokawa, "Group-Communication and Decision-Making Performance: A Continued Test of the Functional Perspective," *Human Communication Research* 14 (1985): 487–515; R. Y. Hirokawa and K. Rost, "Effective Group Decision-Making in Organizations: Field Test of the Vigilant Interaction Theory," *Management Communication Quarterly* 5 (1992): 267–88; R. Y. Hirokawa, "Consensus Group Decision-Making, Quality of Decision and Group Satisfaction: An Attempt to Sort 'Fact' from 'Fiction,'" *Central States Speech Journal* 33 (1982): 407–15.

29. A. B. Hollingshead, "The Rank-Order Effect in Group Decision Making," *Organizational Behavior and Human Decision Process* 68 (1996): 181–93.

30. Federal Electric Corporation, *A Programmed Introduction to PERT* (New York: Wiley, 1963).

31. For example, see R. F. Bales and F. L. Strodtbeck, "Phases in Group Problem-Solving," *Journal of Abnormal and Social Psychology* 46 (1951): 485–95; T. M. Schiedel and L. Crowell, "Idea Development in Small Groups," *Quarterly Journal of*

Speech 50 (1964): 140–45; B. A. Fisher, "Decision Emergence: Phases in Group Decision-Making," *Speech Monographs* 37 (1970): 53–66; and Poole, "Decision Development."

32. Chapter 9 discusses in detail the phases of a group's growth and development.

33. E. G. Bormann, *Discussion and Group Methods: Theory and Practice,* 2nd ed. (New York: Harper & Row, 1975) 282.

34. N. R. F. Maier, *Problem-Solving and Discussions and Conferences* (New York: McGraw-Hill, 1963) 123.

35. B. Schultz, S. M. Ketrow, and D. M. Urban, "Improving Decision Quality in the Small Group: The Role of the Reminder," *Small Group Research* 26 (November 1995): 521–41.

36. A. A. Goldberg and C. E. Larson, *Group Communication: Discussion Processes and Applications* (Englewood Cliffs, NJ: Prentice Hall, 1975) 149.

37. Goldberg and Larson, *Group Communication,* 150.

38. Goldberg and Larson, *Group Communication,* 150.

39. Goldberg and Larson, *Group Communication,* 150.

40. Larson, "Forms of Analysis."

41. For a discussion of Deming's fourteen points, see Scholtes et al., *The Team Handbook.*

42. N. R. F. Maier, "An Experimental Test of the Effect of Training on Discussion Leadership," *Human Relations* 6 (1953): 166–73.

43. D. G. Gouran, "Variables Related to Consensus in Group Discussions of Questions of Policy," *Speech Monographs* 36 (1969): 385–91; T. J. Knutson, "An Experimental Study of the Effects of Orientation Behavior on Small Group Consensus," *Speech Monographs* 39 (1972): 159–65; J. A. Kline, "Orientation and Group Consensus," *Central States Speech Journal* 23 (1972): 44–47; S. A. Beebe, "Orientation as a Determinant of Group Consensus and Satisfaction," *Resources in Education* 13 (October 1978): 19–25.

44. LaFasto and Larson, *When Teams Work Best.*

45. This activity was developed by Russ Wittrup, Department of Speech Communication, Texas State University – San Marcos.

46. See R. Y. Hirokawa and A. J. Salazar, "Task Group Communication and Decision-Making Performance," in L. Frey, ed., *The Handbook of Group Communication Theory and Research* (Thousand Oaks, CA: Sage, 1999) 167–91; Sunwolf and Seibold, "The Impact of Formal Procedure."

47. J. Piven and D. Borgenicht, *The Worst-Case Scenario Survival Handbook* (San Francisco, CA: Chronicle Books, 1999) 120.

48. Robert Bales, *Interaction Process Analysis: A Method for the Study of Small Groups* (Reading, MA: Addison-Wesley, 1950) 59.

49. A. A. Goldberg and C. E. Larson, *Group Communication: Discussion Processes and Applications* (Englewood Cliffs, NJ: Prentice-Hall, 1975) 99–100.

50. J. Keyton, "Observing Group Interaction," in R. Y. Hirokawa, R. S. Cathcart, L. A. Samovar, and L. D. Henman, eds., *Small Group Communication Theory and Practice: An Anthology* (Los Angeles, CA: Roxbury, 2002) 256–66.

CHAPTER 11

1. M. Csikszentmihalyi, *Creativity: Flow and the Psychology of Discovery and Invention* (New York: HarperCollins, 1996).

2. For an excellent discussion and review of the literature about creativity in small groups that informs this chapter, see Sunwolf, "Getting to Group 'Aha!' " in L. R. Frey, ed., *New Directions in Small Group Communication* (Thousand Oaks, CA: Sage, 2002).

3. C. E. Johnson and M. Z. Hackman, *Creative Communication: Principles and Applications* (Prospect Heights, IL: Waveland Press, 1995).

4. P. G. Clampitt, *Communicating for Managerial Effectiveness* (Thousand Oaks, CA: Sage, 2005).

5. J. E. Nemiro, "The Creative Processes in Virtual Teams," *Creativity Research Journal* 14, 1 (2002): 69–83.

6. Nemiro, "The Creative Processes in Virtual Teams."

7. S. J. Parnes and R. B. Noller, "Applied Creativity: The Creative Studies Project: Part II. Results of the Two-Year Program," *Journal of Creative Behavior* 6 (1972): 164–86; R. L. Firestien, "Effects of Creative Problem-Solving Training on Communication Behaviors in Small Groups," *Small Group Research* 21 (1990): 507–22.

8. J. Baer, *Creativity and Divergent Thinking: A Task-Specific Approach* (Hillsdale, NJ: Lawrence Erlbaum, 1993).

9. Firestien, "Effects of Creative Problem Solving Training."

10. Firestien, "Effects of Creative Problem Solving Training."

11. Johnson and Hackman, *Creative Communication.*

12. Johnson and Hackman, *Creative Communication.*

13. S. Jarboe, "Group Communication and Creativity Processes," in L. R. Frey, D. S. Gouran, and M. S. Poole, eds., *The Handbook of Group Communication Theory and Research* (Thousand Oaks, CA: Sage, 1999) 335–68.

14. J. Ayres and T. S. Hopf, "The Long-Term Effect of Visualization in the Classroom: A Brief Research Report," *Communication Education* 39 (1990): 75–78.

15. J. R. Kelly and T. J. Loving, "Time Pressure and Group Performance: Exploring Underlying Processes in the Attentional Focus Model," *Journal of Experimental Social Psychology* 40 (2004): 185–98.

16. J. R. Kelly and S. J. Karau, "Entrainment of Creativity in Small Groups," *Small Group Research* 24 (1993): 179–98.

17. J. R. Kelly and J. E. McGrath, "Effects of Time Limits and Task Types on Task Performance and Interaction of Four-Person Groups," *Journal of Personality and Social Psychology* 49 (1985): 395–407.

18. S. Taggar, "Individual Creativity and Group Ability to Utilize Individual Creative Resources: A Multi-Level Model." *Academy of Management Journal* 45 (April 2002): 315–30.

19. A. B. VanGundy, *Managing Group Creativity: A Modular Approach to Problem Solving* (New York: AMA-COM, 1984).

20. Taggar, "Individual Creativity."

21. J. A. Goncalo and B. M. Staw, "Individualism–Collectivism and Group Creativity," *Organizational Behavior and Human Decision Processes* 100 (2006): 96–109.

22. P. L. McLeod, S. A. Lobel, and T. H. Cox, Jr., "Ethnic Diversity and Creativity in Small Groups," *Small Group Research* 27 (1996): 248–64; A. Miura and M. Hida, "Synergy Between Diversity and Similarity in Group-Idea Generation," *Small Group Research* 35 (2004): 540–64.

23. H. S. Choi and L. Thompson, "Old Wine in a New Bottle: Impact of Membership Change on Group Creativity," *Organizational Behavior and Human Decision Process* 98 (2005): 121–32.

24. A. Chirumbolo, L. Mannetti, A. Pierro, A. Areni, and A. W. Kruglanski, "Motivated Closed-Mindedness and Creativity in Small Groups," *Small Group Research* 36 (2005): 59–82.

25. L. L. Gilson, J. E. Mathieu, C. E. Shalley, and T. M. Ruddy, "Creativity and Standardization: Complementary or Conflicting Driver of Team Effectiveness?" *Academy of Management Journal* 48 (2005): 521–31.

26. Taggar, "Individual Creativity"; P. B. Paulus and H. Yang, "Idea Generation in Groups: A Basis for Creativity in Organizations," *Organizational Behavior and Human Decision Processes* 82 (2000): 76–87.

27. A. F. Osborn, *Applied Imagination* (New York: Scribner's, 1962).

28. T. J. Kramer, G. P. Fleming, and S. M. Mannis, "Improving Face-to-Face Brainstorming Through Modeling and Facilitation," *Small Group Research* 32, 5 (2001) 533–57.

29. E. F. Rietzschel, B. A. Nijstad, and W. Stroebe, "Productivity Is Not Enough: A Comparison of Interactive and Nominal Brainstorming Groups on Idea Generation and Selection," *Journal of Experimental Social Psychology* 42 (2006): 244–51; also see P. B. Paulus and M. T. Dzindolet, "Social Influence Processes in Group Brainstorming," *Journal of Personality and Social Psychology* 64 (1993): 575–86; P. B. Paulus, K. L. Dugosh, M. T. Dzindolet, H. Coskun, and V. K. Putman, "Social and Cognitive Influences in Group Brainstorming: Predicting Production Gains and Losses," *European Review of Social Psychology* 12 (2002): 299–326.

30. R. P. McGlynn, D. McGurk, V. S. Effland, N. L. Johll, and D. J. Harding, "Brainstorming and Task Performance in Groups Constrained by Evidence," *Organizational Behavior and Human Decision Processes* 93 (2004): 75–87.

31. B. A. Nijstad, A. E. M. van Vianen, W. Stroebe, and H. F. M. Lodewijkx, "Persistence in Brainstorming: Exploring Stop Rules in Same-Sex Groups," *Group Processes & Intergroup Relations* 7 (2004): 195–206.

32. Nijstad, van Vianen, Stroebe, and Lodewijkx, "Persistence in Brainstorming."

33. A. L. Delbecq, A. H. Van de Ven, and D. H. Gustafson, *Group Techniques for Program Planning: A Guide to Nominal-Group and Delphi Processes* (Glenview, IL: Scott, Foresman, 1975) 7–16.

34. B. L. Smith, "Interpersonal Behaviors That Damage the Productivity of Creative Problem-Solving Groups," *The Journal of Creative Behavior* 27, 3 (1993): 171–87.

35. G. Philipsen, A. Mulac, and D. Dietrich, "The Effects of Social Interaction on Group Generation of Ideas," *Communication Monographs* 46 (June 1979): 119–25; F. M. Jablin, "Cultivating Imagination: Factors That Enhance and Inhibit Creativity in Brainstorming Groups," *Human Communication Research* 7, 3 (Spring 1981): 245–58; S. Jarboe, "A Comparison of Input-Output, Process-Output, and Input-Process-Output Models of Small Group Problem-Solving Effectiveness," *Communication Monographs* 55 (June 1988): 121–42. The idea of incorporating individual or silent brainstorming into the traditional brainstorming approach emerges from the nominal-group technique suggested by Delbecq, Van de Ven, and Gustafson, *Group Techniques for Program Planning*, 7–16; see also S. Jarboe, "Enhancing Creativity in Groups: Theoretical Boundaries and Pragmatic Limitations," a paper presented at the annual meeting of the Speech Communication Association, Atlanta, Georgia, Nov. 1, 1991; F. M. Jablin and D. R. Seibold, "Implications for Problem-Solving Groups of Empirical Research on 'Brainstorming': A Critical Review of the Literature," *Southern Speech Communication Journal* 43 (1978): 327–56; Philipsen, Mulac, and Dietrich, "The Effects of Social Interaction." See also A. B. VanGundy, *Techniques of Structured Problem Solving* (New York: Van Nostrand Reinhold, 1981).

36. J. J. Sosik, B. J. Avolio, and S. S. Kahai, "Inspiring Group Creativity: Comparing Anonymous and Identified Electronic Brainstorming," *Small Group Research* 29 (1998): 3–31.

37. H. Barki, "Small Group Brainstorming and Idea Quality: Is Electronic Brainstorming the Most Effective Approach?" *Small Group Research* 32, 2 (2001): 158–205.

38. D. H. Gustafson, R. K. Shukla, A. Delbecq, and G. W. Walster, "A Comparative Study of Differences in Subjective Likelihood Estimates Made by Individuals, Interacting Groups, Delphi Groups and Nominal-Groups," *Organizational Behavior and Human Performance* 9 (1973): 280–91; VanGundy, *Techniques of Structured Problem Solving*.

39. Jarboe, "A Comparison of Input-Output, Process-Output, and Input-Process-Output Models."

40. Delbecq, Van de Ven, and Gustafson, *Group Techniques*.

41. M. C. Roy, S. Gauvin, and M. Limayem, "Electronic Group Brainstorming: The Role of Feedback on Productivity," *Small Group Research* 27 (1996): 215–47.

42. J. J. Sosik, B. J. Avolio, and S. S. Kahai, "Inspiring Group Creativity: Comparing Anonymous and Identified Electronic Brainstorming," *Small Group Research* 29 (1998): 3–31; W. H. Cooper, R. B. Gallupe, S. Pollard, and J. Cadsby, "Some Liberating Effects of Anonymous Electronic Brainstorming," *Small Group Research* 29 (1998): 147–77.

43. Sosik, Avolio, and Kahai, "Inspiring Group Creativity."

44. K. L. Dugosh, P. B. Paulus, E. J. Roland, and H. C. Yang, "Cognitive Stimulation in Brainstorming," *Journal of Personality and Social Psychology* 79, 5 (2000): 722–35.

45. Dugosh et al., "Cognitive Stimulation in Brainstorming."

46. Also see B. A. Nijstad, W. Stroebe, and H. F. M. Lodewijkx, "Cognitive Stimulation and Interference in Groups: Exposure

Effects in an Idea-Generation Task," *Journal of Experimental Social Psychology* 38 (2002): 535–44.

47. D. J. York, L. D. Davis, and S. L. Wise, *Virtual Teaming* (Menlo Park, CA: Crisp Publications, 2000) 77.

48. E. K. Aranda, L. Aranda, and K. Conlon, *Teams: Structure, Process, Culture, and Politics* (Englewood Cliffs, NJ: Prentice-Hall, 1998).

49. A. K. Offner, T. J. Kramer, and J. P. Winter, "The Effects of Facilitation, Recording, and Pauses on Group Brainstorming," *Small Group Research* 27 (1996): 283–98; V. Brown and P. B. Paulus, "A Simple Dynamic Model of Social Factors in Group Brainstorming," *Small Group Research* 27 (1996): 91–114; M. W. Kramer, C. L. Kuo, and J. C. Dailey, "The Impact of Brainstorming Techniques on Subsequent Group Processes," *Small Group Research* 28 (1997): 218–42; V. Brown, M. Tumeo, T. S. Larey, and P. B. Paulus, "Modeling Cognitive Interactions During Group Brainstorming," *Small Group Research* 29 (1997): 495–526. For an excellent review of group communication and creativity, see Jarboe, "Group Communication and Creativity Processes," in L. Frey, ed., *The Handbook of Group Communication Theory and Research* (Thousand Oaks, CA: Sage, 1999) 335–68.

50. Kelly and Karau, "Entrainment of Creativity in Small Groups."

51. J. E. Eitington, *The Winning Trainer* (Houston, TX: Gulf Publishing, 1989).

52. Eitington, *The Winning Trainer.*

53. D. A. Romig and L. J. Romig, *Structured Teamwork® Guide* (Austin, TX: Performance Resources, 1990).

54. E. de Bono, *Sur/petition: Creating Value Monopolies When Everyone Is Merely Competing* (New York: HarperBusiness, 1992).

55. S. A. Beebe and K. Barge, "Evaluating Group Discussion," in R. Hirokawa, R. S. Cathcart, L. A. Samovar, and L. A. Henman, eds., *Small Group Communication Theory and Practice: An Anthology* (Los Angeles, CA: Roxbury, 2003) 275–88.

CHAPTER 12

1. D. S. Gouran, "Leadership as the Art of Counteractive Influence in Decision-Making and Problem-Solving Groups," in R. Y. Hirokawa, R. S. Cathcart, L. A. Samovar, and L. D. Henman, eds., *Small Group Communication: Theory and Practice* (Los Angeles: Roxbury, 2003) 172–83.

2. A. P. Hare, *Handbook of Small Group Research,* 2nd ed. (New York: Free Press, 1976).

3. D. Archer, "The Face of Power: Physical Attractiveness as a Non-Verbal Predictor of Small Group Stratification," *Proceedings of the 81st Annual Convention of the American Psychological Association* 8 (1973), Part 1: 177–78.

4. D. Barnlund and F. Haiman, *The Dynamics of Discussion* (Boston: Houghton Mifflin, 1960) 275–79.

5. R. White and R. Lippitt, "Leader Behavior and Member Reaction in Three 'Social Climates,'" in D. Cartwright and A. Zan-

der, eds., *Group Dynamics,* 3rd ed. (New York: Harper & Row, 1968) 319.

6. J. Gastil, "A Meta-Analytic Review of the Productivity and Satisfaction of Democratic and Autocratic Leadership," *Small Group Research* 25 (1994): 384–410.

7. P. Hersey and K. Blanchard, *Management of Organizational Behavior: Utilizing Human Resources,* 6th ed. (Englewood Cliffs, NJ: Prentice Hall, 1992).

8. V. H. Vroom and A. G. Jago, *The New Leadership: Managing Participation in Organizations* (Englewood Cliffs, NJ: Prentice Hall, 1988) 52.

9. S. Trenholm, *Human Communication Theory* (Englewood Cliffs, NJ: Prentice Hall, 1990).

10. Vroom and Jago, *The New Leadership* 52.

11. D. J. York, L. D. Davis, and S. L. Wise, *Virtual Teaming* (Menlo Park, CA: Crisp Publications, 2000) 48–49.

12. D. Gorman, "Conceptual and Methodological Approaches to the Study of Leadership," *Central States Speech Journal* 21 (Winter 1970): 217–23.

13. P. M. Senge, "Leading Learning Organizations," in R. Beckhard et al., eds., *The Leader of the Future* (San Francisco: Jossey-Bass, 1996).

14. P. M. Senge, "The Leader's New Work: Building Learning Organizations," *Sloan Management Review* 32, 1 (Fall 1990): whole issue.

15. L. Little, "Transformational Leadership," *Academic Leadership* 15 (Nov. 1999): 4–5.

16. F. J. Yammarino and A. J. Dubinsky, "Transformational Leadership Theory: Using Levels of Analysis to Determine Boundary Conditions," *Personnel Psychology* 47 (1994): 787–809.

17. B. M. Bass and M. J. Avolio, "Transformational Leadership and Organizational Culture," *International Journal of Public Administration* 17 (1994): 541–54.

18. I. Kotlyar and L. Karakowsky, "Leading Conflict? Linkages Between Leader Behaviors and Group Conflict," *Small Group Research* 37 (2006): 377–403.

19. M. Schminke, D. Wells, J. Peyrefitte, and T. C. Sebora, "Leadership and Ethics in Work Groups," *Group & Organizational Management* 27 (2002): 272–93.

20. J. K. Barge et al., "Relational Competence and Leadership Emergence: An Exploratory Study," paper presented at the annual meeting of the Central States Speech Association, Schaumberg, Illinois, April 14–16, 1988.

21. D. C. Baker, "A Qualitative and Quantitative Analysis of Verbal Style and the Elimination of Potential Leaders in Small Groups," *Communication Quarterly* 38 (1990): 13–26.

22. E. Bormann, *Discussion and Group Methods,* 2nd ed. (New York: Harper & Row, 1975) 256.

23. S. D. Johnson and C. Bechler, "Examining the Relationship Between Listening Effectiveness and Leadership Emergence," *Small Group Research* 29 (1998): 452–71.

24. S. B. Shimanoff and M. M. Jenkins, "Leadership and Gender," in R. Y. Hirokawa, R. S. Cathcart, L. A. Samovar, and L. D. Hen-

man, eds., *Small Group Communication: Theory and Practice* (Los Angeles: Roxbury, 2003) 194.

25. B. L. Bonner, "The Effects of Extroversion on Influence in Ambiguous Group Tasks," *Small Group Research* 31 (2000): 225–44.

26. G. De Souza and H. J. Klein, "Emergent Leadership in the Group Goal-Setting Process," *Small Group Research* 26 (1995): 475–96.

27. M. S. Limon and B. H. La France, "Communication Traits and Leadership Emergence: Examining the Impact of Argumentativeness, Communication Apprehension, and Verbal Aggressiveness in Work Groups," *Southern Communication Journal* 70 (2005): 123–33.

28. For example, see the review of literature in P. H. Andrews, "Sex and Gender Differences in Group Communication: Impact on the Facilitation Process," *Small Group Research* 23 (1992): 74–94.

29. E. I. Megargee, "Influence of Sex Roles on the Manifestation of Leadership," *Journal of Applied Psychology* 53 (1969): 377–82.

30. C. Nemeth, J. Endicott, and J. Wachtler, "From the 50's to the 70's: Women in Jury Deliberations," *Sociometry* 39 (1976): 293–304.

31. J. E. Baird and P. H. Bradley, "Styles of Management and Communication: A Comparative Study of Men and Women," *Communication Monographs* 46 (1979): 101–11.

32. B. Spillman, R. Spillman, and K. Reinking, "Leader Emergence: Dynamic Analysis of the Effects of Sex and Androgyny," *Small Group Behavior* 12 (1981): 139–57.

33. J. R. Goktepe and C. E. Schneier, "Sex and Gender Effects in Evaluating Emergent Leaders in Small Groups," *Sex Roles* 19 (1988): 29–36. See also E. Kushell and R. Newton, "Gender, Leadership Style, and Subordinate Satisfaction: An Experiment," *Sex Roles* 14 (1986): 203–9.

34. See V. P. Hans and N. Eisenberg, "The Effects of Sex Role Attitudes and Group Composition on Men and Women in Groups," *Sex Roles* 12 (1985): 477–90.

35. J. A. Kolb, "Are We Still Stereotyping Leadership? A Look at Gender and Other Predictors of Leader Emergence," *Small Group Research* 28 (1997): 370–93.

36. K. W. Hawkins, "Effects of Gender and Communication Content on Leadership Emergence in Small, Task-Oriented Groups," *Small Group Research* 26 (1995): 234–49.

37. K. B. Knott and E. J. Natalle, "Sex Differences, Organizational Level, and Superiors' Evaluation of Managerial Leadership," *Management Communication Quarterly* 10 (1997): 523–40.

38. M. J. Neubert, "Too Much of a Good Thing or the More the Merrier?" *Small Group Research* 30 (1999): 635–46.

39. S. C. Koch, "Evaluative Affect Display Toward Male and Female Leaders of Task-Oriented Groups," *Small Group Research* 36 (2005): 678–703.

40. D. Tourish and P. Robson, "Sensemaking and Distortion of Critical Upward Communication in Organizations," *Journal of Management Studies* 43 (2006): 711–30.

41. S. B. Glaser, "Teamwork and Communication," *Management Communication Quarterly* 7 (1994): 282–96.

42. R. Spoelde-Claes, "The Effect of Varying Feedback on the Effectiveness of a Small Group on a Physical Task," *Psychologica Belgica* 13, 1 (1973): 61–68.

43. M. Webster, Jr., "Source of Evaluations and Expectations for Performance," *Sociometry* 32, 3 (1969): 243–58.

44. A. B. Hollingshead, "Group and Individual Training: The Impact of Practice on Performance," *Small Group Research* 29 (1998): 254–80.

45. H. E. Gulley and D. Leathers, *Communication and Group Process: Techniques for Improving the Quality of Small-Group Communication*, 3rd ed. (New York: Holt, Rinehart and Winston, 1977) 128.

APPENDIX A

1. Dave Barry, *Dave Barry's Guide to Life* (New York: Wings Books, 1991) 311.

2. "Survive Meetings with High-Tech Tools," *USA Today Online* (January 22, 1999), accessed at http://www. usatoday. com.

3. R. K. Mosvick and R. B. Nelson, *We've Got to Start Meeting Like This!* (Glenview, IL: Scott, Foresman, 1987).

4. S. A. Beebe and J. T. Masterson, "Toward a Model of Small Group Communication: Application for Teaching and Research," *Florida Speech Communication Journal* 8, 2 (1980): 9–15.

5. See D. A. Romig and L. J. Romig, *Breakthrough Teamwork* (Chicago: Irwin, 1996); T. A. Kayser, *Mining Group Gold* (El Segundo, CA: Serif Publishing, 1990).

6. H. L. Ewbank, Jr., *Meeting Management* (Dubuque, IA: Brown, 1968).

7. J. E. Tropman and G. C. Morningstar, *Meetings: How to Make Them Work for You* (New York: Van Nostrand Reinhold, 1985) 56; J. E. Tropman, *Making Meetings Work* (Thousand Oaks, CA: Sage, 1996); see also M. Doyle and D. Straus, *How to Make Meetings Work* (New York: Playboy Press, 1976); Mosvick and Nelson, *We've Got to Start Meeting Like This!*; G. Lumsden and D. Lumsden, *Communicating in Groups and Teams: Sharing Leadership* (Belmont, CA: Wadsworth, 1993); D. B. Curtis, J. J. Floyd, and J. L. Winsor, *Business and Professional Communication* (New York: HarperCollins, 1992); Romig and Romig, *Breakthrough Teamwork*; D. A. Romig and L. Romig, *Structured Teamwork Guide* (Austin, TX: Performances Resources, 1990); Kayser, *Mining Group Gold.*

8. F. Niederman and R. J. Volkema, "The Effects of Facilitator Characteristics on Meeting Preparation, Set Up, and Implementation," *Small Group Research* 30 (1999): 330–60.

9. T. Ludwig and E. S. Geller, "Assigned Versus Participatory Goal Setting and Response Generalization: Managing Injury

Control Among Professional Pizza Deliveries," *Journal of Applied Psychology* 82 (1997): 253–61; for an excellent review of facilitation and collaborative leadership in teams and organizations, see D. A. Romig, *Side by Side Leadership* (Austin, TX: Bard, 2001) 9, 103–10.

10. A. Weitzel and P. Geist, "Parliamentary Procedure in a Community Group: Communication and Vigilant Decision Making," *Communication Monographs* 65 (1998): 244–59.

11. Mosvick and Nelson, *We've Got to Start Meeting Like This!*

12. M. E. Haynes, *Effective Meeting Skills* (Los Altos, CA: Crisp Publications, 1988).

APPENDIX B

1. Our suggestions for helping you plan and present your speech are adapted from S. A. Beebe and S. J. Beebe, *Public Speaking: An Audience-Centered Approach,* 5th ed. (Boston: Allyn and Bacon, 2003).

2. See S. A. Beebe, "Eye Contact: A Nonverbal Determinant of Speaker Credibility," *Speech Teacher* 23 (January 1971): 21–25; S. A. Beebe, "Effects of Eye Contact, Posture, and Vocal Inflection upon Credibility and Comprehension," *Australian Scan Journal of Nonverbal Communication* 7–8 (1979–80): 57–80.

INDEX